TORTS

TORTS: MAJORITY RULE CASES

❖

Second Edition

Learn Law Better, LLC

H. BEAU BAEZ, LAW PROFESSOR

This casebook is designed to help students learn law in an educational setting. The publisher provides educational materials, which are not a substitute for the expertise provided by a licensed lawyer. If you desire legal advice, please hire a licensed professional as nothing in this text should be construed as providing legal advice.

Published in the United States by Learn Law Better, LLC

LearnLawBetter.com

Second Edition

ISBN: 978-0-9861455-4-4

For my colleagues and students, who have helped me become a better teacher.

PREFACE

This casebook is designed for use in a first-year law school Torts course. The cases in this text were selected because they are interesting and pedagogically useful. But unlike most other casebooks, the cases provide the law likely to be encountered on the Multistate Bar Examination®. The bar examiners select rules of law through a rigorous process, generally resulting in questions derived from the law used in a majority of states. This casebook's approach generally provides cases which track the majority rule. In addition to preparing students for the bar exam, majority rule cases allow faculty to focus on teaching fundamental analytical skills—the hallmark of what is meant by the phrase "thinking like a lawyer." Another advantage of this approach is that students are unlikely to get confused on an exam, unsure as to which law the professor wants discussed. After all, in the practice of law almost every lawyer only needs the law in their jurisdiction. While comparing, contrasting, and synthesizing laws from multiple jurisdictions is an important skill, especially for judges and appellate attorneys, it is not necessarily a skill that should be taught extensively in a first year Torts course. However, a few minority approach cases are included to help faculty introduce the skill. Also, several tort classics are retained, such as *United States v. Carroll Towing* and *Brown v. Kendall.*

A second characteristic of this casebook is its student-focus design. Internal citations have been removed, punctuation changed, quotations marks eliminated, archaic words modernized, sentence structure altered, paragraphs rearranged, most author names deleted, and other changes to make cases more accessible to students. The goal is to create a case that reads like a story, which helps increase student learning. For those that want to read the unaltered cases, a basic case citation is provided for each case.

Finally, this casebook does not contain explanations, notes, or problems, which is reminiscent of the approach taken by Christopher Columbus Langdell in the first casebook ever published. This casebook should be supplemented with problems, and because it uses a majority rule approach, works well when assigned along with a concise hornbook. As Langdell noted in his landmark 1871 casebook, *Selection of Cases on the Law of Contracts*: "Law, considered as a science, consists of certain principles or doctrines. To have such a mastery of these as to be able to apply them with constant facility constitutes a true lawyer; and hence to acquire that mastery should be the business of every earnest student of law."

H. Beau Baez, III

TABLE OF CONTENTS

This page left intentionally blank

I. INTRODUCTION

Van Camp v. McAfoos

Supreme Court of Iowa (1968)

This case comes to us on appeal from trial court's action in sustaining defendant's motion to dismiss.

Plaintiff sues Mark McAfoos alleging that at said time and place defendant Mark McAfoos was operating a tricycle on said public sidewalk, and drove the tricycle into the rear of the plaintiff without warning, striking the right leg of the plaintiff thereby causing an injury to the Achilles' tendon of that leg.

Defendant moved to dismiss the petition urging it fails to state a claim upon which relief can be granted, fails to allege negligence and because defendant is only three years one month old.

The question presented is, did plaintiff plead a cause of action?

Plaintiff states her petition contains the following ultimate facts (1) she was rightfully using the public sidewalk (and thus had a right to the reasonably free use thereof and to remain uninjured during such use), (2) defendant used his tricycle on the public sidewalk (and thus had a duty to use the same without injurious interference with others), (3) surprise intrusion of the tricycle into the right rear ankle of plaintiff (thus interfering with plaintiff's right and stating defendant activated the mechanism causing the injury) and (4) damage resulted from the intrusion. She stands firmly on the proposition that invasion of her person is in itself a wrong and she need plead no more. We do not agree.

The extent of plaintiff's allegations were deliberately limited to those heretofore set forth and she so states. She therefore poses our problem independent of Mark's age. The trial court responded in kind and entered judgment on the pleadings without regard to the known allegation that Mark was three years, one month old.

In essence plaintiff urges a person has a right not to be injuriously touched or struck as she lawfully uses a public sidewalk. She was injuriously struck by Mark. Therefore Mark is liable.

She argues that no more need be pleaded. It follows that no more need be proved in order to justify submission of the case. Plaintiff's posture satisfies us she would have us impose liability without fault. We are not prepared to extend this concept to childish acts (by children).

Plaintiff makes it abundantly clear she insists on a right to recovery by proof of an accident caused by another, independent of fault or wrong doing. Where an essential element of the cause of action is missing, the question is not what may be shown under the pleading but whether a cause of action has been pled.

In order to plead a cause of action the pleader must allege ultimate facts from which the fact finder can conclude the essential elements of the cause are present. We agree the conclusion itself need not necessarily be pled if the ultimate facts are contained in the pleading.

We hold liability will not be imposed for use of a tricycle on a public sidewalk without a showing of some fault. Unless and until we are ready to recognize liability without fault for otherwise innocent childish actions, fault must be discernible in the pleading and in proof. No statute or ordinance is cited prohibiting use of a tricycle on a public sidewalk. Intentionally wrongful or negligently wrongful use of the tricycle is neither pled nor can it be made out from the bare allegation defendant operated a tricycle on said public sidewalk and drove the tricycle into the rear of the plaintiff without warning.

Affirmed.

Estevez v. United States

United States District Court, S.D. New York (1999)

This negligence action arises out of an automobile accident resulting in personal injuries to various members of the Estevez family. The car in which plaintiffs were riding collided with a United States postal truck. The following constitutes the court's findings of fact and conclusions of law.

On the evening of October 11, 1996, the Estevez vehicle was driven by Pedro Estevez. All of the passengers sustained injuries in the crash and were taken to the emergency room at the Jacobi Medical Center.

Past Medical Expenses and Pain and Suffering

On the night of the accident, Joseph, age 2, was taken to Jacobi Hospital. He was then transferred to the pediatric intensive care unit of Montefiore Medical Center, where he remained hospitalized for approximately five weeks. During that time he underwent the following surgical procedures: (1) exploratory laparotomy, bowel resection (removal of 8 cm. of the intestine), and repair of perforations in the bowel wall; and (2) aortic endartectomy (removing a clot from the artery), thrombectomy (removing a clot from the vein) and patch angioplasty. During this last procedure a Gortex patch was permanently placed on his aorta. The first surgery was due to a perforation of a section of the small intestine, an abdominal wall hernia and a tear or fracture of the lower pole of the right kidney. The second surgery was due to an intimal tear, which is a tear to the inner lining of the aorta.

The parties agree that Joseph has incurred $138,000 in past hospital and medical costs, the first $50,000 of which has been paid by "no-fault" insurance. The Government suggests that the past pain and suffering award should be $300,000, and that Joseph be awarded past medical expenses in the amount of the lien, namely $88,000. Plaintiff, in turn, argues for a past pain and suffering award of $500,000.

The plaintiff's figures are sound and fully supported by the evidence. In addition, these figures are in general agreement with the past pain and suffering awards submitted by plaintiff's counsel. Thus, Joseph is awarded $88,000 for past medical expenses and $500,000 for past pain and suffering.

Future Medical Expenses and Pain and Suffering

Joseph is entitled to an award for future medical expenses. Based on the totality of the evidence in the record, Joseph is awarded a total of $220,815 in future medical expenses. That award includes the following components: $85,415 for annual cardiology consultations and annual echocardiograms; $1,800 for scannergram's and leg x-rays during the next 5 years; $40,000 for orthotic devices; and $93,600 for physical therapy, assuming that Joseph will need 8 more years of physical therapy. No amount is awarded for any tendon lengthening surgery as no cost estimate was provided for that procedure. An award might also be appropriate for surgery or hospitalization due to abdominal adhesions because Dr. Spigland testified that Joseph was at high risk for developing this condition. However, because there was no figure provided for either surgery or hospitalization, any award would be unduly speculative.

The Government concedes that Joseph is entitled to an award for future pain and suffering, but believes that Joseph is entitled to no more than $100,000 for the pain he will suffer during the remaining 67 years of his life. Plaintiff seeks a larger award for this category of damages.

Joseph is entitled to an award for future pain and suffering. The setting of any such award is by definition speculative. A court must base its determination on comparable cases. Gretchen v. United States, 618 F.2d 177 (2d Cir.1980) ($1.3 million; $1 million awarded for pain and suffering; $300,000 for lost earnings for injuries resulting in a permanent limp, decreased sensation in right arm and shoulder, and partial loss of urinary and sexual function); Ramos v. Pasqua, Verdicts, Settlements & Tactics 9, Vol. 8, No. 1 (Jan.1988) (14 year old boy awarded $1.05 million for a permanently shortened leg, chronic arthritis, chronic pain. Claimant had four surgeries and was scheduled for six more.); Chapman v. Montefiore Hospital, Verdicts, Settlements & Tactics 375, Vol. 10, No. 11 (Nov.1990) ($1.1 million for pain and suffering for injuries resulting in right foot drop, requiring claimant to wear a brace). I conclude based on my review of the evidence, and on cases submitted both by the plaintiff and the Government, that an appropriate award for future pain and suffering is $750,000. I reach this conclusion based on the totality of Joseph's medical problems and his long life expectancy. As noted earlier, Joseph's life expectancy is 67.5 years. This award, then, provides little more than $10,000 per year for a permanent limp and leg shortening, a damaged spine, potential abdominal adhesions, risk of infection of the Gortex patch, and the continued discomfort of medical monitoring and associated procedures.

Future Lost Earnings

Joseph requests an award for future lost earnings. He claims that as a person with a disability, his earning capacity is diminished compared to people who have no disability. He relies on the testimony of Andrew Gluck, who performed a vocational economic assessment. Mr. Gluck testified based on his observations of Joseph, his meeting with Joseph's mother, and his review of the medical records.

Mr. Gluck made several assumptions. First, he assumed that Joseph has a permanent non-severe disability. Second, given the education of Joseph's parents, he assumed that Joseph is likely to obtain a college degree. He next assumed, based on statistical tables made available by the United States Government, that disabled males with a college degree are statistically likely to earn $10,000 less per year than non-disabled males. More specifically, he testified that a non-disabled college graduate can expect to earn an annual salary of $64,610, whereas a disabled college graduate can only expect to earn an annual salary of $54,526. Finally, he concluded that occupationally disabled people have a shorter work life expectancy than non-disabled people. He testified that on average occupationally disabled people work 6.67 years less than those who have no disability.

Based on this evidence, Mr. Gluck concluded that over the course of his work-life, Joseph should be compensated for 31 years of working at an economic loss of $10,000 per year and for 6.67 years of an economic loss of approximately $54,500 per year. According to Mr. Gluck, the sum of these two figures is $920,689 in present value.

The Government argues that Mr. Gluck's testimony should be rejected. It first argues that there is no principled basis to assume that Joseph's disability is comparable to the disability suffered by those in the "non-severely disabled" category of the U.S. Government's statistics. The Government argues that Joseph's permanent disability, viewed in the light most favorable to the plaintiff, is a slight limp, resulting from the foot drop. How does Mr. Gluck, or the Court, conclude that this injury is comparable to those in the non-severely disabled category of the U.S. Government's statistics? The Government asserts that Mr. Gluck never established that this disability will actually constitute a limitation on Joseph's future employment. In short, the Government argues that there are differences in disabilities that were totally ignored by this expert.

The Government's second argument is that Mr. Gluck made certain assumptions concerning Joseph's future medical conditions that were based on his review of the medical records, in which he chose to accept certain medical opinions and reject others. For example, Mr. Gluck testified that "[t]here may be other problems due to internal injuries that would reduce his stamina, all kinds of things that might arise that might interfere with his ability to work."

The Government's final attack on Mr. Gluck is that he relies strictly on statistical probabilities rather than on any specific information concerning Joseph. The Government made the following argument in its summation: "It's a question of not whether he has a limitation in his right leg, but whether that means he will be disabled, and no one has offered a definition of disability in the context of the individual representations that are included in one category versus another."

I agree with the Government that there is no principled way to conclude that Joseph's earning power, given the credible assumption, that he will graduate college, will be any less than that of a healthy person who is a college graduate. Nonetheless, I disagree with the Government with respect to work life expectancy. Based on all of the evidence in the record, I conclude that Joseph has a less than average work life expectancy. I accept Mr. Gluck's testimony that a person with Joseph's complex of medical problems is less likely to work as long or as continuously as a healthy person. According to Mr. Gluck's testimony a non-severely disabled person has a 6.67 year reduced work life expectancy based on reduced job opportunities, limitations on activities of daily living, continuous medical problems, and earlier retirement. Given the $64,610 average annual salary of a 45–year old college educated male, I conclude that Joseph is entitled to a future lost earnings award of $432,887 ($64,610 x 6.7 years).

II. INTENTIONAL TORTS

BATTERY

Snyder v. Turk

Court of Appeals of Ohio, Second District (1993)

The facts in this case occurred during a gall bladder removal operation. The operation took approximately one and one-half hours. The operating surgeon was the defendant-appellee, Dr. Robert Turk. The plaintiff-appellant, Barbara Ann Snyder, was the scrub nurse. Snyder filed a complaint seeking damages from Dr. Turk based upon allegation of civil battery.

The plaintiff has appealed after the trial court removed all issues from jury consideration by granting the defendant a directed verdict at the close of the plaintiff's case.

Dr. Turk began to perform a laparoscopic cholecystectomy. Dr. Turk testified that "I had reached a level of frustration both by the difficulty of the procedure and the difficult exposure and with the instruments." He was also not happy with Snyder's performance.

The plaintiff testified:

Q. Any conversation at this time between you and the defendant?

A. Dr. Turk looked at Dr. Clark at that point and said, 'She's already made three mistakes.'

Q. Did you respond?

A. I said, what have I done Dr. Turk? And he ignored me.

Q. Did there come a time when the defendant asked for a right angle?

A. Yes.

Q. And what did he say?

A. Right angle please.

Q. Did he specify length?

A. No.

Q. What did you hand him?

A. A right angle.

Q. When you hand the right angle to the defendant, what happens?

A. He takes the clamp from me and then he looks at it like he was going to use it and he throws it back at me.

Q. What happens next?

A. That's when I'm standing there and when he reached up and grabbed my shoulder and my gown and pulled me down from a standing position instantly down to the surgical wound and started screaming, can't you see where I'm working? I'm working in a hole. I need long instruments. I need long right angles now.

Q. What part of Dr. Turk's body was in contact with yours?

A. His hand.

Q. And when, you know, right after he makes contact with you, what happens?

A. I'm pulled from a standing position immediately down to like a 90 degree angle, right down onto the surgical field.

Q. Where is your face in the end in relation to the patient there on the table?

A. Looking right down into the surgical wound.

Q. And how far is your face from the wound?

A. Maybe 12 inches.

The plaintiff also testified that she did not suffer any physical injury from her contact with Dr. Turk.

The parties agree that a "battery" is defined as an intentional, unconsented-to contact with another. The appellee contends that there is no liability for the commission of a battery absent proof of an intent to inflict personal injury. Dr. Turk further contends that the directed verdict was properly granted on the battery liability issue because of the absence of evidence that he intended to inflict personal injury.

We believe that reasonable minds could conclude that Dr. Turk intended to commit an offensive contact. We reverse and remand for further proceedings consistent with the opinion.

Cohen v. Smith

Appellate Court of Illinois (1995)

Patricia Cohen was admitted to St. Joseph Memorial Hospital ("Hospital") to deliver her baby. After an examination, Cohen was informed that it would be necessary for her to have a cesarean section. Cohen and her husband allegedly informed her physician, who in turn advised the Hospital staff, that the couple's religious beliefs prohibited Cohen from being seen unclothed by a male. Cohen's doctor assured her husband that their religious convictions would be respected.

During Cohen's cesarean section, Roger Smith, a male nurse on staff at the Hospital, allegedly observed and touched Cohen's naked body. Cohen and her husband filed suit against Nurse Smith and the Hospital. The trial court allowed defendants' motions to dismiss. We reverse.

Historically, battery was first and foremost a systematic substitution for private retribution. Protecting personal integrity has always been viewed as an important basis for battery. Consequently, the defendant is liable not only for contacts which do actual physical harm, but also for those relatively trivial ones which are merely offensive and insulting. This application of battery to remedy offensive and insulting conduct is deeply ingrained in our legal history. As early as 1784, a Pennsylvania defendant was prosecuted for striking the cane of a French ambassador. The court furthered the distinction between harmful offensive batteries and nonharmful offensive batteries:

"As to the assault, this is, perhaps, one of that kind, in which the insult is more to be considered than the actual damage; for, though no great bodily pain is suffered by a blow on the palm of the hand, or the skirt of the coat, yet these are clearly within the definition of assault and battery, and among gentlemen too often induce dueling and terminate in murder." Respublica v. De Longchamps (Pa.1784).

Causing actual physical harm is not an element of battery. A plaintiff is entitled to demand that the defendant refrain from the offensive touching, although the contact results in no visible injury.

CAUSE OF ACTION

According to the complaint, despite being informed of Cohen's religious beliefs, Nurse Smith, an agent and employee of the Hospital, intentionally saw and touched Cohen's naked body.

The allegation that both Nurse Smith and the Hospital were informed in advance of plaintiffs' religious beliefs is important in this case, because the religious convictions of plaintiffs might not be those of most people who enter the hospital to give birth. As a matter of fact, plaintiffs' counsel candidly conceded that there would be no cause of action for battery if Patricia Cohen had been placed in Nurse Smith's and the Hospital's care in an emergency situation in which Patricia had been unable to inform the Hospital or its agents of her beliefs. Plaintiffs' attorney acknowledged that his clients' moral and religious views are not widely held in the community and, because of this, plaintiffs could state a claim against defendants only if the plaintiffs plead that the defendants had knowledge of those beliefs. Specifically, plaintiffs contend that defendants' knowledge is clearly illustrated by an allegation in the plaintiffs' amended complaint that Nurse Smith requested the presence of the Murphysboro City Police at the Hospital to prevent Mr. Cohen from objecting to Nurse Smith's presence in the operating room while Mrs. Cohen was naked, and to physically restrain Mr. Cohen if necessary.

The fact that the plaintiffs hold deeply ingrained religious beliefs which are not shared by the majority of society does not mean that those beliefs deserve less protection than more mainstream religious beliefs. The plaintiffs were not trying to force their religion on other people; they were only insisting that their beliefs be respected by the Hospital and the Hospital staff.

When she informed the Hospital of her moral and religious beliefs against being viewed and touched by males, the Hospital was free to refuse to accede to those demands. But, according to her complaint, when Cohen made her wishes known to the Hospital, it, at least implicitly, agreed to provide her with treatment within the restrictions placed by her beliefs.

Although most people in modern society have come to accept the necessity of being seen unclothed and being touched by members of the opposite sex during medical treatment, the plaintiffs had not accepted these procedures and, according to their complaint, had informed defendants of their convictions. This case is similar to cases involving Jehovah's Witnesses who were unwilling to accept blood transfusions because of religious convictions. Although most people do not share the Jehovah's Witnesses' beliefs about blood transfusions, our society, and our courts, accept their right to have that belief. Similarly, the courts have consistently recognized individuals' rights to refuse medical treatment even if such a refusal would result in an increased likelihood of the individual's death.

A person's right to refuse or accept medical care is not one to be interfered with lightly. As Justice Cardozo stated, "Every human being of adult years and sound mind has a right to determine what shall be done with his own body; and a surgeon who performs an operation without his patient's consent commits an assault, for which he is liable in damages."

Knowing interference with the right of determination is battery. Accepting as true the plaintiffs allegations that they informed defendants of their religious beliefs and that defendants persisted in treating Patricia Cohen as they would have treated a patient without those beliefs, we conclude that the trial court erred in dismissing the battery count.

Garratt v. Dailey

Supreme Court of Washington (1955)

Brian Dailey (age five years, nine months) was visiting with Naomi Garratt, an adult and a sister of the plaintiff, Ruth Garratt, likewise an adult, in the back yard of the plaintiff's home, on July 16, 1951. It is plaintiff's contention that she came out into the back yard to talk with Naomi and that, as she started to sit down in a wood and canvas lawn chair, Brian deliberately pulled it out from under her. The only one of the three persons present so testifying was Naomi Garratt. (Ruth Garratt, the plaintiff, did not testify as to how or why she fell.) The trial court, unwilling to accept this testimony, adopted instead Brian Dailey's version of what happened, and made the following findings: that while Naomi Garratt and Brian Dailey were in the back yard the plaintiff, Ruth Garratt, came out of her house into the back yard. Sometime subsequent thereto defendant, Brian Dailey, picked up a lightly built wood and canvas lawn chair which was then and there located in the back yard of the above described premises, moved it sideways a few feet and seated himself therein, at which time he discovered the plaintiff, Ruth Garratt, about to sit down at the place where the lawn chair had formerly been, at which time he hurriedly got up from the chair and attempted to move it toward Ruth Garratt to aid her in sitting down in the chair; that due to the defendant's small size and lack of dexterity he was unable to get the lawn chair under the plaintiff in time to prevent her from falling to the ground. That plaintiff fell to the ground and sustained a fracture of her hip, and other injuries and damages as hereinafter set forth.

That the preponderance of the evidence in this case establishes that when the defendant, Brian Dailey, moved the chair in question he did not have any willful or unlawful purpose in doing so; that he did not have any intent to injure the plaintiff, or any intent to bring about any unauthorized or offensive contact with her person or any objects appurtenant thereto; that the circumstances which immediately preceded the fall of the plaintiff established that the defendant, Brian Dailey, did not have purpose, intent or design to perform a prank or to effect an assault and battery upon the person of the plaintiff.

In our analysis of the applicable law, we start with the basic premise that Brian, whether five or fifty-five, must have committed some wrongful act before he could be liable for appellant's injuries. It is urged that Brian's action in moving the chair constituted a battery.

A definition (not all-inclusive but sufficient for our purpose) of a battery is the intentional infliction of a harmful bodily contact upon another. In order that an act may be done with the intention of bringing about a harmful or offensive contact or an apprehension thereof to a particular person, either the other or a third person, the act must be done for the purpose of causing the contact or apprehension or with knowledge on the part of the actor that such contact or apprehension is substantially certain to be produced.

We have here the conceded volitional act of Brian, i.e., the moving of a chair. Had the plaintiff proved to the satisfaction of the trial court that Brian moved the chair while she was in the act of sitting down, Brian's action would patently have been for the purpose or with the intent of causing the plaintiff's bodily contact with the ground, and she would be entitled to a judgment against him for the resulting damages

A battery would be established if, in addition to plaintiff's fall, it was proved that, when Brian moved the chair, he knew with substantial certainty that the plaintiff would attempt to sit down where the chair had been. Without such knowledge, there would be nothing wrongful about Brian's act in moving the chair and, there being no wrongful act, there would be no liability.

While a finding that Brian had no such knowledge can be inferred from the findings made, we believe that before the plaintiff's action in such a case should be dismissed there should be no question but that the trial court had passed upon that issue; hence, the case should be remanded for clarification of the findings to specifically cover the question of Brian's knowledge, because intent could be inferred therefrom. If the court finds that he had such knowledge the necessary intent will be established and the plaintiff will be entitled to recover, even though there was no purpose to injure or embarrass the plaintiff. If Brian did not have such knowledge, there was no wrongful act by him and the basic premise of liability on the theory of a battery was not established.

Remanded for clarification.

Baska v. Scherzer

Supreme Court of Kansas (2007)

Baska had given her daughter Ashley, a high school senior, permission to organize a scavenger hunt with some friends. When people returned, a number of them remained at the Baskas' home for a party. Scherzer and Madrigal were both at the party. Around midnight, an altercation broke out between Scherzer and Madrigal. Madrigal approached Scherzer from behind, and the two boys began to push each other and throw punches at one another. Upon being informed of the fight by one of her daughter's friends, Baska yelled at the boys to stop in order to break up the fight. When they continued to fight, Baska placed herself between the boys and was punched in the face, losing several teeth and receiving injuries to her neck and jaw. Baska is certain that Scherzer hit her in the face; she also believes that Madrigal punched her in the back of the head.

The Restatement (Second) of Torts and this court's decisions discuss this situation as being contemplated by the long-standing doctrine of transferred intent. The Restatement explains that the term intent, as it is used in the law of torts, denotes that the actor desires to cause the consequences of his act, or that he believes that the consequences are substantially certain to result from it. Intent is not, however, limited to consequences which are desired. If the actor knows that the consequences are certain, or substantially certain, to result from his act, and still goes ahead, he is treated by the law as if he had in fact desired to produce the result. However, an action need not be directed at the plaintiff in order to give rise to liability for intentional torts. Rather, the doctrine of transferred intent states that the tort of battery may be committed, although the person struck or hit by the defendant is not the one whom he intended to strike or hit. It is enough that the actor intends to produce such an effect upon some other person and that his act so intended is the legal cause of a harmful contact to the other. It is not necessary that the actor know or have reason even to suspect that the other is in the vicinity of the third person whom the actor intends to affect and, therefore, that he should recognize that his act, though directed against the third person, involves a risk of causing bodily harm to the other so that the act would be negligent toward him.

Defendants Madrigal and Scherzer intended to punch someone (the other defendant) and did punch someone (the plaintiff). Although their actions were not specifically directed at the plaintiff, their punches were intentional acts and did injure Baska. If defendant unlawfully aims at one person and hits another, under the doctrine of transferred intent he is guilty of battery on the person hit, the injury being the direct, natural, and probable consequence of the wrongful act. So, if one of two persons fighting unintentionally strikes a third, the person so striking is liable in an action by the third person for a battery.

Polmatier v. Russ

Supreme Court of Connecticut (1988)

The defendant and his two month old daughter visited the home of Arthur Polmatier, his father-in-law. Polmatier lived in East Windsor with his wife, Dorothy, the plaintiff, and their eleven year old son, Robert. During the early evening Robert noticed a disturbance in the living room where he saw the defendant astride Polmatier on a couch beating him on the head with a beer bottle. The defendant then went into Robert's bedroom where he took a 30-30 caliber Winchester rifle from the closet. He then returned to the living room and shot Polmatier twice, causing his death.

The defendant was charged with the crime of murder but was found not guilty by reason of insanity. Dr. Walter Borden, a psychiatrist, testified at both the criminal and this civil proceeding regarding the defendant's sanity. He concluded that the defendant was legally insane and could not form a rational choice but that he could make a schizophrenic or crazy choice.

Connecticut has never directly addressed the issue of whether an insane person is civilly liable for an intentional tort. The majority of jurisdictions that have considered this issue have held insane persons liable for their intentional torts. This liability has been based on a number of grounds, one that where one of two innocent persons must suffer a loss, it should be borne by the one who occasioned it. Another, that public policy requires the enforcement of such liability in order that relatives of the insane person shall be led to restrain him and that tortfeasors shall not simulate or pretend insanity to defend their wrongful acts causing damage to others, and that if he was not liable there would be no redress for injuries, and we might have the anomaly of an insane person having abundant wealth depriving another of his rights without compensation.

Our adoption of the majority rule holding insane persons civilly liable, in appropriate circumstances, for their intentional torts finds support in other Connecticut case law. We have elsewhere recognized the vitality of the common law principle that where one of two innocent persons must suffer loss from an act done, it is just that it should fall on the one who caused the loss rather than upon the other who had no agency in producing it and could not by any means have avoided it.

The issue is whether the defendant intended the act that produced the injury. The defendant argues that for an act to be done with the requisite intent, the act must be an external manifestation of the actor's will. Although the trial court found that the defendant could not form a rational choice, it did find that he could make a schizophrenic or crazy choice. Moreover, a rational choice is not required since an insane person may have an intent to invade the interests of another, even though his reasons and motives for forming that intention may be entirely irrational. The following example is given in the Restatement: "A, who is insane believes that he is Napoleon Bonaparte, and that B, his nurse, who confines him in his room, is an agent of the Duke of Wellington, who is endeavoring to prevent his arrival on the field of Waterloo in time to win the battle. Seeking to escape, he breaks off the leg of a chair, attacks B with it and fractures her skull. A is subject to liability to B for battery."

We recognize that the defendant made conflicting statements about the incident when discussing the homicide. At the hospital on the evening of the homicide the defendant told a police officer that his father-in-law was a heavy drinker and that he used the beer bottle for that reason. He stated he wanted to make his father-in-law suffer for his bad habits and so that he would realize the wrong that he had done. He also told the police officer that he was a supreme being and had the power to rule the destiny of the world and could make his bed fly out of the window. When interviewed by Dr. Borden, the defendant stated that he believed that his father-in-law was a spy for the red Chinese and that he believed his father-in-law was not only going to kill him, but going to harm his infant child so that he killed his father-in-law in self-defense.

Under these circumstances we are persuaded that the defendant's behavior at the time of the beating and shooting of Polmatier constituted an act.

White v. Muniz

Supreme Court of Colorado (2000)

Barbara White placed her eighty-three year-old grandmother, Helen Everly, in an assisted living facility. The caregiver in charge of Everly's wing asked Sherry Lynn Muniz, a shift supervisor, to change Everly's adult diaper. The caregiver informed Muniz that Everly was not cooperating in that effort. This did not surprise Muniz because she knew that Everly sometimes acted obstinately. Indeed, initially Everly refused to allow Muniz to change her diaper, but eventually Muniz thought that Everly relented. However, as Muniz reached toward the diaper, Everly struck Muniz on the jaw and ordered her out of the room.

The next day, Dr. Haven Howell, M.D. examined Everly. Dr. Howell deduced that she had a progressive dementia with characteristic gradual loss of function, loss of higher cortical function including immediate and short term memory, impulse control and judgment. She diagnosed Everly with primary degenerative dementia of the Alzheimer type, senile onset, with depression.

The question we here address is whether an intentional tort requires some proof that the tortfeasor not only intended to contact another person, but also intended that the contact be harmful or offensive to the other person.

Juries may find it difficult to determine the mental state of an actor, but they may rely on circumstantial evidence in reaching their conclusion. No person can pinpoint the thoughts in the mind of another, but a jury can examine the facts to conclude what another must have been thinking. For example, a person of reasonable intelligence knows with substantial certainty that a stone thrown into a crowd will strike someone and result in an offensive or harmful contact to that person. Hence, if an actor of average intelligence performs such an act, the jury can determine that the actor had the requisite intent to cause a harmful or offensive contact, even though the actor denies having such thoughts.

Some courts around the nation have abandoned this dual intent requirement in an intentional tort setting, that being an intent to contact and an intent that the contact be harmful or offensive, and have required only that the tortfeasor intend a contact with another that results in a harmful or offensive touching. Under this view, a victim need only prove that a voluntary movement by the tortfeasor resulted in a contact which a reasonable person would find offensive or to which the victim did not consent. These courts would find intent in contact to the back of a friend that results in a severe, unexpected injury even though the actor did not intend the contact to be harmful or offensive. The actor thus could be held liable for battery because a reasonable person would find an injury offensive or harmful, irrespective of the intent of the actor to harm or offend.

Courts occasionally have intertwined these two distinct understandings of the requisite intent. In most instances when the defendant is a mentally alert adult, this commingling of definitions prejudices neither the plaintiff nor the defendant. However, when evaluating the culpability of particular classes of defendants, such as the very young and the mentally disabled, the intent required by a jurisdiction becomes critical.

In this case, we have the opportunity to examine intent in the context of an injury inflicted by a mentally deficient, Alzheimer's patient. We find that the law of Colorado requires the jury to conclude that the defendant both intended the contact and intended it to be harmful or offensive.

Operating in accordance with this rule, the jury had to find that Everly appreciated the offensiveness of her conduct in order to be liable for the intentional tort of battery. It necessarily had to consider her mental capabilities in making such a finding, including her age, infirmity, education, skill, or any other characteristic as to which the jury had evidence. We presume that the jury looked into the mind of Everly, and reasoned that Everly did not possess the necessary intent to commit an assault or a battery.

A jury can, of course, find a mentally deficient person liable for an intentional tort, but in order to do so, the jury must find that the actor intended offensive or harmful consequences. As a result, insanity is not a defense to an intentional tort according to the ordinary use of that term, but is a characteristic, like infancy, that may make it more difficult to prove the intent element of battery. Our decision today does not create a special rule for the elderly, but applies Colorado's intent requirement in the context of a woman suffering the effects of Alzheimer's.

ASSAULT

Cullison v. Medley

Supreme Court of Indiana (1991)

According to Cullison's deposition testimony, he encountered Sandy, the 16 year old daughter of Ernest, in a grocery store parking lot. They exchanged pleasantries and Cullison, who was thirty-four years old, invited her to have a Coke with him and to come to his home to talk further. A few hours later, someone knocked on the door of his mobile home. Cullison got out of bed and answered the door. He testified that he saw a person standing in the darkness who said that she wanted to talk to him. Cullison answered that he would have to get dressed because he had been in bed. Cullison went back to his bedroom, dressed, and returned to the darkened living room of his trailer. When he entered the living room and turned the lights on, he was confronted by Sandy Medley, as well as by father Ernest, brother Ron, mother Doris, and brother-in-law Terry Simmons. Ernest was on crutches due to knee surgery and had a revolver in a holster strapped to his thigh. Cullison testified that Sandy called him a pervert and told him he was sick, mother Doris berated him while keeping her hand in her pocket, convincing Cullison that she also was carrying a pistol. Ron and Terry said nothing to Cullison, but their presence in his trailer home further intimidated him. Primarily, however, Cullison's attention was riveted to the gun carried by Ernest. Cullison testified that, while Ernest never withdrew the gun from his holster, he "grabbed for the gun a few times and shook the gun" at plaintiff while threatening to "jump astraddle" of Cullison if he did not leave Sandy alone. Cullison testified that Ernest "kept grabbing at it with his hand, like he was going to take it out," and "took it to mean he was going to shoot me" when Ernest threatened to "jump astraddle" of Cullison. Although no one actually touched Cullison, his testimony was that he feared he was about to be shot throughout the episode because Ernest kept moving his hand toward the gun as if to draw the revolver from the holster while threatening Cullison to leave Sandy alone.

As the Medleys were leaving, Cullison suffered chest pains and feared that he was having a heart attack. Approximately two months later, Cullison testified that Ernest glared at him in a menacing manner while again armed with a handgun at a restaurant in Linton. On one of these occasions, Ernest stood next to the booth where Cullison was seated while wearing a pistol and a holster approximately one foot from Cullison's face. Shortly after the incident at his home, Cullison learned that Ernest had previously shot a man. This added greatly to his fear and apprehension of Ernest on the later occasions when Ernest glared at him and stood next to the booth at which he was seated while armed with a handgun in a holster.

Cullison testified that as a result of the incident, he sought psychological counseling and therapy and continued to see a therapist for approximately 18 months. Additionally, Cullison sought psychiatric help and received prescription medication which prevented him from operating power tools or driving an automobile, thus injuring Cullison in his sole proprietorship construction business. Additionally, Cullison testified that he suffered from nervousness, depression, sleeplessness, inability to concentrate and impotency following his run-in with the Medleys.

It is axiomatic that assault, unlike battery, is effectuated when one acts intending to cause a harmful or offensive contact with the person of the other or an imminent apprehension of such contact. It is the right to be free from the apprehension of a battery which is protected by the tort action which we call an assault. As this Court held approximately 90 years ago, an assault constitutes "a touching of the mind, if not of the body." Because it is a touching of the mind, as opposed to the body, the damages which are recoverable for an assault are damages for mental trauma and distress. Any act of such a nature as to excite an apprehension of a battery may constitute an assault. It is an assault to shake a fist under another's nose, to aim or strike at him with a weapon, or to hold it in a threatening position, to rise or advance to strike another, to surround him with a display of force. Additionally, the apprehension must be one which would normally be aroused in the mind of a reasonable person. Finally, the tort is complete with the invasion of the plaintiff's mental peace.

The facts alleged and testified to by Cullison could, if believed, entitle him to recover for an assault against the Medleys.

Dickens v. Puryear

Supreme Court of North Carolina (1981)

The facts brought out at the hearing on summary judgment may be briefly summarized: For a time preceding the incidents in question plaintiff Dickens, a thirty-one year old man, shared sex, alcohol and marijuana with defendants' daughter, a seventeen year old high school student. ON April 2, 1975 defendants, husband and wife, lured plaintiff into rural Johnston County, North Carolina. Upon plaintiff's arrival defendant Earl Puryear, after identifying himself, called out to defendant Ann Puryear who emerged from beside a nearby building and, crying, stated that she "didn't want to see that SOB." Ann Puryear then left the scene. Thereafter Earl Puryear pointed a pistol between plaintiff's eyes and shouted "Ya'll come on out." Four men wearing ski masks and armed with nightsticks then approached from behind plaintiff and beat him into semi-consciousness. They handcuffed plaintiff to a piece of farm machinery and resumed striking him with nightsticks. Defendant Earl Puryear, while brandishing a knife and cutting plaintiff's hair, threatened plaintiff with castration. During four or five interruptions of the beatings defendant Earl Puryear and the others, within plaintiff's hearing, discussed and took votes on whether plaintiff should be killed or castrated. Finally, after some two hours and the conclusion of a final conference, the beatings ceased. Defendant Earl Puryear told plaintiff to go home, pull his telephone off the wall, pack his clothes, and leave the state of North Carolina; otherwise he would be killed. Plaintiff was then set free.

Plaintiff filed his complaint on March 31, 1978. He alleges that he is unable to sleep, afraid to go out in the dark, afraid to meet strangers, afraid he may be killed, suffering from chronic diarrhea and a gum disorder, unable effectively to perform his job, and that he has lost $1000 per month income.

We turn now to the merits of defendants' motions for summary judgment. Defendants contend, and the Court of Appeals agreed, that this is an action grounded in assault and battery. Although plaintiff pleads the tort of intentional infliction of mental distress, the Court of Appeals concluded that the complaint's factual allegations and the factual showing at the hearing on summary judgment support only a claim for assault and battery. The claim was, therefore, barred by the one-year period of limitations applicable to assault and battery. Plaintiff, on the other hand, argues that the factual showing on the motion supports a claim for intentional infliction of mental distress a claim which is governed by the three-year period of limitations. At least, plaintiff argues, his factual showing is such that it cannot be said as a matter of law that he will be unable to prove such a claim at trial. We agree with plaintiff's position.

North Carolina follows common law principles governing assault. An assault is an offer to show violence to another without striking him. The interest protected by the action for assault is freedom from apprehension of a harmful or offensive contact with one's person. The apprehension created must be one of an immediate harmful or offensive contact, as distinguished from contact in the future. As noted in State v. Ingram, in order to constitute an assault there must be:

An overt act or an attempt, or the unequivocal appearance of an attempt, with force and violence, to do some immediate physical injury to the person of another.

The display of force or menace of violence must be such to cause the reasonable apprehension of immediate bodily harm.

A mere threat, unaccompanied by an offer or attempt to show violence, is not an assault.

The apprehension created must be one of imminent contact, as distinguished from any contact in the future. 'Imminent' does not mean immediate, in the sense of instantaneous contact. It means rather that there will be no significant delay. Similarly, words do not make the actor liable for assault unless together with other acts or circumstances they put the other in reasonable apprehension of an imminent harmful or offensive contact with his person.

Ordinarily mere words, unaccompanied by some act apparently intended to carry the threat into execution, do not put the other in apprehension of an imminent bodily contact, and so cannot make the actor liable for an assault. For this reason it is commonly said in the decisions that mere words do not constitute an assault, or that some overt act is required. This is true even though the mental discomfort caused by a threat of serious future harm on the part of one who has the apparent intention and ability to carry out his threat may be far more emotionally disturbing than many of the attempts to inflict minor bodily contacts which are actionable as assaults.

Here much of the factual showing at the hearing related to assaults and batteries committed by defendants against plaintiff. The physical beatings and the cutting of plaintiff's hair constituted batteries. The threats of castration and death, being threats which created apprehension of immediate harmful or offensive contact, were assaults. Plaintiff's recovery for injuries, mental or physical, caused by these actions would be barred by the one-year statute of limitations.

The evidentiary showing on the summary judgment motion does, however, indicate that defendant Earl Puryear threatened plaintiff with death in the future unless plaintiff went home, pulled his telephone off the wall, packed his clothes, and left the state. The Court of Appeals characterized this threat as being an immediate threat of harmful and offensive contact. It was a present threat of harm to plaintiff. The Court of Appeals thus concluded that this threat was also an assault barred by the one-year statute of limitations.

We disagree with the Court of Appeals' characterization of this threat. The threat was not one of imminent, or immediate, harm. It was a threat for the future apparently intended to and which allegedly did inflict serious mental distress; therefore it is actionable, if at all, as an intentional infliction of mental distress.

FALSE IMPRISONMENT

McCann v. Wal-Mart Stores, Inc.

United States Court of Appeals, First Circuit (2000)

This case involves a claim for false imprisonment. Debra McCann and two of her children-Jillian, then 16, and Jonathan, then 12-were shopping at the Wal-Mart store in Bangor, Maine. After they returned a Christmas tree and exchanged a CD player, Jonathan went to the toy section and Jillian and Debra McCann went to shop in other areas of the store. After approximately an hour and a half, the McCanns went to a register and paid for their purchases. One of their receipts was time stamped at 10:10 p.m.

As the McCanns were leaving the store, two Wal-Mart employees, Jean Taylor and Karla Hughes, stepped out in front of the McCanns' shopping cart, blocking their path to the exit. Taylor may have actually put her hand on the cart. The employees told Debra McCann that the children were not allowed in the store because they had been caught stealing on a prior occasion. In fact, the employees were mistaken; the son of a different family had been caught shoplifting in the store about two weeks before, and Taylor and Hughes confused the two families.

Despite Debra McCann's protestations, Taylor said that they had the records, that the police were being called, and that the McCanns "had to go with her." Debra McCann testified that she did not resist Taylor's direction because she believed that she had to go with Taylor and that the police were coming. Taylor and Hughes then brought the McCanns past the registers in the store to an area near the store exit. Taylor stood near the McCanns while Hughes purportedly went to call the police. During this time, Debra McCann tried to show Taylor her identification, but Taylor refused to look at it.

After a few minutes, Hughes returned and switched places with Taylor. Debra McCann told Hughes that she had proof of her identity and that there must be some proof about the identity of the children who had been caught stealing. Hughes then went up to Jonathan, pointed her finger at him, and said that he had been caught stealing two weeks earlier. Jonathan began to cry and denied the accusation. At some point around this time Jonathan said that he needed to use the bathroom and Hughes told him he could not go. At no time during this initial hour or so did the Wal-Mart employees tell the McCanns that they could leave.

Although Wal-Mart's employees had said they were calling the police, they actually called a store security officer who would be able to identify the earlier shoplifter. Eventually, the security officer, Rhonda Bickmore, arrived at the store and informed Hughes that the McCanns were not the family whose son had been caught shoplifting. Hughes then acknowledged her mistake to the McCanns, and the McCanns left the store at approximately 11:15 p.m. In due course, the McCanns brought suit against Wal-Mart for false imprisonment. The jury awarded the McCanns $20,000 in compensatory damages on their claim that they were falsely imprisoned by Wal-Mart employees.

The gist of False Imprisonment is conduct by the actor which is intended to, and does in fact, confine another within boundaries fixed by the actor where, in addition, the victim is either conscious of the confinement or is harmed by it.

While confinement can be imposed by physical barriers or physical force, much less will do-although how much less becomes cloudy at the margins. It is generally settled that mere threats of physical force can suffice, and it is also settled that the threats may be implicit as well as explicit, and that confinement can also be based on a false assertion of legal authority to confine.

Wal-Mart asserts that under Maine law, the jury had to find actual, physical restraint, a phrase it takes from Knowlton, 95 A. at 283; see also Whittaker, 85 A. at 402. While there is no complete definition of false imprisonment by Maine's highest court, this is a good example of taking language out of context. In context, the reference to the necessity of actual, physical restraint is best understood as a reminder that a plaintiff must be actually confined-which Mrs. Knowlton was not.

Taking too literally the phrase "actual, physical restraint" would put Maine law broadly at odds with not only the Restatement but with a practically uniform body of common law in other states that accepts the mere threat of physical force, or a claim of lawful authority to restrain, as enough to satisfy the confinement requirement for false imprisonment (assuming always that the victim submits). We are not required to treat a descriptive phrase as a general rule or attribute to elderly Maine cases an entirely improbable breadth.

Shen v. Daly Company

United States Court of Appeals, Eighth Circuit (2000)

Shen is a United States citizen who retains dual Taiwanese citizenship. In 1989, Shen moved to Taiwan to become managing director of Daly's operation there.

To conduct business in Taiwan, Daly was required to designate a "responsible person," or legal representative in the country, and Shen was so designated. In November 1992, Daly decided to withdraw from Taiwan because of business setbacks. As a result, Shen was terminated but chose to remain in Taiwan. Daly, however, failed to remove Shen as its responsible person.

In December 1993, Shen received a notice from the Taiwan Tax Authority that it wanted to audit Daly's 1992 Taiwan tax returns. Shen, in turn, notified Daly's accounting firm in Taiwan and informed them he was concerned he could be held responsible for any deficiency because his "chop," the Taiwanese equivalent of a signature, was affixed to the returns. Daly responded that it was inconceivable any tax could be owed because Daly had suffered large losses in Taiwan.

Following this request and until mid-October 1995, Shen, through a series of letters to Daly personnel and to Mr. Leo A. Daly III himself, implored Daly to resolve the tax dispute and remove him as the responsible person. In May 1994, the Taiwan Tax Authority assessed a tax liability of approximately $80,000 against Daly for 1991 and 1992. Daly did not appeal the assessment, and it became final in June 1995. In October 1995, the Taiwan Ministry of Finance and the Bureau of Entry and Exit informed Shen he was forbidden from leaving the country until resolution of the Daly tax issue.

Daly's attempt to extricate Shen through diplomatic channels failed. Shen then brought suit for a declaratory judgment in Taiwan to remove himself as Daly's responsible person. Although the court recognized Shen was no longer an employee of Daly, it denied relief because Daly had not replaced him as the responsible person.

In 1997, Shen sued Daly in the United States District Court for the District of Nebraska. He requested a preliminary injunction to force Daly to pay the taxes. The district court entered such an injunction on December 31, 1997. We assume Daly then paid the taxes because Taiwan lifted the travel restriction.

Shen contends the district court erred when it granted Daly's motion for judgment as a matter of law on the false imprisonment claim. False imprisonment is the unlawful restraint against his will of an individual's personal liberty. Shen's liberty was restrained in this case—he was not allowed to leave Taiwan. And, as Shen correctly points out, the term false imprisonment is broader than just confinement within a jail or prison. Shen's confinement, however, was to a whole country. He was free to move about Taiwan, and was not restrained in any way in his daily activities. Although it is difficult to define exactly how close the level of restraint must be, in this case the country of Taiwan is clearly too great an area within which to be falsely imprisoned. Therefore, the district court correctly granted judgment as a matter of law.

Whittaker v. Sandford

Supreme Judicial Court of Maine (1912)

The case shows that for several years prior to 1910, at a locality called Shiloh, in Durham, in this state, there had been gathered together a religious sect, of which the defendant was at least the religious leader. They dwelt in a so-called colony. There was a similar colony under the same religious leadership at Jaffa, in Syria. The plaintiff was a member of this sect, and her husband was one of its ministers. For the promotion of the work of the "movement," as it is called, a Yacht Club was incorporated, of which the defendant was president. The Yacht Club owned two sailing yachts, the "Kingdom" and the "Coronet." So far as this case is concerned, these yachts were employed in transporting members of the movement, back and forth, between the coast of Maine and Jaffa.

The plaintiff, with her four children, sailed on the Coronet to Jaffa in 1905. The plaintiff lived in Jerusalem and Jaffa, as a member of the colony, until March, 1909. At that time she decided to abandon the movement. She made her preparations to return to America by steamer, but did not obtain the necessary funds therefor until December 24, 1909. At that time the Kingdom was in the harbor at Jaffa, and the defendant was on board. On Christmas day he sent a messenger to ask the plaintiff to come on board. She went, first being assured by the messenger that she should be returned to shore. The defendant expressed a strong desire that she should come back to America on the Kingdom, rather than in a steamer, saying, as she says, that he could not bear the sting of having her come home by steamer; he having taken her out. The plaintiff fearing, as she says, that if she came on board the defendant's yacht she would not be let off until she was "won to the movement" again, discussed that subject with the defendant, and he assured her repeatedly that under no circumstances would she be detained on board the vessel after they got into port, and that she should be free to do what she wanted to the moment they reached shore. Relying upon this promise, she boarded the Kingdom and sailed for America with her four children.

The Kingdom arrived in Portland Harbor on the afternoon of Sunday, May 8, 1910. The plaintiff's husband, who was at Shiloh, was telephoned, and went at once to Portland Harbor. The Coronet was also in Portland Harbor at that time. Later both yachts sailed to South Freeport, reaching there Tuesday morning, May 10th. From this time until June 6th following the plaintiff claims that she was prevented from leaving the Kingdom, by the defendant, in such manner as to constitute false imprisonment.

The plaintiff claimed and testified that on two or three occasions the defendant personally refused to furnish her with a boat so that she could leave the Kingdom; that when she wanted to go ashore "they," evidently referring to the defendant and her husband, "had talked against it"; that the defendant "had spoken plainly that it was out of the question"; that when she spoke to him about it he said he would leave it to her husband to do what he wanted to, that he would not take the responsibility of separating families, but that, when she asked her husband to take her ashore, he replied, "we will see Mr. Sandford about it and see what he says." The plaintiff contended that in this way the defendant and her husband in effect played into each other's hands, and shifted the responsibility from one to the other, while she was the victim of this play of battledore and shuttlecock. It was contended that by virtue of the peculiar religious character attributed to the defendant by those who were in the movement, of whom the plaintiff's husband was one, being a minister of that faith, he possessed and exercised supreme control over the members, both on sea and on land, and that his wish was law both to their wills and consciences, and that the plaintiff's husband, whatever part he took in the matter, was either merely the defendant's instrument.

It therefore became pertinent for the plaintiff to show the nature and extent of the defendant's authority and power. This, of course, was only one step; but it was a step. Another would be to show that the defendant exercised that authority and that it was effective in restraining the plaintiff of her liberty.

And the plaintiff was permitted to testify to the following effect: Several years ago the defendant said that God gave him a message that Elijah was here, that he was the second Elijah, and had come to prepare the way for the coming of Christ; that he talked that to the people in the movement for years, and that they knew him as Elijah; that later he said God gave him messages and made him know that the Kingdom of God was established again on earth, and that God made him know that he was to be king among the people, the twelve tribes of Israel scattered out over all the earth, that God scattered them when they were in Palestine after he had brought them out of the land of Egypt, that they sinned and he scattered them, but he said that in the last days they should be restored and brought back to Palestine, and Palestine should be made a glorious land again as God intended it to be, and these people should be gathered up and brought back and restored to the true religion of Jesus Christ, and that God said in the Bible among the prophesies that when these days come and the people are restored He is going to give them a king; he said that a king shall reign and rule in righteousness; he said that God made him know that he was King David, and that he was to reign and rule in righteousness, and that all the earth was going to bow to him. And the witness testified further that all the people in the movement at Shiloh, which seems to have been the original home of the movement, and the place where the plaintiff's husband was minister, know him as King David, and call him so.

In connection with this exception, it may be noticed that one of the defendant's witnesses, a member of the movement, and apparently a frank and intelligent man, being asked on cross-examination to explain why the defendant is sometimes called King David, testified without objection: "We believe that Mr. Sandford is the David that is spoken of as the character that is to appear in the last days to prepare God's people for the coming of Christ."

This is not a religious question, but a question of law. We are not concerned in this case with the beliefs of the defendant and those connected with him. We do not seek to impugn in the slightest degree the grounds of their beliefs. But, whether right or wrong, we think that it is clear that to the trusting and devout followers of such a leader, his influence, his will, his wish, might easily, and probably would, become paramount over their minds, and would control their actions. Besides, the question of the nature and extent of the defendant's control was made relevant by the defendant's contention that the captain and other officers of the yacht, and not the defendant, were in control of the small boats, and that the control was practically independent of the defendant. It must be remembered that this discussion goes only to the admissibility of the evidence, and not to its effect. If in fact the power was not used by the defendant to keep the plaintiff on board the yacht against her will, the possession of the power cannot count against the defendant.

The defendant requested the court to instruct the jury that "to maintain her action the plaintiff must show some actual physical force exercised by the defendant or by someone acting as his agent and by his authority to restrain her of her liberty."

In the remaining counts it is alleged that the unlawful restraint was "by force and against the will of the plaintiff." The court instructed the jury that the plaintiff to recover must show that the restraint was physical, and not merely a moral influence; that it must have been actual physical restraint, in the sense that one intentionally locked into a room would be physically restrained but not necessarily involving physical force upon the person; that it was not necessary that the defendant, or any person by his direction, should lay his hand upon the plaintiff; that if the plaintiff was restrained so that she could not leave the yacht Kingdom by the intentional refusal to furnish transportation as agreed, she not having it in her power to escape otherwise, it would be a physical restraint and unlawful imprisonment. We think the instructions were apt and sufficient. If one should, without right, turn the key in a door, and thereby prevent a person in the room from leaving, it would be the simplest form of unlawful imprisonment. The restraint is physical. The four walls and the locked door are physical impediments to escape. Now is it different when one who is in control of a vessel at anchor, within practical rowing distance from the shore, who has agreed that a guest on board shall be free to leave, there being no means to leave except by rowboats, wrongfully refuses the guest the use of a boat? The boat is the key. By refusing the boat he turns the key. The guest is as effectually locked up as if there were walls along the sides of the vessel. The restraint is physical. The impassable sea is the physical barrier.

A careful study of the evidence leads us to conclude that the jury were warranted in finding that the defendant was guilty of unlawful imprisonment. This, to be sure, is not an action based upon the defendant's failure to keep his agreement to permit the plaintiff to leave the yacht as soon as it should reach shore. But his duty under the circumstances is an important consideration. It cannot be believed that either party to the agreement understood that it was his duty merely to bring her to an American harbor. The agreement implied that she was to go ashore. There was no practical way for her to go ashore except in the yacht's boats. The agreement must be understood to mean that he would bring her to land, or to allow her to get to land, by the only available means. The evidence is that he refused her a boat. His refusal was wrongful. The case leaves not the slightest doubt that he had the power to control the boats, if he chose to exercise it. It was not enough for him to leave it to the husband to say whether she might go ashore or not. She had a personal right to go on shore. If the defendant personally denied her the privilege, as the jury might find he did, it was a wrongful denial.

The defendant did not become a witness, but it is claimed for him that after Tuesday, May 10th, he assumed no responsibility whatever for the plaintiff, and left her in the care of her husband, specifically saying that he would leave it to her husband to say whether she could leave the yacht. From that date, he stayed on the Coronet, only coming aboard the Kingdom once, though on that occasion she says he refused her the use of a boat. From that date she was in the company of her husband, though they were not living in marital relations. She went ashore with him. She visited neighboring islands with him. She was trying to persuade him to leave the movement and make a home for her and their children. He was trying to persuade her to become again a member of the movement. When on shore with him she made no effort to escape. She says she believed it would be useless, and thus went back to the yacht with him. She says that when she did ask her husband to put her ashore to leave, he replied, "We will see Mr. Sandford about it and see what he says." She further says that the defendant had told her that "he" (her husband) "couldn't do it" (put her on shore).

Besides the evidence of express personal refusal on the part of the defendant, we think that a jury might well find upon the evidence that the defendant was strongly desirous that the plaintiff should not leave the yacht, probably for the reason that he hoped her husband's influence might lead her back into the movement, that the husband was strongly desirous of the same end, that if she left the yacht she would be beyond the influence of her husband, that the subject was a matter of conversation between the defendant and the husband, that in view of the relation which the defendant bore to the movement and to the husband, in view of the mystical character attributed to him, in view of the manifest power possessed by him over the minds of the members, growing out of a belief which we have already stated, and which the husband shared in, the husband, if not acting by express mutual understanding with the defendant, was the minister of his known will, with the result that the plaintiff was prevented from leaving the yacht, that the defendant was the superior, the controlling factor, by an influence intentionally used, in keeping her there, that he possessed the key that would unlock the situation, and that in violation of his duty he refused to use it, and thus restrained her of her liberty. If all this was true, the defendant is liable to the plaintiff. The verdict should not be set aside on that ground.

But the damages awarded seem to us manifestly excessive. The plaintiff, if imprisoned, was by no means in close confinement. She was afforded all the liberties of the yacht. She was taken on shore by her husband to do shopping and transact business at a bank. She visited neighboring islands with her husband and children, on one of which they enjoyed a family picnic. The case lacks the elements of humiliation and disgrace that frequently attend false imprisonment. She was respectfully treated as a guest in every way, except that she was restrained from quitting the yacht for good and all.

If the plaintiff remits all of the verdict in excess of $500, within 30 days after the certificate is received by the clerk, motion overruled; otherwise, motion sustained.

Knowlton v. Ross

Supreme Judicial Court of Maine (1915)

The plaintiff claims that she was restrained of her liberty by the defendants under circumstances constituting false imprisonment, until by means of the duress of such imprisonment she delivered to them a valuable diamond ring in pledge as security for the payment of a bill owed by her husband to one of them, and of another bill claimed to be owed by another person.

It appears that the plaintiff's family—that is, her husband, herself, and their two daughters—had been guests for several years at the summer hotel of Mr. Jacobs, one of the defendants, at Ogunquit. The bills for 1907 and 1908 had not been paid. In July, 1909, the family spent two days at the hotel. They had with them a friend, Mr. Lynch. The bills for all were charged to and paid by Mr. Knowlton, the plaintiff's husband. The plaintiff claims that at that time some talk was made about coming back later in the season, and that Mr. Jacobs showed them some rooms in a cottage of which he had the use, and told them that they could have them for $100 a week for all five, the four Knowltons and Lynch. In August, the plaintiff telephoned the management of the hotel for rooms and she was told that they had no rooms available for them. Notwithstanding this, on the next day, August 17th, the family and Mr. Lynch appeared, and after some colloquy were assigned to the cottage, but not to the rooms which the plaintiff says Mr. Jacobs had shown to them in July. From all this the plaintiff contends that Lynch was the guest of the family, and was so understood to be by Mr. Jacobs, and that for that reason Lynch's board was included in the $100 a week which was to be charged for the family. But Mr. Jacobs, denying that there was any arrangement made in July for the family or Lynch, charged Lynch $20 a week for his board, and charged Mr. Knowlton $100 a week for the board of himself wife, and daughters. Mr. Jacobs also claims that, owing to the failure of Knowlton to pay in 1907 and 1908, he declined to receive the family as guests until Mrs. Knowlton had promised to be personally responsible for the bill. This she denies. At the end of two weeks Knowlton gave the bookkeeper a draft for $225, payable September 16th, which was credited on his account. All the foregoing is material only as it tends to throw light on what happened on September 6th.

On that day Mr. Jacobs placed the bill against Knowlton and the one against Lynch in the hands of the defendant Ross for collection. Capias writs were made against these two on the strength of the oath of Jacobs that they were "about to depart and reside beyond the limits of the state," etc. It was later learned that Knowlton had gone to Boston. But Lynch was still at the hotel. Ross, with a deputy sheriff, went into a room, and Lynch was sent for. When he came in he was shown the writ against himself, and informed that he must pay, give bond, or go to jail. He protested that he was there only as a guest of the Knowltons, and therefore that the indebtedness was not his. At Lynch's request, the plaintiff was sent for to explain the matter. She came, and she, too, protested that the indebtedness was not Lynch's, but that it was her husband's. During the interview the writ against Knowlton was produced and shown to the plaintiff.

So far, there is no material disagreement; but as to the other details of the interview, the parties are wholly at variance. The plaintiff claims that when she went into the room the doors were closed, and as she thinks locked. At the same time she says that the deputy sheriff and the hotel manager placed themselves so as to be apparently guarding the exits from the room. She says that Ross said to her, "You people can't come to the state of Maine, and get your board here at a hotel, and leave without paying the bill;" "you know it is a state's prison offense to come into a state and leave without paying;" that he said also, "You don't want to go to jail; you don't want to disgrace yourself and your daughters to go;" and that she replied, "Well, we will go to jail." She says that Lynch then said, "You know what it means; it means for us all to go to jail." She claims that she was asked by Ross if she had any property that she could give as security for the claims; that she showed him the diamond ring, which he took and examined, and put in his pocket, and that "they decided to keep it until the bill was paid"; and that they then told her she might go.

On the other hand, the defendants claim that the doors were neither locked nor guarded, that there was no talk about any state's prison or jail offense, or about anybody's going to jail, except what was said to Lynch; that Lynch besought the plaintiff to "fix it up," and save him from going to jail; that it was arranged that she would take care of that bill; that in the same connection she mentioned the "family" bill, admitted that she had agreed to be responsible for that, and arranged to "fix" that up at the same time she "fixed" the Lynch bill; and as security for the payment of both bills, it is contended, she voluntarily put the ring in question into the possession of Ross. Whatever may have been said or done, it is entirely clear that as the result of the interview the plaintiff left the ring in Ross' possession, with the understanding, and with her assent, unless void by reason of duress, that it should be held by him as security for the payment of both claims; for the plaintiff herself has testified, with respect to the $225 draft which had been received by the bookkeeper, that she "asked Mr. Ross for it after he had taken the ring, and we were out of the room, and they had accepted the ring as a settlement from Mr. Knowlton."

We think, in the first place, that the evidence does not warrant the conclusion that there was any imprisonment of the plaintiff. She was present in the room at the request of Lynch, and not of the defendants. There was a writ against Lynch, and one against her husband, but none against her. She was not touched. She was not told she could not leave the room. The doors were closed, as would be natural under the circumstances. There is no credible evidence that they were locked. There was nothing to prevent her leaving the room, had she chosen to do so. She says the defendants made a show of guarding the exits from the room, that the officer walked back and forth, and that the manager stood for a while at one door. It must be remembered that the plaintiff was not there at the defendants' solicitation, that apparently they had had no purpose of pursuing her that day, that they had no process against her, but that Lynch was practically under arrest. Under these circumstances, the fact that the officer walked back and forth has no significance that she, too, was restrained of her liberty; and the fact, if it was a fact, that the manager stood at the door would be vastly more significant of a purpose of preventing intrusion by others than of preventing the going out of the plaintiff. The room was a public room, to which the guests of the hotel and the servants ordinarily had access; and the presence of outsiders could not have been desired by any of the parties. There was nothing in the conduct of the officer, or of the manager, we think, to justify the belief of the plaintiff that she was, as she terms it, "under arrest." If there were threats, as she claims, they did not constitute imprisonment. They would be evidence of an intention to imprison at some future time. To constitute false imprisonment, there must be actual physical restraint. Whittaker v. Sanford, 110 Me. 77.

Peterson v. Sorlien

Supreme Court of Minnesota (1980)

This action by plaintiff Susan Jungclaus Peterson for false imprisonment arises from an effort by her parents, in conjunction with other individuals, to prompt her disaffiliation from an organization known as The Way Ministry.

This case marks the emergence of a new cultural phenomenon: youth-oriented religious or pseudo-religious groups which utilize the techniques of what has been termed "coercive persuasion" or "mind control" to cultivate an uncritical and devoted following. The word "cult" is not used pejoratively but in its dictionary sense to describe an unorthodox system of belief characterized by "great or excessive devotion or dedication to some person, idea, or thing." Webster's New International Dictionary of the English Language Unabridged. Coercive persuasion is fostered through the creation of a controlled environment that heightens the susceptibility of a subject to suggestion and manipulation through sensory deprivation, physiological depletion, cognitive dissonance, peer pressure, and a clear assertion of authority and dominion. The aftermath of indoctrination is a severe impairment of autonomy and the ability to think independently, which induces a subject's unyielding compliance and the rupture of past connections, affiliations and associations.

At the time of the events in question, Susan Jungclaus Peterson was 21 years old. For most of her life, she lived with her family on a farm near Bird Island, Minnesota. In 1973, she graduated with honors from high school, ranking second in her class. She matriculated that fall at Moorhead State College. A dean's list student during her first year, her academic performance declined and her interests narrowed after she joined the local chapter of a group organized internationally and identified locally as The Way of Minnesota, Inc.

By the end of her freshman year, Susan was devoting many hours to The Way, listening to instructional tapes, soliciting new members and assisting in training sessions. As her sophomore year began, Susan committed herself significantly, selling the car her father had given her and working part-time as a waitress to finance her contributions to The Way. Susan spent the following summer in South Dakota, living in conditions described as appalling and overcrowded, while recruiting, raising money and conducting training sessions for The Way.

On May 24, 1976, defendant Norman Jungclaus, father of plaintiff, arrived at Moorhead to pick up Susan following the end of the third college quarter. Instead of returning to their family home, defendant drove with Susan to Minneapolis to the home of Veronica Morgel. Entering the home of Mrs. Morgel, Susan was greeted by Kathy Mills and several young people who wished to discuss Susan's involvement in the ministry. Each of those present had been in some way touched by the cult phenomenon. It was Kathy Mills, a self-styled professional deprogrammer, to whom the Jungclauses turned, and intermittently for the next sixteen days, it was in the home of Veronica Morgel that Susan stayed.

The avowed purpose of deprogramming is to break the hold of the cult over the individual through reason and confrontation. Initially, Susan was unwilling to discuss her involvement; she lay curled in a fetal position, in the downstairs bedroom where she first stayed, plugging her ears and crying while her father pleaded with her to listen to what was being said. This behavior persisted for two days during which she intermittently engaged in conversation, at one point screaming hysterically and flailing at her father. But by Wednesday Susan's demeanor had changed completely; she was friendly and vivacious and that night slept in an upstairs bedroom. Susan spent all day Thursday reading and conversing with her father and on Saturday night went roller-skating. On Sunday she played softball at a nearby park, afterwards enjoying a picnic lunch. The next week Susan spent in Columbus, Ohio, flying there with a former cult member who had shared with her the experiences of the previous week. While in Columbus, she spoke every day by telephone to her fiancé who, playing tapes and songs from the ministry's headquarters in Minneapolis, begged that she return to the fold. Susan expressed the desire to extricate her fiancé from the dominion of the cult.

Susan returned to Minneapolis on June 9. Unable to arrange a controlled meeting so that Susan could see her fiancé outside the presence of other members of the ministry, her parents asked that she sign an agreement releasing them from liability for their past weeks' actions. Refusing to do so, Susan stepped outside the Morgel residence with the puppy she had purchased in Ohio, motioned to a passing police car and shortly thereafter was reunited with her fiancé in the Minneapolis headquarters of The Way.

The period in question began on Monday, May 24, 1976, and ceased on Wednesday, June 9, 1976, a period of 16 days. The record clearly demonstrates that Susan willingly remained in the company of defendants for at least 13 of those days. During that time she took many excursions into the public sphere, playing softball and picnicking in a city park, roller-skating at a public rink, flying aboard public aircraft and shopping and swimming while relaxing in Ohio. Had Susan desired, manifold opportunities existed for her to alert the authorities of her allegedly unlawful detention; in Minneapolis, two police officers observed at close range the softball game in which she engaged; en route to Ohio, she passed through the security areas of the Twin Cities and Columbus airports in the presence of security guards and uniformed police; in Columbus she transacted business at a bank, went for walks in solitude and was interviewed by an F.B.I. agent who sought assurances of her safety. At no time during the 13-day period did she complain of her treatment or suggest that defendants were holding her against her will. If one is aware of a reasonable means of escape that does not present a danger of bodily or material harm, a restriction is not total and complete and does not constitute unlawful imprisonment.

The trial judge instructed that to deem consent a defense to the charge of false imprisonment for the entire period or for any part therein, a preponderance of the evidence must demonstrate that such plaintiff voluntarily consented. The central issue for the jury, then, was whether Susan voluntarily participated in the activities of the first three days. The jury concluded that her behavior constituted a waiver.

To determine whether the findings of the jury can be supported upon review, the behavior Susan manifested during the initial three days at issue must be considered in light of her actions in the remainder of the period. Because, it is argued, the cult conditioning process induces dramatic and non-consensual change giving rise to a new temporary identity on the part of the individuals whose consent is under examination, Susan's volitional capacity prior to treatment may well have been impaired. Following her readjustment, the evidence suggests that Susan was a different person, "like her old self." As such, the question of Susan's consent becomes a function of time. We therefore deem Susan's subsequent affirmation of defendants' actions dispositive.

Although carried out under colorably religious auspices, the method of cult indoctrination, viewed in a light most favorable to the prevailing party, is predicated on a strategy of coercive persuasion that undermines the capacity for informed consent. While we acknowledge that other social institutions may utilize a degree of coercion in promoting their objectives, none do so to the same extent or intend the same consequences. Society, therefore, has a compelling interest favoring intervention. The facts in this case support the conclusion that plaintiff only regained her volitional capacity to consent after engaging in the first three days of the deprogramming process. As such, we hold that when parents, or their agents, acting under the conviction that the judgmental capacity of their adult child is impaired, seek to extricate that child from what they reasonably believe to be a religious or pseudo-religious cult, and the child at some juncture assents to the actions in question, limitations upon the child's mobility do not constitute meaningful deprivations of personal liberty sufficient to support a judgment for false imprisonment.

TRESPASS

Green Tree Acceptance of Texas, Inc. v. McGrath

Court of Appeals of Texas (1998)

This case revolves around the repossession of a manufactured home. The home was originally purchased by Kelly Junker, who sold it to Arthur and Jenny Dooley. Green Tree Acceptance of Texas, Inc. had a lien on the home. The Dooleys, without telling Green Tree, moved the home to their own property. Eventually, the Dooleys fell behind in their payments. In April, 1990, the McGraths bought the Dooleys' property, but not the manufactured home. Because the Dooleys told the McGraths they did not intend to continue making payments on the home, the McGraths contacted Green Tree about buying the home.

Green Tree told the McGraths it would obtain a Federal Housing Authority (FHA) appraisal to determine the sales price, and that this appraisal would take about three weeks. The McGraths told Green Tree that no one was allowed on the property without notifying them and that the gate to the property was locked.

The McGraths gave Kathy Lucas, a Green Tree employee, permission to meet a neighbor at the property on April 7, 1990, to conduct an FHA appraisal on the home. However, Lucas entered the property on April 5, 1990, by crawling under the fence, and conducted a repossession inspection. On her inspection form, Lucas noted that the home's skirting was solid rock and that the "movers must remove fence and prune trees from drive."

Green Tree hired AAA Transit, an independent contractor, to repossess the home. Bill Capps, inventory control manager for Green Tree, told AAA's owner, Ken Lee, that this home would be difficult to remove because of the rock skirting and the trees. Green Tree sent AAA a map and a landlord's waiver, which AAA required before they would repossess a manufactured home. The map was to the McGraths' property, but the landlord's waiver was signed by Junker, the original purchaser of the home.

When the AAA repossession crew arrived at the McGraths' property, the gate to the property was not locked. They entered the property and removed the home. In doing so, the repossession crew removed the rock skirting surrounding the home and cut down and trimmed trees. The crew also removed the fence by cutting down the fence posts.

The McGraths sued Green Tree and AAA for malicious trespass and damages. The parties stipulated that the proper measure of actual damages was $1,250.00. The McGraths and AAA settled before trial for $7,000.00.

The jury found that Green Tree, through AAA, trespassed on the McGraths' property. The jury awarded the McGraths $1,250.00 for loss of fair market value to the property, $3,000.00 for necessary clean up expenses, and nothing for mental anguish. The jury also found that Green Tree, through AAA, committed the trespass maliciously or in wanton disregard of the McGraths' rights. For the malicious trespass, the jury awarded the McGraths $60,000.00 in exemplary damages. The court reformed the cleanup damages to $1,995.00, to reflect the actual money the McGraths paid for the cleanup. The court also gave Green Tree credit for the $7,000.00 AAA paid the McGraths.

It is well settled that, "One is subject to liability to another for trespass, irrespective of whether he thereby causes harm to any legally protected interest of the other, if he intentionally ... enters land in the possession of the other, or causes a thing or a third person to do so." Thus, Green Tree had notice it would be liable if it caused AAA to trespass.

Furthermore, and more importantly, Green Tree had notice that it could be liable for exemplary damages. A plaintiff is entitled to exemplary damages for trespass if the evidence shows some element of fraud, malice or oppression. The trespass must be initiated by or accompanied with some evil intent or with complete disregard of anyone's rights.

Green Tree argues that the $60,000.00 exemplary damage award was excessive because there were no aggravating factors such as prior complaints or lawsuits against Green Tree based on trespass and because the ratio of exemplary damages to actual damages is excessive.

There are three factors that must be examined to determine if an award of exemplary damages is excessive: the reprehensibility of the defendant's conduct, the ratio of the exemplary damages to the actual harm, and the sanctions for comparable misconduct.

Reprehensibility

While it is true that there was no evidence that Green Tree had trespassed in the past, there was evidence that Green Tree committed this trespass with trickery and deceit. According to the evidence, Green Tree, aware of the type of damages that would occur, knowingly deceived AAA by providing it with an ineffective and inapplicable landlord's waiver, causing AAA to trespass on the McGraths' property in order to repossess the home. AAA's owner, Ken Lee, testified that AAA would not enter property without a landlord's waiver, and thus would not have entered the McGraths' property without a waiver. Further, the evidence shows Green Tree deceived the McGraths, telling them that it would obtain an FHA appraisal on the home so that the McGraths could make an offer on the home. Green Tree never told the McGraths that it planned to repossess the home and it never attempted to obtain the McGraths' consent to enter the property for the purpose of repossessing the home, even though Mr. McGrath told Green Tree at least three times that Green Tree should inform him when it was going to inspect the house so McGrath or someone else could unlock the gate for Green Tree and be present during the inspection. Finally, Larry Simmons, Green Tree's regional manager, testified that it is Green Tree's position that it does not need to obtain permission either from a court or from the property owner to enter onto the property owner's land and repossess a home on which someone other than the property owner has defaulted.

Ratio

The second factor that must be examined is the ratio of the exemplary damages to the actual harm. Whether the ratio of exemplary damages to actual damages is constitutionally acceptable cannot be determined by a mathematical formula. There is no bright line; the reasonableness of the ratio should be judged on the facts of each case.

Sanctions for Comparable Misconduct

The third factor that must be examined to determine if an exemplary damage award is excessive is the amount and type of civil or criminal penalties that could be imposed for comparable misconduct. In Texas, criminal trespass is a Class B misdemeanor, which carries a maximum $2,000 fine. This relatively small comparable sanction is not particularly instructive because Green Tree's conduct was not what the legislature contemplated in passing a criminal trespass statute. The criminal trespass statute is intended to prevent a person from entering or remaining on property without informed consent of the owner. Green Tree's action, through AAA, was an intentional, malicious act, committed through trickery and deceit.

Under these circumstances, where an egregious act has resulted in a fairly small amount of economic damages, we cannot say this award of $60,000.00 was beyond the constitutionally acceptable range.

Intel Corporation v. Hamidi

Supreme Court of California (2003)

Hamidi, a former Intel engineer, formed an organization named Former and Current Employees of Intel (FACE–Intel) to disseminate information and views critical of Intel's employment and personnel policies and practices. FACE–Intel maintained a Web site (which identified Hamidi as Webmaster and as the organization's spokesperson) containing such material. In addition, over a 21–month period Hamidi, on behalf of FACE–Intel, sent six mass e-mails to employee addresses on Intel's electronic mail system. The messages criticized Intel's employment practices, warned employees of the dangers those practices posed to their careers, suggested employees consider moving to other companies, solicited employees' participation in FACE–Intel, and urged employees to inform themselves further by visiting FACE–Intel's Web site. The messages stated that recipients could, by notifying the sender of their wishes, be removed from FACE–Intel's mailing list; Hamidi did not subsequently send messages to anyone who requested removal.

Each message was sent to thousands of addresses. There is no evidence that the receipt or internal distribution of Hamidi's electronic messages damaged Intel's computer system or slowed or impaired its functioning. Intel did present uncontradicted evidence, however, that many employee recipients asked a company official to stop the messages and that staff time was consumed in attempts to block further messages from FACE–Intel.

DISCUSSION

Dubbed by Prosser the "little brother of conversion," the tort of trespass to chattels allows recovery for interferences with possession of personal property not sufficiently important to be classed as conversion, and so to compel the defendant to pay the full value of the thing with which he has interfered.

Though not amounting to conversion, the defendant's interference must, to be actionable, have caused some injury to the chattel or to the plaintiff's rights in it. Trespass to chattels lies where an intentional interference with the possession of personal property has proximately caused injury. In cases of interference with possession of personal property not amounting to conversion, the owner has a cause of action for trespass and may recover only the actual damages suffered by reason of the impairment of the property or the loss of its use. In modern American law generally, trespass remains as an occasional remedy for minor interferences, resulting in some damage, but not sufficiently serious or sufficiently important to amount to the greater tort of conversion.

The dispositive issue in this case, therefore, is whether Hamidi's actions caused or threatened to cause damage to Intel's computer system, or injury to its rights in that personal property, such as to entitle Intel to judgment as a matter of law. To review, the undisputed evidence revealed no actual or threatened damage to Intel's computer hardware or software and no interference with its ordinary and intended operation. Intel was not dispossessed of its computers, nor did Hamidi's messages prevent Intel from using its computers for any measurable length of time. Intel presented no evidence its system was slowed or otherwise impaired by the burden of delivering Hamidi's electronic messages. Nor was there any evidence transmission of the messages imposed any marginal cost on the operation of Intel's computers. In sum, no evidence suggested that in sending messages through Intel's Internet connections and internal computer system Hamidi used the system in any manner in which it was not intended to function or impaired the system in any way. Nor does the evidence show the request of any employee to be removed from FACE–Intel's mailing list was not honored.

Intel's theory would expand the tort of trespass to chattels to cover virtually any unconsented—to communication that, solely because of its content, is unwelcome to the recipient or intermediate transmitter. Damage of this nature—the distraction of reading or listening to an unsolicited communication—is not within the scope of the injury against which the trespass to chattel tort protects, and indeed trivializes it. After all, the property interest protected by the old action of trespass was that of possession; and this has continued to affect the character of the action. Reading an e-mail transmitted to equipment designed to receive it, in and of itself, does not affect the possessory interest in the equipment. Indeed, if a chattel's receipt of an electronic communication constitutes a trespass to that chattel, then not only are unsolicited telephone calls and faxes trespasses to chattel, but unwelcome radio waves and television signals also constitute a trespass to chattel every time the viewer inadvertently sees or hears the unwanted program. While unwelcome communications, electronic or otherwise, can cause a variety of injuries to economic relations, reputation and emotions, those interests are protected by other branches of tort law; in order to address them, we need not create a fiction of injury to the communication system.

Nor may Intel appropriately assert a property interest in its employees' time as employees are not chattels (at least not in the legal sense of the term). Whatever interest Intel may have in preventing its employees from receiving disruptive communications, it is not an interest in personal property, and trespass to chattels is therefore not an action that will lie to protect it. Nor, finally, can the fact Intel staff spent time attempting to block Hamidi's messages be bootstrapped into an injury to Intel's possessory interest in its computers. It is circular to premise the damage element of a tort solely upon the steps taken to prevent the damage. Injury can only be established by the completed tort's consequences, not by the cost of the steps taken to avoid the injury and prevent the tort; otherwise, we can create injury for every supposed tort.

Intel connected its e-mail system to the Internet and permitted its employees to make use of this connection both for business and, to a reasonable extent, for their own purposes. In doing so, the company necessarily contemplated the employees' receipt of unsolicited as well as solicited communications from other companies and individuals. That some communications would, because of their contents, be unwelcome to Intel management was virtually inevitable. Hamidi did nothing but use the e-mail system for its intended purpose—to communicate with employees. The system worked as designed, delivering the messages without any physical or functional harm or disruption. These occasional transmissions cannot reasonably be viewed as impairing the quality or value of Intel's computer system. We conclude, therefore, that Intel has not presented undisputed facts demonstrating an injury to its personal property, or to its legal interest in that property, that support an action for trespass to chattels.

IIED

GTE Southwest v. Bruce

Supreme Court of Texas (1999)

Three GTE employees, Rhonda Bruce, Linda Davis, and Joyce Poelstra, sued GTE for intentional infliction of emotional distress premised on the constant humiliating and abusive behavior of their supervisor, Morris Shields. The supply department was small, consisting of two offices and a store room. There were approximately eight employees other than Shields. Bruce, Davis, and Poelstra ("the employees") worked under Shields. Bruce, Davis, and Poelstra complained to GTE of Shields's conduct, alleging that Shields constantly harassed and intimidated them. The employees complained about Shields's daily use of profanity, short temper, and his abusive and vulgar dictatorial manner. The employees complained that, among other offensive acts, Shields repeatedly yelled, screamed, cursed, and even "charged" at them. In addition, he intentionally humiliated and embarrassed the employees.

To recover damages for intentional infliction of emotional distress, a plaintiff must prove that: (1) the defendant acted intentionally or recklessly; (2) the conduct was extreme and outrageous; (3) the actions of the defendant caused the plaintiff emotional distress; and (4) the resulting emotional distress was severe.

GTE first argues that Shields's conduct is not extreme and outrageous. To be extreme and outrageous, conduct must be so outrageous in character, and so extreme in degree, as to go beyond all possible bounds of decency, and to be regarded as atrocious, and utterly intolerable in a civilized community. Generally, insensitive or even rude behavior does not constitute extreme and outrageous conduct. Similarly, mere insults, indignities, threats, annoyances, petty oppressions, or other trivialities do not rise to the level of extreme and outrageous conduct.

GTE contends that the evidence establishes nothing more than an ordinary employment dispute. To the contrary, the employees produced evidence that, over a period of more than two years, Shields engaged in a pattern of grossly abusive, threatening, and degrading conduct. Shields began regularly using the harshest vulgarity shortly after his arrival at the facility. In response, Bruce and Davis informed Shields that they were uncomfortable with obscene jokes, vulgar cursing, and sexual innuendo in the office. Despite these objections, Shields continued to use exceedingly vulgar language on a daily basis. Several witnesses testified that Shields used the word "f—" as part of his normal pattern of conversation, and that he regularly heaped abusive profanity on the employees. Linda Davis testified that Shields used this language to get a reaction. Gene Martin, another GTE employee, testified that Shields used the words "f—" and "motherf—er" frequently when speaking with the employees. On one occasion when Bruce asked Shields to curb his language because it was offensive, Shields positioned himself in front of her face, and screamed, "I will do and say any damn thing I want. And I don't give a s— who likes it." Another typical example is when Gene Martin asked Shields to stop his yelling and vulgarity because it upset the female employees, and Shields replied "I'm tired of walking on f—ing eggshells, trying to make people happy around here." There was further evidence that Shields's harsh and vulgar language was not merely accidental, but seemed intended to abuse the employees.

More importantly, the employees testified that Shields repeatedly physically and verbally threatened and terrorized them. There was evidence that Shields was continuously in a rage, and that Shields would frequently assault each of the employees by physically charging at them. When doing so, Shields would bend his head down, put his arms straight down by his sides, ball his hands into fists, and walk quickly toward or lunge at the employees, stopping uncomfortably close to their faces while screaming and yelling. The employees were exceedingly frightened by this behavior, afraid that Shields might hit them. Linda Davis testified that Shields charged the employees with the intent to frighten them. At least once, another employee came between Shields and Poelstra to protect her from Shields's charge. A number of witnesses testified that Shields frequently yelled and screamed at the top of his voice, and pounded his fists when requesting the employees to do things. Bruce testified that Shields would "come up fast" and "get up over her"—causing her to lean back—and yell and scream in her face for her to get things for him. Shields included vulgar language in his yelling and screaming. Bruce stated that such conduct was not a part of any disciplinary action against her. Further, the incidents usually occurred in the open rather than in private. Bruce testified that, on one occasion, Shields began beating a banana on his desk, and when he jumped up and slammed the banana into the trash, Bruce thought he would hit her.

Bruce also told of an occasion when Shields entered Bruce's office and went into a rage because Davis had left her purse on a chair and Bruce had placed her umbrella on a filing cabinet in the office. Shields yelled and screamed for Bruce to clean up her office. Shields yelled, "If you don't get things picked up in this office, you will not be working for me."

Bruce also testified that Shields called her into his office every day and would have her stand in front of him, sometimes for as long as thirty minutes, while Shields simply stared at her. Bruce was not allowed to leave Shields's office until she was dismissed, even though Shields would periodically talk on the phone or read papers. This often occurred several times a day. Bruce testified that it made her nauseated and intimidated her. On one occasion, Shields backed Bruce into a corner, leaned over her, and said, "Rumor has it that you know how to get anything you want out here." During an annual review, Shields said to Bruce, "You're mean and you're deadly, very deadly." Davis also testified that Shields would stand over her desk and stare at her.

Shields required Bruce and Davis, both general clerks at GTE, to purchase vacuum cleaners with company funds and to vacuum their offices daily, despite the fact that the company had a cleaning service that performed janitorial services such as vacuuming. The purpose of this seemed not to clean, but to humiliate. Bruce testified that she was ridiculed by other employees. Shields also yelled and screamed when he discovered a spot on the carpet; he made Bruce get on her hands and knees and clean the spots while he stood over her yelling. Poelstra testified that Shields required her to clean tobacco stains from a wall in the warehouse. Poelstra testified that, after she forgot her paperwork for a driving test, Shields ordered her to wear a post-it note on her shirt that said, "Don't forget your paperwork."

We agree with the overwhelming weight of authority in this state and around the country that when repeated or ongoing severe harassment is shown, the conduct should be evaluated as a whole in determining whether it is extreme and outrageous.

GTE argues that the conduct complained of is an ordinary employment dispute because the employees' complaints are really that Shields was a poor supervisor with an objectionable management style. GTE also contends that the actions are employment disputes because Shields committed the acts in the course of disciplining his employees.

We recognize that, even when an employer or supervisor abuses a position of power over an employee, the employer will not be liable for mere insults, indignities, or annoyances that are not extreme and outrageous. But Shields's ongoing acts of harassment, intimidation, and humiliation and his daily obscene and vulgar behavior, which GTE defends as his "management style," went beyond the bounds of tolerable workplace conduct.

Occasional malicious and abusive incidents should not be condoned, but must often be tolerated in our society. But once conduct such as that shown here becomes a regular pattern of behavior and continues despite the victim's objection and attempts to remedy the situation, it can no longer be tolerated. It is the severity and regularity of Shields's abusive and threatening conduct that brings his behavior into the realm of extreme and outrageous conduct. Conduct such as being regularly assaulted, intimidated, and threatened is not typically encountered nor expected in the course of one's employment, nor should it be accepted in a civilized society. An employer certainly has much leeway in its chosen methods of supervising and disciplining employees, but terrorizing them is simply not acceptable. If GTE or Shields was dissatisfied with the employees' performance, GTE could have terminated them, disciplined them, or taken some other more appropriate approach to the problem instead of fostering the abuse, humiliation, and intimidation that was heaped on the employees. Accordingly, the trial court properly submitted the issue to the jury, and there was some evidence to support the jury's conclusion that Shields's conduct was extreme and outrageous.

GTE next contends that any distress the employees suffered was not severe. GTE argues that the employees' complaints of embarrassment, fear, stomach aches, loss of sleep, and headaches are problems that are normally dealt with by each of us in everyday life.

Emotional distress includes all highly unpleasant mental reactions such as embarrassment, fright, horror, grief, shame, humiliation, and worry. Severe emotional distress is distress that is so severe that no reasonable person could be expected to endure it. The employees testified that, as a result of being exposed to Shields's outrageous conduct, they experienced a variety of emotional problems, including crying spells, emotional outbursts, nausea, stomach disorders, headaches, difficulty in sleeping and eating, stress, anxiety, and depression. This evidence is legally sufficient to support the jury's finding that the employees suffered severe emotional distress.

Accordingly, we affirm the court of appeals' judgment.

Nickerson v. Hodges

Supreme Court of Louisiana (1920)

Miss Nickerson was a kinswoman of Burton and Lawson Deck, the exact degree of relationship not being fully shown by the record, and there had been, in the family, a tradition that these two gentlemen, who died many years ago, had prior to their deaths, buried a large amount of gold coin on the place now owned by the defendant John W. Smith. She was employed by the California Perfume Company to solicit orders for their wares and on the occasion of a visit to the city of Shreveport seems to have interviewed a negro fortune teller, who told her that her relatives had buried the gold, and gave her what purported to be a map showing its location on the property of Smith. Thereafter, with the help of some three or four other people, she spent several months digging around the house and on the premises of Smith, who seems to have extended them a cordial welcome, and to have permitted them to dig almost without limit as to time and place, and in addition boarded the fortune hunters without charge. We assume that this was due, perhaps, to the fact that he, too, had a slight hope that they might find something, and he was to receive a part for his concessions. At any rate, the diggers pursued their course with such persistence and at such lengths, digging around the roots of shade trees, the pillars of his house, until finally, his daughter, Minnie Smith, William Baker, and H. R. Hayes conceived the idea of themselves providing a pot of gold for the explorers to find. Accordingly they obtained an old copper kettle, filled it with rocks and wet dirt, and buried it in an old chimney seat on the adjoining place, where the searchers were intending to also prospect for the supposed treasure. Two lids were placed on the pot, the first being fastened down with hay wire; then a note was written by Hayes, dated July 1, 1884, directing whoever should find the pot not to open it for three days, and to notify all the heirs. This note was wrapped in tin, placed between the first and second lids, and the latter was also securely fastened down with hay wire. This took place sometime toward the latter part of March, and, according to these three defendants, was to have been an April fool; but plans miscarried somewhat, and the proper opportunity for the find did not present itself until April 14th. On that day Miss Nickerson and her associates were searching and digging near the point where the pot had been buried, when one Grady Hayes, a brother of H. R. Hayes, following directions from the latter, and apparently helping the explorers to hunt for the gold, dug up the pot and gave the alarm. All of those in the vicinity, of course, rushed to the spot, those who were in on the secret being apparently as much excited as the rest, and, after some discussion, it was decided to remove the lid. When this was done, the note was discovered, and H. R. Hayes advised Miss Nickerson that he thought it proper that its directions should be carried out, and that the bank was the best place to deposit the gold for safe-keeping, until the heirs were notified. Following this suggestion, the pot taken to the bank for deposit. Defendant Gatling was the cashier of the bank, but refused to give a receipt for the deposit as a pot of gold, because he did not know what it contained.

It did not take long for the news to spread that Miss Nickerson had found a pot of gold, and the discussion and interest in the matter became so general that defendant A. J. Hodges, vice president of the bank, decided to examine the pot, so that, in event it did contain gold, proper precautions to guard the bank might be taken. These two undid the wire sufficiently to peep into the pot, and discovered that it apparently contained only dirt. They then replaced the lid and held their tongues until the reappearance of Miss Nickerson.

After depositing the pot in the bank, Miss Nickerson induced Judge R. C. Drew to accompany her to the bank the following Monday for the purpose of seeing that the ceremonies surrounding the opening of the treasure were properly conducted. Judge Drew swears that he had heard in some way that the matter was a joke, and so informed Miss Nickerson, warning her not to place too much faith in the idea that she was about to come into a fortune, but that finally, because of his friendly relations with and kindly feeling toward her, he consented and did go, mainly to gratify her wishes. Some half a dozen other relatives of Burton and Lawson Deck were notified, and accompanied Miss Nickerson to the bank.

With the stage thus set, the parties all appeared at the bank on Monday morning. Judge Drew approached Gatling and informed him that it was desired that the pot be produced for the purpose of opening and examining the contents for the benefit of those assembled. The testimony of the witnesses varies a little as to just when the storm began; some say, as soon as the sack was brought out. Miss Nickerson discovered that the string was tied near the top, instead of down low around the pot, and immediately commenced to shout that she had been robbed; others insist that she was calm until the package was opened and the mocking earth and stones met her view. Be that as it may, she flew into a rage, threw the lid of the pot at Gatling, and for some reason, not clearly explained, turned the force of her wrath upon Hayes to such an extent that he appealed for protection, and Bushong, with another, held her arms to prevent further violence.

Miss Nickerson was a maiden, nearing the age of 45 years, and some 20 years before had been an inmate of an insane asylum, to the knowledge of those who had thus deceived her. She was energetic and self-supporting in her chosen line of employment, as a soap salesperson, until she met the fortune teller who gave her the information which she evidently firmly believed would ultimately enable her to find the fortune. The conspirators, no doubt, merely intended what they did as a practical joke, and had no willful intention of doing the lady any injury. However, the results were quite serious indeed, and the mental suffering and humiliation must have been quite unbearable, to say nothing of the disappointment and conviction, which she carried to her grave some two years later, that she had been robbed.

If Miss Nickerson were still living, we should be disposed to award her damages in a substantial sum, to compensate her for the wrong thus done; but as to the present plaintiffs, her legal heirs, we think that a judgment of $500 will reasonably serve the ends of justice.

Homer v. Long

Court of Special Appeals of Maryland (1992)

The American Psychiatric Association has declared, in clear and unmistakable terms, that sexual intimacies between a psychiatrist and his or her patient are unethical and forbidden. And yet, unfortunately, it occurs. According to Mr. James J. Homer, it occurred between the defendant, S. Eugene Long, M.D., and Mr. Homer's wife, Vicki Homer, and it led, ultimately, to the breakup of the Homer marriage.

The Homers were married in 1966; they have two children who, at the time of the relevant events here, were teenagers. In 1981, Ms. Homer began to suffer from depression which became more pronounced in 1985 following a series of particularly stressful events in her life. On October 25, 1985, she attempted to commit suicide and was taken to the emergency room. Mr. Homer decided to retain a psychiatrist to perform an initial evaluation and he selected Dr. Long. Dr. Long persuaded Mr. Homer to place her under his care, where she would receive appropriate counseling and psychiatric treatment.

At some point, Dr. Long used the personal and confidential information that he had received from Mr. Homer to seduce Mrs. Homer and become sexually intimate with her, apparently as part of his treatment of Mrs. Homer. Homer asserts that his wife, at the time, was dependent, needy, and vulnerable, and that Dr. Long prevented her from seeing her family so that he could embark upon a course of treatment which included an exploitative sexual relationship with her, that he used the personal information supplied by Mr. Homer to manipulate Mrs. Homer's feelings, positively toward Dr. Long, and negatively, toward Mr. Homer, and that he effected and accomplished a transference on the part of Mrs. Homer pursuant to which she came to rely on him and to perceive him as the most important person in her life. As "part of his plan to control Mrs. Homer, in May, 1986, Dr. Long employed her as a typist.

Mr. Homer contends that, although he did not discover the sexual relationship between his wife and Dr. Long until the spring of 1987, the evidence that he then had of it showed that it had been on-going since June, 1986.

To recover in an action for intentional infliction of emotional distress, a plaintiff must show (1) conduct that is intentional or reckless; (2) conduct that is also extreme and outrageous; (3) a causal connection between the wrongful conduct and the emotional distress; and (4) that the emotional distress is severe.

There is no doubt that Dr. Long's conduct, as alleged, would be extreme and outrageous as to Ms. Homer, who, so far at least, has not chosen to complain of it. And, had Mr. Homer also been a patient of Dr. Long, it could be regarded as outrageous to him as well: A jury may find extreme and outrageous conduct where a psychologist who is retained to improve a marital relationship implements a course of extreme conduct which is injurious to the patient and designed to facilitate a romantic, sexual relationship between the therapist and the patient's spouse. But that is not the case here.

There are situations in which conduct directed principally at one person has been regarded as extreme and outrageous as to another, but normally the other person must be present to witness the conduct in order to recover. Where such conduct is directed at a third person, the actor is subject to liability if he intentionally or recklessly causes severe emotional distress (a) to a member of such person's immediate family who is present at the time, whether or not such distress results in bodily harm, or (b) to any other person who is present at the time, if such distress results in bodily harm.

Prosser and Keeton make the same point. In discussing acts directed at third persons they note: "Ordinarily recovery in such cases is limited to plaintiffs who are not only present at the time, but are known by the defendant to be present, so that the mental effect can reasonably be anticipated by the defendant. The distinction between the wife who sees her husband shot down before her eyes, and the one who hears about it five minutes later, may be a highly artificial one; but an argument in justification is the obvious necessity of drawing a line somewhere short of the widow who learns of the decease ten years afterward, when the genuineness and gravity of her distress may very reasonably be doubted."

We see no reason not to apply the general rule. The emotional and economic trauma likely to arise from the seduction of one's spouse is not limited to the case where the seducer is the spouse's therapist. The conduct may be just as outrageous and the harm may be just as great where the seducer is a neighbor, a good friend, a relative, an employee or business associate of the plaintiff, or indeed anyone in whom the plaintiff has imposed trust or for whom he or she has special regard. To relax or abrogate the presence requirement in such cases would greatly expand the scope of the tort, which we are unwilling to do.

Yeager v. Local Union 20

Supreme Court of Ohio (1983)

Plaintiff-appellant, David M. Yeager, was employed as a vice-president and general manager of Browning-Ferris Industries ("BFI") in Toledo, Ohio. His responsibilities included oversight and supervision of BFI employees and operations. Plaintiff alleges that a group from Local 20 entered his office, threatening him with injury, threatening to shut BFI down; made menacing remarks concerning plaintiff and his family; and threatened to "get" plaintiff. As a result, plaintiff alleges that this incident caused him great anxiety for his welfare and that of his family, and led to deleterious physical consequences (*i.e.,* severe stomach pain and discomfort caused by an ulcer or aggravation of a pre-existing ulcerous condition, necessitating a week long hospital stay with medical expenses of nearly $5,000).

Plaintiff also alleges that a picketing and handbilling incident took place outside the confines of the BFI plant. The picket signs and handbills described plaintiff as being a "Little Hitler"; accused him of operating "a Nazi concentration camp" at BFI; alleged that plaintiff did not support the Constitution of the United States; used "Gestapo" tactics; and cheated his employees.

Opinion

Appellant argues that the appellees' conduct caused him severe emotional distress, and that therefore, he should be permitted to state a cause of action for the intentional infliction of emotional distress.

Until today, Ohio was the only jurisdiction in this country that refused to recognize the independent tort of the intentional infliction of serious emotional distress. The reasoning behind this refusal to recognize this cause of action was that " '[t]he damages sought to be recovered are too remote and speculative. The injury is more sentimental than substantial. Being easily simulated and hard to disprove, there is no standard by which it can be justly, or even approximately, compensated.'"

Our prior decisions have explored the reasoning behind the unwillingness of courts to recognize the validity of an action grounded on invasion of emotional tranquillity alone, along with the apprehensions of courts concerning the consequences in allowing recovery for emotional distress. Suffice it to say that we have rejected the skeptical approach embodied in the past cases in favor of conforming the law to the realities of modern medical and psychiatric advancements.

Thus, we hold that in order to state a claim alleging the intentional infliction of emotional distress, the emotional distress alleged must be serious. As Dean Prosser reasoned in his learned treatise, "[i]t would be absurd for the law to seek to secure universal peace of mind, and many interferences with it must of necessity be left to other agencies of social control. 'Against a large part of the frictions and irritations and clashing of temperaments incident to participation in a community life, a certain toughening of the mental hide is a better protection than the law could ever be.' But this is a poor reason for denying recovery for any genuine, serious mental injury." Prosser, Law of Torts (4 Ed.1971) 51, Section 12.

The standard we adopt in our recognition of the tort of intentional infliction of serious emotional distress is succinctly spelled out in the Restatement as follows: "One who by extreme and outrageous conduct intentionally or recklessly causes severe emotional distress to another is subject to liability for such emotional distress, and if bodily harm to the other results from it, for such bodily harm." Restatement of the Law 2d, Torts (1965) 71, Section 46(1).

With respect to the requirement that the conduct alleged be "extreme and outrageous," we find comment *d* to Section 46 of the Restatement, *supra,* at 73, to be instructive in describing this standard:

It has not been enough that the defendant has acted with an intent which is tortious or even criminal, or that he has intended to inflict emotional distress, or even that his conduct has been characterized by 'malice,' or a degree of aggravation which would entitle the plaintiff to punitive damages for another tort. Liability has been found only where the conduct has been so outrageous in character, and so extreme in degree, as to go beyond all possible bounds of decency, and to be regarded as atrocious, and utterly intolerable in a civilized community. Generally, the case is one in which the recitation of the facts to an average member of the community would arouse his resentment against the actor, and lead him to exclaim, 'Outrageous!

We reverse the court of appeals in part and remand the cause to the trial court for further proceedings on the cause of action for intentional infliction of emotional distress.

DEFENSES

Gortarez v. Smitty's Super Valu

Supreme Court of Arizona (1984)

Ernest Gortarez, age 16, and his cousin, Albert Hernandez, age 18, went to Smitty's store. They visited the automotive department, where Hernandez selected a power booster which cost $22.00. While Hernandez was paying for the power booster, Gortarez picked up a 59-cent vaporizer used to freshen the air in cars. Gortarez asked if he could pay for it in the front of the store when he finished shopping. The clerk said yes, but decided that the request was suspicious and had a hunch that Gortarez would try to leave the store without paying for the item.

The two cousins wandered through the store, looking at other merchandise, and finally left the store through an unattended check-out aisle. The clerk, Robert Sjulestad, had followed the two through the store, in aisles parallel to where the young men were walking, so that there were occasions when he could not observe Gortarez below shoulder level. Since Sjulestad did not see them dispose of or pay for the vaporizer, he concluded that Gortarez or Hernandez took the item without paying for it.

Sjulestad then told the assistant manager and the security guard, Daniel Gibson, that "those two guys just ripped us off." According to Gibson's testimony, Sjulestad explained that "they had picked up a vaporizer and asked to pay for it in the front, and then didn't pay for it, as I watched them walk through, and they obviously did not pay for anything at that time."

Gibson and Scott Miller, the assistant manager, along with two other store employees, then ran out of the store to catch the two young men as they were about to get inside their car in the parking lot. Miller went to the passenger side to intercept Gortarez, while Gibson went for Hernandez, who was about to open the car door on the driver's side. Gibson said that he identified himself as an officer by showing his badge as he ran up to Hernandez. (Gibson was an off-duty police officer working as a security guard for Smitty's.) Gibson told Hernandez: "I believe you have something you did not pay for." He then seized Hernandez, put his arms on the car and began searching him. Hernandez offered no resistance even though Gibson did not ask for the vaporizer, nor say what he was looking for. In cross-examination, Gibson admitted that Hernandez did nothing to resist him, and, as Gibson searched him, Hernandez kept repeating that he did not have anything that he had not paid for.

Meanwhile, on the other side of the car, flanked by Miller, Gortarez saw Gibson grab Hernandez, push him up against the car, and search him. Gortarez was outraged at this behavior and used strong language to protest the detention and the search—yelling at Gibson to leave his cousin alone. According to Gortarez, he thought the men were looking for the vaporizer because he heard Gibson tell the others to watch out for the bottle, and to look under the car for the bottle. Gortarez testified that he told the men that Hernandez did not have the vaporizer—it was in the store. No one had stopped to check at the counter through which the two exited, where the vaporizer was eventually found in one of the catch-all baskets at the unattended check-out stand.

Seeing Gibson rousting Hernandez, Gortarez came to the defense of his cousin, ran around the front of the car and pushed Gibson away. Gibson then grabbed Gortarez and put a choke hold around Gortarez' neck until he stopped struggling. Both Hernandez and Gortarez testified that the first time that Gibson identified himself to them was after he had restrained Gortarez in a choke hold. There was testimony that Gortarez was held in the choke hold for a period of time even after Gortarez had advised the store employees that he had left the vaporizer in the store. When a carry-out boy told the store employees that he had found the vaporizer in a basket at the check-out stand, the two cousins were released.

Gortarez later required medical treatment for injuries suffered from the choke hold. Plaintiffs sued Smitty's and Gibson for false arrest, false imprisonment, and assault and battery.

At common law, a private person's privilege to arrest another for a misdemeanor was very limited. The Restatement (Second) of Torts describes the circumstances under which a private person may arrest another without a warrant:

> a) if the other has committed the felony for which he is arrested, or
>
> b) if an act or omission constituting a felony has been committed and the actor reasonably suspects that the other has committed such act or omission, or
>
> c) if the other, in the presence of the actor, is committing a breach of the peace or, having so committed a breach of the peace, he is reasonably believed by the actor to be about to renew it, or
>
> d) if the actor has attempted to commit a felony in the actor's presence and the arrest is made at once or upon fresh pursuit, or
>
> e) if the other knowingly causes the actor to believe that facts existed which would create in him a privilege to arrest under the statement in Clauses (a) to (d).

Arizona has codified the common law. So far as relevant here, the statute provides that a private person may make an arrest for a misdemeanor when the person to be arrested has committed a misdemeanor amounting to a breach of the peace in the presence of the person making the arrest. Thus, at common law and by statute, the privilege to arrest for misdemeanors without a warrant is limited to those misdemeanors which constitute a breach of the peace. In the case of misdemeanors such as shoplifting, there is no breach of the peace, and no common law privilege to arrest. Therefore any common law privilege would exist only for recapture of chattel. There is a limited privilege for an owner whose property has been wrongfully taken, while in fresh pursuit, to use reasonable force to recapture a chattel. An important caveat to this privilege is that the actor must be correct as to the facts which he believes grant him the privilege, and faces liability for damages resulting from any mistake, however reasonable. The force privileged must be reasonable under the circumstances, and not calculated to inflict serious bodily harm.

Thus, privileges for misdemeanor arrest traditionally available at common law recognize no privilege to arrest for ordinary shoplifting. Under this rule a shopkeeper who believed that a customer was shoplifting was placed in an untenable position. Either the shopkeeper allowed the suspect to leave the premises, risking the loss of merchandise, or took the risk of attempting to recapture the chattel by detaining the customer, facing liability for the wrongful detention if the person had not stolen merchandise.

The developing, common law shopkeeper's privilege described by Prosser was incorporated into the second Restatement of Torts as follows: "One who reasonably believes that another has tortiously taken a chattel upon his premises, or has failed to make cash payment for a chattel purchased or services rendered there, is privileged, without arresting the other, to detain him on the premises for the time necessary for a reasonable investigation of the facts."

We have not had occasion to pass upon the applicability of the Restatement rule. Instead Arizona has adopted the shopkeeper's privilege by statute, which provides in pertinent part: "A merchant, or his agent or employee, with reasonable cause, may detain on the premises in a reasonable manner and for a reasonable time any person suspected of shoplifting for questioning or summoning a law enforcement officer."

Reasonable cause is a defense to a civil or criminal action against a peace officer, merchant or an agent or employee of such merchant for false arrest, false or unlawful imprisonment or wrongful detention.

To invoke the privilege, therefore, reasonable cause is only the threshold requirement. Once reasonable cause is established, there are two further questions regarding the application of the privilege. We must ask whether the purpose of the shopkeeper's action was proper (i.e., detention for questioning or summoning a law enforcement officer). The last question is whether the detention was carried out in a reasonable manner and for a reasonable length of time. If the answer to any of the three questions is negative, then the privilege granted by statute is inapplicable and the actions of the shopkeeper are taken at his peril. If the shopkeeper is mistaken and the common law recapture privilege is therefore also inapplicable, the seizure is tortious.

There was a question whether the use of force in the search of Hernandez, and, more importantly, in the restraint of Gortarez, was reasonable. There was no request that the two young men remain. No inquiry was made with regard to whether Hernandez had the vaporizer. Gibson testified that Hernandez gave no indication of resistance and made no attempt to escape. The possible theft of a 59 cent item hardly warrants apprehension that the two were armed or dangerous. There was, arguably, time to make a request to remain before Gibson seized Hernandez and began searching him. Also, there is no indication that such a request would obviously have been futile. The evidence adduced probably would have supported a finding that the manner of detention was unreasonable as a matter of law.

Katko v. Briney

Supreme Court of Iowa (1971)

The primary issue presented here is whether an owner may protect personal property in an unoccupied boarded-up farm house against trespassers and thieves by a spring gun capable of inflicting death or serious injury.

Defendant Bertha L. Briney inherited her parents' farm land, including the house where her grandparents and parents had lived. No one occupied the house thereafter. Her husband, Edward, attempted to care for the land. He kept no farm machinery thereon. The outbuildings became dilapidated.

For about 10 years there occurred a series of trespassing and housebreaking events with loss of some household items, the breaking of windows and "messing up of the property in general."

Defendants through the years boarded up the windows and doors in an attempt to stop the intrusions. They had posted no trespass signs on the land. The nearest one was 35 feet from the house. On June 11, 1967 defendants set a shotgun trap in the north bedroom. After Mr. Briney cleaned and oiled his 20-gauge shotgun, the power of which he was well aware, defendants took it to the old house where they secured it to an iron bed with the barrel pointed at the bedroom door. It was rigged with wire from the doorknob to the gun's trigger so it would fire when the door was opened. Briney first pointed the gun so an intruder would be hit in the stomach but at Mrs. Briney's suggestion it was lowered to hit the legs. He admitted he did so "because I was mad and tired of being tormented" but "he did not intend to injure anyone." He gave no explanation of why he used a loaded shell and set it to hit a person already in the house. Tin was nailed over the bedroom window. The spring gun could not be seen from the outside. No warning of its presence was posted.

Plaintiff worked as a gasoline station attendant seven miles from the old house. About 9:30 p.m. he entered the old house by removing a board from a porch window which was without glass. As he started to open the north bedroom door the shotgun went off striking him in the right leg above the ankle bone. Much of his leg, including part of the tibia, was blown away. He remained in the hospital 40 days.

Plaintiff testified he knew he had no right to break and enter the house with intent to steal bottles and fruit jars. He further testified he had entered a plea of guilty to larceny in the nighttime of property of less than $20 value from a private building. He stated he had been fined $50 and costs and paroled during good behavior from a 60-day jail sentence. Other than minor traffic charges this was plaintiff's first brush with the law.

Prosser on Torts, Third Edition, states: "the law has always placed a higher value upon human safety than upon mere rights in property, it is the accepted rule that there is no privilege to use any force calculated to cause death or serious bodily injury to repel the threat to land or chattels, unless there is also such a threat to the defendant's personal safety as to justify a self-defense. Spring guns and other man killing devices are not justifiable against a mere trespasser, or even a petty thief. They are privileged only against those upon whom the landowner, if he were present in person would be free to inflict injury of the same kind."

Jury verdict for Plaintiff, Affirmed.

Surocco v. Geary

Supreme Court of California (1853)

This was an action, commenced in the court below, to recover damages for blowing up and destroying the plaintiffs' house and property, during the fire of the 24th of December, 1849. Geary, at that time Mayor of San Francisco, justified, on the ground that he had the authority, by virtue of his office, to destroy the building, and also that it had been blown up by him to stop the progress of the conflagration then raging. It was in proof, that the fire passed over and burned beyond the building of the plaintiffs', and that at the time the building was destroyed, they were engaged in removing their property, and could, had they not been prevented, have succeeded in removing more, if not all of their goods.

The only question for our consideration is, whether the person who tears down or destroys the house of another, in good faith, and under apparent necessity, during the time of a conflagration, for the purpose of saving the buildings adjacent, and stopping its progress, can be held personally liable in an action by the owner of the property destroyed.

The right to destroy property, to prevent the spread of a conflagration, has been traced to the highest law of necessity, and the natural rights of man, independent of society or civil government. It is referred by moralists and jurists to the same great principle which justifies the exclusive appropriation of a plank in a shipwreck, though the life of another be sacrificed; with the throwing overboard goods in a tempest, for the safety of a vessel; with the trespassing upon the lands of another, to escape death by an enemy. The common law adopts the principles of the natural law, and places the justification of an act otherwise tortious precisely on the same ground of necessity.

A house on fire, or those in its immediate vicinity, which serve to communicate the flames, becomes a nuisance, which it is lawful to abate, and the private rights of the individual yield to the considerations of general convenience, and the interests of society. Were it otherwise, one stubborn person might involve a whole city in ruin, by refusing to allow the destruction of a building which would cut off the flames and check the progress of the fire, and that, too, when it was perfectly evident that his building must be consumed.

The right of taking individual property for public purposes belongs to the State, by virtue of her right of eminent domain, and is justified on the ground of state necessity; but this is not a taking or a destruction for a public purpose, but a destruction for the benefit of the individual or the city, but not properly of the State.

The counsel for the respondent has asked, who is to judge of the necessity of the destruction of property? This must, in some instances, be a difficult matter to determine. The necessity of blowing up a house may not exist, or be as apparent to the owner, whose judgment is clouded by interest, and the hope of saving his property, as to others. In all such cases the conduct of the individual must be regulated by his own judgment as to the exigencies of the case. If a building should be torn down without apparent or actual necessity, the parties concerned would undoubtedly be liable in an action of trespass. But in every case the necessity must be clearly shown. It is true, many cases of hardship may grow out of this rule, and property may often in such cases be destroyed, without necessity, by irresponsible persons, but this difficulty would not be obviated by making the parties responsible in every case, whether the necessity existed or not.

The legislature of the State possess the power to regulate this subject by providing the manner in which buildings may be destroyed, and the mode in which compensation shall be made; and it is to be hoped that something will be done to obviate the difficulty, and prevent the happening of such events as those supposed by the respondent's counsel.

In the absence of any legislation on the subject, we are compelled to fall back upon the rules of the common law.

The evidence in this case clearly establishes the fact, that the blowing up of the house was necessary, as it would have been consumed had it been left standing. The plaintiffs cannot recover for the value of the goods which they might have saved; they were as much subject to the necessities of the occasion as the house in which they were situate; and if in such cases a party was held liable, it would too frequently happen, that the delay caused by the removal of the goods would render the destruction of the house useless.

Ploof v. Putnam

Supreme Court of Vermont (1908)

It is alleged that the defendant was the owner of an island in Lake Champlain, and of a dock attached thereto; that the plaintiff was then sailing upon the lake on a sloop, on which were the plaintiff and his wife and two minor children; that there then arose a sudden and violent tempest, whereby the sloop and the property and persons therein were placed in great danger of destruction; that, to save these from destruction or injury, the plaintiff was compelled to moor the sloop to defendant's dock; that the defendant, by his servant, unmoored the sloop, whereupon it was driven upon the shore by the tempest, without the plaintiff's fault; and that the sloop and its contents were thereby destroyed, and the plaintiff and his wife and children cast into the lake and upon the shore, receiving injuries.

There are many cases in the books which hold that necessity, and an inability to control movements inaugurated in the proper exercise of a strict right, will justify entries upon land and interferences with personal property that would otherwise have been trespasses. This doctrine of necessity applies with special force to the preservation of human life. One assaulted and in peril of his life may run through the close of another to escape from his assailant. One may sacrifice the personal property of another to save his life or the lives of his fellows. In one case the defendant was sued for taking and carrying away the plaintiff's casket and its contents. It appeared that the ferryman took 47 passengers into his barge to pass to London, among whom were the plaintiff and defendant; and the barge being upon the water a great tempest happened, and a strong wind, so that the barge and all the passengers were in danger of being lost if certain ponderous things were not cast out, and the defendant thereupon cast out the plaintiff's casket. It was resolved that in case of necessity, to save the lives of the passengers, it was lawful for the defendant, being a passenger, to cast the plaintiff's casket out of the barge.

It is clear that an entry upon the land of another may be justified by necessity, and that the declaration before us discloses a necessity for mooring the sloop.

Vincent v. Lake Erie Transportation

Supreme Court of Minnesota (1910)

The steamship Reynolds, owned by the defendant, was for the purpose of discharging her cargo on November 27, 1905, moored to plaintiff's dock. While the unloading of the boat was taking place a storm from the northeast developed, which at about 10 o'clock p. m., when the unloading was completed, had so grown in violence that the wind was then moving at 50 miles per hour and continued to increase during the night.... Navigation was practically suspended from the hour mentioned until the morning of the 29th, when the storm abated, and during that time no master would have been justified in attempting to navigate his vessel. After the discharge of the cargo the Reynolds signaled for a tug to tow her from the dock, but none could be obtained because of the severity of the storm. If the lines holding the ship to the dock had been cast off, she would doubtless have drifted away; but, instead, the lines were kept fast, and as soon as one parted or chafed it was replaced, sometimes with a larger one. The vessel lay upon the outside of the dock, her bow to the east, the wind and waves striking her starboard quarter with such force that she was constantly being lifted and thrown against the dock, resulting in its damage to the amount of $500 [about $16,000 in 2023]

We are satisfied that the character of the storm was such that it would have been highly imprudent for the master of the Reynolds to have attempted to leave the dock or to have permitted his vessel to drift away from it.

The appellant contends, because its conduct during the storm was rendered necessary by prudence and good seamanship under conditions over which it had no control, it cannot be held liable for any injury resulting to the property of others, and claims that the jury should have been so instructed.

The situation was one in which the ordinary rules regulating property rights were suspended by forces beyond human control, and if, without the direct intervention of some act by the one sought to be held liable, the property of another was injured, such injury must be attributed to the act of God, and not to the wrongful act of the person sought to be charged. If during the storm the Reynolds had entered the harbor, and while there had become disabled and been thrown against the plaintiffs' dock, the plaintiffs could not have recovered. Again, if which attempting to hold fast to the dock the lines had parted, without any negligence, and the vessel carried against some other boat or dock in the harbor, there would be no liability upon her owner. But here those in charge of the vessel deliberately and by their direct efforts held her in such a position that the damage to the dock resulted, and, having thus preserved the ship at the expense of the dock, it seems to us that her owners are responsible to the dock owners to the extent of the injury inflicted.

Theologians hold that a starving man may, without moral guilt, take what is necessary to sustain life; but it could hardly be said that the obligation would not be upon such person to pay the value of the property so taken when he became able to do so. And so public necessity, in times of war or peace, may require the taking of private property for public purposes; but under our system of jurisprudence compensation must be made.

Let us imagine in this case that for the better mooring of the vessel those in charge of her had appropriated a valuable cable lying upon the dock. No matter how justifiable such appropriation might have been, it would not be claimed that, because of the overwhelming necessity of the situation, the owner of the cable could not recover its value.

This is not a case where life or property was menaced by any object or thing belonging to the plaintiff, the destruction of which became necessary to prevent the threatened disaster. Nor is it a case where, because of the act of God, or unavoidable accident, the infliction of the injury was beyond the control of the defendant, but is one where the defendant prudently and advisedly availed itself of the plaintiffs' property for the purpose of preserving its own more valuable property, and the plaintiffs are entitled to compensation for the injury done.

Order affirmed.

DISSENT

I am of the opinion that one who constructs a dock to the navigable line of waters, and enters into contractual relations with the owner of a vessel to moor at the same, takes the risk of damage to his dock by a boat caught there by a storm, which event could not have been avoided in the exercise of due care, and further, that the legal status of the parties in such a case is not changed by renewal of cables to keep the boat from being cast adrift at the mercy of the tempest.

III. NEGLIGENCE

DUTY

Stewart v. Motts

Supreme Court of Pennsylvania (1995)

Plaintiff, Jonathon Stewart, stopped at Defendant, Martin Motts' auto repair shop and offered assistance to the Defendant in repairing an automobile fuel tank. In an effort to start and move the car with the gasoline tank unattached, the Plaintiff proceeded to pour gasoline into the carburetor. The Defendant was to turn the ignition key at a given moment. While the exact sequence of events was contested, the tragic result was that the car backfired, caused an explosion and resulted in Plaintiff suffering severe burns to his upper body.

The only issue raised before this Court is the refusal of the trial court to read Stewart's requested point for charge No. 4. This point for charge reads: "We are instructing you that gasoline due to its inflammability, is a very dangerous substance if not properly handled. Therefore, it is incumbent on Mr. Stewart to use care in pouring the gasoline into the motor vehicle. It is also the duty of Mr. Motts to use care in starting the machine to see that the vehicle started without any risk of harm to anyone, particularly Mr. Stewart. The backfiring of engines without the air filter on them does occur. Both Motts, and Stewart, realized, or should have realized the dangerous nature of this substance, and knew, or should have known that the engine may backfire, and/or that the gas may ignite, and burn. With an appreciation of such danger, and under conditions where its existence reasonably should have been known, there follows a high degree of care which circumscribes the conduct of everyone about the danger, and whether the parties acted as reasonable men under the circumstances is for you the jury to decide."

We begin our discussion by reaffirming the principle that there is but one standard of care to be applied to negligence actions involving dangerous instrumentalities. This standard of care is reasonable care. The standard never varies, but the care which it is reasonable to require of the actor varies with the danger involved in his act and is proportionate to it. The greater the danger, the greater the care which must be exercised. Where the reasonable character of an actor's conduct is in question its utility is to be weighed against the magnitude of the risk which it involves. Thus, if an act involves risk of death or bodily injury, the highest attention and caution are required. Therefore, those who deal with firearms, explosives, poisonous drugs or high tension electricity are required to exercise the closest attention and the most careful precautions.

The sole issue presented before us is whether there exists a higher standard of "extraordinary care" for the use of dangerous instrumentalities over and above the standard of "reasonable care" such that the trial court erred for failing to give an instruction to the jury that the Appellee should have used a "high degree of care" in handling gasoline. Because we believe that there is but one standard of care, the standard of "reasonable care", we affirm.

Creasy v. Rusk

Supreme Court of Indiana (2000)

Rusk was admitted to the Brethren Healthcare Center ("BHC") because he suffered from memory loss and confusion. Rusk's primary diagnosis was Alzheimer's disease. Over the course of three years at BHC, Rusk experienced periods of anxiousness, confusion, depression, disorientation, and agitation. Rusk often resisted when staff members attempted to remove him from prohibited areas of the facility. On several occasions, Rusk was belligerent with both staff and other residents. In particular, Rusk was often combative, agitated, and aggressive and would hit staff members when they tried to care for him.

BHC had employed Creasy as a certified nursing assistant for nearly 20 months when the incident at issue occurred. Creasy's responsibilities included caring for Rusk and other patients with Alzheimer's disease. Creasy did not have specialized training on how to care for people with Alzheimer's disease, but she did attend a short BHC presentation on the pathological effects of Alzheimer's. Residents with Alzheimer's had bruised Creasy during the course of her work for BHC, and Creasy knew that Rusk had Alzheimer's disease.

Creasy and another certified nursing assistant, Linda Davis, were working through their routine of putting Rusk and other residents to bed. Creasy knew that Rusk had been very agitated and combative that evening. By Creasy's account: "Davis was helping me put Mr. Rusk to bed. She was holding his wrists to keep him from hitting us and I was trying to get his legs to put him to bed. He was hitting and kicking wildly. During this time, he kicked me several times in my left knee and hip area. My lower back popped and I yelled out with pain from my lower back and left knee."

This case requires us to decide two distinct questions:

(1) Whether the general duty of care imposed upon adults with mental disabilities is the same as that for adults without mental disabilities?

(2) Whether the circumstances of Rusk's case are such that the general duty of care imposed upon adults with mental disabilities should be imposed upon him?

In many, if not most, jurisdictions, the general duty of care imposed on adults with mental disabilities is the same as that for adults without mental disabilities. Adults with mental disabilities are held to the same standard of care as that of a reasonable person under the same circumstances without regard to the alleged tortfeasor's capacity to control or understand the consequences of his or her actions.

The public policy reasons most often cited for holding individuals with mental disabilities to a standard of reasonable care in negligence claims include the following.

(1) Allocates losses between two innocent parties to the one who caused or occasioned the loss.

(2) Provides incentive to those responsible for people with disabilities and interested in their estates to prevent harm and "restrain" those who are potentially dangerous.

(3) Removes inducements for alleged tortfeasors to fake a mental disability in order to escape liability.

(4) Avoids administrative problems involved in courts and juries attempting to identify and assess the significance of an actor's disability.

(5) Forces persons with disabilities to pay for the damage they do if they "are to live in the world.

In balancing the considerations presented in the foregoing analysis, we adopt the following rule. We hold that a person with mental disabilities is generally held to the same standard of care as that of a reasonable person under the same circumstances without regard to the alleged tortfeasor's capacity to control or understand the consequences of his or her actions.

We turn now to the question of whether the circumstances of Rusk's case are such that the general duty of care imposed upon adults with mental disabilities should be found to run from him to Creasy. We find that the relationship between Rusk and Creasy and public policy concerns dictate that Rusk owed no duty of care to Creasy.

Unlike the typical victim, Creasy was not a member of the public at large, unable to anticipate or safeguard against the harm she encountered. Creasy knew of Rusk's violent history. She could have changed her course of action or requested additional assistance when she recognized Rusk's state of mind on the evening when she received the alleged injury.

Rusk's inability to comprehend the circumstances of his relationship with Creasy and others was the very reason Creasy was employed to support Rusk.

We now affirm the trial court, finding that Rusk did not owe a duty to Creasy.

NEGLIGENCE PER SE

O'Guin v. Bingham County

Supreme Court of Idaho (2005)

Shaun and Alex O'Guin were killed while playing at the Bingham County landfill. Apparently, a section of the pit wall collapsed and crushed the children. Earlier that day, the children had been eating lunch at Ridgecrest Elementary School as part of a summer lunch program. As they started walking home, the children went through an unlocked gate at the back of the schoolyard and through a privately owned empty field. The empty field is situated between the landfill and the schoolyard. The border between the empty field and the landfill was unobstructed. At the time of the children's death, the landfill was open to the public one day a week. It was closed on the day the children were killed and no landfill employees were present on the site.

Statutes and administrative regulations may define the applicable standard of care owed, and violations of such statutes and regulations may constitute negligence per se. The effect of establishing negligence per se through violation of a statute is to conclusively establish the first two elements of a cause of action in negligence. In order to replace a common law duty of care with a duty of care from a statute or regulation, the following elements must be met: (1) the statute or regulation must clearly define the required standard of conduct; (2) the statute or regulation must have been intended to prevent the type of harm the defendant's act or omission caused; and (3) the plaintiff must be a member of the class of persons the statute or regulation was designed to protect.

As to the first element, the district court found that the statute and regulations in this case clearly define the County's standard of conduct. Idaho Code Title 39, Chapters 1 and 74 grant authority to the Board of Environmental Quality to adopt solid waste management rules and standards. Those rules require municipal solid waste landfill units to block access by unauthorized persons. The rule in effect at the time of the boys' deaths provided in pertinent part:

"Solid waste management sites shall comply with the following:

> e. Access to the site shall be limited to those times when an attendant is on duty.
>
> > i. Hours of operation and other limitations shall be prominently displayed at the entrance.

ii. The site shall be fenced or otherwise blocked to access when an attendant is not on duty.

iii. Unauthorized vehicles and persons shall be prohibited access to the site."

These regulations require the County to fence or otherwise block access to the landfill when an attendant is not on duty. The Legislature has specifically declared it to be unlawful to fail to comply with the landfill rules. In this case, the record reveals that some of the landfill boundaries were not fenced or blocked. There is also evidence that the landfill was closed and no attendant was on duty. Therefore, the district court was correct that the regulations clearly define the County's required standard of conduct, and the County failed to meet that standard.

The second element asks whether the death of the O'Guin children is the type of harm the statute and regulations were intended to prevent. Idaho Code Section 39–7401(2) states:

"It is the intent of the legislature to establish a program of solid waste management which complies with 40 CFR 258 and facilitates the incorporation of flexible standards in facility design and operation. The legislature hereby establishes the solid waste disposal standards and procedures to effect timely and responsible completion of statutory duties and to ensure protection of human health and the environment, to protect the air, land and waters of the state of Idaho."

Section 3.7.3 entitled "Technical Considerations" relates to the access requirements and provides in part: "Frequently, unauthorized persons are unfamiliar with the hazards associated with landfill facilities, and consequences of uncontrolled access may include injury and even death." This provision indicates a broad definition of what is intended by "protection of human health" and certainly includes possible injury or death to people on the facility grounds. Operators of a landfill have a duty not only to prevent illegal dumping and unauthorized vehicular traffic, but to control public access as well.

The County argues that the intent of these provisions is merely to prevent unauthorized vehicular traffic and illegal dumping. However, the inclusion of physical injury to "unauthorized individuals" by equipment or earth-moving activities, as potential landfill hazards, would indicate otherwise. A similar hazard is presented by a dangerously sloping wall in the landfill. The O'Guin's expert testified that the angle of the slope where the accident occurred was extremely dangerous and violative of EPA and OSHA regulations. These statutes and rules demonstrate that the Legislature intended to safeguard both human health and safety. The injury to the safety of the O'Guin children is the type of harm the Idaho statute and regulations were intended to prevent because the children's deaths relate directly to control of public access and protection of human health and safety.

As to the third element, the O'Guin children are members of the class of persons the regulations were designed to protect. The regulations state "unauthorized vehicles and persons shall be prohibited access to the site." As trespassers, the O'Guin children were certainly "unauthorized persons" and the regulations do not differentiate between the unauthorized person who comes to the landfill to dump improper materials and the unauthorized person who comes to the landfill to play. Furthermore, the regulations require the landfill be fenced or otherwise blocked to access when an attendant is not on duty. This regulation demonstrates the connection between the requirement that the landfill perimeter be fenced or blocked and the protection of persons whose access is unauthorized. Therefore, the regulations controlling access were designed to protect the human health and safety of the unauthorized person who comes to a landfill when an attendant is not on duty and the O'Guin children fit within that category.

Rains v. Bend of the River

Court of Appeals of Tennessee (2003)

Mr. Rains turned eighteen in mid-January. At some point on July 16, Mr. Rains found the key to his father's gun case and removed the .25 caliber handgun. Then, he set out to find ammunition for the pistol because his father did not have any ammunition in the house. His first stop was the sporting goods department at a local K–Mart. He inquired about the minimum age for purchasing .25 caliber ammunition and was told that buyers of that ammunition must be at least twenty-one years old. Mr. Rains showed the clerk his driver's license and commented, "Oh, I'm only eighteen."

After leaving K–Mart, Mr. Rains drove to Bend of the River Shooting Supplies, a store selling firearms, shooting supplies, and ammunition. While at Bend of the River, Mr. Rains purchased a box of ammunition. The store clerk did not ask Mr. Rains for proof of his age. Sometime later Mr. Rains loaded his parents' pistol with the ammunition he had purchased at Bend of the River and fatally shot himself.

Mr. Rains's parents filed a wrongful death lawsuit. They asserted that Bend of the River was negligent per se because it had sold handgun ammunition to a person who was less than twenty-one years of age in violation of the Gun Control Act, 18 U.S.C. §922(b)(1) (2000).

The common-law standard of conduct to which a person must conform to avoid being negligent is the familiar "reasonable person under similar circumstances" standard. As a general matter, this standard requires a person to exercise reasonable care under the circumstances to refrain from conduct that could foreseeably injure others. This standard is flexible, and its contours are inherently fact-sensitive. Therefore, determinations regarding whether particular conduct conforms to the common-law standard of conduct are made on a case-by-case basis.

However, the common law is not the only source of legal duties or standards of conduct in negligence cases. In addition to the general duty to act reasonably to avoid harming others, more specific duties governing particular situations and relationships may be imposed by the General Assembly. Legislatively created legal duties arise in two ways. First, the General Assembly may create a legal duty and then provide a civil cause of action for its breach. Second, the General Assembly may enact a penal statute that does not explicitly provide a civil remedy, and the courts may then derive a civil legal duty from the penal statute. "Negligence per se" is the term used to describe one of the two doctrines associated with the latter process.

The negligence per se doctrine does not create a new cause of action. Rather, it is a form of ordinary negligence, that enables the courts to use a penal statute to define a reasonably prudent person's standard of care. Negligence per se arises when a legislative body pronounces in a penal statute what the conduct of a reasonable person must be, whether or not the common law would require similar conduct.

The negligence per se doctrine is not a magic transformational formula that automatically creates a private negligence cause of action for the violation of every statute. Not every statutory violation amounts to negligence per se. To trigger the doctrine, the statute must establish a specific standard of conduct.

The effect of declaring conduct negligent per se is to render the conduct negligent as a matter of law. Thus, a person whose conduct is negligent per se cannot escape liability by attempting to prove that he or she acted reasonably under the circumstances. However, a finding of negligence per se is not equivalent to a finding of liability per se. Plaintiffs in negligence per se cases must still establish causation in fact, legal cause, and damages.

The fact that the General Assembly has enacted a statute defining criminal conduct does not necessarily mean that the courts must adopt it as a standard of civil liability. Decisions regarding the proper civil standard of conduct rest with the courts. Thus, the courts must ultimately decide whether they will adopt a statutory standard to define the standard of conduct of reasonable persons in specific circumstances.

The two threshold questions in every negligence per se case are whether the plaintiff belongs to the class of persons the statute was designed to protect and whether the plaintiff's injury is of the type that the statute was designed to prevent.

The Tennessee Supreme Court has, over the years, been quick to invoke the negligence per se doctrine with regard to violations of penal statutes designed to protect the public. In addition, another panel of this court has implied that the sale of handgun ammunition to a person under twenty-one years of age is negligence per se under Tennessee law. Accordingly, we will presume that the sale of handgun ammunition to an eighteen year old purchaser in violation of 18 U.S.C. § 922(b)(1) is negligence per se.

Concluding that Bend of the River was negligent per se for its violation of 18 U.S.C. §922(b)(1) does not end the inquiry. To maintain a successful negligence per se action, Mr. Rains's parents must prove not only that Bend of the River violated a penal statute designed to protect the public but also that the violation of the statute was the legal cause of Mr. Rains's death.

The concept of "legal cause" was formerly known as "proximate cause." It connotes a policy decision made by the judiciary to establish a boundary of legal liability, and to deny liability for conduct that could otherwise be actionable. These decisions are based on consideration of logic, common sense, policy, precedent, and other more or less inadequately expressed ideas of what justice demands or of what is administratively possible and convenient. An actor's negligent conduct is the legal cause of harm to another if the conduct is a substantial factor in bringing about the harm and there is no rule of law relieving the actor from liability because of the manner in which the actor's negligence resulted in the harm

Foreseeability is the key here because no person is expected to protect against harms from events that he or she cannot reasonably anticipate or foresee or which are so unlikely to occur that the risk, although recognizable, would commonly be disregarded. In cases brought against persons who supplied a suicide victim the means to commit suicide, the foreseeability question hinges on the victim's behavior and demeanor at the time of the sale.

None of Mr. Rains's family or acquaintances had any suspicion that he was suicidal, and there is no evidence that his conduct or demeanor when he purchased the ammunition should have given the clerk at Bend of the River reason to foresee or anticipate that he intended to use the ammunition to commit suicide or to misuse it in any other way.

The undisputed facts in this record provide no basis for concluding that Bend of the River knew or should have known that Mr. Rains intended to use the ammunition he purchased on July 16, 1997 to commit suicide. As tragic as Mr. Rains's death is, we have no basis for holding Bend of the River to a different standard of foreseeability than his family.

The claims against Bend of the River are dismissed.

Eisenhuth v. Moneyhon

Ohio Supreme Court (1954)

Before argument, at the request of counsel for plaintiff, the court gave the following special charge:

"I charge you that Section 6307-38 of the General Code of Ohio provides as follows:

> (a) No person shall turn a vehicle or trackless trolley from a direct course upon a highway unless and until such person shall have exercised due care to ascertain that such movement can be made with reasonable safety to other users of the highway and then only after giving a clearly audible signal by sounding the horn if any pedestrian may be affected by such movement or after giving an appropriate signal in the event any traffic may be affected by such movement.
>
> (b) A signal of intention to turn right or left shall be given in sufficient time in advance of the movement indicated to give ample warning to other users of the highway who would be affected by such movement."

In the general charge the court gave the following instruction to the jury:

"if you find by a preponderance of the evidence that the defendant, Moneyhon, did make a left turn across the center line of the highway without giving any signal of his intention to make a left turn in sufficient time in advance of the left turn to give ample warning to the other users of the highway, including the driver of the automobile in which the plaintiff was riding, then the defendant, Moneyhon, would be guilty of negligence as a matter of law."

Comprehensively stated, the rule is that where a legislative enactment imposes upon any person a specific duty for the protection of others, and his failure to perform that duty proximately results in injury to another, he is liable per se or as a matter of law to such other for the injury. The violation of any specific legislative enactment enacted for the protection of private persons is of itself such a breach of duty as to constitute negligence.

However, a legislative enactment which does not purport to define a civil liability but merely makes provision to secure the safety or welfare of the public is not to be construed as establishing such a liability. In such cases, no standard of care other than the common-law standard of due care under the circumstances is fixed by the enactment, and the standard of due care is that exercised by a reasonably prudent person under the circumstances of the particular case.

The determination whether any legislative enactment prescribes a specific course of conduct, the violation of which is negligence per se, or only a rule of conduct, compliance with which is to be tested by the conduct of a reasonably prudent person, often presents a problem of grant difficulty. Where there exists a legislative enactment commanding or prohibiting for the safety of others the doing of a specific act and there is a violation of such enactment solely by one whose duty it is to obey it, such violation constitutes negligence per se; but where there exists a legislative enactment expressing for the safety of others, in general or abstract terms, a rule of conduct, negligence per se has no application, and liability must be determined by the application of the test of due care as exercised by a reasonably prudent person under the circumstances of the case.

There remains the application of these tests to the statute in question, Section 6307-38, General Code, and the determination whether its violation constitutes negligence per se. Subdivision (a) of the section definitely requires the operator of a motor vehicle or trackless trolley, before turning the 'vehicle from a direct course upon a highway, to give a clearly audible signal by sounding the horn if any pedestrian may be affected by such movement. Concededly, the defendant at the time of the collision and accident was turning his car from a direct course on the highway to make a left turn.

If a pedestrian were here 'affected,' which is not the case, clearly a failure of the defendant to give any signal by sounding the horn would be a violation of a definite requirement of the statute and would be negligence per se.

But the duty of the defendant to obey the requirements of the statute as to 'other users of the highway' was subject to a variety of variable facts which must be considered and determined before liability of the defendant may be 'ascertained.' The statute requires the operator of a vehicle, before turning it 'from a direct course upon a highway', to exercise 'due care to ascertain that such movement can be made with reasonable safety to other users of the highway and then only after giving an appropriate signal in the event any traffic may be affected by such movement', and subdivision (b) of the section provides that 'A signal of intention to turn right or left shall be given in sufficient time in advance of the movement indicated to give ample warning to other users of the highway who would be affected by such movement.

It will be noted that these variables must be ascertained by the jury, and if present their operative effect must be determined before the ultimate fact of liability can be resolved.

Clearly, these qualifying requirements are not definite specific requirements and do not depend upon the sole conduct or responsibility of the operator of the vehicle. On the contrary, they constitute rules of conduct or rules of the road which for their consideration and application to the ultimate question of liability must be submitted to the jury.

The judgment of the Court of Appeals, as well as that of the Common Pleas Court, is reversed, and the cause is remanded to the latter court for retrial.

Ornella v. Robertson

Ohio Supreme Court (1968)

Plaintiff, Beatrice Ornella, executed a left turn at a point in a highway divided into two roadways by angled concrete dividers.

Section 4511.35, Revised Code, provides in full text, as follows:

Whenever any highway has been divided into two roadways by an intervening space, or by a physical barrier, or clearly indicated dividing section so constructed as to impede vehicular traffic, every vehicle shall be driven only upon the right-hand roadway, and no vehicle shall be driven over, across, or within any such dividing space, barrier, or section, except through an opening, crossover, or intersection established by public authority. This section does not prohibit the occupancy of such dividing space, barrier, or section for the purpose of an emergency stop or in compliance with an order of a police officer.

That Section 4511.35, Revised Code, was intended as a safety measure to protect those persons traveling in the opposite direction on a divided highway is obvious. But safety statutes are of two types-those which provide a specific standard of conduct and those which provide a general standard of conduct. A violation of the former type constitutes negligence per se whereas a violation of the latter type does not.

The distinction between negligence and negligence per se is the means and method of ascertainment. The first must be found by the jury from the facts, the conditions, and circumstances disclosed by the evidence; the latter is a violation of a specific requirement of law or ordinance; the only fact for determination by the jury being the commission or omission of the specific act inhibited or required.

Where a specific requirement is made by statute and an absolute duty thereby imposed, no inquiry is to be made whether the defendant acted as a reasonably prudent man, or was in the exercise of ordinary care. In such a situation, the obligation and requirement has been fixed and established by law, and the conduct of any person which is violative of such specific statutory requirement is illegal, and, if it proximately results in injury to one to whom a legal duty is owed, the transgressor is liable for the resulting damage. In such case, the jury is not called upon to determine whether the conduct constituted negligence; it determines only whether the act prohibited was committed or the act required by law was omitted, as the case may be. The violator of such specific requirement of law is liable, irrespective of the question as to whether his act is such as is deemed to meet and satisfy the test of ordinary or reasonable care which would be applied in the absence of such statutory definition and imposition of absolute duty, such as, for instance, the absolute and specific requirement as to headlights. Where the standard of duty is thus fixed and absolute, it being the same under all circumstances, the failure to observe that requirement is clearly negligence per se. But, where duties are undefined, or defined only in abstract or general terms, leaving to the jury the ascertainment and determination of reasonableness and correctness of acts and conduct under the proven conditions and circumstances, the phrase 'negligence per se' has no application.

It being clear that the standard of duty imposed by Section 4511.35, Revised Code, is a specific requirement, which is fixed and absolute, the same under all circumstances and is imposed upon all users of motor vehicles on divided highways, it follows that a violation of that section constitutes negligence per se.

Since the opening statement of counsel admits of acts by plaintiff, Beatrice Ornella, which constitute a violation of Section 4511.35, Revised Code, it only remains to be determined if that violation proximately contributed to cause her injuries, for if it did, she may not recover.

It may be said that the law imposes a duty upon persons to protect themselves from injury. Sometimes that duty may consist only in the obligation to conduct themselves as reasonably prudent persons would under the same or similar circumstances. Sometimes that duty might rise to the level of an even higher obligation-that of refraining from conduct which might appear reasonably prudent under the circumstances. This latter type of obligation, may, of course, be imposed only where there is a clear statutory mandate.

When this duty imposed by law is breached, and the violation proximately contributes to cause an injury also proximately caused in part by negligence for which another party is responsible, no recovery may be had under the law in this state.

Being able to arrive at no other conclusions, from the allegations contained in the petition and the remarks made by counsel for the plaintiffs during opening statement, except that plaintiff, Beatrice Ornella, was negligence as a matter of law, for a violation of Section 4511.35, Revised Code, we cannot determine otherwise than that plaintiff's violation proximately contributed to cause her injuries, which precludes her recovery altogether. If she had not engaged in the forbidden endeavor, to wit, making the left turn across a physical barrier in a divided highway at a place otherwise than provided by public authority, then she would not have placed herself in a position of peril to be hit by someone proceeding in the opposite direction as was defendant.

The term, proximate cause, is often difficult of exact definition as applied to the facts of a particular case. However, it is generally true that, where an original act is wrongful or negligent and in a natural and continuous sequence produces a result which would not have taken place without the act, proximate cause is established, and the fact that some other act unites with the original act to cause injury does not relieve the initial offender from liability.

It is because what constitutes a 'natural and continuous sequence' is insusceptible of determination other than in the context of a particular case that the issue of proximate cause is ordinarily one for determination by the jury. However, where reasonable minds could not differ with respect to the matter because the circumstances clearly indicate an obvious cause and effect relationship, the issue may be determined as a matter of law.

In granting the motion for judgment on the pleadings and opening statement of plaintiffs' counsel, the Common Pleas Court necessarily made the determination that, were plaintiffs to prove all that they set out to prove, no right to recover would be established. Since, for all of the foregoing reasons, we are of the opinion that that is a correct determination, we affirm the judgment below.

BREACH OF DUTY

Indiana Consolidated Insurance v. Mathew

Court of Appeals of Indiana (1980)

Mathew's brother was out of town for the weekend. The two brothers lived across the street from each other and took turns mowing both lawns. In the late afternoon Mathew decided to mow both lawns and went to his brother's garage where a twelve horsepower Toro riding lawnmower was stored. The mower was approximately eight years old, was kept in good mechanical condition, and had required only minor tune-ups and belt replacements for the rotary mower assembly. Mathew pulled the mower away from the side wall of the garage and after checking the gas gauge filled the lawnmower approximately three-fourths full with gasoline using a funnel. He then went back across the street to his home for approximately twenty minutes. Upon returning to the garage Mathew started the lawnmower. However, he noticed a flame in the engine area under the hood and immediately shut the engine off. He opened the hood and saw a flame four to five inches tall under the gas tank. Using some clean towels Mathew tried to snuff out the flame but was unsuccessful. He could find no other means to extinguish the fire. The flames continued to grow and the machine began spewing gasoline, so he ran to his home to call the fire department. He returned to find the garage totally engulfed in flames. At trial Mathew testified that he was afraid to try to push the flaming machine outside the garage for fear that the tank would explode in his face.

Indiana Consolidated brought this action against Mathew alleging that he breached a duty owed to his brother to exercise due care in starting the lawnmower and therefore stands liable for the damages resulting from his negligence. After a bench trial the Court below entered the following finding: "The Court now finds from the evidence concerning the past activities concerning the defendant in this cause and his involvement with the mower in question and the practices which he followed and from all of the circumstances present in this case that the defendant, Robert D. Mathew, did not act in any manner other than a reasonable prudent person would act under the same or similar circumstances; the Court further finds that there is no evidence of negligence on the part of the defendant, Robert D. Mathew, and that the plaintiff should take nothing by its complaint."

On appeal appellant contends that the judgment is contrary to law because Mathew was negligent in filling the gas tank, in starting the mower in an enclosed area, and in failing to push the flaming mower out of the garage. The standard by which Mathew's conduct is to be measured is whether he exercised the duty to use due care in operating the mower that an ordinary prudent man would exercise under the same or similar circumstances.

The record amply supports the finding that Mathew did not act in a negligent manner in filling the gas tank. He testified that he did so carefully, with the use of a funnel. He did not fill the tank full, and he was adamant in his belief that he did not spill any gasoline. He hypothesized that even had any gas been spilled it would have evaporated in the cool air during the twenty-minute period before he started the mower. Appellant is merely asking this Court to reweigh the evidence in regard to any gasoline spillage due to Mathew's admission on cross-examination that he could have spilled some fuel. The trier of fact resolved this issue in favor of Mathew, finding that he exercised due care in fueling the mower, and it must remain undisturbed upon appeal.

Appellant's further allegation that Mathew negligently failed to push the flaming mower out of the garage area is refuted by the evidence that the machine was spewing gasoline and that he was afraid for his safety should the tank explode. Mathew therefore chose to leave and summon help from the local fire department. One who is confronted with a sudden emergency not of his own making is not chargeable with negligence if he acts according to his best judgment. The law values human life above property. Greater risk of one's person is justified to save life than is reasonable in protecting property. If Mathew had tried to push the riding mower ten feet into an open area the machine might have exploded and caused much graver damage to his person than was suffered by the destruction of the garage.

Stinnett v. Buchele

Court of Appeals of Kentucky (1980)

This is a tort action filed by an employee against his employer for injuries sustained during the course and scope of his employment. The lower court granted summary judgment to the employer on the ground that there was no showing that the injury was caused by the negligence of the employer. We affirm.

Buchele is a practicing physician and Stinnett is a farm laborer. Mr. Stinnett undertook to repair the roof on a barn located at one of Dr. Buchele's farms. The repairs were to consist of nailing down the edges of the roof that had been loosened by the wind and painting the roof with a coating. Stinnett was severely injured when he fell from the roof while applying the coating with a paint roller. Stinnett urges in his brief to this court that Dr. Buchele was negligent for failing to comply with occupational and health regulations and also for his failure to provide a safe place to work.

We do not find any evidence that Dr. Buchele was negligent in failing to provide Stinnett with a safe place to work. We agree with Stinnett when he states that Dr. Buchele had the obligation to furnish him: "a place reasonably safe having regard for the character of work and reasonably safe tools and appliances for doing the work. The measure of duty is to exercise ordinary or reasonable care to do so. The standard is the care exercised by prudent employers in similar circumstances." Although we may consider that painting a barn roof is dangerous work, we cannot say that Dr. Buchele can be held liable for failing to provide a safe place to work solely because he asked Stinnett to work on the roof. We hold, therefore, that there was no showing of any negligence on the part of Dr. Buchele arising solely out of the fact that he had asked Stinnett to paint the barn roof.

Stinnett next argues that a reasonable and prudent employer would have provided safety devices of some kind even though not required to by statute or regulation. Stinnett had been in the painting business with his brother-in-law for two years before he began working for Dr. Buchele. Although the record is not clear whether Stinnett, his brother-in-law or both did the painting, they did paint a church steeple and an undetermined number of barn roofs. On occasion safety belts and safety nets had been used while painting the barn roofs. Dr. Buchele had purchased the material that Stinnett was applying to the roof when he fell. Stinnett did not ask Dr. Buchele to procure a safety net nor did he check to see if one was available. He admitted he could have used a safety rope around his waist but he did not think any were available.

In short, we find no evidence of negligence on the part of Dr. Buchele to submit to a jury.

Bernier v. Boston Edison

Supreme Judicial Court of Massachusetts (1980)

The plaintiffs Arthur Bernier, Jr., and Patricia J. Kasputys, then eighteen and fifteen years old, were let out of school and sauntered to an ice cream parlor on Massachusetts Avenue, one of the town's major shopping areas. A half hour later, Alice Ramsdell entered her 1968 Buick Skylark automobile parked, pointed east, on the south side of Massachusetts Avenue (which here runs west-east), in the last metered space about fifteen to twenty feet short of where the avenue meets Muzzey Street, a one-way street beginning at the avenue and running south. No traffic signals were posted at the junction with Muzzey Street.

As Ramsdell started her car, she noted, checking her rear-view and side-view mirrors, that there was a car later identified as a Cadillac convertible driven by John Boireau some seventy-five feet behind her. She wanted to make a right turn on Muzzey Street. Just before pulling out, Ramsdell observed that the Cadillac was much closer to her than before. Boireau, too, wished to turn right onto Muzzey Street. As there were no cars ahead of her before the intersection, Ramsdell thought she could make the turn before the Cadillac interfered.

As Ramsdell was pulling left slightly away from the curb, Boireau passed her traveling (as he said) about five miles an hour. Whether Ramsdell's car then bolted out and struck Boireau's car as he was negotiating the right turn, or Boireau turned into Ramsdell's car as the two attempted to make the turn, was the subject of conflicting testimony. So, too, the estimates of Ramsdell's speed on impact with Boireau varied from five to thirty miles an hour. Both drivers said they recognized the trouble and braked, but not before a minor collision occurred some ten to fifteen feet into Muzzey Street intersection, Boireau's right front fender being slightly dented by contact with Ramsdell's left front fender.

What might have been a commonplace collision turned into a complicated accident. On impact, Ramsdell, a woman of sixty-nine, hit her head against her steering wheel and suffered a bloody nose. She testified she lost complete control of that car. Dazed, she unknowingly let her foot slip from the power brake to the gas pedal. In the result, after veering right around Boireau's car she accelerated across the remaining twenty feet of Muzzey Street, bounced to the south sidewalk, about nine feet wide, of Massachusetts Avenue, and moved about fifty-five feet down the sidewalk. On this passage the car scraped the front of a camera store, hit and levelled a parking meter, struck and damaged extensively the right rear section of a Chevrolet Chevelle automobile (the third parked car beyond Muzzey Street), knocked down an electric light pole owned by the defendant Boston Edison Company (Edison), and struck the plaintiffs who had left the ice cream parlor and were walking side by side west, into the face of the oncoming car. There was much confusion at trial whether, after hitting the meter and car, Ramsdell first hit the pole and then the plaintiffs, or first the plaintiffs and then the pole, but no one denied she hit all three.

The electric light pole, when hit, fell away from Ramsdell's car toward the east, struck a Volkswagen automobile parked along Massachusetts Avenue (the fourth car from Muzzey Street), and came down across the legs of Bernier. Bernier's thighs and left shin bone were broken, the latter break causing a permanently shortened left leg. Kasputys lay within two feet of the pole further in from the curb than Bernier. She was unconscious and vomiting. She suffered a skull fracture on the right side of her head where pieces of metal and a length of wire were found imbedded, and developed permanent pain in her left lower leg.

The jury returned verdicts clearing Boireau but holding Ramsdell and Edison liable. Only Edison appealed. The plaintiffs did not claim that an otherwise acceptable pole had been rendered dangerous through damage or that a well-designed pole had been carelessly constructed. Rather the gravamen of the plaintiffs' case, as it appeared at trial, was that

Edison had failed through negligence to design a pole that was accommodated reasonably to foreseeable vehicular impacts so as to avoid pedestrian injuries, and that the continued use of the pole created an unreasonable risk of such injuries.

As designer of the pole and in control of its maintenance, Edison must anticipate the environment in which its product will be used, and it must design against the reasonably foreseeable risks attending the product's use in that setting. Certainly the evidence showed that a risk of automobiles colliding with Edison poles in particular No. 6 poles was not only foreseeable but well known to the company. About 100 to 120 Edison poles a year were knocked down in such collisions in Edison's Northeast Service Center, which included Lexington. A so-called "knock down truck" worked steadily replacing downed poles in the district and installing new ones, and there were estimates by employees that in their years of field work they had replaced thousands of Edison poles. One employee said he had been personally involved in replacing at least a hundred poles of the type involved in the accident.

As in the case of vehicles, design should take into account foreseeable participation in collisions. And for the speeds to be encountered and consequences entailed in collisions, one analyzes the whole setting. This was a busy shopping area with heavy pedestrian and vehicular traffics. Parked cars often lined the street but this was not a safety factor that could be greatly relied on.

What precautions were taken in the design to guard against the risk of pedestrian injury through collapse of a No. 6 pole upon impact by a vehicle? According to the evidence, the problem was not seriously adverted to. Symptomatic was evidence that no head of a relevant engineering department had authorized a test of Edison poles to determine impact resistance, or knew of such a test. No attempt had been made to design against the risk to pedestrians and no specifications took the impact resistance factor into account. Overall, the major considerations in Edison's design of poles (including their materials) seemed to be cost, adaptability to Edison's existing system of power supply and connecting apparatus, and capacity of Edison employees to install the poles safely.

Edison's failure to pay serious attention to the risk of pedestrian injury in designing poles is probative of the actual quality of the poles in that respect, but adequate poles might come about by happenstance. It became necessary to examine the design of the poles in relation to possible impacts and, if that yielded unsatisfactory estimates, to consider what alternative designs were available and feasible and at what costs or with what other effects. To begin with, since injuries might be serious (as the present case indeed indicated), the likelihood of accidents need not be high to warrant careful consideration of safety features.

The plaintiffs' major witness concerning design safety was Howard Simpson, who had a doctorate in engineering and practiced as a consulting structural engineer. In his opinion, the concrete of the thickness specified for No. 6 poles lacked ductility, the quality which would allow a pole, when struck by a car, to absorb part of the impact and bend without breaking. No. 6 would shatter when hit with sufficient force; indeed, one of the Edison supervisors testified about No. 6 that the concrete all crumbles at the point of impact. As the exposed steel rods could not then support the weight of the pole, it would fall. As to the force sufficient to break No. 6 in this fashion, Simpson testified that the pole would succumb to a 1968 Buick Skylark with a passenger, spare tire, and full gas tank going as slowly as six m.p.h. A medium-sized truck weighing 10,000 pounds could level No. 6 when traveling at 1.5 m.p.h.

Simpson went on to say that the strength of the pole could have been substantially improved by using steel rods of larger diameter or by placing steel spirals perpendicular to those vertical rods. In his opinion the latter device would have enabled the pole to withstand the impact of the Buick at 11 m. p. h. an important advance, as a car going 9 m.p.h. has an energy considerably greater than that at 6 m.p.h. Such hoops and spirals had been in use since the early 1900's in columns for buildings. Simpson calculated the cost per pole of the hoops at $5.75 and the spirals at $17.50.

Edison argues that a finding of negligence here left it in the grip of a polycentric problem. If it chose to protect pedestrians by using stronger poles, motorists might be more seriously injured when they hit poles which did not break. If it chose to protect motorists, pedestrians would claim recovery when poles fell on them. No designer or owner, Edison added, is required to make or use a product wholly accident-free. There is some disingenuousness in this argument as the evidence shows Edison paid scant attention in the design of the No. 6 pole to the safety either of motorists or pedestrians. But we think there is nothing in the argument to relieve Edison of a duty to take precautions against knockdowns by cars, and it would seem reasonable for Edison to consider pedestrian safety with particular seriousness. Persons in a car are protected by a metal and glass shield sometimes three times as heavy as the pole's entire weight; pedestrians are exposed. Whether drivers are hurt any less by impact at similar speeds with poles that topple than with poles that bend rather than fall is unknown to us and apparently to Edison as well. To be sure, many more cars will hit poles than poles will hit pedestrians, but a six m.p.h. threshold for cars, and less for trucks, seems little protection indeed.

To conclude. Here the jury could rationally find negligence of design and maintenance. They could find that the vehicular speed at which No. 6 would topple was grievously low, creating an unacceptable risk of grave injury to persons at the scene (who in shopping areas such as Lexington Center might be numerous). The impact resistance of the pole could have been improved by relatively minor alterations available at the time and not inconveniencing Edison or the public, or possibly by the use of another type of pole with greater resistance.

In balancing all the pertinent factors, the jury made a judgment as to the social acceptability of the design.

Judgments affirmed.

United States v. Carroll Towing Co.

Court of Appeals, Second Circuit (1947)

L. HAND, Circuit Judge

These appeals concern the sinking of the barge, 'Anna C,' on January 4, 1944. The Conners Marine Co., Inc., was the owner of the barge; the Grace Line, Inc., was the charterer of the tug, 'Carroll,' of which the Carroll Towing Co. was the owner.

On January 2, 1944, the barge, which had lifted the cargo of flour, was made fast off the end of Pier 58 on the Manhattan side of the North River, whence she was later shifted to Pier 52. At some time not disclosed, five other barges were moored outside her, extending into the river; her lines to the pier were not then strengthened. At the end of the next pier north (called the Public Pier), lay four barges; and a line had been made fast from the outermost of these to the fourth barge of the tier hanging to Pier 52. The purpose of this line is not entirely apparent, and in any event it obstructed entrance into the slip between the two piers of barges. The Grace Line, which had chartered the tug, Carroll, sent her down to drill out one of the barges which lay at the end of the Public Pier; and in order to do so it was necessary to throw off the line between the two tiers. On board the Carroll at the time were not only her master, but a harbormaster employed by the Grace Line. Before throwing off the line between the two tiers, the Carroll nosed up against the outer barge of the tier lying off Pier 52, ran a line from her own stem to the middle bit of that barge, and kept working her engines against the tide. The captain of the Carroll put a deckhand and the harbormaster on the barges, told them to throw off the line which barred the entrance to the slip; but, before doing so, to make sure that the tier on Pier 52 was safely moored. The harbormaster and the deckhand went aboard the barges and readjusted all the fasts to their satisfaction, including those from the Anna C., to the pier.

After doing so, they threw off the line between the two tiers and again boarded the Carroll, which backed away from the outside barge, preparatory to drilling out the barge she was after off the Public Pier. She had only got about seventy-five feet away when the tier off Pier 52 broke adrift. The tide and wind carried down the six barges, still holding together, until the Anna C hit a tanker, whose propeller broke a hole in her at or near her bottom. Shortly thereafter she careened, dumped her cargo of flour, and sank. The tug, Grace, owned by the Grace Line, and the Carroll, came to the help of the flotilla after it broke loose; and, as both had syphon pumps on board, they could have kept the Anna C afloat, had they learned of her condition; but the bargee had left her on the evening before, and nobody was on board to observe that she was leaking.

Since there are occasions when every vessel will break from her moorings, and since, if she does, she becomes a menace to those about her; the owner's duty, as in other similar situations, to provide against resulting injuries is a function of three variables: (1) The probability that she will break away; (2) the gravity of the resulting injury, if she does; (3) the burden of adequate precautions. Possibly it serves to bring this notion into relief to state it in algebraic terms: if the probability be called P; the injury, L; and the burden, B; liability depends upon whether B is less than L multiplied by P (i.e., whether B less than PL). Applied to this situation, the likelihood that a barge will break from her fasts and the damage she will do, vary with the place and time; for example, if a storm threatens, the danger is greater; so it is, if she is in a crowded harbor where moored barges are constantly being shifted about. On the other hand, the barge must not be the bargee's prison, even though he lives aboard; he must go ashore at times. We need not say whether, even in such crowded waters as New York Harbor a bargee must be aboard at night at all. But we hold that it is not in all cases a sufficient answer to a bargee's absence without excuse, during working hours, that he has properly made fast his barge to a pier, when he leaves her. In the case at bar the bargee left at five o'clock in the afternoon of January 3rd, and the flotilla broke away at about two o'clock in the afternoon of the following day, twenty-one hours afterwards. The bargee had been away all the time, and we hold that his fabricated story was affirmative evidence that he had no excuse for his absence. During this time, especially during the short January days and in the full tide of war activity, barges were being constantly drilled in and out. Certainly it was not beyond reasonable expectation that, with the inevitable haste and bustle, the work might not be done with adequate care. In such circumstances we hold that it was a fair requirement that the Conners Company should have a bargee aboard (unless he had some excuse for his absence), during the working hours of daylight.

Pipher v. Parsell

Supreme Court of Delaware (2007)

The plaintiff, Kristyn Pipher ("Pipher"), appeals from the Superior Court's judgment as a matter of law in favor of the defendant, Johnathan Parsell ("Parsell"). Pipher argues that the Superior Court erred when it ruled that, as a matter of law, Parsell was not negligent. We agree and hold that the issue of Parsell's negligence should have been submitted to the jury.

Around 6 p.m., Pipher, Parsell and Johnene Beisel ("Beisel") were traveling south in Parsell's pickup truck. All three were sitting on the front seat. Parsell was driving, Pipher was sitting in the middle, and Beisel was in the passenger seat next to the door. They were all sixteen-years-old at the time.

As they were traveling at 55 mph, Beisel unexpectedly grabbed the steering wheel causing the truck to veer off onto the shoulder of the road. Parsell testified that Beisel's conduct caused him both shock and surprise. Although Beisel's conduct prompted him to be on his guard, Parsell further testified that he did not expect Beisel to grab the wheel again. Nevertheless, his recognition of how serious Beisel's conduct was, shows he was aware that he now had someone in his car who had engaged in dangerous behavior.

Parsell testified that he did nothing in response to Beisel's initial action. Approximately thirty seconds later, Beisel again yanked the steering wheel, causing Parsell's truck to leave the roadway, slide down an embankment and strike a tree. Pipher was injured as a result of the collision.

The trial judge concluded that, as a matter of law, Parsell had no duty to do anything after Beisel yanked the wheel the first time because it would be reasonable for the driver to assume that it would not happen again. The trial judge also ruled that (1) there was no negligence in failing to discharge the dangerous passenger and (2) that failing to admonish the dangerous passenger was not negligence and could not be considered a proximate cause of Pipher's injuries.

A driver owes a duty of care to her or his passengers because it is foreseeable that they may be injured if, through inattention or otherwise, the driver involves the car she or he is operating in a collision. Almost forty-five years ago, this Court held that a minor who operates a motor vehicle on the highways will be held to the same standard of care and must accord his or her own passengers the same diligence and protection which is required of an adult motorist under similar circumstances. The following year, this Court recognized an important correlative principle: One riding as a passenger in a motor vehicle has the right to assume that the driver will exercise reasonable care and caution and is under no duty to supervise the driving in the absence of knowledge that the driver is unfit or incompetent to drive.

Pipher argues that after Beisel grabbed the steering wheel initially, Parsell was on notice that a dangerous situation could reoccur in the truck. Pipher further argues that once Parsell had notice of a possibly dangerous situation, he had a duty to exercise reasonable care to protect his passengers from that harm. Finally, Pipher concludes that Parsell was negligent when he kept driving without attempting to remove, or at least address, that risk.

In general, where the actions of a passenger that cause an accident are not foreseeable, there is no negligence attributable to the driver. But, when actions of a passenger that interfere with the driver's safe operation of the motor vehicle are foreseeable, the failure to prevent such conduct may be a breach of the driver's duty to either other passengers or to the public. Under the circumstances of this case, a reasonable jury could find that Parsell breached his duty to protect Pipher from Beisel by preventing Beisel from grabbing the steering wheel a second time.

The issue of Parsell's alleged breach of duty to Pipher, the foreseeability of Beisel's repeat conduct, and the proximate cause of Pipher's injuries were all factual determinations that should have been submitted to the jury. Accordingly, the judgment of the Superior Court, that was entered as a matter of law, is reversed.

Chambers v. Village of Moreauville

Supreme Court of Louisiana (2012)

Arlene Chambers ("Chambers") and a friend, Annette Bowman ("Bowman"), were walking from a former co-worker's funeral at Simpson Baptist Church to Chambers' home. During most of this walk, Bowman walked slightly in front of Chambers on the left portion of the sidewalk, while Chambers walked on the right portion of the sidewalk. When adjacent to 2 Tassin Street, Chambers noticed one panel of the sidewalk sloped down and the adjacent panel sloped upward and began navigating these slopes. However, she did not see a one-and-one-quarter to one-and-one-half inch ledge at the top of the upward slope on the right edge of the sidewalk, and she tripped and fell when her boot caught the ledge. As a result, Chambers sustained a comminuted fracture of the radius of her right arm. The claim was tried as a bench trial, resulting in a judgment in favor of the plaintiff, finding Moreauville one hundred percent at fault, and assessing damages in the amount of $349,214.39

After discussing the expert testimony and case law relating to whether this defect constituted an unreasonable risk of harm, the trial judge stated in his oral reasons for judgment:

The deviation is not important to me. What is important is the cost factor and it's important in my ruling. I cannot allow a municipality to say the cost factor will be our escape clause. But a municipality can say it would cost ... too much. I am not saying it's a judicially imposed duty on a municipality but if you got sidewalks in your custody and guard your[sic] responsible for them not the landowners. The law is clear. They've got to be reasonably safe for pedestrians. The municipality has to budget and prepare for this. They just got to. They can't just let them go and then say well you got an escape clause. It's a cross[sic] factor. We can't fix them all over town. We've got to. I mean if we don't, if a municipality can play that card every time and say the cost factor well then they ... no longer have to keep them reasonably safe. So for those reasons, I find the City of Moreauville one hundred percent at fault for the accident at issue.

The court of appeal affirmed the portion of the trial court's ruling which provided that the elevated differential created an unreasonable risk of harm.

LAW AND DISCUSSION

We find the trial court applied incorrect principles of law because it failed to consider a necessary component of the risk-utility balancing test in determining whether the instant deviation created an unreasonable risk of harm. Specifically, the trial judge erred when he expressly declined to consider cost, an indispensable component of the risk-utility balancing test.

Courts have adopted a risk-utility balancing test to determine whether a condition is unreasonably dangerous, wherein the trier of fact balances the gravity and the risk of harm against the individual and societal utility and the cost and feasibility of repair. This Court has applied the risk-utility balancing test to determine whether a defect in a sidewalk creates an unreasonable risk of harm, and determined there is no fixed rule in determining whether a defect in a sidewalk is unreasonably dangerous. Instead, the facts and surrounding circumstances of each case control. However, the test applied requires the consideration of whether or not the sidewalk was maintained in a reasonably safe condition for persons exercising ordinary care and prudence. Therefore, although municipalities have a duty to maintain its sidewalks in a reasonably safe condition, they are not insurers of the safety of pedestrians and are not required to maintain sidewalks in perfect condition. To be liable for damages caused by a defect, the defect must be dangerous or calculated to cause injury. Moreover, when traveling down a sidewalk a pedestrian is not required to exercise the care required in traversing a jungle, but he must exercise ordinary care, keeping in mind that irregularities exist in sidewalks.

Another factor relevant to the risk of harm in a sidewalk case is the number of years the defect has existed relative to the pedestrian traffic and the number of incidents reported. Accordingly, we find the risk of harm is not great because the deviation is relatively small, there have been no reported complaints in the approximately forty years that the deviation has been in existence in spite of this area being traveled by twenty-five pedestrians a day, and the deviation was not deliberately created by the defendant.

As stated earlier, the risk-utility balancing test requires balancing the gravity and the risk of harm against the individual and societal utility and the cost and feasibility of repair. As part of the cost analysis, the physical and financial inability of a municipality to maintain its things in anything more than a reasonably safe condition has been considered by this Court as a factor in determining whether such condition creates an unreasonable risk of harm. This includes not only the cost to fix the instant deviation, but also all similar deviations.

Moreover, even though the record does not reveal precisely the number of sidewalks in Moreauville or exactly how many similar deviations exist on these sidewalks, such evidence is not critical here. Instead, central to our ruling is the fact that the cost of fixing all deviations similar to the instant deviation is out of proportion to the gain in fixing such deviations because the risk of someone being seriously injured by such a small sidewalk defect is so slight. This is evident here by the fact that Chambers is the only person who has reported tripping on this defect in the approximately forty years the defect has existed. Therefore, although it may be fiscally possible for Moreauville to fix such deviations, there would be little gained in fixing them. In effect, a ruling finding the deviation creates an unreasonable risk of harm would be sending a message out to the State and all of its municipalities that they are burdened with the fiscally exorbitant task of fixing all sidewalk deviations of one-and-one-half to one-and-one-quarter inches, even though the risk of someone being injured by such a defect is minimal. For the aforementioned reasons, we find the cost factor weighs heavily in favor of finding the instant deviation does not create an unreasonable risk of harm.

Considering the moderate gravity of the harm, the small size of the defect, the absence of complaints regarding this area of the sidewalk for the forty years the condition has been in existence, the development of the defect due to natural causes, the cost to fix all similar deviations, the high utility of the sidewalk, the overt nature of the defect, and Chambers' failure to exercise the requisite standard of care while traversing this area of the sidewalk, we conclude that the instant deviation does not present an unreasonable risk of harm.

For the reasons stated herein, the judgments of the court of appeal and trial court are reversed and judgment is rendered in favor of the defendant, dismissing the plaintiff's claim against the Village of Moreauville with prejudice.

DISSENT

Here, both the plaintiff's expert and the mayor agreed the proposed repairs would have cost between five and six hundred dollars. While this amount is not exactly trivial for a small municipality such as Moreauville, neither is it so expensive that the proposed repairs would be impractical. Considering the obvious trip hazard presented by the sidewalk and the mayor's firsthand knowledge of the sidewalk's poor condition, a reasonable municipality would have made the appropriate repairs.

The majority opinion places great weight on the lack of prior reported injuries on this section of the sidewalk. However, as plaintiff points out, this is not proof that no one has ever tripped there before. At best, we know no one has tripped on this section and suffered a serious injury. Most sidewalk trips result in nothing more than a minor embarrassment and perhaps a skinned knee, and would never be reported. Although the absence of prior reported incidents may be a factor for the trier of fact to consider, it is not an absolute bar to recovery. Numerous courts have found unreasonable risk of harm even where plaintiff's injury was the first reported injury at a certain place. The majority suggests a municipality has no duty to repair a hazard until someone has already been injured, which is a classic example of shutting the barn door after the horse has escaped.

PROOF OF BREACH

Santiago v. First Student, Inc.

Supreme Court of Rhode Island (2004)

This personal injury action arises out of an alleged motor vehicle accident that occurred between November 17 and November 21, 1997. The plaintiff alleges that, between 3:30 p.m. and 4:30 p.m. on an unspecified day, she was injured when defendants school bus, in which she was a passenger, collided with an unidentified vehicle. At the time of the accident, plaintiff was returning to her home from school, where she was in the eighth grade. According to her complaint, the accident occurred at or about Charles Street or a street along her bus route in Providence between her school and her home.

When plaintiff was deposed as part of pretrial discovery in this case, she testified that she could not remember the street or the neighborhood where the accident occurred. She also admitted that she could not find the street today if she wanted to. The plaintiff did, however, offer a brief description of her recollection of the events. She remembered that the bus was driving on a one-way street approaching a stop sign. According to plaintiff, she saw the unidentified vehicle approaching the intersection, coming toward the bus from the right. She was then jerked forward when the bus driver applied the brakes and the bus collided with the unidentified vehicle. As a result of the collision, plaintiff says, the right side of her face hit the seat in front of her. Police did not respond to the accident and, consequently, there is no police report describing the incident.

Admitting that she did not see the collision occur, plaintiff was unable to offer any details about it. She was unable to say whether the unidentified car had a stop sign. She did not know whether the bus was damaged or the extent of the damage to the other vehicle, other than that its side mirror was knocked off. Although she rode the bus every school day, plaintiff was unable to remember the names of other students who rode the bus with her, except one girl whom she knew only as Daiquiri.

Unfortunately, plaintiff has not spoken with Daiquiri in three years and Daiquiri has since moved away. To identify the bus driver, all plaintiff could provide was his physical description and the fact that he was from the Dominican Republic and did not speak English. Additionally, plaintiff did not know any witnesses to the accident.

Arguing that it is entitled to summary judgment, defendant points to an absence of any evidence of its negligence. This Court has held that the mere occurrence of an accident, without more, does not warrant an inference that a defendant has been negligent. Rather, a party's negligence must affirmatively be established by competent evidence and may not be based on conjecture or speculation.

Reviewing the evidence in the light most favorable to plaintiff, we must accept her assertion that she was injured in an accident. To assign negligence to defendant based on the evidence in the record, however, would impermissibly cross the line from reasonable inference and venture into the realm of rank speculation. The plaintiff admitted that she did not see how the collision occurred. Although she testified that a stop sign controlled the flow of traffic coming from the bus's direction, she does not allege that the bus driver failed to stop at the sign as directed. The plaintiff is unable to describe any actions on the part of the driver of the unidentified vehicle or unidentified bus driver relating to the accident. Indeed, there is no evidence of the interaction between the bus and the unidentified car, except that the two vehicles collided. Furthermore, plaintiff can provide no other witnesses capable of offering a meaningful description of the accident.

The fact that the plaintiff's case may be extremely difficult to prove, however, does not relieve her of the burden of presenting sufficient evidence to demonstrate the existence of a material question of fact. The plaintiff has not met that burden in this case and the defendant, therefore, is entitled to judgment as a matter of law.

Upchurch v. Rotenberry

Supreme Court of Mississippi (2000)

This case arises out of a one-car accident. The plaintiff, Beverly Ann Upchurch (Upchurch), filed a Complaint against the defendant, Teresa Rotenberry (Rotenberry). The Complaint alleges that Rotenberry negligently lost control of her vehicle while driving, which resulted in the death of Upchurch's son, Timothy Adam Upchurch (Adam).

On the night of October 5, 1992, the decedent, Timothy Adam Upchurch, was riding in the passenger seat of Teresa Rotenberry's car while Rotenberry was driving. Adam was the only passenger in the car. The car was traveling west on Highway 182 when Rotenberry lost control of her vehicle. Upchurch claims Teresa left the road suddenly without warning, causing injuries and damages to the decedent that resulted in his death. Rotenberry, however, maintains that she saw a small animal and swerving to avoid hitting it, left the road and lost control of her car. The vehicle struck a tree on the side of the road, and Adam was killed. There were no eyewitnesses to the collision.

Upchurch presented three witnesses on the issue of liability: Kirk Rosenhan, Larry Guyton and Teresa Rotenberry, who was called as an adverse witness. Kirk Rosenhan is a part-time instructor in engineering mechanics at Mississippi State University. He is also a fire services coordinator for Oktibbeha County. Rosenhan came to the accident scene in his capacity as fire services coordinator. He surveyed the scene, including the roadway and the area between the point where the vehicle left the road and where it struck the tree. Rosenhan testified at trial as both an accident reconstructionist and a fact witness to the accident investigation. He testified that according to the absence of markings he observed, Rotenberry's vehicle traveled in a straight line from the point it left the road to the point it hit the tree. Rosenhan testified that on the night of the accident he walked the area with lights and could find no scuff marks or skid marks on the road. Rosenhan further testified that he estimated the speed of Rotenberry's vehicle to be 60 mph when it struck the tree. Finally, Rosenhan testified that the vehicle traveled 160 feet after leaving the road and before making impact with the tree. Rosenhan opined that Rotenberry had sufficient time to react once the vehicle left the roadway before it hit the tree.

The speed the vehicle was traveling when it struck the tree, as well as, whether the vehicle left any marks either on the roadway or the area between leaving the road and striking the tree is also disputed in this case. Rotenberry's expert, Thomas Shaeffer, testified that there were tire marks which began on the road and proceeded off the road, through the grass, and down toward the tree. Shaeffer identified these marks as yaw marks. Shaeffer defines yaw marks as a mark a tire makes when it is still rotating but not traveling in the direction that it is oriented. In other words, if you're driving down the road and you-you steer to one direction, the tires are going to go where the steering wheel tells them to go, but the car may not be able to maneuver as quickly as you, uh-as your steering angle that you've just input it, so the tires are still turning, but they're sliding sideways a little bit and what happens then is it typically leaves a-a narrow black mark called a yaw mark on the road surface if it's paved or some sort of concrete surface or something like that.

On direct examination, Shaeffer testified that the car was traveling approximately 25 to 35 mph when it hit the tree. However, on cross examination, Shaeffer testified that the car was going 42 to 50 mph when it made impact with the tree.

Shaeffer also testified that he observed small pebbles wedged between the rim and tire on both the front left and rear left wheels of the vehicle. This is additional evidence that the vehicle made an extreme right hand turn. All of the evidence presented at trial by Shaeffer was consistent with the vehicle making an evasive maneuver to the right in order to avoid an object on the roadway. Shaeffer's final determination was that the car struck the tree and flipped over on its top, which undoubtedly caused additional damage to the vehicle.

Throughout the discovery proceedings and at the trial itself, Rotenberry testified that she could not remember the events leading up to the accident including a two-day period just prior to the accident. However, on November 13, 1992 (about 5 weeks after the accident), Rotenberry did sign a written statement detailing the accident. In this statement, Rotenberry testified that a large animal, either a deer or a dog, ran across the road and into her lane ultimately causing her to leave the road.

In her brief, Upchurch raises the issue that Kirk Rosenhan, plaintiff's expert, testified that he smelled alcohol on the defendant at the accident scene. However, on direct examination of Rosenhan the following exchange occurred.

Q. Did you get close to Teresa Rotenberry?

A. Not really.

Q. Did you get close enough to smell her?

A. No, I didn't.

Q. Did you smell any odor of intoxicant on her?

A. Uh, not on her....

On redirect examination after an overnight recess, Rosenhan changed his testimony to say that he had not been specific as to the driver of the vehicle the day before and that he did smell alcohol on the driver the night of the accident. The above exchange, however, makes it clear that Rosenhan was perfectly specific on direct examination in denying that he smelled alcohol on Rotenberry at the scene of the accident. It is noteworthy that Rosenhan did testify on direct examination that he smelled alcohol in the area. Also, the presence of beer in the car is not disputed in the facts of this case.

Larry Guyton, a trooper with the Mississippi Highway Patrol, also testified for the plaintiff. Officer Guyton testified that he arrived on the scene after Rotenberry had been taken away by ambulance. Officer Guyton spoke to Rotenberry by telephone in her hospital room two days after the accident. Rotenberry was able to remember the accident at this point. She appeared alert during the conversation. Officer Guyton testified that Rotenberry told him that she was traveling westbound on Highway 182 near Starkville when she saw an animal coming into her lane from the opposite side of the road. She swerved to the right to avoid hitting the animal. In Officer Guyton's opinion, Rotenberry appeared to be telling him the truth.

Further, Officer Guyton testified on direct examination that Rotenberry told him that she had two beers earlier in the evening. On cross examination, however, Officer Guyton testified that Rotenberry did not tell him about drinking beer. He just asked her how the accident occurred, and she told him.

DISCUSSION

This Court's review must be considered from the last point raised at trial-in the instant case judgment notwithstanding the verdict ("JNOV"). Where, as here, the trial judge has refused to grant a motion for JNOV, we examine all of the evidence-not just evidence which supports the non-movant's case-in the light most favorable to the party opposed to the motion. All credible evidence tending to support the non-movant's case and all favorable inferences reasonably drawn therefrom are accepted as true and redound to the benefit of the non-mover. If the facts and inferences so considered point so overwhelmingly in favor of the movant that reasonable men could not have arrived at a contrary verdict, the motion should be granted. On the other hand, if there is substantial evidence opposed to the motion, that is, evidence of such quality and weight that reasonable and fair-minded men in the exercise of impartial judgment might reach different conclusions, the jury verdict should be allowed to stand and the motion denied, and, if it has been so denied, we have no authority to reverse.

Examining all of the evidence in the light most favorable to Rotenberry and accepting all favorable credible evidence tending to support Rotenberry's case and all favorable inferences drawn therefrom as true, this Court concludes that reasonable and fair-minded jury members could reach different conclusions. Consequently, the jury verdict stands, and the motion for JNOV is denied.

This Court will not intrude into the realm of the jury by determining the credibility of a witness and making findings of fact. The jury is the judge of the weight of the evidence and the credibility of the witnesses. Through her statement and the testimony of other witnesses, Rotenberry offered evidence explaining the events of that tragic night. The jury considered this evidence, weighed it, and found in favor of Rotenberry.

The resolution of disputed facts such as this is a duty that devolves upon the jury sitting as finders of fact. They are charged with listening to the witnesses, observing their demeanor, and coming to their own conclusions of which evidence they find more credible. Our system of jurisprudence has determined that citizen jurors, employing their native intelligence and collective life experiences, are best qualified to make those judgments. Absent some clear indication that the jurors in a particular case somehow ignored that duty, neither the trial court, nor this Court reviewing the record on appeal, are permitted to interfere in the conclusions reached by these jurors.

Accepting as true all of the evidence which supports the jury verdict in this case, we conclude that the trial court did not abuse its discretion in failing to grant Upchurch a new trial. The jury finding in this case is not contrary to the overwhelming weight of the evidence. Therefore, this issue is without merit.

AFFIRMED

Wal-Mart Stores, Inc. v. Wright

Supreme Court of Indiana (2002)

Ruth Ann Wright sued for injuries she sustained when she slipped on a puddle of water at the Wal-Mart "Outdoor Lawn and Garden Corral." Wright alleged Wal–Mart was negligent in the maintenance, care and inspection of the premises, and Wal–Mart asserted contributory negligence. By stipulation of the parties, a number of Wal–Mart's employee documents assembled as a "Store Manual" were admitted into evidence at the jury trial that followed. At the end of the trial, Wright tendered the following instruction:

"There was in effect at the time of the Plaintiff's injury a store manual and safety handbook prepared by the Defendant, Wal–Mart Stores, Inc., and issued to employees. You may consider the violation of any rules, policies, practices and procedures contained in these manuals and safety handbook along with all of the other evidence and the Court's instructions in deciding whether Wal–Mart was negligent. The violation of its rules, policies, practices and procedures are a proper item of evidence tending to show the degree of care recognized by Wal–Mart as ordinary care under the conditions specified in its rules, policies, practices and procedures."

The jury found Wal–Mart liable and assessed Wright's total damages at $600,000, reduced to $420,000 by 30% comparative fault attributed to Wright. Wal–Mart appealed, contending that the jury instruction was an improper statement of law that incorrectly altered the standard of care from an objective one to a subjective one.

Explicit in the second paragraph of the instruction, is the assumption that the Manual in fact "tends to show the degree of care recognized by Wal–Mart as ordinary care under the conditions specified in the Manual." Wal–Mart objected to this assumption, contending "you can set standards for yourself that exceed ordinary care and the fact that you've done that shouldn't be used as evidence tending to show the degree that you believe is ordinary." We agree. The second paragraph of the instruction told the jurors that because Wal–Mart has established certain rules and policies, those rules and policies are evidence of the degree of care recognized by Wal–Mart as ordinary care. But Wal–Mart is correct that its rules and policies may exceed its view of what is required by ordinary care in a given situation. Rules and policies in the Manual may have been established for any number of reasons having nothing to do with safety and ordinary care, including a desire to appear more clean and neat to attract customers, or a concern that spills may contaminate merchandise.

There is a second problem with the instruction. Even if the Manual reflected Wal–Mart's subjective view of ordinary care, the second paragraph of the instruction incorrectly states the law because it invites jurors to apply Wal–Mart's subjective view—as evidenced by the Manual—rather than an objective standard of ordinary care. It is axiomatic that in a negligence action the standard of conduct which the community demands must be an external and objective one, rather than the individual judgment, good or bad, of the particular actor. An individual actor's belief that he is using reasonable care is immaterial. A defendant's belief that it is acting reasonably is no defense if its conduct falls below reasonable care. Similarly, a defendant's belief that it should perform at a higher standard than objective reasonable care is equally irrelevant.

Wright cites four cases in support of the instruction. These authorities support the admissibility of the Manual, which Wal–Mart does not contest. They do not support an instruction to consider any violation of the Manual as evidence tending to show the degree of care recognized by Wal–Mart as ordinary care under the conditions. We conclude that the Instruction was an improper invitation to deviate from the accepted objective standard of ordinary care and therefore incorrectly stated the law.

The judgment of the trial court is reversed. This action is remanded for a new trial.

RES IPSA LOQUITUR

Byrne v. Boadle

Court of the Exchequer Chamber (1863)

TRIAL

At the trial the evidence adduced on the part of the plaintiff was as follows: A witness named Critchley said "On the 18th July, I was in Scotland Road, on the right side going north, defendant's shop is on that side. When I was opposite to his shop, a barrel of flour fell from a window above in defendant's house and shop, and knocked the plaintiff down. He was carried into an adjoining shop. A horse and cart came opposite the defendant's door. Barrels of flour were in the cart. I do not think the barrel was being lowered by a rope. I cannot say: I did not see the barrel until it struck the plaintiff. It was not swinging when it struck the plaintiff. It struck him on the shoulder and knocked him towards the shop. No one called out until after the accident." The plaintiff said "On approaching Scotland Place and defendant's shop, I lost all recollection. I felt no blow. I saw nothing to warn me of danger. I was taken home in a cab. I was helpless for a fortnight." Another witness said "I saw a barrel falling. I don't know how, but from defendant's." It was admitted that the defendant was a dealer in flour.

It was submitted, on the part of the defendant, that there was no evidence of negligence for the jury. The trial judge was of that opinion, and held for the defendant.

SUMMARY OF ORAL ARGUMENT: DEFENSE COUNSEL & COMMENTS FROM JUDGES

The defendant argues that first, there was no evidence to connect the defendant or his servants with the occurrence. It is not suggested that the defendant himself was present, and it will be argued that upon these pleadings it is not open to the defendant to contend that his servants were not engaged in lowering the barrel of flour. But the declaration alleges that the defendant, by his servants, so negligently lowered the barrel of flour, that by and through the negligence of the defendant, by his servants, it fell upon the plaintiff. That is tantamount to an allegation that the injury was caused by the defendant's negligence, and it is competent to him, under the plea of not guilty, to contend that his servants were not concerned in the act alleged. The plaintiff could not properly plead to this declaration that his servants were not guilty of negligence, or that the servants were not his servants. If it had been stated by way of inducement that at the time of the grievance the defendant's servants were engaged in lowering the barrel of flour, that would have been a traversable allegation, not in issue under the plea of not guilty. Then, assuming the point is open upon these pleadings, there was no evidence that the defendant, or any person for whose acts he would be responsible, was engaged in lowering the barrel of flour. It is consistent with the evidence that the purchaser of the flour was superintending the lowering of it by his servant, or it may be that a stranger was engaged to do it without the knowledge or authority of the defendant. [Pollock, C. B. The presumption is that the defendant's servants were engaged in removing the defendant's flour; if they were not it was competent to the defendant to prove it.]

Secondly, assuming the facts to be brought home to the defendant or his servants, these facts do not disclose any evidence for the jury of negligence. The plaintiff was bound to give affirmative proof of negligence. But there was not a scintilla of evidence, unless the occurrence is of itself evidence of negligence. There was not even evidence that the barrel was being lowered by a jigger-hoist as alleged in the declaration. [Pollock, C. B. There are certain cases of which it may be said *res ipsa loquitur*, and this seems one of them.] Unless a plaintiff gives some evidence which ought to be submitted to the jury, the defendant is not bound to offer any defense. The plaintiff cannot, by a defective proof of his case, compel the defendant to give evidence in explanation. [Pollock, C. B. I have frequently observed that a defendant has a right to remain silent unless a prima facie case is established against him. But here the question is whether the plaintiff has not shown such a case.] In a case of this nature, in which the sympathies of a jury are with the plaintiff, it would be dangerous to allow presumption to be substituted for affirmative proof of negligence.

SUMMARY OF ORAL DECISION FROM THE BENCH

POLLOCK, Chief Baron: We are all of opinion that the rule must be absolute to enter the verdict for the plaintiff. The learned counsel was quite right in saying that there are many accidents from which no presumption of negligence can arise, but I think it would be wrong to lay down as a rule that in no case can presumption of negligence arise from the fact of an accident. Suppose in this case the barrel had rolled out of the warehouse and fallen on the plaintiff, how could he possibly ascertain from what cause it occurred. It is the duty of persons who keep barrels in a warehouse to take care that they do not roll out, and I think that such a case would, beyond all doubt, afford prima facie evidence of negligence. A barrel could not roll out of a warehouse without some negligence, and to say that a plaintiff who is injured by it must call witnesses from the warehouse to prove negligence seems to me preposterous.

So in the building or repairing a house, or putting pots on the chimneys, if a person passing along the road is injured by something falling upon him, I think the accident alone would be prima facie evidence of negligence. Or if an article calculated to cause damage is put in a wrong place and does mischief, I think that those whose duty it was to put it in the right place are prima facie responsible, and if there is any state of facts to rebut the presumption of negligence, they must prove them. The present case upon the evidence comes to this, a man is passing in front of the premises of a dealer in flour, and there falls down upon him a barrel of flour. I think it apparent that the barrel was in the custody of the defendant who occupied the premises, and who is responsible for the acts of his servants who had the control of it; and in my opinion the fact of its falling is prima facie evidence of negligence, and the plaintiff who was injured by it is not bound to shew that it could not fall without negligence, but if there are any facts inconsistent with negligence it is for the defendant to prove them.

Commonwealth Edison Company and Northern Illinois Gas Company v. Cosgrove

Appellate Court of Illinois (2000)

Cosgrove and her roommate, William Bozic, noticed the power lines sparking in the alley behind their residence. The lines were still sparking when Cosgrove and Bozic went to bed. At approximately 3 a.m. a fire erupted in the alley behind Cosgrove's home. Bozic saw an electrical wire fall to the ground during a storm and a nearby tree catch on fire. Both Cosgrove and Bozic also observed a tall blue flame shooting into the air.

Cosgrove argues that the trial court erred in granting summary judgment in favor of the defendants, which alleged res ipsa loquitur against ComEd and NiGas, respectively. The doctrine of res ipsa loquitur allows an inference or presumption of negligence to be raised by circumstantial evidence. When res ipsa loquitur is invoked, the plaintiff bears the burden of proving that (1) the occurrence is one that would not ordinarily occur in the absence of negligence; and (2) the defendant had exclusive control of the instrumentality that caused the event. Res ipsa loquitur does not apply if the injury can be as readily attributed to pure accident as to the defendant's negligence.

The trial court concluded that the fire at issue here was of the kind that would not occur absent negligence of some kind on the part of ComEd. We disagree. Negligence is not ordinarily the sole reason for a downed power line. Other forces may cause a downed power line, such as wind, lightning, storm, or an animal chewing through the wire. During the night in question, there had been strong storms, and rain was still falling when the fire crew arrived at the scene. There are injuries that may result from occurrences without fault on the part of anyone. A fire caused by a fallen power line may not result solely from negligence; therefore, res ipsa loquitur did not lie against ComEd in this case.

As to NiGas, we conclude that the trial court erred in granting summary judgment in their favor. A ruptured gas line feeding a fire does not ordinarily occur in the absence of negligence. Gas mains are buried beyond the reach and interference of the general public, and the probability is great that breaks therein are occasioned by defects in the pipes or improper utilization thereof. In the ordinary course of events, gas explosions and fires do not occur; when one does occur, an inference of fault is justifiable. This inference may be explained or rebutted. However, even if the gas company is blameless, its superior knowledge of the facts at hand and its responsibility to the community create a duty to come forward and make an explanation.

NiGas argues that res ipsa loquitur is inapplicable when one of the instrumentalities that cause the injury is not under the control or management of the defendant. NiGas does not argue that it was not in exclusive control of its pipeline; however, it argues that it was not in control of the power line, which was a cause of the fire. However, it has long been held that, if escaping gas is a proximate cause of the plaintiff's injury, the immediate cause of ignition is irrelevant. The sparking provided by the power line would have been merely a condition that acted upon the release of the gas, no more the cause than if Cosgrove had been standing near the gas line smoking a cigarette that then ignited the gas. Furthermore, the presence of some control or possession in a person other than defendant does not necessarily destroy the application of res ipsa loquitur. One must look at the nature of the surrounding circumstances and the intervening control of another. Here, ComEd's possession of the power line is irrelevant. The spark provided by that line does not negate NiGas's duty to safely transport gas through its pipeline. Res ipsa loquitur was properly pleaded against NiGas, and the trial court erred in granting summary judgment in NiGas's favor.

Koch v. Norris Public Power District

Court of Appeals of Nebraska (2001)

Verdell Koch (Koch) and Priscilla Koch sued the Norris Public Power District (Norris) for damages they suffered from a fire that started when a high voltage power line maintained by Norris fell into their field and started a fire. The Koches appeal from the trial court's order granting a directed verdict in favor of Norris upon the basis that the doctrine of res ipsa loquitur did not apply to establish Norris' negligence as the cause of the power line falling.

Res ipsa loquitur operates as a type of circumstantial evidence, that is, facts or circumstances, proved or known, from which existence or nonexistence of another fact may be logically inferred or deduced through a rational process. Regarding res ipsa loquitur, the requirement that the occurrence be one which ordinarily does not happen without negligence is of course only another way of stating an obvious principle of circumstantial evidence: that the event must be such that in the light of ordinary experience it gives rise to an inference that someone must have been negligent.

The essence of res ipsa loquitur is that the facts speak for themselves and lead to a proper inference of negligence by the fact finder without further proof. Res ipsa loquitur is an exception to the general rule that negligence cannot be presumed from the mere occurrence of an accident.

Res ipsa loquitur is not a matter of substantive law, but, as a form of circumstantial evidence, is a procedural matter. The plaintiff must prove in order to invoke the doctrine of res ipsa loquitur: (1) The occurrence is one which would not, in the ordinary course of things, happen in the absence of negligence; (2) the instrumentality that produced the occurrence was under the exclusive control and management of the defendant; and (3) there is an absence of an explanation by the alleged wrongdoer.

First, we observe that the trial court appears to have resolved the case under the second element. The trial court stated that the Koches must show that there was no possibility that a third party, not Norris, could have caused the injury. Of course, the evidence does not show there is no possibility that a third party could have caused the injury. Clearly, the Koches could not carry that burden, and therefore the trial court granted Norris' motion for a directed verdict. For the reasons stated below, we do not believe the Koches have the burden assigned to them by the trial court. We shall proceed to analyze this case under the three elements for the application of res ipsa loquitur listed above.

1. Was Occurrence One Which Would Not, in Ordinary Course of Things, Happen in Absence of Negligence?

It is declared to be a matter of common knowledge that high-voltage wires do not ordinarily fall upon the highway without negligence on the part of those in control of such wires, and in order to overcome the prima facie case presented when injury occurs by coming in contact with a fallen wire, the company must make a showing of the condition of the wire at the time it fell, as well as a showing of proper installation.

All the cases we found on the subject, is that power lines do not normally fall without fault on behalf of the company that maintains them and that res ipsa loquitur is applied in the absence of a substantial, significant, or probable explanation. Generally in the cases which hold the doctrine does not apply, the reasons cited for that conclusion have to do with the power lines not being under the exclusive control of the power company, which is really a consideration under the second element of res ipsa loquitur, or that the power line was caused to be down by the act of the plaintiff, of nature, or of some third party, which is a reason usually treated under the third element of res ipsa loquitur. However, all of the above-cited cases seem to be based upon the proposition that, and the majority rule seems to be, if a power line falls without explanation, then the fall is attributed to the power company if that line is under the exclusive control of the power company. In other words, power lines do not, in the ordinary course of events, fall in the absence of negligence.

Koch testified that the weather was sunny but windy. There is no evidence or claim that a 40-mile-per-hour wind in this area is abnormally high. Koch testified that he had never seen weather factors, except tornadoes and ice storms, damage power lines. Pollard admitted that power lines do not ordinarily fall down and that something has to cause them to fall. The fact that Norris felt it necessary to introduce evidence of possible damages by vandals shooting the line show that Norris cannot seriously maintain that the line did not fall on its own without its being either built or maintained in a negligent manner. Norris does not contend that nature is a cause of the downed line in this case. We believe the effect of the act or possible act of a third party is properly considered under either the second or the third elements of res ipsa loquitur. We therefore conclude that the first of the three elements for the application of res ipsa loquitur is established.

2. Was Instrumentality That Produced Occurrence Under Defendant's Exclusive Control and Management?

The plaintiff is not required to eliminate with certainty all other possible causes or inferences, which would mean that the plaintiff must prove a civil case beyond a reasonable doubt. All that is needed is evidence from which reasonable persons can say that on the whole it is more likely that there was negligence associated with the cause of the event than that there was not. It is enough that the court cannot say that the jury could not reasonably come to that conclusion. Where no such balance of probabilities in favor of negligence can reasonably be found, res ipsa loquitur does not apply.

In the case at hand, the evidence shows without dispute that the wire which fell was placed high into the air by Norris and that of course, it was obviously regularly charged with high voltage. To expect anyone to interfere with Norris' control, except perhaps by throwing or shooting something, is ridiculous. Pollard admitted that it was up to Norris to take care of the line, that its customers do not climb the line poles and it is common knowledge that people do not do so, and that no one except Norris employees and those entities it has contracts with are allowed to have any control over the line. Except for the possibility of vandalism, there is no reasonable possibility that the wire fell as the result of anything other than Norris' not properly building or maintaining the line. We conclude that for purposes of the doctrine of res ipsa loquitur, Norris had exclusive control and management of the power line.

3. Is There Absence of Explanation by Alleged Wrongdoer?

The only explanation that Norris came up with was the possibility that either vandals or hunters damaged the line. The possibility of damage from hunters or vandals seems weak at best. There is no evidence of vandals being in the area or that general vandalism was so common as to justify the assumption that vandals shot the line. There is no evidence that the guns used by squirrel hunters or dove hunters are of a type that are likely to damage a high line, but general notions of hunting and the firearms used to accomplish it leaves us wondering what a gun of sufficient power to damage a high line would do to either a squirrel or a dove. To allow Norris to escape liability as a matter of law solely upon the unsupported claim that vandals caused the break seems to allow the finder of fact to decide an important question on guess and speculation. In any case, recovery under res ipsa loquitur should not be denied as a matter of law solely as the result of that type of evidence.

For the reasons given, we find that the trial court should not have granted Norris' motion for a directed verdict. We therefore reverse, and remand for a new trial.

Warren v. Jeffries

Supreme Court of North Carolina (1965)

Defendant drove to Terry's home to see Terry's father and parked his car in the yard. Terry's father was not at home and defendant went in the house and waited for his return. The car was left standing on an incline. During the time there were in and around the house about a dozen children, including Terry; their ages ranged from 18 months to 20 years. The car remained parked for about an hour prior to the accident, and during this interval no one had gone to the car or touched it for any purpose. One of the children needed shoe polish and defendant gave Terry's mother the keys to his automobile so she could drive it to a store for the polish. She and five children, including Terry, started to the car. It was raining and Terry didn't want to wear his glasses; he gave them to his mother and she went back in the house to put them up. The five children (eldest, 20 years) got in the rear seat of the car; it was a 4-door sedan, and none of them got in the front seat. They did not touch any of the control mechanisms of the car. Terry was the last to get in and when he closed the door something clicked in the front and the car started rolling backwards in the direction of a large ditch. One of the older children opened the door and told the others to jump out. All jumped out, Terry first. When he jumped out he fell, and the front wheel ran over his chest, resulting in his death.

The mother's graphic description of her son is so typical of an alert and active little boy that it is worthy of preservation. "He was full of fun at all times, he never was still unless he was asleep, he was either laughing or playing or doing something to let you know he was around. One thing I remember, the lady I worked for give him a little puppy and he was crazy about this little dog."

Plaintiff alleges defendant was negligent in that (1) he failed to set the hand brake, (2) failed to engage the transmission, and (3) neglected to maintain adequate brakes. There is no evidence as to the condition of the brakes, whether the hand brake had been set, or whether the car was in gear. Apparently the car was not examined after the accident. What caused it to make a clicking sound and begin rolling backwards is pure speculation. The doctrine of res ipsa loquitur is not applicable.

Widmyer v. Southeast Skyways, Inc.

Supreme Court of Alaska (1978)

On November 15, 1974, a DeHavilland Beaver airplane, owned by Southeast Skyways, Inc. crashed in the waters of False Bay, Chichagof Island, Alaska. The pilot and three passengers were killed in the crash. A jury returned a verdict for Skyways.

William Bernhardt, who piloted another plane from Juneau on the 15th bound for Basket Bay, testified that the weather at Juneau International Airport was generally good on that day. Both planes proceeded toward their destinations and, in so doing, travelled in a southerly direction down Chatham Strait which separates Admiralty and Chichagof Islands. Bernhardt observed Skyways' airplane in a parallel flight pattern near Hawk Inlet on Admiralty Island. A heavy snow squall was encountered by both airplanes. Bernhardt overtook Skyways' craft near Point Marsden on Admiralty Island; and, at that time, both airplanes were flying at an altitude of 50 to 100 feet. Bernhardt lost sight of the Skyways' craft when it executed a turn to the right, away from the Admiralty Island beach, and disappeared from view.

The Skyways' craft was next sighted on the Chichagof side of the Chatham Strait by Charles and Esther Kaze. The airplane was flying at low altitude near their cabin, and it crashed a few seconds after they observed it. There was no change in the audible pitch of the motor prior to impact. It was snowing very hard, and visibility was poor. They found the craft wreckage in a vertical, nose down position in rough tidal water; there were no survivors.

Skyways' evidence focused on inclement weather as a cause of the accident. Harold Searby, a defense witness and an expert in meteorology, testified that the weather in Southeast Alaska on the day of the crash was unstable; and that, in his opinion, strong and severe turbulence existed in False Bay at the time of the crash.

Ray Renshaw, a defense witness and an expert on aviation in Southeast Alaska, testified to his opinion that Richard Norvell, whom he had supervised and trained, was an experienced pilot with approximately 3,000 hours of flight. He then testified to his opinion that, after completing his turn from the Admiralty side of the Chatham Strait, Norvell was in clear air; that he crossed the Strait and proceeded down a corridor on the Chichagof side in clear air; that he encountered a snow squall and attempted to land in False Bay when the craft was struck by an unexpected gust of wind; and that the crash was not due to pilot error.

Plaintiffs allege error in the superior court's denial of their proposed instruction on the doctrine of Res ipsa loquitur. The doctrine of Res ipsa loquitur, meaning "the thing or transaction speaks for itself," permits a finding of negligence from the circumstances surrounding the injury. It does not allow negligence to be established from the mere fact of injury itself. The doctrine, where applicable, is a bridge, dispensing with the requirement that a plaintiff specifically prove breach of duty, once that duty and proximate cause have been established.

Traditionally, the doctrine has been applied when the following requirements are met: 1) the accident is one which ordinarily does not occur in the absence of someone's negligence; 2) the agency or instrumentality is within the exclusive control of the defendant; 3) the injurious condition or occurrence was not due to any voluntary action or contribution on the part of the plaintiff.

We now return to analysis of the three traditional prerequisites to the applicability of Res ipsa loquitur: an accident that normally does not happen without negligence; exclusive control of the instrumentality by the defendant; and absence of voluntary action or contribution by the plaintiff.

Since it is not the mere fact of injury itself, but the circumstances surrounding the injury, which justify the application of the doctrine, the applicability of the doctrine must depend on the peculiar facts and circumstances of each case.

Skyways relies primarily on the weather conditions incident to the crash to refute plaintiffs' argument that the requirements have been met. Weather conditions, however, are not material to the issue of plaintiff contribution. Accordingly, we shall first address this prerequisite.

Plaintiff contribution is not the equivalent of contributory negligence. Instead, the former term refers to the question of control: the doctrine of Res ipsa loquitur will not apply if the plaintiff had control of the instrumentality. Skyways argues that plaintiffs have not established lack of plaintiff contribution, since the passengers could have interfered with the controls. Here, however, there was no evidence regarding passenger interference presented by any of the parties.

If the requirement of no plaintiff contribution is strictly applied, no Res ipsa loquitur instruction could be given where the plaintiff lacks sufficient evidence, or any evidence, upon which to prove a negative. We believe that there must be some evidence upon which a jury could find plaintiff contribution before a Res ipsa loquitur instruction can be denied for this reason. In the face of a silent record, the conclusion that a passenger did not interfere with the operation of an aircraft is much more compelling than the conclusion that he did interfere.

While it is clear that Res ipsa loquitur is applicable in general to aviation cases, it is not necessarily applicable to every such case since the specific circumstances will vary. Weather may impinge upon the first prerequisite for Res ipsa loquitur in that it may contribute to a set of circumstances in which it is not more likely than not that the crash was caused by the defendant's negligence. To require a plaintiff to show that a crash was not caused by weather, as a prerequisite to the application of Res ipsa loquitur, presents the problems inherent in proving a negative. We will not require a plaintiff to negate the possibility of weather as a cause of an airplane crash in order to obtain the benefit of a Res ipsa loquitur instruction.

The general safety record of air travel and the present state of air technology compel us to conclude that air crashes do not normally occur absent negligence, even in inclement weather. In Alaska Airlines, Inc. v. Sweat, we stated: "Air travel may no longer be regarded as inherently dangerous and flights aboard certified carriers do not involve an unreasonable risk of harm.

Thus, under the circumstances of this case, we find no reason to preclude the applicability of the doctrine of Res ipsa loquitur. We find the lack of an instruction on the doctrine to be error.

Wolfe v. Feldman

City Court, City of New York (1936)

Defendant's story is that plaintiff was strapped to the operating chair; that a short time later, after plaintiff was in the excitement stage of nitrous oxide anesthesia and as he moved closer to the chair to adjust the suction aspirator, plaintiff, despite the limited movement of the strapped wrist, clutched his testicles with a painful grip, which required the use of great force to release. Thereafter he proceeded with the operation and when the patient had recovered from the anesthetic she complained of pain in the right little finger. The following day an X-ray of the finger showed on the second phalanx a narrow line which looked like a fracture.

Defendant testified that he had present two assistants, a doctor and a nurse. The straps were applied to the chest, legs, and wrists of the patient after the anesthetic gas had begun to take effect; that being the most considerate policy. Wrist straps allow the patient's arm to hang over the side of chair, but there is no rigid close strapping which would defeat normal circulation in the hand.

Where the defendant tacitly admits causing the injury, the acute problem is this: Has the defendant satisfactorily explained the occurrence of the accident? The rule of res ipsa loquitur applies, and while the plaintiff must sustain the burden of proof of defendant's lack of proper care, the defendant is obliged to come forward with proof that he observed reasonable care in the performance of these dental services. If, as claimed by the plaintiff, defendant alone was present at the time of the administration of the anesthetic and no restraining straps were applied to control the actions of plaintiff after she became unconscious, it is clear that there was such lack of care and diligence by defendant as constitutes negligence. If, on the other hand, as claimed by the defense, wrist straps were applied, it is quite evident that such application or fastening must not have been properly performed, else the very purpose for which such strapping is done was not accomplished. Nor does the claim that it was impracticable to so fasten the straps as to prevent certain freedom of movement of the wrists and hands of the patient help defendant, for in such case it was incumbent on him, during the time the patient was in the so-called "fighting stage" reached by patients undergoing anesthesia by nitrous oxide, not to place his body in such a position as to permit plaintiff's hands to interfere with him to such extent as to require the application of force sufficiently severe to cause her physical injury. The nonobservance of such duty constituted negligence. In Keily v. Colton the court stated: "There was nothing hurtful in the anesthetic administered to the plaintiff, and the fact that he was put under its influence is material only in determining the amount of care which the defendants were called upon to exercise. They knew that the plaintiff, while under the influence of the anesthetic, had no control of his faculties; that they were powerless to act, and that he was unable to exert the slightest effort to protect himself from any of the probable or possible consequences of the operation which they had undertaken to perform. He was in their charge and under their control to such an extent that they were required to exercise the highest professional skill and diligence to avoid every possible danger, for the law imposes duties upon men according to the circumstances in which they are called to act. In this case skill and diligence must be considered as indissolubly associated. The professional man, no matter how skillful, who leaves an essential link wanting or a danger unguarded in the continuous chain of treatment is guilty of negligence, and if the omission results in injury to the patient, the practitioner is answerable."

For defendant's failure to satisfactorily explain the absence of his negligence for his failure to observe the degree of care necessary under the circumstances, plaintiff should have judgment.

Kerns v. Sealy

United States District Court, S.D. Alabama (2007)

This action arises from a fire on November 8, 2005 that caused substantial damage to a partially constructed house in Gulf Shores, Alabama, belonging to plaintiffs, Melvin and Pauline Kerns. Plaintiffs maintain that defendants Mark Sealy and Pro–Foam of South Alabama, Inc. caused the fire while applying spray-on foam insulation in the attic of that house.

The Fire

Plaintiffs were building a nearly 4,000 square-foot home in Gulf Shores, Alabama. Plaintiffs contacted defendant Pro–Foam of South Alabama, Inc. ("Pro–Foam") to request an estimate for application of spray-on polyurethane foam insulation in the attic of the Gulf Shores house. Defendant Paul Mark Sealy, owner of Pro–Foam, came to the home site to meet with the Kernses, examine the house, and provide an estimate.

Sealy and another Pro–Foam representative, non-party John Frank, went to plaintiffs' house to apply the foam. Although Pro–Foam was a side business for them, Sealy and Frank were experienced in this kind of work, having done literally "hundreds of jobs" prior to this one. The parties agree that this kind of insulation is applied by mixing two chemicals, an "A" component and a "B" component, through a spray gun. The mixing of the chemicals causes an exothermic chemical reaction, producing both heat and foam, which rises like shaving cream after being expelled from the gun. Sealy and Frank were unable to complete the application that day because they encountered a temperature problem with the raw material, in that the B component was too cold—and therefore too thick to be pumped out of the drum effectively—because of chilly weather, resulting in poor foam. Upon observing this problem, Sealy and Frank ceased work on the plaintiffs' job after proceeding "not far," and contacted their distributor to troubleshoot the matter.

On the morning of November 8, 2005, Sealy and Frank returned to the Kernses' house to perform the foam insulation job. No one else was present at the construction site that day. Defendants anticipated being able to complete the entire job in a single eight-hour day, spraying two two-inch layers, or "lifts," of foam over the entire roof deck of the house. In general, defendants' procedure was to spray a two-inch lift for 30 to 40 minutes, then go back to the beginning and spray a second two-inch lift directly over the same area that had been previously sprayed, for a total depth of 4 inches. According to defendants' expert, "[i]ndustry standards recommend that you not put foam on any thicker than two inches in one pass" for safety purposes. Defendants subscribed to that general rule. Their protocol for applying foam was to have one person actually spraying in the attic, while the other one monitored the chemical drums and kept an eye on the person doing the spraying, with the two individuals swapping responsibilities every 45 minutes to an hour so that the person doing the spraying would not get too tired.

Defendants do not recall whether they used lighting or fans on the jobsite, although they had used them on other jobs and were working in an unventilated attic with poor visibility in places. Sealy testified that he could not see into an eve area at the corner of the roof where they applied foam (and where the fire appears to have ignited). Moreover, there is no evidence in the record as to what, if any, steps Sealy and Frank took to ensure that each lift did not exceed two inches. In that regard, defendants' expert Larry Creel testified that applying these two-inch lifts is not an exact science and that there may be areas where more than two inches of foam are inadvertently applied in a given lift by the applicator. As evidence that this actually happened here, plaintiffs point to post-fire photographs that, while difficult to interpret, might reasonably be construed as depicting unburned foam in the roof area at depths exceeding 4 inches in places.

At some point before noon, Sealy left the premises for a lunch break, while Frank remained on site and continued applying foam. When Sealy returned, he and Frank noticed a "light haze" that they had never observed previously in their hundreds of foam insulation jobs. This haze was light in color, not a dark smoke. Sealy also could detect a burning odor. Upon noticing the haze, they stopped spraying, but the haze "started getting more and more and more and more." Sealy and Frank isolated the region of the house which was smoldering, an area where they already had applied two two-inch lifts of foam. They attempted to remove the smoldering foam material by hand, even going outside and pulling down the eve to separate it from other combustible materials in the area. Industry standards dictate that when "you have a hot spot or foam that you know is hot, then you need to take measures to correct it, which generally means opening up that hot spot to vent the heat out so that you don't have a fire." Approximately 20 to 30 minutes after they first noticed the haze, Sealy and Frank saw flames. The fire started in the southeast corner of the roof, in the eve area where they had previously applied foam. As Sealy and Frank were both off-duty, trained, experienced, professional firefighters who did Pro–Foam work in their spare time, they attempted to douse the blaze themselves using a garden hose. It is undisputed that they "tried their dangedest to put that fire out" at risk to their own safety; unfortunately, their efforts were unsuccessful. At some point after the flames broke out, Sealy called 9–1–1 while Frank stayed in the attic with the hose, and the Gulf Shores Fire Department was summoned to the scene. The Fire Department report reflects that firefighters were dispatched at 12:20 p.m., that they arrived on the scene at 12:28 p.m., and that they had the fire under control at 12:52 p.m.

Cause(s) of the Fire

The Gulf Shores Fire Department performed an investigation of the fire in an attempt to determine its cause. Fire investigators could not find any source of ignition in the roof area where the fire began. Indeed, Sealy and Frank do not smoke, no electricity had been connected in the house, and there were no lightning strikes in the area, such that there were no conventional ignition sources on site. Indeed, the only materials present were normal construction materials and the freshly-sprayed foam insulation. On that basis, George T. Blakemore, Fire Chief for the City of Gulf Shores, informed plaintiffs as follows: "The only thing we can conclude as a source of ignition is a possible spontaneous ignition. We were not able to locate any normal source of ignition at the point of origin."

Although no definitive cause of the fire has been determined, several theories have been posited by witnesses in this case. Both Blakemore and Posey recognize the possibility of spontaneous combustion of the foam (which could occur if the foam were applied in a manner not in compliance with industry standards, such as in lifts that were too thick or that were repeated in accelerated time intervals, thereby trapping the heat generated by the exothermic reaction or otherwise preventing it from dissipating). Defense expert Creel reiterated this possibility, observing that "[a]ll polyurethane foam if it's installed improperly is flammable" because of the exothermic reaction when the chemicals are combined. Nonetheless, Creel mentioned as other possible causes static electricity, an ignition source on the eve (such as a lit, smoldering cigarette or cigar), or a chemical defect in this batch of foam's formula that caused it to overheat.

Negligence / Res Ipsa Loquitur Claims

Alabama courts have explained "that direct evidence is not necessary to prove negligence on the part of a defendant and that proof of negligence may be established completely through circumstantial evidence." "A fact is established by circumstantial evidence if it can be reasonably inferred from the facts and circumstances adduced."

To prevail on a claim of negligence under Alabama law, a plaintiff must prove: "(1) a duty to a foreseeable plaintiff; (2) a breach of that duty; (3) proximate causation; and (4) damage or injury." Defendants argue that the second and third elements are not satisfied. Specifically, defendants maintain that there is no evidence that Sealy and Frank acted in a negligent manner on November 8, 2005; to the contrary, defendants contend, defense expert Creel has opined that their conduct comported with industry standards. Even if defendants breached some duty of care, they assert, there is no evidence that such breach caused the fire, particularly where both plaintiffs' expert Posey and the Gulf Shores Fire Department have opined that the cause of the fire is unknown and where all witnesses apparently agree that there are multiple possible causes, some of which (e.g., manufacturing defect in the foam, foreign object/ignition source left concealed in the eve by an unknown third party) would not be attributable to defendants.

The elements of res ipsa loquitur are as follows: "(1) [T]he defendant must have had full management and control of the instrumentality which caused the injury; (2) the circumstances must be such that according to common knowledge and the experience of mankind the accident could not have happened if those having control of the management had not been negligent; (3) the plaintiff's injury must have resulted from the accident."

This is not a res ipsa loquitur case. The second element poses an insuperable obstacle for plaintiffs here because it is undisputed that there are a number of different potential causes of the fire at the Kernses' house that are extrinsic to defendants, including for example a manufacturing defect in the foam. The foam applied on plaintiffs' house was manufactured by a third party, Isotec. If Isotec manufactured that foam with a core temperature problem that rendered it susceptible to overheating, then the fire could have occurred even if Sealy and Pro–Foam were not negligent at all. That very real, very plausible alternative explanation—which plaintiffs have proffered no competent evidence to disprove—precludes the res ipsa loquitur inference here. After all, "[i]f one can reasonably conclude that the accident could have happened without any negligence on the part of the defendant, then the res ipsa loquitur presumption does not apply." From the summary judgment record, one could reasonably conclude that the fire at the Kernses' home could have happened even if Sealy and Pro–Foam were not negligent because, for example, the batch of foam might have had a core temperature problem; therefore, the presumption of res ipsa loquitur is plainly inapplicable.

As the res ipsa loquitur doctrine is not properly a part of this case, plaintiffs must show breach of duty by defendants through the ordinary means, by adducing sufficient evidence from which a reasonable factfinder could conclude that defendants were in fact negligent. Construed in the light most favorable to plaintiffs, the record reveals the following evidence of negligence: (a) defendants' expert testified that improper application of polyurethane foam insulation can start a fire because of the exothermic reaction when the chemicals are mixed; (b) industry safety standards call for polyurethane foam insulation to be applied in no more than two inches per pass, and a thicker foam application heightens the likelihood of a runaway exothermic reaction; (c) defendants applied the foam at the Kernses' home in two passes, so the total thickness of the foam should not exceed four inches to comply with industry safety standards; (d) there are post-fire photographs from which a reasonable factfinder could conclude that the thickness of the unburned foam exceeded four inches in depth, suggesting that defendants might have applied the foam in a manner that exceeded the industry safety standard of two inches per pass; (e) Sealy and Frank applied foam into or near an eave area where they could not see, such that it is unclear how they could know the thickness of each pass as they worked in that area; (f) the fire originated in that eave area; (g) although fans may be helpful in dissipating excess heat from the foam's exothermic reaction and lights may aid visibility, defendants do not recall using either on the Kernses' job; (h) although their standard protocol was for one person to spray foam while the other person monitored the area, Frank continued spraying in the Kernses' attic while Sealy went on a lunch break across the street; (i) Sealy noticed the haze and smelled the burning odor that were symptoms of a runaway exothermic reaction immediately after returning from his lunch break; (j) defendants had never seen this kind of haze before in their hundreds of jobs; (k) industry standard for treating hotspots calls for foam appliers to cut them open to vent excess heat; (l) instead of cutting open hotspots, defendants resorted to scooping up foam with their hands and pulling down eaves; (m) no fire erupted for 20 or 30 minutes after defendants noticed the haze; (n) the haze grew worse and worse during that time period, yet defendants failed to call for help, failed to vent hotspots effectively, and otherwise failed to alleviate the problem; and (o) defendants failed to call for help at that time to prevent the fire even though they were both off-duty firefighters who were keenly aware of the fire hazards attendant to the foam insulation application process.

Viewing these facts in their totality, a reasonable finder of fact could determine that defendants breached a duty of care to defendants by failing to utilize adequate safety equipment at the jobsite, exceeding the industry standard of two inches per pass in applying foam, applying foam in or near an area where defendants could not see, continuing to apply foam while one member of the team was off the premises at lunch, and failing to take adequate measures to prevent the fire or call for help during the 20 to 30 minute interval after they first noticed the haze and smelled the burning odor that signaled a runaway exothermic reaction. A reasonable factfinder could further conclude that this breach of duty proximately caused the fire that resulted in heavy damage to plaintiffs' house. Accordingly, defendants are not entitled to summary judgment on the negligence cause of action set forth in Count I of the Amended Complaint.

HARM & ACTUAL CAUSE

Right v. Breen

Supreme Court of Connecticut (2006)

The issue in this certified appeal is whether a plaintiff in a negligence action must be awarded nominal damages when the defendant admits liability but denies having caused the alleged injury, and the fact finder thereafter concludes that the plaintiff failed to prove that he suffered any injury as a result of the defendant's conduct.

In May, 2000, the plaintiff had stopped his automobile at a red traffic light when it was struck from behind by a vehicle driven by the defendant. There was minor damage to the plaintiff's vehicle, but no physical injuries were reported at the accident scene. Thereafter, the plaintiff brought this action, alleging that, as a result of the defendant's negligence, he had suffered bodily injury leading to both economic and noneconomic damages.

At trial, the plaintiff presented evidence concerning his injuries that allegedly had resulted from the impact of the collision. Because the defendant contended that the plaintiff's injuries were the result of various other automobile accidents, the plaintiff also presented evidence concerning accidents in which he had been involved prior to the May, 2000 collision with the defendant-a 1989 head-on collision, an incident in the early 1990s in which he backed a vehicle into a pole, and a 1995 high impact collision in which the plaintiff's vehicle was hit from behind on the highway-as well as accidents that occurred after the May, 2000 collision-a 2001 rear impact collision, and a 2002 low impact collision. The jury returned a verdict of zero economic damages and zero noneconomic damages.

The essential elements of a cause of action in negligence are well established: duty; breach of that duty; causation; and actual injury. Without proof of each of these elements, a plaintiff's cause fails entirely, and he is not entitled to have the question of damages considered. This is because conduct that is merely negligent, without proof of an actual injury, is not considered to be a significant interference with the public interest such that there is any right to complain of it, or to be free from it. If actual damage is necessary to the cause of action, as in negligence, nominal damages are not awarded.

Salintero v. Nystrom

District Court of Appeal of Florida (1977)

Anna Salinetro sustained back injuries in an automobile accident and applied for personal injury benefits from her insurer, State Farm Mutual Automobile Insurance Company. State Farm required Anna to submit to a medical examination and on December 10 x-rays were taken by Dr. Nystrom of her lower back and abdominal area. Although unknown to her, Anna was approximately four-six weeks pregnant at the time; however, neither Dr. Nystrom nor his receptionist or his x-ray technician inquired whether or not she was pregnant or the date of her last menstrual period. Thereafter, upon suspecting she was pregnant, on December 12 Anna visited her gynecologist, Dr. Emilio Aldereguia, who, after running some tests, confirmed her pregnancy. In January Dr. Aldereguia learned that Dr. Nystrom had taken x-rays of Anna's pelvis and advised her to terminate her pregnancy because of possible damage to the fetus by the x-rays. Anna underwent a therapeutic abortion and the pathology report stated that the fetus was dead at the time of the abortion. Thereafter, Anna filed the instant lawsuit against Dr. Nystrom for medical malpractice. The trial judge granted the motion and entered judgment for Dr. Nystrom.

Assuming arguendo that Dr. Nystrom's conduct fell below the standard of care in failing to inquire of Anna whether she was pregnant or not on the date of her last menstrual period, this omission was not the cause of her injury. Anna herself testified that even if asked about being pregnant, she would have answered in the negative. Anna further testified to the effect that being a few days late with her menstrual period was not unusual and did not indicate to her that she may have been pregnant at the time she went to Dr. Nystrom; that six days prior thereto she had visited Dr. Aldereguia, and he had found no evidence that she was pregnant. We further note that simply because Anna was late with her menstrual period would not in and of itself mean that she was pregnant because further tests were required to ascertain whether she was pregnant.

Landers v. East Texas Salt Water Disposal Co.

Supreme Court of Texas (1952)

In his petition plaintiff alleged that he was the owner of a small lake which he had drained, cleaned and stocked with fish at considerable expense; that defendant East Texas Salt Water Disposal Company was the owner of a pipe line which traversed land adjoining plaintiff's land on the west and into which the defendant pumped approximately 1500 barrels of salt water daily; that on or about April 1, 1949, such pipe line broke and the defendant Disposal Company negligently permitted some 10,000 to 15,000 barrels of salt water to escape from the line and to flow over plaintiff's land and into his lake, killing his fish and otherwise injuring and damaging him. Plaintiff further alleged that the defendant Sun Oil Company was the owner of an oil well, located a short distance from plaintiff's property line, from which the defendant pumped small quantities of oil and large quantities of salt water each day, the oil and salt water being carried off through a pipe line which for some distance ran parallel to a spring branch; that the branch crossed plaintiff's property and emptied into his lake; that on or about April 1, 1949, the pipe line broke and the defendant Sun Oil Company negligently permitted large quantities of oil and salt water to escape and run into the branch and thence into plaintiff's lake, killing his fish and otherwise injuring and damaging him.

Did the plaintiff in his pleading allege facts which, if established by evidence, made the defendants jointly and severally liable for plaintiff's damages? From the face of the petition it appears that there was no concert of action nor unity of design between the defendants in the commission of their alleged tortious acts, an absence said by the court in the case of Sun Oil Co. v. Robicheaux, to be determinative of the nonexistence of joint liability. In that case the rule was thus stated:

"The rule is well established in this state, and supported by almost universal authority, that an action at law for damages for torts cannot be maintained against several defendants jointly, when each acted independently of the others and there was no concert or unity of design between them. In such a case the tort of each defendant is several when committed, and it does not become joint because afterwards its consequences, united with the consequences of several other torts committed by other persons in producing damages. Under such circumstances, each tortfeasor is liable only for the part of the injury or damages caused by his own wrong; that is, where a person contributes to an injury along with others, he must respond in damages, but if he acts independently, and not in concert of action which other persons in causing such injury, he is liable only for the damages which directly and proximately result from his own act, and the fact that it may be difficult to define the damages caused by the wrongful act of each person who independently contributed to the final result does not affect the rule."

The rule of the Robicheaux case, strictly followed, has made it impossible for a plaintiff, though gravely injured, to secure relief in the nature of damages through a joint and several judgment by joining in one suit as defendants all wrongdoers whose independent tortious acts have joined in producing an injury to the plaintiff, which, although theoretically divisible, as a practical matter and realistically considered is in fact but a single indivisible injury. If such has been the law, from the standpoint of justice it should not have been; if it is the law now, it will not be hereafter. The case of Sun Oil Co. v. Robicheaux is overruled. Where the tortious acts of two or more wrongdoers join to produce an indivisible injury, that is, an injury which from its nature cannot be apportioned with reasonable certainty to the individual wrongdoers, all of the wrongdoers will be held jointly and severally liable for the entire damages and the injured party may proceed to judgment against any one separately or against all in one suit. If fewer than the whole number of wrongdoers are joined as defendants to plaintiff's suit, those joined may by proper cross action under the governing rules bring in those omitted. To permit the joinder as defendants of such wrongdoers without at the same time imposing joint liability upon them would not relieve the inequities of the situation nor cure the ills of the plaintiff. Simple procedural joinder of the defendants would put the plaintiff in no better position to produce the required proof of the portion of the injury attributable to each of the defendants. In most such cases, under the decisions heretofore cited, he would still be the victim of an instructed verdict. It would be of no comfort or advantage to the plaintiff that the instructed verdict relieved all of the defendants of liability in one suit and at one time rather than in separate suits and one at a time.

Anderson v. Minneapolis, St. Paul Railway Company

Supreme Court of Minnesota (1920)

The complaint alleged that sparks from one of defendant's locomotive engines set a fire on or near the right of way, and that this fire spread until it finally reached plaintiff's land, where it destroyed some of his property. The answer was a general denial, followed by an allegation that, if plaintiff was damaged by fire, the fire was not due to any act of defendant, was of unknown origin, and, by reason of extraordinary weather conditions, became a huge conflagration.

Plaintiff's case in chief was directed to proving that in August, 1918, one of defendant's engines started a fire in a bog near the west side of plaintiff's land; that it smoldered there until October 12, 1918, when it flared up and burned his property, shortly before it was reached by one of the great fires which swept through Northeastern Minnesota at the close of that day. Defendant introduced evidence to show that on and prior to October 12th fires were burning west and northwest of, and were swept by the wind towards, plaintiff's premises. It did not show how such fires originated, neither did it clearly and certainly trace the destruction of plaintiff's property to them. By cross-examination of defendant's witnesses and by his rebuttal evidence plaintiff made a showing which would have justified the jury in finding that the fires proved by defendant were started by its locomotive on or near its right of way in the vicinity of Kettle River.

Defendant contends that it made a showing from which the jury might have found that fires of unknown origin, coming from the west and northwest, destroyed plaintiff's property independently of the bog fire. For the purposes of the case we will assume that there was sufficient evidence to warrant the jury in so finding.

The thought expressed in the general charge to the jury is this: Assume that defendant's engine did set the bog fire, but that some greater fire swept over it before it reached plaintiff's land; then and in that event defendant is not liable, unless the bog fire was a substantial factor in causing plaintiff's damage. We are of the opinion that the law was correctly stated in the instructions.

The court was justified in refusing to give the requested instruction for another reason. Neither the drought nor the wind would or could have destroyed plaintiff's property without the fire. The result was one which might reasonably be anticipated as a natural consequence of setting a fire and permitting it to burn for days in a country abnormally dry. Hence, if it can be said that an extraordinary wind coupled with an unusual drought were proximate causes of the injury, still the fire was a material concurring cause, without which there would have been no damage to plaintiff, and defendant is liable under the established rules of law.

The following proposition is stated in defendant's brief and relied on for a reversal: "If plaintiff's property was damaged by a number of fires combining, one being the fire pleaded, and the others being of no responsible origin, but of such sufficient or superior force that they would have produced the damage to plaintiff's property, regardless of the fire pleaded, then defendant was not liable."

If a fire set by the engine of one railroad company unites with a fire set by the engine of another company, there is joint and several liability, even though either fire would have destroyed plaintiff's property.

We find no error requiring a reversal, and hence the order appealed from is affirmed.

Dillon v. Twin State Gas & Electric Co.

Supreme Court of New Hampshire (1932)

It was in evidence that at one time the defendant's construction foreman had complained to the city marshal about the bridge's use by boys as a playground, and in his complaint had referred to the defendant's wires. The only wires were those over the bridge superstructure. From this evidence and that relating to the extent of the practice for boys to climb up to and upon the horizontal girders an inference that the defendant had notice of the practice was reasonable.

The use of the girders brought the wires leading to the lamp close to those making the use, and as to them it was in effect the same as though the wires were near the floor of the bridge. While the current in the wires over the bridge was mechanically shut off during the daytime, other wires carried a commercial current, and there was a risk from many causes of the energizing of the bridge wires at any time.

The circumstances of the decedent's death give rise to an unusual issue of its cause. In leaning over from the girder and losing his balance he was entitled to no protection from the defendant to keep from falling. Its only liability was in exposing him to the danger of charged wires. If but for the current in the wires he would have fallen down on the floor of the bridge or into the river, he would without doubt have been either killed or seriously injured. Although he died from electrocution, yet, if by reason of his preceding loss of balance he was bound to fall except for the intervention of the current, he either did not have long to live or was to be maimed. In such an outcome of his loss of balance, the defendant deprived him, not of a life of normal expectancy, but of one too short to be given pecuniary allowance, in one alternative, and not of normal, but of limited, earning capacity, in the other.

If it were found that he would have thus fallen with death probably resulting, the defendant would not be liable, unless for conscious suffering found to have been sustained from the shock. In that situation his life or earning capacity had no value. To constitute actionable negligence there must be damage.

Summers v. Tice

Supreme Court of California (1948)

Plaintiff and the two defendants were hunting quail on the open range. Each of the defendants was armed with a 12 gauge shotgun loaded with shells containing 7 1/2 size shot. Prior to going hunting plaintiff discussed the hunting procedure with defendants, indicating that they were to exercise care when shooting and to keep in line. In the course of hunting plaintiff proceeded up a hill, thus placing the hunters at the points of a triangle. The view of defendants with reference to plaintiff was unobstructed and they knew his location. Defendant Tice flushed a quail which rose in flight to a ten foot elevation and flew between plaintiff and defendants. Both defendants shot at the quail, shooting in plaintiff's direction. At that time defendants were 75 yards from plaintiff. One shot struck plaintiff in his eye and another in his upper lip. Finally it was found by the court that as the direct result of the shooting by defendants the shots struck plaintiff as above mentioned and that defendants were negligent in so shooting and plaintiff was not contributorily negligent.

The problem presented in this case is whether the judgment against both defendants may stand. It is argued by defendants that they are not joint tortfeasors, and thus jointly and severally liable, as they were not acting in concert, and that there is not sufficient evidence to show which defendant was guilty of the negligence which caused the injuries the shooting by Tice or that by Simonson. Tice argues that there is evidence to show that the shot which struck plaintiff came from Simonson's gun because of admissions allegedly made by him to third persons and no evidence that they came from his gun. Further in connection with the latter contention, the court failed to find on plaintiff's allegation in his complaint that he did not know which one was at fault did not find which defendant was guilty of the negligence which caused the injuries to plaintiff.

Considering the last argument first, we believe it is clear that the court sufficiently found on the issue that defendants were jointly liable and that thus the negligence of both was the cause of the injury. It found that both defendants were negligent and that as a direct and proximate result of the shots fired by defendants, and each of them, a birdshot pellet was caused to and did lodge in plaintiff's right eye and that another birdshot pellet was caused to and did lodge in plaintiff's upper lip. Implicit in such finding is the assumption that the court was unable to ascertain whether the shots were from the gun of one defendant or the other or one shot from each of them. The one shot that entered plaintiff's eye was the major factor in assessing damages and that shot could not have come from the gun of both defendants. It was from one or the other only.

When two or more persons by their acts are possibly the sole cause of a harm, or when two or more acts of the same person are possibly the sole cause, and the plaintiff has introduced evidence that the one of the two persons, or the one of the same person's two acts, is culpable, then the defendant has the burden of proving that the other person, or his other act, was the sole cause of the harm. The real reason for the rule that each joint tortfeasor is responsible for the whole damage is the practical unfairness of denying the injured person redress simply because he cannot prove how much damage each did, when it is certain that between them they did all; let them be the ones to apportion it among themselves.

When we consider the relative position of the parties and the results that would flow if plaintiff was required to pin the injury on one of the defendants only, a requirement that the burden of proof on that subject be shifted to defendants becomes manifest. They are both wrongdoers both negligent toward plaintiff. They brought about a situation where the negligence of one of them injured the plaintiff, hence it should rest with them each to absolve himself if he can. The injured party has been placed by defendants in the unfair position of pointing to which defendant caused the harm. If one can escape the other may also and plaintiff is remediless. Ordinarily defendants are in a far better position to offer evidence to determine which one caused the injury.

Under the circumstances here presented, each defendant is liable for the whole damage whether they are deemed to be acting in concert or independently.

Mohr v. Grantham

Supreme Court of Washington (2011)

Linda Mohr suffered a trauma-induced stroke and is now permanently disabled. She and her husband, Charles, claim that negligent treatment by her health care providers diminished her chances of avoiding or greatly minimizing her disability. In other words, they claim that negligence caused Mrs. Mohr a loss of the chance of a better outcome. This case compels consideration of whether, in the medical malpractice context, there is a cause of action for a lost chance, even when the ultimate result is some serious harm short of death.

Mrs. Mohr suffered a hypoglycemic event that caused her to run her car into a utility pole. She was taken by ambulance to the emergency room. Having visible lacerations on her face from the car accident, Mrs. Mohr was given a neurological assessment upon arrival and a computerized tomography (CT) scan of her brain about an hour later. The results were normal.

Following those neurological tests, however, Mrs. Mohr reported and was observed to have neurological symptoms, including being wobbly on her feet and having severe pain after being administered pain medication. Dr. Grantham informed one of Mrs. Mohr's physician sons, Dr. Brandt Mohr, by phone that he would carry out another neurological assessment before discharging her. He did not. Instead, he prescribed a narcotic, Darvocet, and sent Mrs. Mohr home with her husband. At that point, Mrs. Mohr could not walk herself to or from the car and had to be carried to bed by her husband when they arrived home.

Mrs. Mohr was again transported to the emergency room because her husband was concerned that she remained very lethargic through the night. Mrs. Mohr was diagnosed as having a stroke. A magnetic resonance imaging (MRI) examination confirmed that Mrs. Mohr was in fact having a stroke. However, Dr. Dawson did not provide any anticoagulant or antithrombotic treatment or therapy.

Before the transfer, Mrs. Mohr's two physician sons had arrived to be by her side. They tried to get both Dr. Dawson and then, after her transfer, Dr. Watson to order a CT angiogram. A CT angiogram was not done until 2:30 p.m., after the Mohr sons had Dr. Watson repeatedly paged. Then, although the results were available at 3:27 p.m., Dr. Watson was not located or informed until 4:50 p.m. that the CT angiogram showed a dissected carotid artery. He still did not order anyone to administer anticoagulant therapy, antiplatelet agents, or any other treatment. Dr. Watson had prescribed aspirin around 2:00 p.m. but did not order its immediate administration.

Mrs. Mohr's sons finally arranged a transfer and transport to Harborview Medical Center. Dr. Watson signed the transfer form as a formality. Only shortly before her transport at 6:00 p.m. was Mrs. Mohr finally given aspirin, though it had to be administered in suppository form because, by then, she could no longer swallow. Mrs. Mohr is now permanently brain damaged; a quarter to a third of her brain tissue was destroyed. In particular, the portions of her brain that were damaged are involved with motor control, sensation, and spatial reasoning.

Mrs. Mohr and her husband filed suit, claiming that Mrs. Mohr received negligent treatment, far below the recognized standard of care. They argue that the doctors' negligence substantially diminished her chance of recovery and that, with nonnegligent care, her disability could have been lessened or altogether avoided. The Mohrs' claim relies, at least in part, on a medical malpractice cause of action for the loss of a chance. In support of their claim, the Mohrs presented the family's testimony, including her two sons who are doctors, and the testimony of two other doctors, Kyra Becker and A. Basil Harris. The testimony included expert opinions that had Mrs. Mohr received nonnegligent treatment she would have had a 50 to 60 percent chance of a better outcome. The better outcome would have been no disability or, at least, significantly less disability. The Benton County Superior Court granted summary judgment for the defendants on the basis that the Mohrs did not show "but for" causation.

ANALYSIS

1. Lost Chance of a Better Outcome

The medical malpractice statute requires the same elements of proof as traditional tort elements of proof: duty, breach, injury, and proximate cause. The standard formulation for proving proximate causation in tort cases requires, first, a showing that the breach of duty was a cause in fact of the injury, and, second, a showing that as a matter of law liability should attach. In a medical malpractice case, for example, a plaintiff would traditionally seek to prove "cause in fact" by showing that he or she would not have been injured but for the health care provider's failure to use reasonable care. However, the word cause has a notoriously elusive meaning. For this reason, and in service of underlying tort principles, this court and others have recognized some limited exceptions to the strict tort formula, including recognition of lost chance claims.

The Herskovits case involved a survival action following an allegedly negligent failure to diagnose lung cancer. Over the course of a year, Leslie Herskovits repeatedly sought treatment for persistent chest pains and a cough, for which he was prescribed only cough medicine. When he finally sought another medical opinion, Herskovits was diagnosed with lung cancer within three weeks. His diagnosing physician testified that the delay in diagnosis likely diminished Herskovits's chance of long-term survival from 39 percent to 25 percent. Less than two years after his diagnosis, then 60 years old, Herskovits died. The trial court dismissed the case on summary judgment on the basis that Herskovits's estate, which brought suit, failed to establish a prima facie case of proximate cause: it could not show that but for his doctor's negligence he would have survived because he probably would have died from lung cancer even if the diagnosis had been made earlier. This court reversed the trial court, finding that Herskovits's lost chance was actionable.

The opinion in Herskovits explained: "To decide otherwise would be a blanket release from liability for doctors and hospitals any time there was less than a 50 percent chance of survival, regardless of how flagrant the negligence." They similarly noted that traditional all-or-nothing causation in lost chance cases subverts the deterrence objectives of tort law.

Rather than looking to the causation element, Herskovits focused instead on the nature of the injury. The best resolution of the issue before us is to recognize the loss of a less than even chance as an actionable injury. The court noted among its concerns about the "all or nothing" traditional tort approach to recovery that it creates pressure to manipulate and distort other rules affecting causation and damages in an attempt to mitigate perceived injustices.

We find no persuasive rationale to distinguish Herskovits from a medical malpractice claim where the facts involve a loss of chance of avoiding or minimizing permanent disability rather than death. To limit Herskovits to cases that result in death is arbitrary; the same underlying principles of deterring negligence and compensating for injury apply when the ultimate harm is permanent disability.

We hold that Herskovits applies to lost chance claims where the ultimate harm is some serious injury short of death. We also formally adopt the reasoning of the Herskovits plurality. Under this formulation, a plaintiff bears the burden to prove duty, breach, and that such breach of duty proximately caused a loss of chance of a better outcome. This reasoning of the Herskovits plurality has largely withstood many of the concerns about the doctrine, particularly because it does not prescribe the specific manner of proving causation in lost chance cases. Rather, it relies on established tort theories of causation, without applying a particular causation test to all lost chance cases. Instead, the loss of a chance is the compensable injury.

In Herskovits the court discussed limiting damages. Rather than full damages for the adverse outcome, the plaintiff is only compensated for the lost opportunity. The lost opportunity may be thought of as the adverse outcome discounted by the difference between the ex-ante probability of the outcome in light of the defendant's negligence and the probability of the outcome absent the defendant's negligence. Treating the loss of a chance as the cognizable injury permits plaintiffs to recover for the loss of an opportunity for a better outcome, an interest that we agree should be compensable, while providing for the proper valuation of such an interest.

We find no meaningful basis to distinguish permanent disability from death for the purposes of raising a loss of chance claim. Accordingly, we hold that Herskovits applies to medical malpractice cases that result in harm short of death and formally adopt the rationale of the plurality opinion that the injury is the lost chance. For the reasons discussed next, as it relates to the facts of this case, we reverse the order of summary judgment.

PROXIMATE CAUSE

Palsgraf v. Long Island Railroad

Court of Appeals of New York (1928)

CARDOZO, C. J.

Plaintiff was standing on a platform of defendant's railroad after buying a ticket to go to Rockaway Beach. A train stopped at the station, bound for another place. Two men ran forward to catch it. One of the men reached the platform of the car without mishap, though the train was already moving. The other man, carrying a package, jumped aboard the car, but seemed unsteady as if about to fall. A guard on the car, who had held the door open, reached forward to help him in, and another guard on the platform pushed him from behind. In this act, the package was dislodged, and fell upon the rails. It was a package of small size, about fifteen inches long, and was covered by a newspaper. In fact it contained fireworks, but there was nothing in its appearance to give notice of its contents. The fireworks when they fell exploded. The shock of the explosion threw down some scales at the other end of the platform many feet away. The scales struck the plaintiff, causing injuries for which she sues.

The conduct of the defendant's guard, if a wrong in its relation to the holder of the package, was not a wrong in its relation to the plaintiff, standing far away. Relatively to her it was not negligence at all. Nothing in the situation gave notice that the falling package had in it the potency of peril to persons thus removed. Negligence is not actionable unless it involves the invasion of a legally protected interest, the violation of a right. Proof of negligence in the air, so to speak, will not do. Negligence is the absence of care, according to the circumstances. The plaintiff, as she stood upon the platform of the station, might claim to be protected against intentional invasion of her bodily security. Such invasion is not charged. She might claim to be protected against unintentional invasion by conduct involving in the thought of reasonable men an unreasonable hazard that such invasion would ensue. If no hazard was apparent to the eye of ordinary vigilance, an act innocent and harmless, at least to outward seeming, with reference to her, did not take to itself the quality of a tort because it happened to be a wrong, though apparently not one involving the risk of bodily insecurity, with reference to someone else. In every instance, before negligence can be predicated of a given act, back of the act must be sought and found a duty to the individual complaining, the observance of which would have averted or avoided the injury.

A different conclusion will involve us, and swiftly too, in a maze of contradictions. A guard stumbles over a package which has been left upon a platform. It seems to be a bundle of newspapers. It turns out to be a can of dynamite. To the eye of ordinary vigilance, the bundle is abandoned waste, which may be kicked or trod on with impunity. Is a passenger at the other end of the platform protected by the law against the unsuspected hazard concealed beneath the waste? If not, is the result to be any different, so far as the distant passenger is concerned, when the guard stumbles over a valise which a truckman or a porter has left upon the walk? The passenger far away, if the victim of a wrong at all, has a cause of action, not derivative, but original and primary. His claim to be protected against invasion of his bodily security is neither greater nor less because the act resulting in the invasion is a wrong to another far removed. In this case, the rights that are said to have been violated, are not even of the same order. The man was not injured in his person nor even put in danger. The purpose of the act, as well as its effect, was to make his person safe. It there was a wrong to him at all, which may very well be doubted it was a wrong to a property interest only, the safety of his package. Out of this wrong to property, which threatened injury to nothing else, there has passed, we are told, to the plaintiff by derivation or succession a right of action for the invasion of an interest of another order, the right to bodily security. The diversity of interests emphasizes the futility of the effort to build the plaintiff's right upon the basis of a wrong to someone else.

The argument for the plaintiff is built upon the shifting meanings of such words as wrong and wrongful, and shares their instability. What the plaintiff must show is "a wrong" to herself; i.e., a violation of her own right, and not merely a wrong to someone else, nor conduct wrongful because unsocial, but not "a wrong" to anyone. We are told that one who drives at reckless speed through a crowded city street is guilty of a negligent act and therefore of a wrongful one, irrespective of the consequences. Negligent the act is, and wrongful in the sense that it is unsocial, but wrongful and unsocial in relation to other travelers, only because the eye of vigilance perceives the risk of damage. If the same act were to be committed on a speedway or a race course, it would lose its wrongful quality. The risk reasonably to be perceived defines the duty to be obeyed, and risk imports relation; it is risk to another or to others within the range of apprehension. This does not mean, of course, that one who launches a destructive force is always relieved of liability, if the force, though known to be destructive, pursues an unexpected path. It was not necessary that the defendant should have had notice of the particular method in which an accident would occur, if the possibility of an accident was clear to the ordinarily prudent eye. Some acts, such as shooting are so imminently dangerous to anyone who may come within reach of the missile however unexpectedly, as to impose a duty of prevision not far from that of an insurer. Even today, and much oftener in earlier stages of the law, one acts sometimes at one's peril. These cases aside, wrong is defined in terms of the natural or probable, at least when unintentional. The range of reasonable apprehension is at times a question for the court, and at times, if varying inferences are possible, a question for the jury. Here, by concession, there was nothing in the situation to suggest to the most cautious mind that the parcel wrapped in newspaper would spread wreckage through the station. If the guard had thrown it down knowingly and willfully, he would not have threatened the plaintiff's safety, so far as appearances could warn him. His conduct would not have involved, even then, an unreasonable probability of invasion of her bodily security. Liability can be no greater where the act is inadvertent.

The law of causation, remote or proximate, is thus foreign to the case before us. The question of liability is always anterior to the question of the measure of the consequences that go with liability. If there is no tort to be redressed, there is no occasion to consider what damage might be recovered if there were a finding of a tort.

ANDREWS, J. (dissenting)

Assisting a passenger to board a train, the defendant's servant negligently knocked a package from his arms. It fell between the platform and the cars. Of its contents the servant knew and could know nothing. A violent explosion followed. The concussion broke some scales standing a considerable distance away. In falling, they injured the plaintiff, an intending passenger.

Upon these facts, may she recover the damages she has suffered in an action brought against the master? The result we shall reach depends upon our theory as to the nature of negligence. Is it a relative concept—the breach of some duty owing to a particular person or to particular persons? Or, where there is an act which unreasonably threatens the safety of others, is the doer liable for all its proximate consequences, even where they result in injury to one who would generally be thought to be outside the radius of danger? This is not a mere dispute as to words. We might not believe that to the average mind the dropping of the bundle would seem to involve the probability of harm to the plaintiff standing many feet away whatever might be the case as to the owner or to one so near as to be likely to be struck by its fall. If, however, we adopt the second hypothesis, we have to inquire only as to the relation between cause and effect. We deal in terms of proximate cause, not of negligence.

Negligence may be defined roughly as an act or omission which unreasonably does or may affect the rights of others, or which unreasonably fails to protect one's self from the dangers resulting from such acts. Here I confine myself to the first branch of the definition. Nor do I comment on the word unreasonable. For present purposes it sufficiently describes that average of conduct that society requires of its members.

But we are told that "there is no negligence unless there is in the particular case a legal duty to take care, and this duty must be one which is owed to the plaintiff himself and not merely to others." This I think too narrow a conception. Where there is the unreasonable act, and some right that may be affected there is negligence whether damage does or does not result. That is immaterial. Should we drive down Broadway at a reckless speed, we are negligent whether we strike an approaching car or miss it by an inch. The act itself is wrongful. It is a wrong not only to those who happen to be within the radius of danger, but to all who might have been there—a wrong to the public at large. Such is the language of the street. Such again and again their language in speaking of the duty of some defendant and discussing proximate cause in cases where such a discussion is wholly irrelevant on any other theory. As was said by Mr. Justice Holmes many years ago: "The measure of the defendant's duty in determining whether a wrong has been committed is one thing, the measure of liability when a wrong has been committed is another."

Due care is a duty imposed on each one of us to protect society from unnecessary danger, not to protect A, B, or C alone. It may well be that there is no such thing as negligence in the abstract. "Proof of negligence in the air, so to speak, will not do." In an empty world negligence would not exist. It does involve a relationship between man and his fellows, but not merely a relationship between man and those whom he might reasonably expect his act would injure; rather, a relationship between him and those whom he does in fact injure. If his act has a tendency to harm someone, it harms him a mile away as surely as it does those on the scene.

The proposition is this: Every one owes to the world at large the duty of refraining from those acts that may unreasonably threaten the safety of others. Such an act occurs. Not only is he wronged to whom harm, might reasonably be expected to result, but he also who is in fact injured, even if he be outside what would generally be thought the danger zone. There needs be duty due the one complaining, but this is not a duty to a particular individual because as to him harm might be expected. Harm to someone being the natural result of the act, not only that one alone, but all those in fact injured may complain. We have never, I think, held otherwise. Unreasonable risk being taken, its consequences are not confined to those who might probably be hurt.

The right to recover damages rests on additional considerations. The plaintiff's rights must be injured, and this injury must be caused by the negligence. We build a dam, but are negligent as to its foundations. Breaking, it injures property downstream. We are not liable if all this happened because of some reason other than the insecure foundation. But, when injuries do result from out unlawful act, we are liable for the consequences. It does not matter that they are unusual, unexpected, unforeseen, and unforeseeable. But there is one limitation. The damages must be so connected with the negligence that the latter may be said to be the proximate cause of the former.

These two words have never been given an inclusive definition. What is a cause in a legal sense, still more what is a proximate cause, depend in each case upon many considerations, as does the existence of negligence itself. Any philosophical doctrine of causation does not help us. A boy throws a stone into a pond. The ripples spread. The water level rises. The history of that pond is altered to all eternity. It will be altered by other causes also. Yet it will be forever the resultant of all causes combined. Each one will have an influence. How great only omniscience can say. You may speak of a chain, or, if you please, a net. An analogy is of little aid. Each cause brings about future events. Without each the future would not be the same. Each is proximate in the sense it is essential. But that is not what we mean by the word. Nor on the other hand do we mean sole cause. There is no such thing.

Should analogy be though helpful, however, I prefer that of a stream. The spring, starting on its journey, is joined by tributary after tributary. The river, reaching the ocean, comes from a hundred sources. No man may say whence any drop of water is derived. Yet for a time distinction may be possible. Into the clear creek, brown swamp water flows from the left. Later, from the right comes water stained by its clay bed. The three may remain for a space, sharply divided. But at last inevitably no trace of separation remains. They are so commingled that all distinction is lost.

A cause, but not the proximate cause. What we do mean by the word proximate is that, because of convenience, of public policy, of a rough sense of justice, the law arbitrarily declines to trace a series of events beyond a certain point. This is not logic. It is practical politics. We may regret that the line was drawn just where it was, but drawn somewhere it had to be. Cause it surely was. The words we used were simply indicative of our notions of public policy. Other courts think differently. But somewhere they reach the point where they cannot say the stream comes from any one source.

There are no fixed rules to govern our judgment. There are simply matters of which we may take account. We have in a somewhat different connection spoken of the stream of events. We have asked whether that stream was deflected—whether it was forced into new and unexpected channels. This is rather rhetoric than law. There is in truth little to guide us other than common sense.

There are some hints that may help us. The proximate cause, involved as it may be with many other causes, must be, at the least, something without which the event would not happen. The court must ask itself whether there was a natural and continuous sequence between cause and effect. Was the one a substantial factor in producing the other? Was there a direct connection between them, without too many intervening causes? Is the effect of cause on result not too attenuated? Is the cause likely, in the usual judgment of mankind, to produce the result? Or, by the exercise of prudent foresight, could the result be foreseen? Is the result too remote from the cause, and here we consider remoteness in time and space. We draw an uncertain and wavering line, but draw it we must as best we can. Once again, it is all a question of fair judgment, always keeping in mind the fact that we endeavor to make a rule in each case that will be practical and in keeping with the general understanding of mankind.

The act upon which defendant's liability rests is knocking an apparently harmless package onto the platform. The act was negligent. For its proximate consequences the defendant is liable. If its contents were broken, to the owner; if it fell upon and crushed a passenger's foot, then to him; if it exploded and injured one in the immediate vicinity, to him also as to A in the illustration. Mrs. Palsgraf was standing some distance away. How far cannot be told from the record—apparently 25 or 30 feet, perhaps less. Except for the explosion, she would not have been injured. We are told by the appellant in his brief, "it cannot be denied that the explosion was the direct cause of the plaintiff's injuries." So it was a substantial factor in producing the result—there was a natural and continuous sequence—direct connection. The only intervening cause was that, instead of blowing her to the ground, the concussion smashed the weighing machine which in turn fell upon her. There was no remoteness in time, little in space. And surely, given such an explosion as here, it needed no great foresight to predict that the natural result would be to injure one on the platform at no greater distance from its scene than was the plaintiff. Just how no one might be able to predict. Whether by flying fragments, by broken glass, by wreckage of machines or structures no one could say. But injury in some form was most probable.

Under these circumstances I cannot say as a matter of law that the plaintiff's injuries were not the proximate result of the negligence.

Derdiarian v. Felix Contracting Corp.

Court of Appeals of New York (1980)

As a general rule, the question of proximate cause is to be decided by the finder of fact, aided by appropriate instructions. There is no basis on this record for concluding, as a matter of law, that a superseding cause or other factor intervened to break the nexus between defendant's negligence and plaintiff's injury.

Defendant Felix Contracting Corporation was performing a contract to install an underground gas main for defendant Con Edison. Defendant James Dickens suffered an epileptic seizure and lost consciousness, allowing his vehicle to careen into the work site and strike plaintiff with such force as to throw him into the air. When plaintiff landed, he was splattered over his face, head and body with 400 degree boiling hot liquid enamel from a kettle struck by the automobile. The enamel was used in connection with sealing the gas main. Although plaintiff's body ignited into a fire ball, he miraculously survived the incident.

At trial, plaintiff's theory was that defendant Felix had negligently failed to take adequate measures to insure the safety of workers on the excavation site. Plaintiff's evidence indicates that the accident occurred on a two-lane roadway. The excavation was located in the eastbound lane, and ran from approximately one foot south of the center line to within 2 or 3 feet of the curb. When plaintiff arrived on the site, he was instructed by Felix' foreman to park his truck on the west side of the excavation, parallel to the curb. As a result, there was a gap of some 7 1/2 feet between the side of the truck and the curb line. Derdiarian testified that he made a request to park his truck on the east side of the hole, so he could set up the kettle away from the oncoming eastbound traffic. The Felix foreman instructed him to leave his truck where it was, and plaintiff then put the kettle near the curb, on the west side of the excavation.

To support his claim of an unsafe work site, plaintiff called as a witness Lawrence Lawton, an expert in traffic safety. According to Lawton, the usual and accepted method of safeguarding the workers is to erect a barrier around the excavation. Such a barrier, consisting of a truck, a piece of heavy equipment or a pile of dirt, would keep a car out of the excavation and protect workers from oncoming traffic. The expert testified that the barrier should cover the entire width of the excavation. He also stated that there should have been two flagmen present, rather than one, and that warning signs should have been posted advising motorists that there was only one lane of traffic and that there was a flagman ahead.

The concept of proximate cause, or more appropriately legal cause, has proven to be an elusive one, incapable of being precisely defined to cover all situations. This is, in part, because the concept stems from policy considerations that serve to place manageable limits upon the liability that flows from negligent conduct (e. g., Palsgraf v. Long Island R.R., (Andrews, J., dissenting)). Depending upon the nature of the case, a variety of factors may be relevant in assessing legal cause. Given the unique nature of the inquiry in each case, it is for the finder of fact to determine legal cause, once the court has been satisfied that a prima facie case has been established. To carry the burden of proving a prima facie case, the plaintiff must generally show that the defendant's negligence was a substantial cause of the events which produced the injury. Plaintiff need not demonstrate, however, that the precise manner in which the accident happened, or the extent of injuries, was foreseeable.

Where the acts of a third person intervene between the defendant's conduct and the plaintiff's injury, the causal connection is not automatically severed. In such a case, liability turns upon whether the intervening act is a normal or foreseeable consequence of the situation created by the defendant's negligence. If the intervening act is extraordinary under the circumstances, not foreseeable in the normal course of events, or independent of or far removed from the defendant's conduct, it may well be a superseding act which breaks the causal nexus. Because questions concerning what is foreseeable and what is normal may be the subject of varying inferences, as is the question of negligence itself, these issues generally are for the fact finder to resolve.

There are certain instances, to be sure, where only one conclusion may be drawn from the established facts and where the question of legal cause may be decided as a matter of law. Those cases generally involve independent intervening acts which operate upon but do not flow from the original negligence. Thus, for instance, we have held that where an automobile lessor negligently supplies a car with a defective trunk lid, it is not liable to the lessee who, while stopped to repair the trunk, was injured by the negligent driving of a third party. Although the renter's negligence undoubtedly served to place the injured party at the site of the accident, the intervening act was divorced from and not the foreseeable risk associated with the original negligence. And the injuries were different in kind than those which would have normally been expected from a defective trunk. In short, the negligence of the renter merely furnished the occasion for an unrelated act to cause injuries not ordinarily anticipated.

By contrast, in the present case, we cannot say as a matter of law that defendant Dickens' negligence was a superseding cause which interrupted the link between Felix' negligence and plaintiff's injuries. From the evidence in the record, the jury could have found that Felix negligently failed to safeguard the excavation site. A prime hazard associated with such dereliction is the possibility that a driver will negligently enter the work site and cause injury to a worker. That the driver was negligent, or even reckless, does not insulate Felix from liability. Nor is it decisive that the driver lost control of the vehicle through a negligent failure to take medication, rather than a driving mistake. The precise manner of the event need not be anticipated. The finder of fact could have concluded that the foreseeable, normal and natural result of the risk created by Felix was the injury of a worker by a car entering the improperly protected work area. An intervening act may not serve as a superseding cause, and relieve an actor of responsibility, where the risk of the intervening act occurring is the very same risk which renders the actor negligent.

In a similar vein, plaintiff's act of placing the kettle on the west side of the excavation does not, as a matter of law, absolve defendant Felix of responsibility. Serious injury, or even death, was a foreseeable consequence of a vehicle crashing through the work area. The injury could have occurred in numerous ways, ranging from a worker being directly struck by the car to the car hitting an object that injures the worker. Placement of the kettle, or any object in the work area, could affect how the accident occurs and the extent of injuries. That defendant could not anticipate the precise manner of the accident or the exact extent of injuries, however, does not preclude liability as a matter of law where the general risk and character of injuries are foreseeable.

Sheehan v. City of New York

Court of Appeals of New York (1976)

On a clear morning an eastbound bus operated by appellant Timothy Sheehan and owned by appellant Manhattan and Bronx Surface Transit Operating Authority (MABSTOA) was brought to a gradual stop for the purpose of permitting any passengers who wished to do so to board or alight. [The bus stopped on the road and not in the designated bus stop area by the curb]. While so stopped, the bus was struck from the rear by a sanitation truck operated by respondent Anthony Loria and owned by respondent the City of New York (City). Sheehan and respondent Walter Novak, Jr., a passenger in the bus, were injured.

The street where the injury occurred is a two-way street; in each direction it has two lanes, one along the curb where vehicles generally parked and the second along the center line where moving vehicles usually traveled. The block on which the bus had been proceeding before it reached the corner was about 300 feet long. It is undisputed that Sheehan's brake lights had signaled his intended stop and that it had been a slow and gradual one. The truck driver had noticed the brake lights where he was still 150 feet behind the bus. Loria testified that when he attempted to stop his brakes did not hold. A designated bus stop was located at the southeast curb but Sheehan testified he did not pull into it.

Though negligence and proximate cause frequently overlap in the proof and theory which support each of them, they are not the same conceptually. Evidence of negligence is not enough by itself to establish liability. It must also be proved that the negligence was the cause of the event which produced the harm sustained by one who brings the complaint.

Both sides agree that the truck struck the bus in the rear, that the bus had been within the truck driver's uninterrupted view continually for a long distance before the impact and long after the signal of its intended stop had been transmitted to the truck, that it at no time had left the truck's path, that its stop was engineered slowly so that no element of surprise was involved and that it was the failure of its brakes which propelled the truck into the bus.

The only factual dispute was as to whether other automobiles then occupied the designated bus stop, a matter which here is irrelevant to the determination of proximate cause.

Assuming the designated stop was available for the bus's use, if it had in fact stopped there and, having discharged or boarded its passengers, pulled back into the traveling lane before proceeding across the intersection, it would, properly, have been in exactly the same position at which it found itself when it was hit. Or, if observing no prospective passengers in the stop and having none who wished to alight at that corner, the bus driver had decided not to go through the proper practice of pulling in and out of the stop, but, preparatory to crossing, had merely stopped in the traveling lane at the corner before doing so, his bus would have been in precisely the same position. In short, the bus at the time of the accident appears merely to have been at one point in the street where it had a right to be (the traveling lane) rather than at another point in the street where it had a right to be (the bus stop). The result of the sanitation truck's brake failure would have been no different, if, perchance, a pedestrian or a vehicle other than the bus had been using the street at that point at that time and had instead become the target of the truck's faulty brakes.

In addition, it appears quite clear that, if the bus's stop in the traveled lane could, on any view of the circumstances here, be regarded as a proximate cause of the accident, the failure of the truck's brakes might have been an independent, supervening cause. Though, where either of two independent acts of negligence may be found to be concurring, that is, direct causes of an accident, the perpetrator of either or both may be found responsible for the whole harm incurred.

Novak's complaint against MABSTOA and Sheehan should therefore have been dismissed before the cases went to the jury, and a verdict on the issue of liability should then have been directed in favor of Sheehan in his affirmative case.

Marshall v. Nugent

United States Court of Appeals, First Circuit (1955)

A car owned and operated by Walter G. Harriman was proceeding on a public highway. Marshall was riding as a passenger in the front seat. Harriman was a son-in-law of Marshall and also his employee in an insurance business conducted under the name of the Frank E. Marshall Agency.

As Harriman was driving his car on the right-hand side at 30 to 35 miles per hour, he approached a curve in the road. At this point the highway ran uphill and curved rather sharply to Harriman's right. Proceeding in the opposite direction was a heavy oil truck owned by Socony-Vacuum Oil Co., Inc., and driven by Warren K. Prince. After the oil truck loomed over the crest of the hill it cut the corner by swinging over to the westerly side of the highway (to Prince's left) and proceeded down the banked curve in that manner. In this situation the truck and the car were headed for a collision. Harriman turned to the right into the snowbank at the west side of the road to slow down; the car went into a skid for about 50 ft. and came to a stop completely off the highway. Prince stopped his oil truck and inquired if they were okay—which they were at that time—and offered to yank the car back into the highway if Harriman had a chain.

At this time the oil truck, blocking as it was the eastern lane of the highway, was stopped in a dangerous place. Prince, who was very familiar with this particular portion of the highway, recognized the danger inherent in the situation, for he remarked to Messrs. Harriman and Marshall that his truck was stopped in a rather dangerous position and that someone ought to go up the grade to warn any approaching northbound traffic.

In response to this obviously reasonable suggestion from Prince, Marshall undertook to go up the hill to warn any cars that might be approaching. Harriman continued the operation of getting out his chain and affixing it to the spring shackle of his car. Meanwhile, Prince let the truck stand still on the east side of the highway, when it might have been safer to have pulled over in a matter of moments to the other side of the highway to await the towing operation. Having proceeded for perhaps 75 or 80 ft., walking on his right-hand side of the highway Marshall perceived coming over the crest of the hill a car driven by Robert H. Nugent. This car would have presented no danger to Marshall if it could have proceeded on its right-hand or easterly lane, but this was impossible because the oil truck was blocking this lane. Marshall waved his arms in warning. Nugent turned his car toward the left. It soon went into a skid, crossing to the left-hand side of the banked curve, crashing into a plank guard fence on the westerly side of the highway, and immediately thereafter striking and severely injuring Marshall. It all happened so quickly that Marshall was unable to get out of the way.

Coming then the contention dealing with the doctrine of proximate causation, a doctrine which appellant's arguments tend to make out to be more complex and esoteric than it really is. To say that the situation created by the defendant's culpable acts constituted merely a condition, not a cause of plaintiff's harm, is to indulge in mere verbiage, which does not solve the question at issue, but is simply a way of stating the conclusion, arrived at from other considerations, that the causal relation between the defendant's act and the plaintiff's injury is not strong enough to warrant holding the defendant legally responsible for the injury.

The adjective proximate, as commonly used in this connection, is perhaps misleading, since to establish liability it is not necessarily true that the defendant's culpable act must be shown to have been the next or immediate cause of the plaintiff's injury. In many familiar instances, the defendant's act may be more remote in the chain of events; and the plaintiff's injury may more immediately have been caused by an intervening force of nature, or an intervening act of a third person whether culpable or not, or even an act by the plaintiff bringing himself in contact with the dangerous situation resulting from the defendant's negligence.

Whatever may be the New Hampshire law in the foregoing respect, the case at bar presents a quite different situation. Plaintiff Marshall was a passenger in the oncoming car, and thus was one of the persons whose bodily safety was primarily endangered by the negligence of Prince in cutting the corner with the Socony truck. In that view, Prince's negligence constituted an irretrievable breach of duty to the plaintiff. Though this particular act of negligence was over and done with when the truck pulled up alongside of the stalled car without having actually collides with it, still the consequences of such past negligence were in the bosom of time, as yet unrevealed.

If the car had been pulled back onto the highway, and Harriman and Marshall, having got in it again, had resumed their journey and had had a collision with another car five miles down the road, in which Marshall suffered bodily injuries, it could truly be said that such subsequent injury to Marshall was a consequence in fact of the earlier delay caused by the defendant's negligence, in the sense that but for such delay the car would not have been at the fatal intersection at the moment the other car ran into it. But on such assumed state of facts, the courts would no doubt conclude that Prince's earlier negligence in cutting the corner was not the proximate cause of this later injury received by the plaintiff. That would be because the extra risks to which such negligence by Prince had subjected the passengers in the car were obviously entirely over; the situation had been stabilized and become normal, and, so far as one could foresee, whatever subsequent risks the car might have to encounter in its resumed journey were simply the inseparable risks, no more and no less, that were incident to the car's being out on the highway at all. But in the case at bar, the circumstances under which Marshall received the personal injuries complained of presented no such clear-cut situation.

Moum v. Maercklein

Supreme Court of North Dakota (1972)

Evan Dockter, deceased, was an employee of the defendant Soo Line Railway Company, working as a probationary brakeman out of Harvey, North Dakota. He lived in Minot, a distance of approximately seventy miles from Harvey, and traveled to and from his work by car over U.S. Highway No. 52. The yard clerk of the defendant called Dockter in Minot, at approximately 7:15 o'clock, and asked him to report in Harvey at 9:10 a.m. Dockter left Minot at 7:40 a.m. It was snowing when he left home. On route to Harvey, he encountered adverse weather conditions and was involved in an automobile accident and was killed. Also fatally injured in the collision were the father, the mother, and the baby sister of the minor plaintiff, who herself suffered personal injuries.

The plaintiff claims that a severe blizzard was raging between Minot and Harvey at the time that the defendant Soo Line ordered Dockter to report for work. Visibility on the highway was bad and there was some wind and blowing snow, making travel extremely hazardous. Dockter attempted to pass an automobile traveling in the same direction, and due to his negligence he killed plaintiff's parents, her baby sister, and himself.

The plaintiff alleges that the negligence of the Soo Line consisted in ordering the deceased employee to report for work, knowing the unsafe and hazardous weather, road, and driving conditions then existing, and knowing that the employee would have to travel approximately seventy miles under such conditions in less than two hours; that the defendant Soo Line knew, or should have known, that the deceased employee would have to drive his automobile in an unsafe manner in order to report on time, and further knowing that because he was a probationary employee he would be afraid of losing his job if he did not report on time. The jury returned a verdict for the plaintiff.

The defendant Soo Line Railway Company can be held liable to the plaintiff only if it has failed to exercise that degree of care demanded by the circumstances. The term negligence is relative, and its application depends on the situation of the party and the degree of care that the circumstances reasonably impose. To constitute negligence, there must be a causal connection between the negligence and the injury sustained; for the negligence to be the proximate cause of the injury, the defendant must owe to the plaintiff a duty, and the injury to the plaintiff must have resulted as a direct consequence of the negligent breach of that duty. Proximate cause of an injury is a cause which in natural and continuous sequence, unbroken by any controlling, intervening cause, produces injury, and without which it would not have occurred. Thus, to render the defendant liable, it must appear not only that the injury complained of was a natural and probable consequence of the negligent act of the defendant, but that such consequence ought reasonably to have been anticipated by a person of ordinary intelligence in the light of attending circumstances.

One of the tests of proximate cause is the defendant's duty to reasonable foresee the consequence of his negligence. If the person had no knowledgeable ground to anticipate that his act would or might result in injury to anyone, the act is not negligent at all. The law requires that a person reasonably guard against probabilities-not against all possibilities. The law will not hold a person liable for the unusual. Thus a party is not chargeable with all possible consequences of his negligent act, and he is not responsible for a consequence which is possible according to occasional experiences. He is liable only for the consequences which are probable according to the ordinary, usual experiences of mankind.

In this case, the employee, Dockter, resided in Minot, approximately seventy miles from Harvey, where he was to report for work. He was given less than two hours to make the trip. It was snowing and blowing, and at times visibility was almost zero. Did the action of the Soo Line in requesting him to report for work constitute negligence, and, if so, was such negligent act the proximate cause of the accident which occurred? We believe that the act of the defendant in asking its employee to report for work was a remote cause, and not the proximate cause of the accident. It was an act which created a condition which was followed by an independent, unforeseeable act, that of the employee, Dockter, in trying to pass another car without due care. Even though the Soo Line's requesting the employee to report for work indirectly resulted in injury to the plaintiff, such injury was not a probable result of the defendant's order, but was only a possible result. Here, the collision would not have happened if the Soo Line had not requested Dockter to report for work, but that does not make the Soo Line liable for the remote result of its order.

There were many cars on the highway on the day of the accident. If being on the road was so hazardous that merely driving on the highway under existing conditions and circumstances in itself was negligence, then the plaintiff's parents were negligent for venturing out under such conditions. Although the accident which occurred would not have occurred if the defendant Soo Line had not ordered Dockter to report for work, and although the accident which took place was possible, it was not a probable result of the act of the defendant; and an alleged wrongdoer is responsible only for the probable results of his wrongful act. We find that the yard clerk of the defendant could not reasonably have foreseen that the deceased would recklessly try to pass a car at a moment when visibility was poor and thus cause an accident. In other words, we conclude that there was no evidence upon which the jury could find that the action of the yard clerk in calling Dockter to report for work was the proximate cause of the accident. Liability cannot be based upon a prior remote cause which may have provided the conditions that resulted in injury, where the injury itself was the result of an intervening, unrelated cause, which in this case was the negligence of Dockter.

For reasons stated, the judgment of the trial court is reversed, and the complaint of the plaintiffs is ordered dismissed.

DEFENSES

Wassell v. Adams

United States Court of Appeals, Seventh Circuit (1989)

POSNER, Circuit Judge

The plaintiff, Susan Wassell, grew up in a small town in a poor coal-mining region of Pennsylvania—a town so small and obscure that it has no name. After graduating from high school she worked briefly as a nurse's aide, then became engaged to Michael Wassell, also from Pennsylvania. Michael joined the Navy and was sent to Great Lakes Naval Training Station, just north of Chicago, for basic training. He and Susan had decided to get married as soon as he completed basic training. The graduation was scheduled for a Friday. Susan, who was 21 years old, traveled to Chicago with Michael's parents for the graduation. The three checked into a double room at the Ron–Ric motel. The Ron–Ric is a small and inexpensive motel that caters to the families of sailors at the Great Lakes Naval Training Station a few blocks to the east.

Four blocks to the west of the Ron–Ric motel is a high-crime area: murder, prostitution, robbery, drugs—the works. The Adamses occasionally warned women guests not to walk alone in the neighborhood at night. They did not warn the Wassells or Susan.

On Saturday the Wassells checked out and left for Pennsylvania, and at the Wassells' suggestion Susan moved from the double room that she had shared with them to a single room in the Ron–Ric. Michael spent Saturday night with her but had to return to the base on Sunday for several days. She remained to look for an apartment where they could live after they were married (for he was scheduled to remain at the base after completing basic training).

Upon returning to her room at the motel, she locked the door, fastened the chain, and went to bed. She fell into a deep sleep, from which she was awakened by a knock on the door. She turned on a light and saw by the clock built into the television set that it was 1:00 a.m. She went to the door and looked through the peephole but saw no one. Next to the door was a pane of clear glass. She did not look through it. The door had two locks plus a chain. She unlocked the door and opened it all the way, thinking that Michael had come from the base. It was not Michael at the door. It was a respectably dressed black man whom Susan had never seen before. He asked for Cindy. She told him there was no Cindy there. Then he asked for a glass of water. She went to the bathroom, which was at the other end of the room, to fetch the glass of water. When she came out of the bathroom, the man was sitting at the table in the room. (The room had a screen door as well as a solid door, but the screen door had not been latched.) He took the water but said it wasn't cold enough. He also said he had no money, and Susan remarked that she had $20 in her car. The man went into the bathroom to get a colder glass of water. Susan began to get nervous. She was standing between the bathroom and the door of her room. She hid her purse, which contained her car keys and $800 in cash that Michael had given her. There was no telephone in the room. There was an alarm attached to the television set, which would be activated if someone tried to remove the set, but she had not been told and did not know about the alarm, although a notice of the alarm was posted by the set. The parking lot on which the motel rooms opened was brightly lit by floodlights.

A few tense minutes passed after the man entered the bathroom. He poked his head out of the doorway and asked Susan to join him in the bathroom, he wanted to show her something. She refused. After a while he emerged from the bathroom—naked from the waist down. Susan fled from the room, and beat on the door of the adjacent room. There was no response. The man ran after her and grabbed her. She screamed, but no one appeared. The motel had no security guard; the Adamses lived in a basement apartment at the other end of the motel and did not hear her screams.

The man covered Susan's mouth and dragged her back to her room. There he gagged her with a wash cloth. He raped her. These outrages occupied more than an hour. Eventually Susan persuaded the rapist to take a shower with her. After the shower, she managed to get out of the bathroom before he did, dress, and flee in her car. To save herself after the rapes, she had tried to convince him that she liked him, and had succeeded at least to the extent that his guard was down. The Adamses' lawyer tried halfheartedly to show that she had consented to the rapes, but backed off from this position in closing argument.

There had been a rape at the motel several years previously. There had also been a robbery, and an incident in which an intruder kicked in the door to one of the rooms. These were the only serious crimes committed during the seven years that the Adamses owned the motel.

Susan married Michael, but the rape had induced post trauma stress that has, according to her testimony and that of a psychologist testifying as her expert witness, blighted her life. She brought this suit against the Adamses. A jury composed of four women and three men found that the Adamses had indeed been negligent and that their negligence had been a proximate cause of the assault, and the jury assessed Susan's damages at $850,000, which was the figure her lawyer had requested in closing argument. But in addition the jury found that Susan had been negligent too—and indeed that her negligence had been 97 percent to blame for the attack and the Adamses' only 3 percent. So, the jury awarded Susan only $25,500 in damages. This happens to be approximately the midpoint of the psychologist's estimate—$20,000 to $30,000—of the expense of the therapy that the psychologist believes Susan may need for her post-traumatic stress.

Susan Wassell's counsel argues that the jury's verdict reflected a chastened, hardened, urban mentality—that lurking behind every door is evil and danger, even if the guest is from a small town unfamiliar with the area. He points out that a person awakened from a deep sleep is not apt to be thinking clearly and that once Susan opened the door the fat was in the fire—if she had slammed the door in the rapist's face he might have kicked the door in. The Adamses' counsel argued to the jury (perhaps with the wisdom of hindsight) that Susan's tragic mistake was failing to flee when the man entered the bathroom. Susan's counsel insists that Susan was not negligent at all but that, if she was, she was at most 5 percent responsible for the catastrophe, which, he argues, could have been averted costlessly by a simple warning from the Adamses. To this the Adamses' counsel replies absurdly that a warning would have been costly—it might have scared guests away! The loss of business from telling the truth is not a social loss; it is a social gain.

It is careless to open a motel or hotel door in the middle of the night without trying to find out who is knocking. Still, people aren't at their most alert when they are awakened in the middle of the night, and it wasn't crazy for Susan to assume that Michael had returned without telling her, even though he had said he would be spending the night at the base. So it cannot be assumed that the cost—not to her (although her testimony suggests that she is not so naive or provincial as her lawyer tried to convince the jury she was), but to the reasonable person who found himself or herself in her position, for that is the benchmark in determining plaintiff's as well as defendant's negligence was zero, or even that it was slight. As innkeepers the Adamses had a duty to exercise a high degree of care to protect their guests from assaults on the motel premises. And the cost to the Adamses of warning all their female guests of the dangers of the neighborhood would have been negligible. Surely a warning to Susan would not have cost the Adamses 32 times the cost to her of schooling herself to greater vigilance.

But this analysis is incomplete. It is unlikely that a warning would have averted the attack. Susan testified that she thought the man who had knocked on the door was her fiancé. Thinking this, she would have opened the door no matter how dangerous she believed the neighborhood to be. The warning that was not given might have deterred her from walking alone in the neighborhood. But that was not the pertinent danger. Of course, if the Adamses had told her not to open her door in the middle of the night under any circumstances without carefully ascertaining who was trying to enter the room, this would have been a pertinent warning and might have had an effect. But it is absurd to think that hoteliers are required to give so obvious a warning, any more than they must warn guests not to stick their fingers into the electrical outlets. Everyone, or at least the average person, knows better than to open his or her door to a stranger in the middle of the night. The problem was not that Susan thought that she should open her bedroom door in the middle of the night to anyone who knocked, but that she wasn't thinking clearly. A warning would not have availed against a temporary, sleep-induced lapse.

Giving the jury every benefit of the doubt, as we are required to do especially in a case such as this where the jury was not asked to render either a special verdict or a general verdict with answers to written interrogatories, we must assume that the jury was not so muddle-headed as to believe that the Adamses' negligence consisted in failing to give a futile warning. Rather, we must assume that the jury thought the Adamses' negligence consisted in failing to have a security guard, or telephones in each room, or alarms designed to protect the motel's patrons rather than just the owners' television sets. (The Adamses did, however, have an informal agreement with the local police that the police would cruise through the parking lot of the Ron–Ric whenever they drove down the street at night—and this was maybe three or four times a night.) The only one of these omitted precautions for which there is a cost figure in the record was the security guard. A guard would have cost $50 a night. That is almost $20,000 a year. This is not an enormous number. The plaintiff suggests that it would have been even lower because the guard would have been needed only on busy nights. But the evidence was in conflict on whether the Sunday night after a Friday graduation, which is the night that Susan was attacked, was a busy night. And the need for a security guard would seem to be greater, the less busy rather than the busier the motel; if there had been someone in the room adjacent to Susan's, she might have been saved from her ordeal. In any event the cost of the security guard, whether on all nights or just on busy nights might be much greater than the monetary equivalent of the greater vigilance on the part of Susan that would have averted the attack.

The assumption that the jury was clear-thinking and instruction-abiding is artificial. During its deliberations, the jury sent the judge a question about the duty to warn (the judge did not answer it). This is some indication that the jury thought that the Adamses' negligence consisted in failing to warn Susan. But it is equally plausible that the jury didn't think the Adamses were negligent at all toward Susan, but, persuaded that she had suffered terribly, wanted to give her a token recovery. The issue for us is not whether this jury was rational and law-abiding but whether a rational jury could, consistently with the evidence, have returned the verdict that this jury did.

If we were the trier of fact, persuaded that both parties were negligent and forced to guess about the relative costs to the plaintiff and to the defendants of averting the assault, we would assess the defendants' share at more than 3 percent. But we are not the trier of fact, and are authorized to upset the jury's apportionment only if persuaded that the trial judge abused his discretion in determining that the jury's verdict was not against the clear weight of the evidence. We are not so persuaded. It seems probably wrong to us, but we have suggested an interpretation of the evidence under which the verdict was consistent with the evidence and the law. And that is enough to require us to uphold the district judge's refusal to set aside the verdict. AFFIRMED.

Pohl v. County of Furnas

United States Court of Appeals, Eighth Circuit (2012)

Juston Pohl, a resident of Michigan, traveled to rural Furnas County, Nebraska in December for a hunting trip. Pohl mistakenly turned west onto Drive 719, which is a gravel road that does not have a posted speed limit but is subject to a general statutory limit of 50 miles per hour. Drive 719 has a ninety degree curve one mile after its intersection with Highway 47. At the time of Pohl's accident, a posted sign was placed at least 110 feet in front of the curve. The sign was two feet square with a yellow background and contained a black arrow with a ninety degree bend.

After turning onto Drive 719, Pohl accelerated to 63 mph, traveling with his high beam headlights on. When Pohl neared the warning sign, he braked too late to prevent the car from missing the curve and going off the road. The car hit an embankment, rolled, and came to rest upside down in a culvert. Pohl lost consciousness. When he came to, he realized he could not move his legs. Since he was unable to walk, he remained in the car all night hoping to be rescued. No help had arrived by daybreak, and Pohl managed to drag himself to a nearby farmhouse where the residents called an ambulance. It was later determined that he had a fracture and cord compression in his thoracic spine as well as frostbite in his feet.

Pohl sued the county for common law negligence. He alleged that his injuries were the result of the county's negligent placement of the sign warning about the curve and its negligent failure to maintain it. He sought damages for his medical expenses, physical pain and mental suffering, and lost wages.

In its findings of fact, the district court determined that the sign was abraded and lacked retro reflective paint. It was therefore not legible to a nighttime driver traveling with headlights until the driver was within 100 feet of the sign. The court also found that Pohl had reacted to the left-hand turn warning sign—or to some other indicia of danger—when his car was closely aligned with the sign. Had Pohl been traveling at the speed limit of 50 mph and all other variables remained constant, the court determined that his car would have gone off the road at the same location at a speed of 15 miles per hour. If the car reached the embankment at all, the impact would have been much less severe, and, in any event, the car would have come to rest before reaching the culvert.

The district court found that the county was negligent because of the combination of the sign's lack of retro reflectivity and its placement. Had the sign been retro reflective, its placement in proximity to the curve may have been adequate. It further found that this negligence and Pohl's negligence in driving 13 miles over the speed limit were the proximate causes of his accident and injuries. In assessing the responsibility for the accident and Pohl's injuries the court allocated 60% of the negligence to the county and 40% to Pohl. The district court then calculated that Pohl was entitled to $678,606.14 in damages for medical expenses and pain and suffering, and awarded him $407,163.38 following a reduction for his comparative negligence.

We address the county's argument that even if its placement of the sign was negligent and a proximate cause of the accident, the district court erred by undervaluing Pohl's contributory negligence. Contributory negligence occurs where the plaintiff breaches a duty of care and his breach concurs and cooperates with the defendant's negligence to form a proximate cause of the injury. Under Nebraska law, a plaintiff is barred from recovery if his negligence is equal to or greater than that of the defendant. Contributory negligence is an affirmative defense that must be proved by the party asserting it.

The county first contends that the trial court erred in its assessment of contributory negligence because it should have found that Pohl's contributory negligence in speeding exceeded the county's negligence, thus barring recovery. In support of this argument, it points to testimony indicating that had Pohl been traveling at the speed limit, he would have been able to negotiate the curve successfully if he had braked when aligned with the sign. This testimony was contradicted, however, by testimony that had Pohl been traveling at the speed limit, his speed at the curve would have still been too great to negotiate it successfully. Given this conflicting testimony, we cannot say that the district court clearly erred by not finding that Pohl's negligence exceeded that of the county.

The county further contends that the district court should have found that Pohl was contributorily negligent in two additional ways. First it argues that he was negligent by driving faster than conditions allowed because it was snowing on the night of the accident and he was unfamiliar with Drive 719. It also urges that he was negligent by failing to maintain a proper lookout. We conclude that the district court did not commit clear error by not making these findings. Multiple witnesses testified that the snow on the night of the accident did not impede visibility or cause slippery road surfaces. As for the county's argument that Pohl failed to maintain a proper lookout, the only evidence would be the fact that his vehicle left the roadway. Given the county's negligence in placing and maintaining the warning sign, the fact that Pohl left the roadway does not necessarily indicate that he was not keeping a proper lookout.

As discussed above, the evidence supported the district court's finding that the negligence of both parties contributed to Pohl's injuries. Attributing 40% of the negligence to Pohl was reasonable considering the evidence that the accident would still have happened at a lower speed but with less severe injuries.

Accordingly, we affirm the judgment of the district court.

Mercer v. Vanderbilt University

Supreme Court of Tennessee (2004)

Larry T. Qualls was seriously injured in a single-vehicle accident in which he sustained a mild-to-moderate concussion and multiple facial fractures. Upon arriving at the trauma center at Vanderbilt University Medical Center ("Vanderbilt") nearly four hours after the accident, Qualls had a blood alcohol level of .13%, which extrapolated to approximately .20% at the time of the accident. Qualls was connected to a ventilator to assist his breathing and remained on a ventilator while at Vanderbilt.

Two days later, CT scans were ordered for reconstructive surgery to treat his facial fractures. Upon arriving at the CT suite Nurse Starks administered a paralytic drug to Qualls in preparation for the CT scans. As a result, Qualls was unable to move or breathe on his own and became completely dependent on the portable ventilator. Nurse Starks never informed the other health care providers that she had given Qualls the drug.

Qualls was then moved from his hospital bed to the CT table. After Qualls was secured on the table, Nurse Starks, Ms. Turner, and the CT technician, Wayman Bean, moved to the adjoining control room, and Ms. Fowler returned to the neuro-intensive care unit to obtain fresh linens for Qualls's bed. From the control room, Nurse Starks and Ms. Turner could see the CT table through a glass window and could observe Qualls's face on a television monitor. Neither of them looked at the cardiac monitor or the ventilator while Qualls was in the CT scanner. [At some point after being placed in the room, both the oxygen tank and secondary oxygen tank the patient was using ran out of oxygen].

Shortly after Qualls was moved to his bed, however, someone noticed that he had turned gray and was not breathing. Nurse Starks and Ms. Turner looked at the cardiac monitor and discovered that Qualls's heart had stopped. Nurse Starks and Ms. Turner disconnected Qualls from the ventilator and immediately began administering CPR. Ms. Fowler called a "code" for additional personnel and within minutes, the "code team" arrived and took over the resuscitation effort.

Although Qualls was successfully resuscitated, he sustained severe and permanent brain damage. Prior to his discharge from Vanderbilt, Qualls's facial fractures were successfully treated. Since his discharge, Qualls has been a patient at NHC Healthcare, a skilled nursing facility and has remained in a persistent vegetative state.

At trial, Vanderbilt admitted that Nurse Starks had violated the applicable standard of care in her treatment of Qualls on the night in question [by not checking the oxygen tank]. However, Vanderbilt asserted that her violation of the standard of care was not the cause of Qualls's permanent brain injury. Instead, Vanderbilt's theory was that Qualls suffered a catastrophic event, such as a seizure or a malignant heart arrhythmia, which was caused by his alcohol withdrawal. Vanderbilt contends that it was this event that caused Qualls's brain injury. The jury returned a verdict in favor of the plaintiff, setting damages in the amount of $7,366,000. The jury apportioned 70% of the fault to Vanderbilt and 30% of the fault to Qualls.

Comparative Fault

The plaintiff makes a strong argument that Qualls's brain injury was separate and distinct from the injuries he sustained in the automobile accident. The plaintiff acknowledges that the mild-to-moderate concussion and facial fractures that Qualls sustained in the automobile accident were a result of his own negligence. However, the plaintiff argues that the brain injury that left Qualls in a persistent vegetative state occurred nearly four days after Qualls was admitted to Vanderbilt and was not a result of the accident or any negligence on Qualls's part. An equally strong argument, however, could be made that Qualls suffered one, indivisible injury. Qualls's negligence caused his facial fractures, and the incident that resulted in his brain injury occurred during the treatment of those fractures. Similarly, in Gray, the Court's conclusion that the decedent had sustained an indivisible injury evidently was based on the fact that the decedent's own negligence had caused the very injury that the physician negligently misdiagnosed. However, a valid argument could be made that the decedent suffered two separate injuries: her ruptured spleen, which was caused by her negligent operation of a motor vehicle, and her death, which was caused by her physician's negligent misdiagnosis of her ruptured spleen.

It would be anomalous to posit, on the one hand, that a health care provider is required to meet a uniform standard of care in its delivery of medical services to all patients, but permit, on the other hand, the conclusion that, where a breach of that duty is established, no liability may exist if the patient's own preinjury conduct caused the illness or injury which necessitated the medical care.

We also agree that patients who may have negligently injured themselves are nevertheless entitled to subsequent non-negligent medical treatment and to an undiminished recovery if such subsequent non-negligent treatment is not afforded. We therefore hold that a patient's negligent conduct that occurs prior to a health care provider's negligent treatment and provides only the occasion for the health care provider's subsequent negligence may not be compared to the negligence of the health care provider.

In the present case, Qualls's negligence merely provided the occasion for the medical care, attention, and treatment that gave rise to this medical malpractice action. We therefore hold that the principles of comparative fault do not apply so as to allow fault to be assessed to Qualls. We recognize that Qualls's medical treatment was complicated by his alcohol withdrawal and that evidence concerning his alcohol consumption was clearly relevant to his treatment and to Vanderbilt's theory of causation. We hold, however, that Qualls's antecedent negligence should not have been considered by the jury in assessing fault.

Leroy Fibre Company v. Chicago, Milwaukee, & Saint Paul Railway

Supreme Court of the United States (1914)

The LeRoy Fibre Company, plaintiff, brought an action against defendant to recover the value of flax straw alleged to have been negligently burned and destroyed by defendant. One of the grounds of negligence was that a locomotive engine of defendant, while passing the premises of plaintiff, was so negligently managed and operated by defendant's employees that it emitted and threw sparks and coals of unusual size upon the stacks of flax straw, and thereby set fire to and destroyed them.

Some years after defendant had constructed and commenced operating its line of railroad through Grand Meadow, Minnesota, the plaintiff established at that village a factory for the manufacture of tow from flax straw. The plaintiff had adjacent to its factory premises, a tract of ground abutting upon the railroad right of way and approximately 250 by 400 feet in dimension, upon which it stored flax straw it purchased for use in its manufacturing business. There were about 230 stacks, arranged in two rows, parallel with the right of way. The distance from the center of the railroad track to the fence along the line of the right of way was 50 feet, from the fence to the nearest row of stacks, 20 or 25 feet, and from the fence to the second row of stacks, about 35 feet. During a high wind, a fire started upon one of the stacks in the second row, and as a result all were consumed.

There was substantial evidence to show that the fire was started by a locomotive engine of defendant which had just passed, and that through the negligent operation of defendant's employees in charge, it emitted large quantities of sparks and live cinders, which were carried to the straw stack by a high wind then prevailing. It was contended by defendant, that plaintiff itself was negligent, and that its negligence contributed to the destruction of its property. There was no evidence that plaintiff was negligent save that it had placed its property of a flammable character upon its own premises so near the railroad. In other words, the character of the property and its proximity to an operated railroad, for which plaintiff was responsible, was the sole evidence of plaintiff's contributory negligence.

The doctrine of contributory negligence is entirely out of place. Depart from the simple requirement of the law, that everyone must use his property so as not to injure others, and you pass to refinements and confusing considerations. There is no embarrassment in the principle even to the operation of a railroad. Such operation is a legitimate use of property; other property in its vicinity may suffer inconveniences and be subject to risks by it, but a risk from wrongful operation is not one of them.

The legal conception of property is of rights. If you declare a right is subject to a wrong, you confound the meaning of both. It is difficult to deal with the opposing contention. There are some principles that have axiomatic character. The tangibility of property is in its uses, and that the uses by one owner of his property may be limited by the wrongful use of another owner of his is a contradiction.

Allred v. Capital Area Soccer League

Court of Appeals of North Carolina (2008)

Plaintiffs' complaint alleged that she attended a women's professional soccer match. Plaintiff was in the stands located immediately behind one of the soccer goals during the players' pre-game warm-ups. During the warm-ups many balls were directed towards the nets in a relatively short period of time. One of these balls sailed over the soccer goal, into the stands, striking plaintiff and causing serious injury. Plaintiff alleged that she had never attended a soccer game at the subject facility prior to her injury, had no knowledge or underlying information that there was a significant risk of being struck by a soccer ball.

Plaintiffs' complaint asserts that defendants were negligent in: (1) failing to warn patrons of the risk of being struck by a soccer ball leaving the field of play; (2) failing to provide a safe environment for patrons; and (3) failing to install protective netting behind the goals to protect spectators.

The cases previously decided in North Carolina deal with spectators being struck by balls at baseball games. These cases have been uniformly decided against the spectator, either on the basis that the stadium operator was not negligent or that the spectator assumed the risk of being hit by a baseball.

We further note that the cases in this area have tended to intermingle the legal concepts of the duty owed by the sports facility owner to the patron and the patron's assumption of known and obvious risks of attending a sporting event. While these legal theories are interrelated and contain common concepts, they are nonetheless separate. We will treat the duty of the facility owner and the patron's assumption of risk as separate concepts.

The duty of the operator of a baseball park to exercise reasonable care to protect its patrons does not extend to the common hazards incident to the game. In baseball, the patron participates in the sport as a spectator and in so doing subjects himself to certain risks necessarily and usually incident to and inherent in the game; risks that are obvious and should be observed in the exercise of reasonable care. This does not mean that he assumes the risk of being injured by the proprietor's negligence but that by voluntarily entering into the sport as a spectator he knowingly accepts the reasonable risks and hazards inherent in and incident to the game. There is no duty to warn against dangers either known or so obvious and apparent that they should have reasonably been discovered by plaintiff.

Assumption of risk is an affirmative defense which must be pled by the party seeking to invoke it. The party asserting an affirmative defense has the burden of proof to establish all elements of the defense. The two elements of the common law defense of assumption of risk are: (1) actual or constructive knowledge of the risk, and (2) consent by the plaintiff to assume that risk.

It is clear that plaintiff did not expressly consent to accept the hazard which caused her injury. However, consent may be implied from conduct under the circumstances. By entering freely and voluntarily into any relation or situation which presents obvious danger, the plaintiff may be taken to accept it, and to agree that he will look out for himself, and relieve the defendant of responsibility. Those who participate or sit as spectators at sports and amusements assume all the obvious risks of being hurt by roller coasters, and flying balls. Thus, a plaintiff's consent to assume a risk may be either express or implied.

Defendants contend that plaintiffs' complaint clearly reveals that she assumed the risk of being struck by the soccer ball when she attended the soccer match. We first note that assumption of risk is an affirmative defense upon which defendants have the burden of proof. Second, the first element of assumption of risk is the plaintiff's actual or constructive knowledge of the risk. As discussed above, the allegations of plaintiffs' complaint do not affirmatively establish either actual or constructive knowledge of the danger. Thus, it was improper for the trial court to dismiss the plaintiffs' complaint at the motion to dismiss stage of the proceedings.

The doctrine of assumption of risk has been generally limited to cases where there was a contractual relationship between the parties. We have discussed assumption of risk in detail because it was raised and discussed extensively by the parties in their briefs. Plaintiffs' complaint alleges that she was a lawful visitor and spectator at the soccer match and makes a passing reference to ticket stubs. At this early stage of the proceedings, we treat these allegations as sufficient to support some type of contractual relationship which would make the doctrine of assumption of risk applicable.

REVERSED AND REMANDED

Bass v. Aetna Insurance Company

Supreme Court of Louisiana (1979)

Mr. and Mrs. Loyd Bass sued Aetna Insurance Company, insurer of Mr. Kenneth Fussell under a homeowner's policy, and Southern Farm Bureau Casualty Insurance Company, insurer of Shepard's Fold Church of God, seeking damages for personal injuries suffered by Mrs. Bass when Mr. Fussell, a member of the Shepard's Fold Church, ran down the church aisle and collided with Mrs. Bass, also a member of the church, who was in the aisle praying. The defendants denied all allegations of negligence on the part of their insureds, and, alternatively, pleaded the affirmative defenses of assumption of the risk and contributory negligence. After trial on the merits, the Twenty-Second Judicial District Court dismissed plaintiffs' suit.

During a revival service, the Shepard's Fold Church of God was very crowded with not enough seats to accommodate all the parishioners. Consequently, Mrs. Bass and other parishioners who could not find seats were standing in the aisles of the church. Reverend Rodney Jeffers, in the course of preaching to the congregation, stated that the doors of the church should be opened and referred to the possibility of running. Immediately afterward, Mr. Fussell began running up the aisle and ran into Mrs. Bass, who was in the aisle praying with her head bowed. As a result, Mrs. Bass fell and was injured.

The issues are whether Mr. Fussell was negligent, whether the Shepard's Fold Church of God was negligent, and, if so, whether the plaintiffs' action is barred by either the defenses of assumption of the risk or contributory negligence. Although Mr. Fussell testified that he was "trotting" under the Spirit of the Lord and does not remember actually running into Mrs. Bass, another witness testified that she saw Mr. Fussell run into Mrs. Bass and knock her down. If Fussell's defense is that he was not in control of his actions, it can be compared to voluntary intoxication, which will not exonerate one from delictual responsibility. A worshiper in church has no more right to run over a fellow worshiper in the aisle than a passerby on the sidewalk. Mr. Fussell breached this duty and was negligent when he trotted or ran down the aisle of the church without regard for the safety of other parishioners in the aisles.

Actionable negligence also results from the creation or maintenance of an unreasonable risk of injury to others. In determining whether the risk is unreasonable, not only the seriousness of the harm that may be caused is relevant, but also the likelihood that harm may be caused. In the instant case, according to both Mrs. Bass and Reverend Jeffers, there were approximately three hundred fifty to three hundred seventy-five parishioners in the church on the night of the accident, and many of the parishioners were standing in the aisles. Reverend Jeffers recognized the likelihood that harm might be caused by this crowded condition because he testified that he asked that the aisles be cleared, that he encouraged "open response to the Spirit," and that running or moving "in the Spirit" were common forms of religious expression in Shepard's Fold Church. Another defense witness testified that Reverend Jeffers, recognizing the crowded aisles, asked if somebody would run for him (which apparently is what Mr. Fussell did). Reverend Jeffers did not stop the service to clear the aisles, but continued to maintain an unreasonable risk of injury to the parishioners. The Shepard's Fold Church is responsible for the negligence of its pastor, Reverend Jeffers, under these circumstances.

Concluding that both Mr. Fussell and the church were negligent, we next consider the defenses of assumption of the risk and contributory negligence. The Court of Appeal, in affirming the trial court, concluded that Mrs. Bass assumed the risk by remaining in the aisle with her eyes closed, and that she was contributorily negligent by remaining after having been alerted that running might occur.

Assumption of the risk and contributory negligence are affirmative defenses, and as we stated: The determination of whether a plaintiff has assumed a risk is made by subjective inquiry, whereas contributory negligence is determined objectively under the reasonable man standard.

Knowledge is the mainstay of this assumption of the risk defense, and this court will impute knowledge to a plaintiff, not because he was in a position to make certain observations, but only when the plaintiff actually made those observations and from those observations should reasonably have known that a risk was involved. Assumption of the risk therefore is properly applicable to those situations where the plaintiff, with knowledge of the peril, voluntarily enters into a relationship with defendant involving danger to himself because of defendant's contemplated conduct.

We cannot agree with the Court of Appeal's conclusion that Mrs. Bass assumed the risk. Although Mrs. Bass had belonged to the Church of God faith for approximately fifty-five years and the Shepard's Fold Church for approximately twenty-five years, neither she nor any other witness had seen or heard of any injury or collision in any Church of God church. Before the accident, no one, including Mrs. Bass, felt endangered by worshiping in this church. Mrs. Bass unequivocally testified that she had never seen anyone run in the church. The evidence fails to persuade us that Mrs. Bass actually, subjectively comprehended that by praying in the aisle she was incurring a risk of being run over, or that she could or should have known or understood that she was incurring such a risk.

The defense failed to prove that Mrs. Bass voluntarily assumed or exposed herself to this risk. Movement in the aisles was not an extraordinary condition in this church because worshipers frequently went to the altar, the very central focal point in the church, for prayer. Heedless running in the aisle was an unusual and extraordinary hazard, to which plaintiff did not knowingly expose herself.

Contributory negligence is also an affirmative defense; the defendants bear the burden of proving contributory negligence by a preponderance of the evidence. Contributory negligence is objectively determined under the reasonable man standard. It is not contributory negligence to bow one's head when praying in a church, whether in the pew or in the aisle.

For the reasons assigned, the judgments of the district court and of the Court of Appeal are reversed.

Stelluti v. Casapenn Enterprises

Supreme Court of New Jersey (2010)

While participating in a spinning class at a private fitness center, the handlebars on plaintiff Gina Stelluti's spin bike dislodged from the bike, causing her to fall and suffer injuries. In this appeal we must determine whether plaintiff should be bound to a pre-injury waiver of liability that she executed in connection with her membership application and agreement.

POWERHOUSE FITNESS (The Club)

WAIVER & RELEASE FORM

You agree that if you engage in any physical exercise or activity, or use any club amenity on the premises or off premises including any sponsored club event, you do so entirely at your own risk. You agree that you are voluntarily participating in these activities and use of these facilities and premises and assume all risks of injury, illness, or death.

This waiver and release of liability includes, without limitation, all injuries which may occur as a result of, (a) your use of all amenities and equipment in the facility and your participation in any activity, class, program, personal training or instruction, (b) the sudden and unforeseen malfunctioning of any equipment, (c) our instruction, training, supervision, or dietary recommendations, and (d) your slipping and/or falling while in the club, or on the club premises, including adjacent sidewalks and parking areas.

You acknowledge that you have carefully read this "waiver and release" and fully understand that it is a release of liability. You expressly agree to release and discharge the health club, and all affiliates, employees, agents, representatives, successors, or assigns, from any and all claims or causes of action and you agree to voluntarily give up or waive any right that you may otherwise have to bring a legal action against the club for personal injury or property damage.

To the extent that statute or case law does not prohibit releases for negligence, this release is also for negligence on the part of the Club, its agents, and employees.

Signed: /s/ Gina Stelluti

As a threshold matter, to be enforceable an exculpatory agreement must "reflect the unequivocal expression of the party giving up his or her legal rights that this decision was made voluntarily, intelligently and with the full knowledge of its legal consequences." When a party enters into a signed, written contract, that party is presumed to understand and assent to its terms, unless fraudulent conduct is suspected. Although Stelluti argues that she did not know what she was signing, she does not claim that she signed the waiver form as the result of fraud, deceit, or misrepresentation. Therefore, the trial court was well within reason to presume that she understood the terms of the agreement, and the finding to that effect is unassailable.

It is well recognized that the common law imposes a duty of care on business owners to maintain a safe premises for their business invitees because the law recognizes that an owner is in the best position to prevent harm. That standard of care encompasses a duty "to guard against any dangerous conditions on the property that the owner either knows about or should have discovered, and to conduct a reasonable inspection to discover latent dangerous conditions." That said, the law recognizes that for certain activities conducted by operation of some types of business, particularly those that pose inherent risks to the participant, the business entity will not be held liable for injuries sustained "so long as the business has acted in accordance with 'the ordinary duty owed to business invitees, including exercise of care commensurate with the nature of the risk, foreseeability of injury, and fairness in the circumstances.' " When it comes to physical activities in the nature of sports—physical exertion associated with physical training, exercise, and the like—injuries are not an unexpected, unforeseeable result of such strenuous activity.

By its nature, exercising entails vigorous physical exertion. Injuries from exercise are common; indeed minor injuries can be expected—for example, sore muscles following completion of a tough exercise or workout may be indicative of building or toning muscles. Those injuries and others may result from faulty equipment, improper use of equipment, inadequate instruction, inexperience or poor physical condition of the user, or excessive exertion.

Although there is public interest in holding a health club to its general common law duty to business invitees—to maintain its premises in a condition safe from defects that the business is charged with knowing or discovering—it need not ensure the safety of its patrons who voluntarily assume some risk by engaging in strenuous physical activities that have a potential to result in injuries. Any requirement to so guarantee a patron's safety from all risk in using equipment, which understandably is passed from patron to patron, could chill the establishment of health clubs. Health clubs perform a salutary purpose by offering activities and equipment so that patrons can enjoy challenging physical exercise. There has been recognized a "positive social value" in allowing gyms to limit their liability in respect of patrons who wish to assume the risk of participation in activities that could cause an injury. And, further, it is not unreasonable to encourage patrons of a fitness center to take proper steps to prepare, such as identifying their own physical limitations and learning about the activity, before engaging in a foreign activity for the first time.

Although it would be unreasonable to demand that a fitness center inspect each individual piece of equipment after every patron's use, it would be unreasonable, and contrary to the public interest, to condone willful blindness to problems that arise with the equipment provided for patrons' use. Thus, had Powerhouse's management or employees been aware of a piece of defective exercise equipment and failed to remedy the condition or to warn adequately of the dangerous condition, or if it had dangerously or improperly maintained equipment, Powerhouse could not exculpate itself from such reckless or gross negligence. That showing was not made on this record.

We hold business owners to a standard of care congruent with the nature of their business, which is to make available the specialized equipment and facility to their invitees who are there to exercise, train, and to push their physical limits. That is, we impose a duty not to engage in reckless or gross negligence.

For the foregoing reasons, we affirm the judgment of the Appellate Division that sustained the award of summary judgment to defendant.

DUTY: LANDOWNERS

Gladon v. Greater Cleveland Regional Transit Authority

Supreme Court of Ohio (1996)

[Gladon was lying on RTA train tracks and hit by a train. He does not know how he ended up on the tracks—he may have been drunk or pushed onto the tracks by strangers].

Ohio adheres to the common-law classifications of invitee, licensee, and trespasser in cases of premises liability. In Ohio, the status of the person who enters upon the land of another (i.e., trespasser, licensee, or invitee) continues to define the scope of the legal duty that the landowner owes the entrant. Invitees are persons who rightfully come upon the premises of another by invitation, express or implied, for some purpose which is beneficial to the owner.

The status of an invitee is not absolute but is limited by the landowner's invitation. The visitor has the status of an invitee only while he is on the part of the land to which his invitation extends-or in other words, the part of the land upon which the possessor gives him reason to believe that his presence is desired for the purpose for which he has come. If the invitee goes outside of the area of his invitation, he becomes a trespasser or a licensee, depending upon whether he goes there without the consent of the possessor, or with such consent.

Gladon was an invitee when he purchased an RTA ticket, rode the rapid transit train and waited at RTA's platform. However, RTA's invitation to Gladon to use its premises did not extend to the area on or near the tracks. In fact, Gladon acknowledged that RTA did not permit the public in the area on or near the tracks. Although the result seems harsh, the common law on this subject is well grounded and we are not inclined to reject it. Accordingly, we hold that where an entrant upon another's land exceeds the scope of the landowner's invitation, the entrant will lose the status of an invitee, and become either a licensee or trespasser.

Gladon contends that he retained his invitee status because there was no evidence that he intentionally or purposely entered upon the track area. So far as the liability of the possessor of the land to the intruder is concerned, however, the possessor's duty, and liability, will be the same regardless of the manner of entry, so long as the entry itself is not privileged.

In determining whether the person is a trespasser within the meaning of this section, the question whether his entry has been intentional, negligent or purely accidental is not material, except as it may bear on the existence of a privilege. Without the consent or privilege to enter the area of the tracks, the law views such entry from the aspect of the landowner whose duties to the entrant flow from the parameters of his permission to be there. As a result, the determining fact is the presence or absence of a privilege to enter or to remain on the land, and the status of an accidental trespasser is still that of a trespasser.

Furthermore, whether Gladon was privileged to enter the tracks is immaterial. A person privileged to enter the land is owed the same duties as a licensee. Because the duties owed to a licensee and trespasser are the same, whether Gladon was privileged to enter the land does not change the standard of care RTA owed to him.

Even though his entry may have been unintentional and against Gladon's wishes, once on the tracks, Gladon exceeded the scope of his invitation and lost his status as an invitee. Because Gladon then became either a licensee or a trespasser for purposes of determining the duty RTA owed to him, the trial court erred in instructing the jury that he was an invitee as a matter of law.

We now turn to the duty owed to Gladon by RTA as a result of Gladon's change in status from invitee to either licensee or trespasser. A landowner owes a duty to an invitee to exercise ordinary care for the invitee's safety and protection. Conversely, a landowner owes no duty to a licensee or trespasser except to refrain from willful, wanton or reckless conduct which is likely to injure him. When a trespasser or licensee is discovered in a position of peril, a landowner is required to use ordinary care to avoid injuring him. The duty to exercise ordinary care arises after the landowner knows, or from facts within his knowledge should know or believe, that a trespasser or licensee is on the land.

Having instructed the jury as a matter of law that Gladon was an invitee, the trial court assigned RTA a duty of ordinary care to discover and to avoid danger. These instructions erred in two respects. First, the instructions imposed upon RTA a duty to use ordinary care to discover Gladon's presence. To the contrary, RTA was under no duty to anticipate trespassers and could only be liable for injuries resulting from willful or wanton conduct. Second, the instructions imposed upon RTA a duty to use ordinary care to avoid injuring Gladon prior to the operator's discovery of him. Rather, RTA's duty to use ordinary care to avoid injuring Gladon did not arise until RTA knew or should have known that Gladon was on the tracks. Whether the operator knew or should have known a person was on the tracks upon observing the tennis shoe remains a question for the jury.

Given that the instructions were erroneous and prejudicial, we reverse the judgment of the court of appeals and remand this cause for a new trial.

Bennett v. Stanley

Supreme Court of Ohio (2001)

When Rickey G. Bennett, plaintiff-appellant, arrived home in the late afternoon he found his two young daughters crying. The three-year-old, Kyleigh, told him that Mommy and Chance, her five-year-old half-brother, were drowning in the water. Bennett ran next door to his neighbors' house to find mother and son unconscious in the swimming pool. Both died.

The Bennetts had moved next door to defendants-appellees, Jeffrey and Stacey Stanley. The Stanleys had purchased their home the previous June. At the time of their purchase, the Stanleys' property included a swimming pool that had gone unused for three years. At that time, the pool was enclosed with fencing and a brick wall. After moving in, the Stanleys drained the pool once but thereafter they allowed rainwater to accumulate in the pool to a depth of over six feet. They removed a tarp that had been on the pool and also removed the fencing that had been around two sides of the pool. The pool became pond-like: it contained tadpoles and frogs, and Mr. Stanley had seen a snake swimming on the surface. The pool contained no ladders, and its sides were slimy with algae. The Bennetts rented the house next to the Stanleys. The houses were about one hundred feet apart. There was some fencing with an eight-foot gap between the two properties.

The Stanleys were aware that the Bennetts had moved next door and that they had young children. They had seen the children outside unsupervised. Stacey Stanley had once called Chance onto her property to retrieve a dog. The Stanleys testified, however, that they never had any concern about the children getting into the pool. They did not post any warning or no trespassing signs on their property.

Kyleigh told her father that she and Chance had been playing at the pool on the afternoon of the tragedy. The sheriff's department concluded that Chance had gone to the pool to look at the frogs and somehow fell into the pool. His mother apparently drowned trying to save him.

Ohio has long recognized a range of duties for property owners vis-à-vis persons entering their property. Currently, to an invitee the landowner owes a duty to exercise ordinary care and to protect the invitee by maintaining the premises in a safe condition. To licensees and trespassers, on the other hand, a landowner owes no duty except to refrain from willful, wanton or reckless conduct which is likely to injure the licensee or trespasser. Today, we face the issue of whether child trespassers should become another class of users who are owed a different duty of care.

This court has consistently held that children have a special status in tort law and that duties of care owed to children are different from duties owed to adults. The amount of care required to discharge a duty owed to a child of tender years is necessarily greater than that required to discharge a duty owed to an adult under the same circumstances. This is the approach long followed by this court and we see no reason to abandon it. Children of tender years, and youthful persons generally, are entitled to a degree of care proportioned to their inability to foresee and avoid the perils that they may encounter. The same discernment and foresight in discovering defects and dangers cannot be reasonably expected of them, that older and experienced persons habitually employ; and therefore the greater precaution should be taken, where children are exposed to them.

Recognizing the special status of children in the law, this court has even accorded special protection to child trespassers by adopting the dangerous instrumentality doctrine. The dangerous instrumentality exception to nonliability to trespassers imposes upon the owner or occupier of a premises a higher duty of care to a child trespasser when such owner or occupier actively and negligently operates hazardous machinery or other apparatus, the dangerousness of which is not readily apparent to children.

Thus, the court adopted as early as 1932 some of the hallmarks of the attractive nuisance doctrine. Elements such as knowledge of children's presence, the maintenance of a potentially dangerous force, and an exercise of care by the owner commensurate with the danger are a part of the attractive nuisance doctrine in most states.

Despite the fact that in premises liability cases a landowner's duty is defined by the status of the plaintiff, and that children, even child trespassers, are accorded special protection in Ohio tort law, this court has never adopted the attractive nuisance doctrine. A possessor of land is subject to liability for physical harm to children trespassing thereon caused by an artificial condition upon land if (a) the place where the condition exists is one upon which the possessor knows or has reason to know that children are likely to trespass, and (b) the condition is one of which the possessor knows or has reason to know and which he realizes or should realize will involve an unreasonable risk of death or serious bodily harm to such children, and (c) the children because of their youth do not discover the condition or realize the risk involved in intermeddling with it or in coming within the area made dangerous by it, and (d) the utility to the possessor of maintaining the condition and the burden of eliminating the danger are slight as compared with the risk to children involved, and (e) the possessor fails to exercise reasonable care to eliminate the danger or otherwise to protect the children.

Ohio is one of only three states that have not either created a special duty for trespassing children or done away with distinctions of duty based upon a person's status as an invitee, licensee, or trespasser. We therefore use this case to adopt the attractive nuisance doctrine.

Smith v. Kuligring

Supreme Court of North Dakota (2005)

Kulig owns a four-story building in Minot with two commercial businesses on the main floor and four apartments leased on the second floor. There is a separate door for residential tenants to enter the building. The door is kept locked at all times so that only tenants and invited guests may enter the premises, and all tenants have a key to the front door. Attached to the back east side of the building is a fire escape. Access to the fire escape can be gained through a second floor door onto a landing. At the bottom of the fire escape, a ladder is located approximately seven feet above the ground and, therefore, access from the ground is limited. Kulig instructed tenants of the building, including Michael Spotted Wolf, who rented one of the second floor apartments, they were not to use the fire escape for entering or exiting the building. It was to be used only in the case of an emergency. Kulig posted "no trespassing" signs on both sides of the second floor door leading to the fire escape landing, on the landing itself, and on the ladder between the landing and the ground.

Kelly Smith and Sonny Smith were visiting Spotted Wolf in his apartment in Kulig's building and were drinking most of the afternoon in the apartment. Sometime around 10:00 p.m., Kelly Smith visited a relative at another location in Minot. While Kelly Smith was visiting the relative, Sonny Smith phoned and invited Kelly Smith to come back to Spotted Wolf's apartment. Kelly Smith was later seen by a witness at a local bar around its closing time of 1:00 a.m. No one saw Smith again until approximately 2:00 a.m., when his body was discovered lying in the alley beneath the fire escape on the east side of Kulig's apartment building.

Rhonda Smith filed a wrongful death action against Kulig, alleging Kelly Smith was killed while walking on the fire escape when attachment bolts securing the fire escape came out of the wall. She alleged the death was the result of Kulig's negligent failure to provide a safe environment and to keep the fire escape serviced in a safe manner. The case was tried to the court. Dr. John Smith testified the cause of Kelly Smith's death was "a fall from a balcony of a fire escape." Clint Wolf, an investigator with the Minot Police Department, testified that attachment bolts were missing from the fire escape, which allowed it to swing away from the wall, presumably causing Smith to fall to the street. The trial court found that Smith, while using the fire escape to enter or exit the building, was a trespasser to whom Kulig did not owe a duty other than to refrain from harming him in a willful or wanton manner. The court determined Kulig did not breach his duty to Smith, and the court dismissed the action.

II. Rhonda Smith argues the trial court erred in finding Kelly Smith was a trespasser when he presumably fell off the fire escape of Kulig's building. Landowners owe a general duty to lawful entrants to maintain their property in a reasonably safe condition under the circumstances. However, a landowner's only duty to a trespasser is to refrain from harming the trespasser in a willful and wanton manner.

It is undisputed Kulig had informed tenants they and their guests were not entitled to use the fire escape to enter or exit the building. Although Kelly Smith may have been invited to Spotted Wolf's apartment as a guest, the evidence supports the trial court's finding Smith became a trespasser on Kulig's property when he attempted to enter or exit the building via the fire escape, in spite of the no trespass signs forbidding its usage in that manner when there was no emergency necessitating its use.

The word "trespasser" is legally defined as a person who enters or remains upon premises in possession of another without a privilege to do so created by the possessor's consent, either express or implied.

Here, the trial court found the fire escape on the back side of Kulig's building contained "no trespass" signs, as did the doors leading to and from the fire escape at the second and third levels. The court also found that the ladder to the fire escape had a no trespassing sign mounted on it. The court found that Kelly Smith was a trespasser on the premises, because Smith did not have a right to use the fire escape as an entry or exit to the building and there was no emergency situation which would reasonably require him to have used it for that purpose. No trespassing signs on the property negated any implied consent upon which Kelly Smith could claim to have been a lawful occupant of the premises while using the fire escape in contravention of the warnings against such use. We, therefore, hold the trial court's finding Kelly Smith was a trespasser is not clearly erroneous.

III. For purposes of determining landowner liability for injury caused to occupants upon the land, this Court has eliminated the distinction between an invitee and a licencee, but has retained the distinction with regard to trespassers:

An occupier of premises owes no duty to a trespasser other than to refrain from harming the trespasser in a willful and wanton manner until such time as the trespasser's presence in a place of danger becomes known, at which point the occupier's duty is to exercise ordinary care to avoid injuring him.

IV. Rhonda Smith argues the trial court's finding Tony Kulig did not harm Kelly Smith in a willful and wanton manner is clearly erroneous, because the undisputed evidence is that

Kulig did not inspect the fire escape and consequently neither knew the attachment bolts were missing nor took any action to remedy that situation to make the fire escape safe for use.

Willful and wanton actions are reckless, heedless, malicious; characterized by extreme recklessness or foolhardiness; recklessly disregardful of the rights or safety of others or of consequences.

With respect to trespassers, a landowner is not under any affirmative duty to give a trespasser warning of concealed perils, although, by the exercise of reasonable care, the owner might have discovered the defect or danger which caused the injury. The person in charge only owes a duty to not knowingly or willfully expose a trespasser to hidden danger or peril. In Werth, a landowner was sued for injuries sustained by the plaintiff, who fell into the landowner's basement stairwell when a railing attached to the basement entrance of the building collapsed as the plaintiff leaned on it while talking to another person. This Court held that when the defendant did not know of the dangerous condition of the railing and there was no showing of facts from which the defendant could have inferred that the railing was dangerous, the defendant was not liable to the plaintiff for the injuries sustained. Similarly, in this case, there is no evidence that Kulig knew or had reason to know the fire escape was in a dangerous condition.

Kelly Smith also argues Kulig's failure to inspect the fire escape and maintain it in a reasonably good condition constitutes willful and wanton misconduct, as a matter of law. Kulig testified he had discussions with fire department personnel, who acquiesced in allowing him to use "a thin wire" to discourage access to the fire escape from the second floor but which, at the same time, would allow someone to "step through" in the event they needed to use the fire escape in an emergency. Kulig testified he had recently used the fire escape several times to replace no trespass signs, and he had informed tenants that they and their guests were not to use the fire escape for building entry or exit. He also testified fire department inspections of the building did not disclose, to his knowledge, any safety problems with the fire escape:

Q The yearly inspections by the Minot Fire Department basically included the whole building?

A Yes.

Q It included the fire escape?

A Yes. I believe it did.

Q If they made recommendations or requirements for anything that needed repair or maintenance you followed up and did it, didn't you?

A Yes.

Q Did you have any reason to believe there was any problem with this fire escape, that it was dangerous in any way?

A Not at all.

We hold the trial court's finding that Kulig did not harm Kelly Smith in a willful and wanton manner is not clearly erroneous. While Kulig's lack of knowledge may not have precluded his liability for injuries sustained by an occupant lawfully using the fire escape, it does insulate Kulig in this limited instance from liability toward Kelly Smith, who was merely a trespasser.

We affirm the judgment dismissing the wrongful death action.

Rowland v. Christian

Supreme Court of California (1968)

Plaintiff alleged that Miss Christian told the lessors of her apartment that the knob of the porcelain cold water faucet on the bathroom basin was cracked and should be replaced; that plaintiff entered the apartment at the invitation of Miss Christian; that he was injured while using the bathroom fixtures, suffering severed tendons and nerves of his right hand; and that he has incurred medical and hospital expenses. He further alleged that the bathroom fixtures were dangerous, that Miss Christian was aware of the dangerous condition, and that his injuries were proximately caused by the negligence of Miss Christian. Plaintiff sought recovery of his medical and hospital expenses, loss of wages, damage to his clothing, and general damages. It does not appear from the complaint whether the crack in the faucet handle was obvious to an ordinary inspection or was concealed.

One of the areas where this court and other courts have departed from the fundamental concept that a man is liable for injuries caused by his carelessness is with regard to the liability of a possessor of land for injuries to persons who have entered upon that land. The departure from the fundamental rule of liability for negligence has been accomplished by classifying the plaintiff either as a trespasser, licensee, or invitee and then adopting special rules as to the duty owed by the possessor to each of the classifications. Generally speaking a trespasser is a person who enters or remains upon land of another without a privilege to do so; a licensee is a person like a social guest who is not an invitee and who is privileged to enter or remain upon land by virtue of the possessor's consent, and an invitee is a business visitor who is invited or permitted to enter or remain on the land for a purpose directly or indirectly connected with business dealings between them.

In refusing to adopt the rules relating to the liability of a possessor of land for the law of admiralty, the United States Supreme Court stated: the distinctions which the common law draws between licensee and invitee were inherited from a culture deeply rooted to the land, a culture which traced many of its standards to a heritage of feudalism. In an effort to do justice in an industrialized urban society, with its complex economic and individual relationships, modern common-law courts have found it necessary to formulate increasingly subtle verbal refinements, to create sub classifications among traditional common-law categories, and to delineate fine gradations in the standards of care which the landowner owes to each. Yet even within a single jurisdiction, the classifications and sub classifications bred by the common law have produced confusion and conflict. As new distinctions have been spawned, older ones have become obscured. Through this semantic morass the common law has moved, unevenly and with hesitation, towards imposing on owners and occupiers a single duty of reasonable care in all circumstances.

There is another fundamental objection to the approach to the question of the possessor's liability on the basis of the common law distinctions based upon the status of the injured party as a trespasser, licensee, or invitee. Complexity can be borne and confusion remedied where the underlying principles governing liability are based upon proper considerations. Whatever may have been the historical justifications for the common law distinctions, it is clear that those distinctions are not justified in the light of our modern society and that the complexity and confusion which has arisen is not due to difficulty in applying the original common law rules—they are all too easy to apply in their original formulation—but is due to the attempts to apply just rules in our modern society within the ancient terminology.

A man's life or limb does not become less worthy of protection by the law nor a loss less worthy of compensation under the law because he has come upon the land of another without permission or with permission but without a business purpose. Reasonable people do not ordinarily vary their conduct depending upon such matters, and to focus upon the status of the injured party as a trespasser, licensee, or invitee in order to determine the question whether the landowner has a duty of care, is contrary to our modern social mores and humanitarian values. The common law rules obscure rather than illuminate the proper considerations which should govern determination of the question of duty.

It bears repetition that the basic policy of this state is that everyone is responsible for an injury caused to another by his want of ordinary care or skill in the management of his property. The factors which may in particular cases warrant departure from this fundamental principle do not warrant the wholesale immunities resulting from the common law classifications, and we are satisfied that continued adherence to the common law distinctions can only lead to injustice or, if we are to avoid injustice, further fictions with the resulting complexity and confusion. We decline to follow and perpetuate such rigid classifications. The proper test to be applied to the liability of the possessor of land is whether in the management of his property he has acted as a reasonable man in view of the probability of injury to others, and, although the plaintiff's status as a trespasser, licensee, or invitee may in the light of the facts giving rise to such status have some bearing on the question of liability, the status is not determinative.

Once the ancient concepts as to the liability of the occupier of land are stripped away, the status of the plaintiff relegated to its proper place in determining such liability, and ordinary principles of negligence applied, the result in the instant case presents no substantial difficulties. As we have seen, when we view the matters presented on the motion for summary judgment as we must, we must assume defendant Miss Christian was aware that the faucet handle was defective and dangerous, that the defect was not obvious, and that plaintiff was about to come in contact with the defective condition, and under the undisputed facts she neither remedied the condition nor warned plaintiff of it. Where the occupier of land is aware of a concealed condition involving in the absence of precautions an unreasonable risk of harm to those coming in contact with it and is aware that a person on the premises is about to come in contact with it, the trier of fact can reasonably conclude that a failure to warn or to repair the condition constitutes negligence. Whether or not a guest has a right to expect that his host will remedy dangerous conditions on his account, he should reasonably be entitled to rely upon a warning of the dangerous condition so that he, like the host, will be in a position to take special precautions when he comes in contact with it.

Pagelsdorf v. Safeco Insurance Company of America

Supreme Court of Wisconsin (1979)

The defendant Richard J. Mahnke owned a two-story, two-family duplex. There were four balcony porches: one in front and one in back of each flat. Mahnke rented the upper unit to John and Mary Katherine Blattner who lived there with their three children. Eventually they left the apartment and moved to Kansas. She left her furniture in the apartment and paid her rent for the month of May, having arranged with the Mahnkes to have her brothers move the furniture. When Mrs. Blattner's two brothers arrived to move her belongings to Kansas they rented a truck and parked it behind the duplex. While moving the furniture out of the duplex, they felt they would need help with the heavier items. They asked Carol Pagelsdorf, a next-door neighbor who had been packing Mrs. Blattner's belongings, to ask her husband James to help them. He agreed to help.

While moving the bedroom furniture, Pagelsdorf and one of Mrs. Blattner's brothers felt that the box spring was too cumbersome to be taken down the back stairway. The Blattner brother decided that the best way to remove it from the apartment would be to lower it from the rear balcony to the ground. While letting the spring down, Pagelsdorf applied pressure straight down on the railing with his body. After both men released the box spring, Pagelsdorf began to straighten up, placing his hands on the railing, and bending his knees slightly. His knees then touched the 2 X 2 spokes in the railing, and the bottom swung out as if on a hinge. The entire railing section came loose, and Pagelsdorf fell to the ground below, suffering injuries. Mahnke testified that after the incident he examined the 4 X 4 posts and the railing section which gave way and found that the railing ends had dry rot in them. He stated that wood with dry rot would retain its form but not its strength.

The parties agree that the extent of Mahnke's duty toward Pagelsdorf turns on whether Pagelsdorf was an invitee or a licensee with respect to Mahnke. Pagelsdorf maintains he was Mahnke's invitee; if he was, the jury should have been instructed that Mahnke owed him a duty of ordinary care. The defendants contend that the trial court properly determined that Pagelsdorf was Mahnke's licensee and, therefore, properly instructed the jury that he owed Pagelsdorf only a duty to warn of known hazards.

These arguments overlook the effect on a landowner's common law duty upon transfer of the premises from the owner to a lessee. The classification of visitors identified the degree of duty of the possessor or occupier of the premises. When the property is leased, the duty of the landlord was controlled by a different rule. That, with certain exceptions, a landlord is not liable for injuries to his tenants and their visitors resulting from defects in the premises. The general rule of nonliability was based on the concept of a lease as a conveyance of property and the consequent transfer of possession and control of the premises to the tenant.

There are exceptions to this general rule of nonliability. The landlord is liable for injuries to the tenant or his visitor caused by a dangerous condition if he contracts to repair defects, or if, knowing of a defect existing at the time the tenant took possession, he conceals it from a tenant who could not reasonably be expected to discover it. Additionally, the general rule is not applicable where the premises are leased for public use, or are retained in the landlord's control, or where the landlord negligently makes repairs.

None of the exceptions to the general rule are applicable to the facts of this case. The premises were not leased for public use, nor was the porch within Mahnke's control, nor did he negligently repair the railing. The plaintiffs argue that Mahnke contracted to repair defects; but according to Mrs. Blattner's testimony, Mahnke's promise extended only to items the Blattners reported as being in disrepair. Therefore, error cannot be predicated on the trial court's failure to give an instruction concerning Mahnke's constructive knowledge where the asserted contract was to repair defects of which Mahnke actually knew. Finally, the concealed-defect exception does not apply because there was no evidence that the dry rot existed when the Blattners moved in and because Mrs. Blattner testified that she knew of the rot in the railing.

Therefore, if we were to follow the traditional rule, Pagelsdorf was not entitled to an instruction that Mahnke owed him a duty of ordinary care. We believe, however, that the better public policy lies in the abandonment of the general rule of nonliability and the adoption of a rule that a landlord is under a duty to exercise ordinary care in the maintenance of the premises.

Scurti v. City of New York

Court of Appeals of New York (1976)

Today the court has held that the liability of a landowner to one injured upon his property should be governed, not by the ancient and antiquated distinctions between trespassers, licensees, and invitees decisive under common law, but rather by the standard applicable to negligence cases generally, i.e., the standard of reasonable care under the circumstances whereby foreseeability shall be a measure of liability. This case involves the further application of that standard and consideration of those factors, conclusive under prior law, which may continue to have some relevance in determining a landowner's liability for injury to one who concededly entered his property without permission.

John Scurti, a 14-year-old high school student accompanied by another boy, entered a railroad yard through a hole in the fence at the rear of a playground. He then climbed on the top of a freight car and was electrocuted when he came in contact with a high-voltage wire used to supply power to the locomotives. It is conceded that Scurti did not have permission to enter the yard or to climb upon the train.

The starting point at common law was the fact that the injury, no matter how foreseeable, had occurred on the defendant's property. At a time when landowners were a dominant class and ownership of land was considered akin to a sacred right, the fact that the plaintiff was a trespasser was of the utmost importance. Thus the landowner was held to owe no duty to a trespasser other than the obligation to refrain from willfully or wantonly injuring him. This simply proscribed certain criminal or quasi-criminal acts such as shooting or setting traps, and did little more than serve as a reminder that it was not open season on trespassers.

Under the standard of reasonable care adopted by the court today the factors which sustained the landowner's immunity and inspired the exceptions under prior law will no longer be considered decisive. But, as indicated, most of them have some probative value and to that extent they will continue to have some relevance in determining whether, under all the facts and circumstances, there has been a breach of duty.

The fact that the injury occurred on the defendant's property is certainly a relevant circumstance in assessing the reasonableness of the defendant's conduct. The defendant has the right to use his property and to develop it for his profit and enjoyment. That often means that he must conduct dangerous activities or permit dangerous instruments and conditions to exist on the premises. However under those circumstances he must take reasonable measures to prevent injury to those whose presence on the property can reasonably be foreseen. Whether the threat is posed by a dangerous condition or a dangerous activity is of little significance in itself. It may have some bearing on the effort required to prevent the injury, but that depends on the facts of the particular case. In this connection it is important to note that the elimination of the immunity conferred by prior law should not pose an unreasonable burden on the use of the property since all that is now required is the exercise of reasonable care under the circumstances. The defendant can always show that it would have been unduly burdensome to have done more.

The fact that the plaintiff entered without permission is also a relevant circumstance. It may well demonstrate that the plaintiff's presence was not foreseeable at the time and place of the injury. However the likelihood of one entering without permission depends on the facts of the case including the location of the property in relation to populated areas, its accessibility and whether there have been any prior incidents of trespassing in the area where the injury occurred. The age of the plaintiff is also significant in view of the well- known propensities of children to climb about and play. And, of course, the fact that the entry was unauthorized may be of little or no importance if the plaintiff's presence was discovered by the owner in time to avoid the injury.

In sum, several of the factors considered decisive under prior law may be usefully integrated into the general theory of tort liability so as to provide standards and guidelines in determining a landowner's liability.

Flowers v. Rock Creek Terrace Limited Partnership

Court of Appeals of Maryland (1987)

David Flowers was a fireman with the Kensington Volunteer Fire Department. Flowers and other members of the Kensington Volunteer Fire Department responded to a fire alarm at the Rock Creek Apartments. In the course of the fire, the twelfth-floor lobby became filled with smoke making it nearly impossible to see. As Flowers and other firefighters evacuated tenants from apartments adjoining the twelfth-floor lobby, Flowers fell down an open elevator shaft and sustained severe permanent injuries.

The history of the fireman's rule in Maryland is like that in many other states. Earlier cases in this country involving firemen's attempts to recover for negligently caused injuries sustained while firefighting largely focused on the status of the firemen on the premises where the injuries occurred. These cases indicated that firemen came upon the premises under a privilege conferred by legal authority, and, not being invited by the landholder, took the property as they found it. Later cases, while still sounding in premises liability law, recognized that it is a fireman's job to fight fires, and as such he normally takes the risk of fire-related injuries which may be attributable to the landowner or occupier's negligence. Thus, whether purporting to apply premises liability law, or under a rationale based on the relationship between firemen and the public whom they serve, courts held that landowners and occupiers ordinarily owed firemen no duty of reasonable care.

When a fire department is called to fight a blaze, the cause of the blaze is immaterial. It may be the result of actual negligence on the part of the property owner, such as the dropping of a lighted match, or of his negligence in the maintenance of his property, as in permitting a known defective condition of the wiring to remain uncorrected. In either case, if the fireman is injured by the flames or gases of the conflagration, apart from unusual factors operative after the fire has begun, he cannot recover. Fighting the fire, however caused, is his occupation. Compensation for injuries sustained in the fulfilment of his duties, absent other circumstances, is the obligation of society.

A premises liability rationale does not encompass cases in which a fireman is injured by a fire caused by the negligence of someone other than the owner or occupier of the premises. In the present case, Westinghouse and Sting Security are not landowners or occupiers but have invoked the fireman's rule. In addition, other public employees, such as postmen and building inspectors, are generally held to be entitled to due care even though their counterparts in the fire and police departments are not. Nevertheless, postal workers and building inspectors, like firemen and policemen, often enter land pursuant to legal authority rather than expressed invitation. Nothing in traditional premises liability law, however, furnishes a ground for classifying some of these public employees as invitees and others as licensees. Moreover, although prior cases sounding in premises liability law had begun to define the extent to which firemen are deemed to anticipate certain occupational risks, the premises liability rationale itself does not provide a basis for delimiting the duties owed to firemen. Instead, it is an analysis of the relationship between firemen and the public whom they serve which best explains the fireman's rule.

With few exceptions, courts elsewhere have retained the fireman's rule but have based the rule on public policy considerations. Some of these courts emphasize a public policy somewhat analogous to the assumption of risk doctrine applied in negligence cases. Firemen are engaged by the public to encounter risks inherent in firefighting; they assume those risks, and therefore they should not recover for fire-related injuries.

Many cases emphasize a public policy derived from the unique relationship between firefighters and the public. The courts reason that firemen cannot recover for negligence in starting fires because it is precisely their duty to take all reasonable measures to protect lives and property from fires. In addition, some courts have pointed out that firemen receive compensation, such as salary, workers' compensation, and special injury compensation, to fight fires for the public, and that taxpayers should not have to pay such moneys for the firefighting service and then be subject to liability if they call upon the service.

We agree that the fireman's rule is best explained by public policy. It is the nature of the firefighting occupation that limits a fireman's ability to recover in tort for work-related injuries. Instead of continuing to use a rationale based on the law of premises liability, we hold that, as a matter of public policy, firemen and police officers generally cannot recover for injuries attributable to the negligence that requires their assistance. This public policy is based on a relationship between firemen and policemen and the public that calls on these safety officers specifically to confront certain hazards on behalf of the public. A fireman or police officer may not recover if injured by the negligently created risk that was the very reason for his presence on the scene in his occupational capacity. Someone who negligently creates the need for a public safety officer will not be liable to a fireman or policeman for injuries caused by this negligence.

We reiterate, however, that firemen and policemen are not barred from recovery for all improper conduct. Negligent acts not protected by the fireman's rule may include failure to warn the firemen of pre-existing hidden dangers where there was knowledge of the danger and an opportunity to warn. They also may include acts which occur subsequent to the safety officer's arrival on the scene and which are outside of his anticipated occupational hazards. The fireman's rule should not apply when the fireman sustains injuries after the initial period of his anticipated occupational risk, or from perils not reasonably foreseeable as part of that risk. In these situations a fireman or policeman is owed a duty of due care. Moreover, the fireman's rule does not apply to suits against arsonists or those engaging in similar misconduct.

PROFESSIONAL STANDARD

Walski v. Tiesenga

Supreme Court of Illinois (1978)

This appeal involves an action in malpractice against two doctors, Marvin Tiesenga and James Walsh, for personal injuries arising from the alleged negligence of the doctors during an operation on plaintiff's thyroid gland in which her left recurrent laryngeal nerve was cut. At the close of the plaintiff's case, the defendants moved for a directed verdict contending that plaintiff had failed to present evidence that the defendants' actions did not conform to the standard of care in the medical community. The trial court directed a verdict in favor of the defendants.

The plaintiff, Harriet Walski, had a long-standing history of problems with her thyroid gland. Dr. Walsh detected that plaintiff's thyroid gland was enlarged and was pressing on her trachea. Dr. Walsh arranged for Dr. Tiesenga, a general surgeon, to perform a subtotal thyroidectomy, and Dr. Walsh assisted in the surgery. After surgery, plaintiff experienced problems in breathing and speaking.

Dr. Tiesenga testified that a recurrent laryngeal nerve lies on either side of the thyroid gland. If that nerve is severed, cut or crushed, paralysis of the vocal chords would be expected. Dr. Tiesenga testified that prior to surgery he was aware of plaintiff's medical history and, in particular, the fact that she had had prior surgery on her thyroid gland. He testified that as a result of the prior surgery and radioactive treatment, there was scar tissue or adhesions around the gland and that the anatomical landmarks used to locate the recurrent laryngeal nerves were not in their normal positions, although the nerves themselves would be more or less in their usual locations. He stated he made no attempt to identify the nerve on the left but, in removing tissue from the left side of the gland, made a wide cut so as to avoid the area where the nerve might possibly be. Dr. Tiesenga testified that basically it is better practice to identify the nerve when doing an extensive thyroidectomy, certainly in the case of a thyroid which had never been operated upon before. According to the testimony, however, plaintiff's thyroidectomy was the most difficult thyroid surgery which can be performed. Because plaintiff's gland was very large and firmly adherent to the surrounding structures and because the nerve is a delicate structure which could be damaged in the process of identifying it, Dr. Tiesenga determined it was more prudent to avoid the area where the nerve might possibly be, rather than try to identify it. Dr. Tiesenga also indicated he agreed with the textbook procedure of first exposing and identifying the recurrent laryngeal nerve in those cases where the patient had had no previous thyroid surgery.

Dr. David M. Berger testified as an expert witness on plaintiff's behalf. Dr. Berger testified that there are always options available in surgery but that in his own mind it was not a proper option to skirt the left recurrent laryngeal nerve. He stated he could not testify generally but only on the basis of his own opinion as to what he considered a proper option. When asked on cross-examination if there existed a contemporary school of surgeons that will skirt the nerve when they encounter a host of adhesions, Dr. Berger responded that "in the institutions in which I trained that is not the teaching. And I can't speak for other institutions or other areas of training. I can only speak for my own." Defense counsel read a quotation to Dr. Berger from a medical textbook which indicated that there existed a certain amount of controversy in the medical community concerning deliberate exposure of the laryngeal nerve. The quotation concluded with the remark that the situation remained one in which each surgeon will find the approach which suits him best. Dr. Berger indicated that he did not fully agree with that statement, but indicated the decision whether or not to expose the nerve depends on the surgeon and the technique and care he uses.

One element of a cause of action for medical malpractice is proof of the standard of care by which the defendant physician's conduct is to be measured. The appellate decisions in this State have held that the plaintiff in a medical malpractice action generally must establish the standard of care through expert testimony. The plaintiff must then prove that, judged in the light of these standards, the doctor was unskillful or negligent and that his want of skill or care caused the injury to the plaintiff.

Plaintiff here had the burden of establishing that the defendant doctors were guilty of malpractice. She failed, however, to introduce evidence of the standard of care to which the defendants were bound to adhere. Plaintiff's expert, Dr. Berger, testified only concerning his own personal preference for isolating the laryngeal nerve under the facts presented to him in the hypothetical question. He at no time testified that there was a generally accepted medical standard of care, or skill which required the identification of the laryngeal nerve under the circumstances. Plaintiff's witness Dr. Kowal testified that the decision whether to isolate the nerve varied from case to case.

Other jurisdictions, when presented only, as we are here, with conflicting opinions by testifying physicians of what they personally consider correct technique under the circumstances, have concluded that the plaintiff has failed to present sufficient evidence of a standard of care in the medical community to submit the case to the jury. It is insufficient for plaintiff to establish a Prima facie case merely to present testimony of another physician that he would have acted differently from the defendant, since medicine is not an exact science. It is rather a profession which involves the exercise of individual judgment within the framework of established procedures. Differences in opinion are consistent with the exercise of due care.

Without evidence of a standard of care to which the defendant doctors were bound to adhere there is nothing against which a jury would measure the defendants' conduct and no means for it to resolve the factual question of whether the defendants deviated from the established standard and, therefore, were negligent.

Bruni v. Tatsumi

Supreme Court of Ohio (1976)

Plaintiffs, Dorothy Bruni and her husband, Joseph Bruni, filed suit against Dr. Tetsuo Tatsumi and his associate, Dr. Francis C. Boyer, for alleged medical malpractice committed by both defendant doctors while Dorothy Bruni was a patient.

At the conclusion of all the evidence, the trial court sustained a motion for a directed verdict in favor of both defendants. Plaintiffs thereupon appealed to the Court of Appeals which affirmed the judgment of the Court of Common Pleas.

In August 1968, plaintiff experienced some difficulty with her right eye. It became red and painful, and she was admitted to Aultman General Hospital where Dr. Tatsumi, a neurosurgeon, performed a series of arteriograms and a diagnosis was made of 'carotid artery cavernous sinus fistula.' This condition behind her right eye caused a leakage of blood. A surgical procedure was performed which involved the insertion of a selverstone clamp in her neck around plaintiff's right carotid artery. Complications later developed and plaintiff suffered a stroke. A craniotomy was later performed.

At the trial, as part of plaintiffs' case, a neurosurgeon, Dr. Wilbur George Bingham, Jr., from Columbus testified by deposition. He testified that certain surgical procedures used upon plaintiff by defendant, Dr. Tatsumi, were not accepted medical practice in Columbus. Then he was asked:

'Q. Would your opinion still hold true, Doctor, for any moderately large, or large metropolitan area in which neurosurgery is practiced throughout this country?

'A. I believe it would.'

Plaintiffs contend that this answer establishes the standard of care in the medical community where this patient was treated, Canton.

Earlier in his deposition, the witness, when asked his opinion about certain things done by one defendant in connection with the treatment of plaintiff and 'whether he is using accepted and good medical technique and procedure,' answered, 'Well, I do not have an opinion about anything that goes on in Canton. '

Later in his deposition, when asked if his opinions as to standard of care and as to good medical practice would apply as well to the vicinity of Cleveland, Ohio, he replied, 'I do not know how they do cases like this in Cleveland.' One of the expert witnesses testifying for defendant was a Cleveland neurosurgeon, Dr. William Trowbridge.

In evaluating the conduct of a physician and surgeon charged with malpractice, the test is whether the physician, in the performance of his service, either did some particular thing or things that physicians and surgeons, in that medical community, of ordinary skill, care and diligence would not have done under the same or similar circumstances, or failed or omitted to do some particular thing or things which physicians and surgeons of ordinary skill, care and diligence would have done under the same or similar circumstances. He is required to exercise the average degree of skill, care and diligence exercised by members of the same medical specialty community in similar situations.

As early as 1897, Circuit Judge William H. Taft (later Chief Justice of the United States Supreme Court) wrote as follows in interpreting the Ohio law on malpractice:

'Before the plaintiff can recover, she must show by affirmative evidence-first, that defendant was unskillful or negligent: and, second, that his want of skill or care caused injury to the plaintiff. If either element is lacking in her proof, she has presented no case for the consideration of the jury. But when a case concerns the highly specialized art of treating an eye for cataract, or for the mysterious and dread disease of glaucoma, with respect to which a layman can have no knowledge at all, the court and jury must be dependent on expert evidence. There can be no other guide, and, where want of skill or attention is not thus shown by expert evidence applied to the facts, there is no evidence of it proper to be submitted to the jury.'

Under Ohio law, in order to establish medical malpractice, it must be shown by a preponderance of the evidence that the injury complained of was caused by the doing of some particular thing or things that a physician or surgeon of ordinary skill, care and diligence would not have done under like or similar conditions or circumstances, or by the failure or omission to do some particular thing or things that such a physician or surgeon would have done under like or similar conditions and circumstances, and that the injury complained of was the direct result of such doing or failing to do some one or more of such particular things.

Failure to establish the recognized standards of the medical community has been fatal to the presentation of a prima facie case of malpractice by the plaintiffs

Proof of the recognized standards must necessarily be provided through expert testimony. This expert must be qualified to express an opinion concerning the specific standard of care that prevails in the medical community in which the alleged malpractice took place, according to the body of law that has developed in this area of evidence. Courts generally have adopted one of four rules governing the standard of care with which a medical witness from one locality must be familiar in order to be competent to testify in a malpractice action against another physician or surgeon in a different locality.

Another important consideration in this case is that the procedure in question was in the field of neurosurgery and both the defendant and the expert witness were board-certified neurosurgeons. The broad issue facing this court is whether any locality rule of evidence in connection with expert medical testimony in a specialty is operative in Ohio. In this case, the trial court granted defendants' motion for directed verdict at the conclusion of all of the testimony.

In ruling on defendants' motion, the trial court, in part, said:

'In evaluating the conduct of a physician charged with malpractice, the test is whether, in the performance of his services, he either did some thing or things that physicians in that medical community of ordinary skill, care and diligence would not have done under the same or similar circumstances, or failed or omitted to do some particular thing or things that physicians in that medical community would have done under the same or similar circumstances.

'In nearly all malpractice cases and certainly in the instant case, as is evident from the fact that plaintiffs presented only one witness, a neurosurgeon from Columbus, Ohio, the testimony of an expert was necessary to meet this burden.

'Plaintiffs' expert stated that he did not have an opinion of 'anything that goes on in Canton, Ohio,' and he did not know 'how they do cases like this in Cleveland.' There was no other testimony presented by plaintiffs on this issue and the quoted statements of this witness nullified his other testimony that his methods of procedure were followed in 'metropolitan areas.'

"Failure to establish the recognized standards of the medical community is fatal to the presentation of a prima facie case of malpractice by the plaintiff.'

The rationale for the locality rule was first expressed in Small v. Howard (1880), 128 Mass. 131, 136, in the following language:

'It is a matter of common knowledge that a physician in a small country village does not usually make a specialty of surgery, and, however well informed he may be in the theory of all parts of his profession, he would, generally speaking, be but seldom called upon as a surgeon to perform difficult operations. He would have but few opportunities of observation and practice in that line such as public hospitals or large cities would afford. The defendant was applied to, being the practitioner in a small village, and we think it was correct to rule that 'he was bound to possess that skill only which physicians and surgeons of ordinary ability and skill, practicing in similar localities, with opportunities for no larger experience, ordinarily possess; and he was not bound to possess that high degree of art and skill possessed by eminent surgeons practicing in large cities, and making a specialty of the practice of surgery."

The basis for this rule was that a physician at that time in a small town lacked the opportunity to keep abreast of the advances in the medical profession and that he did not have the most modern facilities to provide care and treatment for his patients. Under these circumstances it would be unfair to hold such a doctor to the same standards of care as doctors who have such opportunities and facilities in larger cities.

Admittedly, there was ample justification for a local-standard rule then and for many years following. But in this modern era means of transportation facilitate opportunities for physicians and surgeons from small communities to attend up-to-date medical seminars; the general circulation of medical journals makes new developments readily available to them and they can easily communicate with the most advanced medical centers in the country.

So, the locality rule has been increasingly eroded as being antiquated and unrealistic, especially in the medical specialties field.

What the trial court had before it in this case was truly the competency of a board-certified neurosurgeon, an acknowledged specialist from Columbus, testifying about the practice of another neurosurgeon, the defendant, in Canton. The latter is 'obligated to bring to the discharge of his duty that degree of skill and knowledge possessed by physicians who are specialists in the light of present-day scientific knowledge.' Accordingly, the standard of care in this case is that owed to a patient by the community of neurosurgeons. Geographical conditions or circumstances do not control either the standard of the specialist's care or the competence of the expert's testimony.

Here, the credentials of the expert, Dr. Wilbur George Bingham, Jr., are flawless. His testimony, in part, at the trial was that some of the procedures used by Dr. Tetsuo Tatsumi in treating the plaintiff were not accepted medical procedures. A jury question was presented thereby and the jury should have been permitted to pass on it under a proper charge of the court. For the reasons stated, it was error to direct a verdict for defendant.

Arato v. Avedon

Supreme Court of California (1993)

Miklos Arato was a successful 42–year–old electrical contractor and part-time real estate developer when, early in 1980, his internist diagnosed a failing kidney. On July 21, 1980, in the course of surgery to remove the kidney, the operating surgeon detected a tumor on the tail or distal portion of Mr. Arato's pancreas. Concerned that the cancer could recur and might have infiltrated adjacent organs, Mr. Arato's surgeon referred him to a group of oncology practitioners for follow-up treatment.

During his initial visit to the oncologists, Mr. Arato filled out a multipage questionnaire. Among the some 150 questions asked was whether patients "wished to be told the truth about their condition" or whether they wanted the physician to "bear the burden" for them. Mr. Arato checked the box indicating that he wished to be told the truth. However, neither the operating surgeon nor the treating oncologists specifically disclosed to the patient or his wife the high statistical mortality rate associated with pancreatic cancer.

Mr. Arato's treating physicians justified not disclosing statistical life expectancy data to their patient on disparate grounds. According to the testimony of his surgeon, Mr. Arato had exhibited great anxiety over his condition, so much so that his surgeon determined that it would have been medically inappropriate to disclose specific mortality rates. All of the treating physicians testified that statistical life expectancy data had little predictive value when applied to a particular patient with individualized symptoms, medical history, character traits and other variables. A year and four days following surgery, Mr. Arato died. [As Mr. Arato did not appreciate that he might die soon, he did nothing to wrap up his business affairs, causing significant economic damages to his business].

Sensitivity to context seems appropriate in the case of life expectancy projections for cancer patients based on statistical samples. Without exception, the testimony of every physician-witness at trial confirmed what is evident even to a nonprofessional: statistical morbidity values derived from the experience of population groups are inherently unreliable and offer little assurance regarding the fate of the individual patient; indeed, to assume that such data are conclusive in themselves smacks of a refusal to explore treatment alternatives and the medical abdication of the patient's well-being. Certainly the jury here heard evidence of articulable grounds for the conclusion that the particular features of Mr. Arato's case distinguished it from the typical population of pancreatic cancer sufferers and their dismal statistical probabilities—a fact plaintiffs impliedly acknowledged at trial in conceding that the oncologic referral of Mr. Arato and ensuing chemotherapy were not in themselves medically negligent.

Rather than mandate the disclosure of specific information as a matter of law, the better rule is to instruct the jury that a physician is under a legal duty to disclose to the patient all material information—that is, information which the physician knows or should know would be regarded as significant by a reasonable person in the patient's position when deciding to accept or reject a recommended medical procedure—needed to make an informed decision regarding a proposed treatment.

Here, the evidence was more than sufficient to support the jury's finding that defendants had reasonably disclosed to Mr. Arato information material to his decision whether to undergo the proposed chemotherapy/radiation treatment.

Winkjer v. Herr

Supreme Court of North Dakota (1979)

Medical Malpractice

Generally, a prima facie case of medical malpractice must consist of evidence establishing the applicable standard of care, violation of that standard, and a causal relationship between the violation and the harm complained of. A physician is required to exercise such reasonable care and skill as are exercised ordinarily by physicians practicing in similar localities in the same general line of practice.

Defendant in this case diagnosed the plaintiff as having glaucoma. Plaintiff alleged that defendant's diagnosis of and treatment for glaucoma was negligent because plaintiff actually had ocular hypertension. Defendant's experts agreed, however, that defendant's diagnosis of and treatment for glaucoma was proper. In addition to having elevated intraocular pressure, plaintiff was a myope and not only is glaucoma more common in myopes but also a myope having elevated intraocular pressure is more likely to have subsequent damage to his optic nerve. Also, plaintiff's mother had glaucoma and it is known that if there is a history of glaucoma in a family there is an increased likelihood that a given individual will have glaucoma and if that history is on the maternal side the probability increases even further, the experts stated in their depositions there are also a number of judgmental factors which affect a physician's decision on whether or not a patient has glaucoma such as excessive pigmentation, the shape of the optic disc, whether or not the discs are symmetric or if there have been changes in the discs over a period of time. Based upon these various indications of glaucoma, the experts stated the defendant's decision to treat the plaintiff for glaucoma rather than wait and watch whether or not plaintiff developed disc damage was proper. We conclude this information was sufficient to show there was no genuine issue of whether or not defendant exercised the proper degree of care and skill and thus shifted the burden of proving the existence of a genuine issue of fact to the plaintiff. We now examine plaintiff's argument to determine if he met that burden.

Evidence as to the degree of care and skill required of a physician in diagnosing or treating one's ailment, as well as any departure from that standard, must generally be established by expert testimony. The exception to this general rule is "such expert testimony is not necessary where the matters to be proved fall within an area of common knowledge and developing lay comprehension of medical techniques and where the results of surgical or medical treatment, viewed in light of all the circumstances, provide a sufficient evidentiary basis to support an inference of negligence."

The rule as to the proper standard of care and skill is but an adaptation of the general standard of negligence to a group required to act as reasonable men possessing their medical talents presumably would. Thus where a physician's activity constitutes a blunder so egregious that a layman is capable of comprehending its enormity, medical testimony is not necessary to test the propriety of that activity.

Plaintiff argued that defendant's prescription of phospholine iodide for plaintiff's condition, which time has proven was ocular hypertension, was a blunder so egregious a layman is capable of comprehending its enormity without the assistance of expert medical testimony. In support of his argument, plaintiff offered a letter that was written by the defendant at the request of the plaintiff to the Federal Aviation Administration stating that defendant's diagnosis of plaintiff's condition had changed from chronic open angle glaucoma to ocular hypertension. Plaintiff also offered statements from the physicians desk reference, warnings from the Food and Drug Administration's clearance of phospholine iodide, and instructions for administration accompanying the drug, that phospholine iodide was not recommended for ocular hypertension.

Although plaintiff may be correct in his contention that the published warnings and recommendations, combined with the common knowledge doctrine, may have been sufficient to present a prima facie case of negligence in the prescription of phospholine iodide for a diagnosis of ocular hypertension, those are not the facts of this case. Rather, there was a prescription for a condition diagnosed as glaucoma. Expert statements in the form of depositions agreed, and plaintiff's published material was not to the contrary, that phospholine iodide is a proper drug to be used in the treatment of glaucoma. The real issue, then, is whether or not defendant was negligent in diagnosing glaucoma as plaintiff's condition which time has shown was actually ocular hypertension. Treatment of a patient with the right drug for the wrong disease is not negligence unless the diagnosis of the disease was negligent. The mere fact that a physician was mistaken in his diagnosis is not alone sufficient to warrant a finding of negligence.

We conclude the factors relied upon by the defendant in the diagnosis and treatment for glaucoma were not those commonly susceptible of understanding by a lay person without the assistance of expert medical testimony. We also conclude plaintiff has failed to meet his burden of refuting the showing made by the defendant that there was no genuine issue of fact that defendant's diagnosis and treatment was not carried on with the required degree of due care and skill.

Informed Consent

Plaintiff also alleged defendant was negligent under the doctrine of informed consent for not warning the plaintiff that treatment with phospholine iodide could cause cataracts. A major element of any negligence action is the existence and extent of a duty owed the defendant by the plaintiff. Generally there exists the duty of reasonable disclosure of the available choices with respect to the proposed therapy and of the material and known risks potentially involved in each. A more difficult question arises in this case as to the extent of the duty and the standard by which it should be measured.

The test for determining whether a particular peril must be divulged is its materiality to the patient's decision: all risks potentially affecting the decision must be unmasked. Failure to disclose a risk that would have been disclosed under accepted medical practice thus should be a sufficient, but not a necessary, condition of liability. No reason appears to justify withholding information from a patient, in light of his right to self-determination, if medical practice dictates disclosure. But even if his disclosure conforms to accepted medical practice, a physician nevertheless should be liable if he fails to inform the patient of a significant risk of treatment or of an alternative treatment.

A duty to disclose can arise only if the physician knew or should have known of the risks to be disclosed. Also, a physician is not required to disclose all possible risks and dangers of the proposed procedure but only those that are significant in terms of their seriousness and likelihood of occurrence. There is no need to disclose risks of little consequence, those that are extremely remote, or those that are common knowledge as inherent in the treatment. If a risk was not known to exist, clearly a physician cannot be held liable for failure to inform his patient.

Defendant's experts in their depositions and affidavits agreed that although there was evidence that phospholine iodide was cataractous, there was no evidence indicating phospholine iodide was cataractous in the levels and lengths of time prescribed by the defendant. The plaintiff did not offer expert testimony to refute the showing of the defendant that there was no genuine issue of fact as to a known risk to be disclosed. Even if we consider the material offered by the plaintiff that phospholine iodide was cataractous, that information does not indicate at what levels and over what length of time the drug has been shown to possibly cause cataracts. There can be no liability for a physician to disclose a risk that was unknown in the manner in which a particular drug or treatment was prescribed.

The judgment of the district court is affirmed.

NO DUTY AND EXCEPTIONS

Estate of Cilley v. Lane

Supreme Judicial Court of Maine (2009)

In 2003, Jennifer Lane and Joshua Cilley began a romantic relationship that continued over the next year and one-half. Although the two had discussed marriage, they had also broken up and reunited several times during those months. On January 30, 2005, Lane told Cilley that they needed to take some time off from their relationship, but that they would still be friends. During the late afternoon of the next day, January 31, 2005, Lane was drinking beer and eating pizza with two friends who lived near her at a trailer park. In the early evening, after drinking four or five beers, Lane left her friend's trailer and walked a short distance to her own trailer to call her daughter.

Approximately five minutes after Lane reached her home, Cilley arrived and entered. Lane told him to leave; Cilley refused and initially blocked Lane's attempt to exit the trailer. Lane claims that she tried to use her cell phone to call a neighbor for help with removing Cilley from her home. Lane also claims that, while she was on the phone, Cilley went out to his car, and returned carrying a small caliber rifle. He then grabbed her cell phone, threw it against the wall, and broke it.

Lane walked out of her trailer. As she was doing so, she heard a loud pop, which she later described as sounding like a firecracker. Lane looked back, and saw Cilley fall to the floor. She then heard him say that "it was an accident" and "it was not supposed to happen." Lane, who did not see any blood, did not investigate or attempt to assess whether Cilley was injured. She returned to her friend's trailer and told her two friends that Cilley had pretended to shoot himself inside her trailer.

Lane's friends looked out the window and saw Cilley lying on the steps to Lane's trailer, halfway outside the door. They went over to Cilley, and noted that he was mumbling, "It was an accident." One of the friends picked up the gun lying near Cilley, and asked him if he had been shot. She noted that Cilley was turning white, and had difficulty breathing. The other friend went to a neighboring trailer and called 911. Cilley could not be resuscitated at the hospital. He died as a result of a single gunshot wound to his abdomen. According to the physician who treated him, Cilley could have been resuscitated if he had arrived at the hospital five to ten minutes earlier.

A duty is an obligation, to which the law will give recognition and effect, to conform to a particular manner of conduct toward another. The law does not impose a general obligation to protect others from harm not created by the actor. The fact that the actor realizes or should realize that action on his part is necessary for another's aid or protection does not of itself impose upon him a duty to take such action. Because Cilley was a trespasser at the time of the incident, Lane's only duty to him was to refrain from wanton, willful, or reckless behavior. To entitle a trespasser to recover for an injury, he must do more than show negligence. It must appear that a wanton or intentional injury was inflicted on him. Lane's failure to contact emergency assistance for Cilley immediately after she heard the pop does not rise to the level of wanton, willful, or reckless behavior because Lane did not create the danger to Cilley, nor commit any act that led to his initial injury. Our cases are devoid of any precedent that would require a landowner to affirmatively act to help a trespasser injured through no fault or act of the landowner.

With its second argument, the Estate urges us to recognize a new common law duty: the duty to seek affirmative emergency assistance through reasonable means. The Estate contends that the mores of the community and the abundance of technology mandate recognition of this duty in order to enhance public safety. A person who witnesses another's injury, the Estate contends, although not required to render any aid herself, must contact emergency assistance as long as she can do so in a safe manner. In the alternative, the Estate argued that the duty could be limited, so that the duty to seek emergency assistance would apply only when a homeowner witnesses injury to another on her property, regardless of the injured person's legal status. In support of both alternatives, the Estate asserts that a special relationship arises when the witness observes injury to the other party, and it is this relationship that imposes a duty to act, regardless of any other relationship between the parties and regardless of whether the witness caused or could have foreseen the harm.

We have held that a party does not have an affirmative duty to aid or warn another person in peril unless the party created the danger or the two people had a special relationship that society recognizes as sufficient to create the duty. The Estate has asked us to add a new relationship to this list, and to impose a narrow but unlimited duty to contact emergency assistance.

The duty proposed by the Estate stands in direct opposition to the principle that a person does not have an affirmative duty to aid or warn another person in peril. Broadly, this rule is known as the "no duty to rescue" rule. In response to a few notorious instances of bystander inaction, some state legislatures have enacted laws imposing criminal or civil liability for failing to render reasonable assistance to a person in danger or to immediately report a crime that has been committed. Although Cilley's family did ask the Maine Legislature to enact a law imposing criminal sanctions and creating civil liability for persons who observe that another has received a serious injury and then fails to immediately report and request first aid for that person, the Legislature did not enact the requested law. In accordance with our precedent, we also must decline the Estate's request that we recognize a new common law duty.

Wakulich v. Mraz

Supreme Court of Illinois (2003)

Following the death of her 16–year–old daughter Elizabeth Wakulich, plaintiff Mary Louise Wakulich as special administrator of Elizabeth's estate, brought an action alleging claims under the Wrongful Death Act. According to the Complaint, during the evening of June 15 and continuing into the early morning hours of June 16, Elizabeth was at the home of defendants, Michael Mraz, his brother Brian Mraz, and their father Dennis Mraz. At that time, Michael was 21 years old, and Brian was 18 years old. Plaintiff alleged that Michael and Brian induced Elizabeth, by offering monies, by goading and by applying great social pressure, to drink a quart bottle of Goldschlager, a highly alcoholic and dangerous beverage, and that Michael and Brian knew, or should have known, that Elizabeth, a minor, could not appreciate the dangers associated with consumption of excessive amounts of alcoholic beverages.

After consuming the entire bottle of Goldschlager, Elizabeth lost consciousness. Michael and Brian placed her in the family room of their home, where they observed her vomiting profusely and making gurgling sounds. They later removed her vomit-saturated blouse and placed a pillow under her head to prevent aspiration. Brian and Michael allegedly refused to drive Elizabeth home, did not contact her parents, did not seek medical attention, and actually prevented other individuals at the home from calling 911 or seeking other medical intervention. During the morning of June 16, Dennis ordered Michael and Brian to remove Elizabeth from their home, which they did. Elizabeth died later that day.

We consider first those counts which alleged that Michael and Brian were negligent in providing an alcoholic beverage to Elizabeth and inducing her to consume a dangerous amount. Relying on over a century of precedent, we hold Illinois has no common law cause of action for injuries arising out of the sale or gift of alcoholic beverages; that the legislature has preempted the field of alcohol-related liability; and that any change in the law governing alcohol-related liability should be made by the General Assembly, or not at all. We thus decline to adopt any form of social host liability for serving alcohol.

We next consider whether, as defendants argue, those counts of the complaint alleging a voluntary undertaking by Michael and Brian are fatally defective. Generally, pursuant to the voluntary undertaking theory of liability, one who undertakes, gratuitously or for consideration, to render services to another is subject to liability for bodily harm caused to the other by one's failure to exercise due care in the performance of the undertaking.

Plaintiff alleged that Michael and Brian voluntarily undertook to care for Elizabeth after she became unconscious. As an initial matter, defendants argue that plaintiff's voluntary undertaking theory is simply an attempt to circumvent the rule against social host liability. This argument fails. The liability of defendants, if any, is not contingent on their status as social hosts. Indeed, it is irrelevant for purposes of plaintiff's voluntary undertaking counts whether defendants were acting as social hosts on the evening of June 15, and supplied the alcohol which Elizabeth consumed. Rather, based on the allegations of the complaint, defendants' liability arises by virtue of their voluntary assumption of a duty to care for Elizabeth after she became unconscious, irrespective of the circumstances leading up to that point. Thus, plaintiff's voluntary undertaking theory does not circumvent the rule against social host liability.

In a related argument, defendants maintain that there is no special relationship between a social host and a guest which would impose a duty upon the social host to seek medical assistance. This argument, like the one before it, necessarily fails. Plaintiff did not allege that defendants were under a legal duty to seek medical assistance for Elizabeth, or to otherwise care for her, by virtue of their status as social hosts or their relationship with Elizabeth. Plaintiff alleged that defendants voluntarily undertook to care for Elizabeth. By undertaking to act, defendants became subject to a duty with respect to the manner of performance. In other words, having undertaken to care for Elizabeth, defendants were obligated to exercise due care in the performance of that undertaking.

Here, plaintiff has alleged that defendants failed to summon aid by contacting Elizabeth's parents, failed to otherwise obtain medical assistance that evening or the following morning when she was still unconscious, and prevented other persons from obtaining aid, proximately causing her death. These allegations, liberally construed, sufficiently allege that defendants' conduct increased the risk of harm to Elizabeth.

Importantly, plaintiff's theory in this case is not that defendants failed to perform at all and are liable for their nonfeasance. Plaintiff's theory is that defendants negligently performed their voluntary undertaking and are liable for their misfeasance. Although defendant's alleged failure to summon medical assistance is itself inaction, it is also one of the ways in which plaintiff claims defendants negligently performed their voluntary undertaking to care for Elizabeth, which is affirmative misconduct.

In any event, defendants overlook that part of the complaint which states that defendants actually prevented other individuals at the home from calling 911 or seeking other medical intervention. Thus, plaintiff has alleged an affirmative act by defendants, not simply a failure to act.

We conclude that the allegations of plaintiff's complaint sufficiently stated a cause of action based on a voluntary undertaking theory.

Farwell v. Keaton

Supreme Court of Michigan (1976)

Siegrist and Farwell drove to a trailer rental lot to return an automobile which Siegrist had borrowed from a friend who worked there. While waiting for the friend to finish work, Siegrist and Farwell consumed some beer. Two girls walked by the entrance to the lot. Siegrist and Farwell attempted to engage them in conversation; they left Farwell's car and followed the girls to a drive-in restaurant down the street.

The girls complained to their friends in the restaurant that they were being followed. Six boys chased Siegrist and Farwell back to the lot. Siegrist escaped unharmed, but Farwell was severely beaten. Siegrist found Farwell underneath his automobile in the lot. Ice was applied to Farwell's head. Siegrist then drove Farwell around for approximately two hours, stopping at a number of drive-in restaurants. Farwell went to sleep in the back seat of his car. Around midnight Siegrist drove the car to the home of Farwell's grandparents, parked it in the driveway, unsuccessfully attempted to rouse Farwell, and left. Farwell's grandparents discovered him in the car the next morning and took him to the hospital. He died three days later of an epidural hematoma.

At trial, plaintiff contended that had Siegrist taken Farwell to the hospital, or had he notified someone of Farwell's condition and whereabouts, Farwell would not have died. A neurosurgeon testified that if a person in Farwell's condition is taken to a doctor before, or within half an hour after, consciousness is lost, there is an 85 to 88 per cent chance of survival.

Siegrist contends that he is not liable for failure to obtain medical assistance for Farwell because he had no duty to do so. Courts have been slow to recognize a duty to render aid to a person in peril. Where such a duty has been found, it has been predicated upon the existence of a special relationship between the parties; in such a case, if defendant knew or should have known of the other person's peril, he is required to render reasonable care under all the circumstances.

Farwell and Siegrist were companions on a social venture. Implicit in such a common undertaking is the understanding that one will render assistance to the other when he is in peril if he can do so without endangering himself. Siegrist knew or should have known when he left Farwell, who was badly beaten and unconscious, in the back seat of his car that no one would find him before morning. Under these circumstances, to say that Siegrist had no duty to obtain medical assistance or at least to notify someone of Farwell's condition and whereabouts would be shocking to humanitarian considerations and fly in the face of the commonly accepted code of social conduct. Courts will find a duty where, in general, reasonable men would recognize it and agree that it exists. Farwell and Siegrist were companions engaged in a common undertaking; there was a special relationship between the parties. Because Siegrist knew or should have known of the peril Farwell was in and could render assistance without endangering himself he had an affirmative duty to come to Farwell's aid.

Podias v. Mairs

Superior Court of New Jersey, Appellate Division (2007)

In the evening of September 27 and early morning hours of September 28, eighteen-year old Michael Mairs was drinking beer at the home of a friend Thomas Chomko. He eventually left with two other friends, defendants Swanson and Newell, both also eighteen years of age, to return to Monmouth University where all three were students. Mairs was driving. Swanson was in the front passenger seat and Newell was seated in the rear of the vehicle where he apparently fell asleep. It was raining and the road was wet.

At approximately 2:00 a.m., while traveling on the Garden State Parkway, Mairs lost control of the car, struck a motorcycle driven by Antonios Podias, and went over the guardrail. All three exited the vehicle and huddled around the car. Swanson saw Podias lying in the roadway and because he saw no movement and heard no sound, told Mairs and Newell that he thought Mairs had killed the cyclist. At that time, there were no other cars on the road.

Even though all three had cell phones, no one called for assistance. Instead they argued about whether the car had collided with the motorcycle. And, within minutes of the accident, Mairs called his girlfriend on Newell's cell phone since his was lost when he got out of the car. Swanson also used his cell phone, placing seventeen calls in the next one-and-one-half hours. Twenty-six additional calls were made from Newell's cell phone in the two-and-one-half hours after the accident, the first just three minutes post-accident. None of these, however, were emergency assistance calls. As Swanson later explained: "I didn't feel responsible to call the police." And Newell just "didn't want to get in trouble."

After about five or ten minutes, the trio all decided to get back in the car and leave the scene. Swanson directed, "we have to get to an exit." Upon their return to the car, Swanson instructed Mairs "not to bring up his name or involve him in what occurred" and "don't get us [Swanson and Newell] involved, we weren't there." The three then drove south on the parkway for a short distance until Mairs' car broke down. Mairs pulled over and waited in the bushes for his girlfriend to arrive, while Swanson and Newell ran off into the woods, where Newell eventually lost sight of Swanson. Before they deserted him, Swanson again reminded Mairs that "there was no need to get Swanson and Newell in trouble." Mairs thought Swanson was "just scared" and that both defendants were concerned about Mairs "drinking and driving." Meanwhile, a motor vehicle operated by Patricia Uribe ran over Podias, who died as a result of injuries sustained in these accidents.

Traditional tort theory emphasizes individual liability, which is to say that each particular defendant who is to be charged with responsibility must be proceeding negligently. Ordinarily, then, mere presence at the commission of the wrong, or failure to object to it, is not enough to charge one with responsibility inasmuch as there is no duty to take affirmative steps to interfere. Because of this reluctance to countenance inaction as a basis of liability, the common law has persistently refused to impose on a stranger the moral obligation of common humanity to go to the aid of another human being who is in danger, even if the other is in danger of losing his life. Thus, the common law rule imposes no independent duty of rescue at all and relieves a bystander from any obligation to provide affirmative aid or emergency assistance, even if the bystander has the ability to help.

Of course, exceptions are as longstanding as the rule. For instance, if one already has a pre-existing legal duty to render assistance, who either by statute or "public calling" has undertaken a duty to give service, then it is that duty which impels him to act, for which omission he may be liable. So too, at common law, those under no pre-existing duty may nevertheless be liable if they choose to volunteer emergency assistance for another but do so negligently. Over the years, liability for inaction has been gradually extended still further to a limited group of relations, in which custom, public sentiment, and views of social policy have led courts to find a duty of affirmative action. Thus, a duty to render assistance may either be contractual, relational or transactional.

To establish liability, however, such relationships need not be limited to those where a pre-existing duty exists, or involving economic ties, or dependent on the actor's status as, for instance, a landowner or business owner. Rather, it may only be necessary to find some definite relation between the parties of such a character that social policy justifies the imposition of a duty to act. So, for instance, the general duty which arises in many relations to take reasonable precautions for the safety of others may include the obligation to exercise control over the conduct of third persons with dangerous propensities.

Actually, the extension of liability based on these and other relational features mirrors evolving notions of duty, which are no longer tethered to rigid formalisms or static historical classifications. This progression is not surprising. The assessment of duty necessarily includes an examination of the relationships between and among the parties. The fundamental question is whether the plaintiff's interests are entitled to legal protection against the defendant's conduct. In this regard, the determination of the existence of duty is ultimately a question of fairness and public policy, which in turn draws upon notions of fairness, common sense, and morality.

The duty determination, which is a judicial one, involves a complex analysis that weighs and balances several related factors, including the nature of the underlying risk of harm, that is, its foreseeability and severity, the opportunity and ability to exercise care to prevent the harm, the comparative interests of, and the relationships between or among the parties, and, ultimately, based on considerations of public policy and fairness, the societal interest in the proposed solution.

Governed by these principles, we are satisfied that the record admits of sufficient facts from which a reasonable jury could find defendants breached a duty which proximately caused the victim's death. In our view, given the circumstances, the imposition of a duty upon defendants does not offend notions of fairness and common decency and is in accord with public policy.

South v. Amtrak

Supreme Court of North Dakota (1980)

An action was commenced by South for damages sustained as a result of a collision between a pickup truck, owned and driven by South, and the Railroad's train at the Barrett Avenue crossing in Larimore, North Dakota, on January 17, 1976. South sustained serious injuries in the collision. He sued the Railroad for damages on a theory of negligence, and his wife, Delores, also sued the Railroad for damages allegedly incurred by the loss of her husband's consortium.

South lived in Larimore, and on the morning of the collision he, for the first time, was driving to work at a new missile site location to which he had been assigned. To drive to the old work site South crossed the railroad tracks in Larimore at the Towner Avenue crossing, but in order to drive to the new work site South took a route which crossed the tracks at the Barrett Avenue crossing. As South approached the Barrett Avenue crossing traveling south at approximately 20 miles per hour, a westbound Amtrak passenger train was also approaching the Barrett Avenue crossing traveling at approximately 68 miles per hour. Both the train and South's pickup reached the crossing at approximately the same instant and the front of the train engine collided with the left front portion of South's vehicle.

The Railroad asserts that it was not negligent in the operation of its train and that the maintenance of the crossbuck sign was not a material issue because South was aware of the location of the railroad tracks running through Larimore. Several witnesses testified, on behalf of the Railroad, that the train whistle did blow a warning on the morning of the collision. The Railroad also attempted to prove that South was negligent in failing to ascertain the presence of the train and in failing to safely stop his vehicle prior to reaching the railroad tracks.

At the conclusion of the trial the jury returned a verdict in favor of South and his wife, Delores, against the Railroad. The jury, upon finding that the Railroad was 100 percent negligent and that South was not negligent, awarded general and special damages of $935,000 to South and $125,000 to Delores South.

Prior to opening argument the Railroad made a motion to exclude all evidence referring to the train engineer's failure to cover South with his parka or to otherwise assist South at the scene of the accident, on the ground that such evidence was prejudicial. The engineer who was operating the train at the time of the accident died prior to the commencement of the trial in this case. Prior to his death, the Souths' counsel had taken the engineer's deposition, and it was part of this deposition testimony that the Railroad sought to exclude in its motion.

The motion was denied, and during opening argument the Souths' counsel made the following statement:

The evidence will show that as he was lying there, and I'm taking the deposition of Mr. Decker, the engineer, I says to Mr. Decker, 'Did you have anything to cover him up with?' 'No, I told the police,' he says. 'Was it cold out? What did you do?' 'I went to the cab.' I said, 'Did you have anything to cover him up with?' He said, 'My new jacket.' I says, 'Why didn't you go and cover him up?' He says, 'That was a brand-new jacket. It cost $55. I wasn't going to get it bloody. The hood cost me $7 alone and I was going to be in Devils Lake the next day and I didn't want to get cold. I wasn't going to get a jacket bloody for anybody.' I said, 'If you'd have known he was alive, would you have covered him up?' He said, 'No, I wouldn't ruin that jacket.'

Subsequent to opening arguments, the trial court ruled in chambers that he would not allow certain parts of the engineer's deposition testimony regarding the parka incident to be read to the jury because its prejudicial effect outweighed its probative value.

In its instructions to the jury the trial court stated that if the jury found by a fair preponderance of the evidence that the Railroad failed to provide any necessary care for South after the accident he could recover for damages proximately resulting from such failure.

The Railroad asserts that counsel's opening statement was highly prejudicial and constitutes grounds for a new trial. The Railroad also asserts that it was improper for the Souths' counsel to comment on the parka incident during closing argument after the court had ruled to exclude such matters. The Railroad's latter assertion is based on an inaccurate premise of the trial court's ruling. The foregoing quoted portions of the deposition which were read to the jury demonstrate that the trial court did not exclude all testimony regarding the parka incident. Only certain statements made by the engineer which the court concluded were highly prejudicial and of little or no probative value were deleted from the deposition testimony. Provided the trial court did not err in admitting this evidence of the engineer's failure to assist South, then plaintiff counsel's comments during closing argument were not improper.

In order to determine whether it was error for the trial court to admit evidence of the engineer's failure to render assistance after the accident this Court must resolve, as a matter of first impression, whether there is an affirmative duty to render assistance to an injured person, and, if so, under what circumstances. Unless the engineer in this case had such an affirmative duty to assist South, all testimony regarding his failure to cover South with his parka or to otherwise assist was improperly admitted evidence – irrelevant and immaterial to any issue in the case.

During trial the Souths contended that the engineer had an affirmative duty to assist South by virtue of § 39-08-06, N.D.C.C., which imposes upon "the driver of any vehicle involved in an accident" a duty to render reasonable assistance to any person injured in such accident. We disagree that the engineer incurred a duty to assist under § 39-08-06, N.D.C.C. Trains are excluded from the definition of "vehicle" under Title 39, N.D.C.C, as follows:

39-01-01.Definitions. In this title, unless the context or subject matter otherwise requires: ...

72. 'Vehicle' shall include every device in, upon, or by which any person or property may be transported or drawn upon a public highway, except devices moved by human power or used exclusively upon stationary rails or tracks. We conclude that the requirements of § 39-08-06, N.D.C.C., do not pertain to trains, and no duty was imposed upon the engineer of the train in the instant case by virtue of that section.

On the subject of whether there is a common law duty to assist one in peril Prosser comments as follows in his treatise, Prosser, Law of Torts, Section 56 (4th Ed. 1971):

Because of this reluctance to countenance nonfeasance as a basis of liability, the law has persistently refused to recognize the moral obligation of common decency and common humanity, to come to the aid of another human being who is in danger, even though the outcome is to cost him his life.

Thus far the difficulties of setting any standards of unselfish service to fellow men, and of making any workable rule to cover possible situations where fifty people might fail to rescue one, has limited any tendency to depart from the rule to cases where some special relation between the parties has afforded a justification for the creation of a duty, without any question of setting up a rule of universal application.

It also is recognized that if the defendant's own negligence has been responsible for the plaintiff's situation, a relation has arisen which imposes a duty to make a reasonable effort to give assistance, and avoid any further harm. Where the original danger is created by innocent conduct, involving no fault on the part of the defendant, it was formerly the rule that no such duty arose; but this appears to have given way, in recent decisions, to a recognition of the duty to take action, both where the prior innocent conduct has created an unreasonable risk of harm to the plaintiff, and where it has already injured him.

The Restatement (Second) of Torts S 322 (1965) takes the following position:

§ 322. Duty to Aid Another Harmed by Actor's Conduct

If the actor knows or has reason to know that by his conduct, whether tortious or innocent, he has caused such bodily harm to another as to make him helpless and in danger of further harm, the actor is under a duty to exercise reasonable care to prevent such further harm.

Thus, the Restatement view is that one who harms another has an affirmative duty to exercise reasonable care to prevent further harm.

We believe that the position expressed by § 322, Restatement (Second) of Torts (1965), reflects the type of basic decency and human thoughtfulness which is generally characteristic of our people, and we therefore, adopt the standard imposed by that section. Accordingly, we hold that a person who knows or has reason to know that his conduct, whether tortious or innocent, has caused harm to another has an affirmative duty to render assistance to prevent further harm. One who breaches such duty is subject to liability for damages incurred as a result of the additional harm proximately caused by such breach. We further hold that, in the instant case, the trial court did not err in the admission of the engineer's testimony regarding the assistance, or lack thereof, to South at the scene of the accident, nor did the court abuse its discretion in refusing to admit those portions of the testimony which the court determined were highly prejudicial and irrelevant.

During opening argument to the jury, the Souths' counsel referred to statements made by the engineer as to why he did not cover South with his jacket. As part of its instruction to the jury the trial court gave a standard instruction that the arguments or other remarks of the attorneys were not to be considered as evidence in the case and that any comments by counsel concerning the evidence which were not warranted by the evidence actually admitted were to be wholly disregarded. We recognize the reality of a situation such as this wherein inflammatory comments made by counsel during opening argument, once impressed upon the minds of the jurors, can perhaps never be totally erased or their effect completely negated by an instruction that such comments are not evidence and should be wholly disregarded. Nevertheless, in view of the instruction as given and in view of the proper limited admission into evidence of the engineer's testimony regarding his failure to assist South after the accident we hold that the disputed comments of the Souths' counsel in opening argument did not constitute prejudicial error entitling the Railroad to a new trial.

Tarasoff v. Regents of the University of California

Supreme Court of California (1976)

On October 27, Prosenjit Poddar killed Tatiana Tarasoff. Plaintiffs, Tatiana's parents, allege that two months earlier Poddar confided his intention to kill Tatiana to Dr. Lawrence Moore, a psychologist employed by the Cowell Memorial Hospital at the University of California at Berkeley. They allege that on Moore's request, the campus police briefly detained Poddar, but released him when he appeared rational. They further claim that Dr. Harvey Powelson, Moore's superior, then directed that no further action be taken to detain Poddar. No one warned plaintiffs of Tatiana's peril.

Plaintiffs can state a cause of action against defendant therapists for negligent failure to protect Tatiana. In analyzing this issue, we bear in mind that legal duties are not discoverable facts of nature, but merely conclusory expressions that, in cases of a particular type, liability should be imposed for damage done. Duty is not sacrosanct in itself, but only an expression of the sum total of those considerations of policy which lead the law to say that the particular plaintiff is entitled to protection.

The most important of these considerations in establishing duty is foreseeability. As a general principle, a defendant owes a duty of care to all persons who are foreseeably endangered by his conduct, with respect to all risks which make the conduct unreasonably dangerous. As we shall explain, however, when the avoidance of foreseeable harm requires a defendant to control the conduct of another person, or to warn of such conduct, the common law has traditionally imposed liability only if the defendant bears some special relationship to the dangerous person or to the potential victim. Since the relationship between a therapist and his patient satisfies this requirement, we need not here decide whether foreseeability alone is sufficient to create a duty to exercise reasonably care to protect a potential victim of another's conduct.

Although, as we have stated above, under the common law, as a general rule, one person owed no duty to control the conduct of another nor to warn those endangered by such conduct, the courts have carved out an exception to this rule in cases in which the defendant stands in some special relationship to either the person whose conduct needs to be controlled or in a relationship to the foreseeable victim of that conduct. Applying this exception to the present case, we note that a relationship of defendant therapists to either Tatiana or Poddar will suffice to establish a duty of care. Although plaintiffs' pleadings assert no special relation between Tatiana and defendant therapists, they establish as between Poddar and defendant therapists the special relation that arises between a patient and his doctor or psychotherapist. Such a relationship may support affirmative duties for the benefit of third persons. Thus, for example, a hospital must exercise reasonable care to control the behavior of a patient which may endanger other persons. A doctor must also warn a patient if the patient's condition or medication renders certain conduct, such as driving a car, dangerous to others.

Although the California decisions that recognize this duty have involved cases in which the defendant stood in a special relationship both to the victim and to the person whose conduct created the danger, we do not think that the duty should logically be constricted to such situations.

Defendants contend, however, that imposition of a duty to exercise reasonable care to protect third persons is unworkable because therapists cannot accurately predict whether or not a patient will resort to violence. In support of this argument amicus representing the American Psychiatric Association and other professional societies cites numerous articles which indicate that therapists, in the present state of the art, are unable reliably to predict violent acts; their forecasts, amicus claims, tend consistently to over predict violence, and indeed are more often wrong than right. Since predictions of violence are often erroneous, amicus concludes, the courts should not render rulings that predicate the liability of therapists upon the validity of such predictions.

The role of the psychiatrist, who is indeed a practitioner of medicine, and that of the psychologist who performs an allied function, are like that of the physician who must conform to the standards of the profession and who must often make diagnoses and predictions based upon such evaluations. Thus the judgment of the therapist in diagnosing emotional disorders and in predicting whether a patient presents a serious danger of violence is comparable to the judgment which doctors and professionals must regularly render under accepted rules of responsibility.

We recognize the difficulty that a therapist encounters in attempting to forecast whether a patient presents a serious danger of violence. Obviously we do not require that the therapist, in making that determination, render a perfect performance; the therapist need only exercise that reasonable degree of skill, knowledge, and care ordinarily possessed and exercised by members of that professional specialty under similar circumstances. Within the broad range of reasonable practice and treatment in which professional opinion and judgment may differ, the therapist is free to exercise his or her own best judgment without liability; proof, aided by hindsight, that he or she judged wrongly is insufficient to establish negligence.

In the instant case, however, the pleadings do not raise any question as to failure of defendant therapists to predict that Poddar presented a serious danger of violence. On the contrary, the present complaints allege that defendant therapists did in fact predict that Poddar would kill, but were negligent in failing to warn.

We realize that the open and confidential character of psychotherapeutic dialogue encourages patients to express threats of violence, few of which are ever executed. Certainly a therapist should not be encouraged routinely to reveal such threats; such disclosures could seriously disrupt the patient's relationship with his therapist and with the persons threatened. To the contrary, the therapist's obligations to his patient require that he not disclose a confidence unless such disclosure is necessary to avert danger to others, and even then that he do so discreetly, and in a fashion that would preserve the privacy of his patient to the fullest extent compatible with the prevention of the threatened danger. The protective privilege ends where the public peril begins.

Our current crowded and computerized society compels the interdependence of its members. In this risk-infested society we can hardly tolerate the further exposure to danger that would result from a concealed knowledge of the therapist that his patient was lethal. If the exercise of reasonable care to protect the threatened victim requires the therapist to warn the endangered party or those who can reasonably be expected to notify him, we see no sufficient societal interest that would protect and justify concealment. The containment of such risks lies in the public interest. For the foregoing reasons, we find that plaintiffs' complaints can be amended to state a cause of action against defendants Moore, Powelson, Gold, and Yandell and against the Regents as their employer, for breach of a duty to exercise reasonable care to protect Tatiana.

Ward v. Inishmaan Associates Limited Partnership

Supreme Court of New Hampshire (2007)

The defendants, Inishmaan Associates Limited Partnership (Inishmaan) and JCM Management Company (JCM), appeal the denial for a directed verdict and for summary judgment made during the trial of this personal injury action.

Inishmaan owns the Osprey Landing Apartment Community, a 329–unit mixed income housing complex. JCM manages Osprey Landing on behalf of Inishmaan. The plaintiff, Kristin Ward, individually and as next friend of her son, Casey Miller, brought suit against the defendants. The plaintiff sought damages for injuries that occurred as the result of an alleged criminal assault on her by her neighbor, Merry Sommers (Sommers), when the plaintiff was living in the housing complex. Casey witnessed the attack but was not injured. We refer hereinafter to Kristin and Casey collectively as the plaintiff.

On July 12, 2002, Sommers assaulted the plaintiff outside the plaintiff's apartment, stabbing her several times. Friction between Sommers and the plaintiff had begun in September 1999.

Sommers frequently made offensive verbal comments to the plaintiff, persistently banged on a common wall that separated their two apartments, and made numerous and unsubstantiated complaints to the management of excessive noise, slamming of doors and purported drug dealing in the plaintiff's apartment. In March 2002, Sommers pushed the plaintiff's car door into her while the plaintiff was in the process of removing Casey from his car seat. The plaintiff reported the incident to the police, but they apparently concluded that no criminal activity had taken place. The plaintiff regularly registered her complaints about Sommers' behavior with JCM personnel.

After the stabbing incident, Sommers was arrested and charged with attempted murder. The plaintiff brought suit against Inishmaan and JCM alleging that they failed to protect her from Sommers' purported criminal assault. Sommers died before being brought to trial on the criminal charges.

On one hand lies the accepted maxim that all persons, including landlords, have a duty to exercise reasonable care not to subject others to an unreasonable risk of harm. On the other hand, a competing rule holds that private persons have no general duty to protect others from the criminal acts of third persons. We agree with numerous courts that as a general principle, landlords have no duty to protect tenants from criminal attack. Our review of the law suggest four possible exceptions.

The first exception arises when a special relationship exists between the parties. Explaining that courts have repeatedly held that a landlord-tenant relationship is not a special relationship engendering a duty on the part of the landlord to protect tenants from criminal attack, we reject liability based solely on the landlord-tenant relationship.

The second exception arises where an especial temptation and opportunity for criminal misconduct brought about by the defendant, will call upon him to take precautions against it. This means that a party who realizes or should realize that his conduct has created a condition which involves an unreasonable risk of harm to another has a duty to exercise reasonable care to prevent the risk from taking effect. According to the majority of cases, this exception is generally limited in landlord-tenant cases to situations where a known physical defect on the premises foreseeably enhanced the risk of that attack. Thus we conclude that a duty to protect tenants from criminal attack may arise when a landlord has created, or is responsible for, a known defective condition on a premises that foreseeably enhanced the risk of criminal attack.

The third exception is the existence of overriding foreseeability, which would hold landlords to a duty to protect tenants from criminal attacks that were clearly foreseeable, even if not causally related to physical defects on the premises. We reject liability based upon that principle.

The fourth exception arises from the general tort principle that one who voluntarily assumes a duty thereafter has a duty to act with reasonable care. A landlord who undertakes, either gratuitously or by contract, to provide security will thereafter have a duty to act with reasonable care.

Therefore, of four possible exceptions to the general rule that landlords have no duty to protect tenants from criminal attack, we have accepted two and rejected the others. Thus, a duty may arise when a landlord has created, or is responsible for, a known defective condition on a premises that foreseeably enhances the risk of criminal attack. In addition, a landlord who undertakes to provide security has a duty to act with reasonable care. Where, however, a landlord has made no affirmative attempt to provide security, and is not responsible for a physical defect that enhances the risk of crime, we will not find such a duty. We reject liability based solely on the landlord-tenant relationship or on a doctrine of overriding foreseeability.

The plaintiff's evidence failed to establish that the defendants created or were responsible for a physical defect on the premises that foreseeably enhanced the risk of criminal attack. Nor did the plaintiff's evidence establish that the defendants undertook to provide security against criminal attacks. Therefore, we hold that the trial court's denial of the defendants' motion for a directed verdict constituted an unsustainable exercise of discretion, and we reverse that ruling.

GOVERNMENT

Birnbaum v. U.S.

United States Court of Appeals, Second Circuit (1978)

For twenty years (from approximately 1953 to 1973), the Central Intelligence Agency ("CIA") covertly opened first class mail which American citizens sent to, or received from, the Soviet Union. Letters destined for the U.S.S.R., or originating there, were selected by agents in New York, photocopied, and then returned to postal authorities for ultimate delivery. During the existence of the project over 215,000 pieces of mail were inspected and copied in this fashion. The CIA released photocopies of some letters to the FBI in aid of that agency's mission with respect to suspected domestic subversion.

Norman Birnbaum, whose mail was opened and copied, sued the United States for compensatory damages under the Federal Tort Claims Act ("FTCA") for a single opened letter that had been intercepted en route to the U.S.S.R. in 1970.

The District Judge, as required, tried the case himself, and found that the United States was liable to the plaintiff for damages in the amount of $1,000. The United States was also required to send a letter of apology to the plaintiff. From this judgment the United States appeals.

I. Before the Act was passed in 1946, the United States, as sovereign, possessed complete immunity against suit for torts committed by its agents and employees. The only redress was by private bill in the Congress. The purpose of the Act was generally to waive the sovereign immunity of the United States for torts of its employees committed within the scope of their employment, if such torts committed in the employ of a private person would have given rise to liability under state law. Thus, recovery under the Act could only be predicated upon such a state tort cause of action. Moreover, in groping for a formula that would eliminate the nuisance of private bills and yet interfere only minimally with government functions, Congress created statutory exceptions to the general waiver of immunity in the Act. Three of these are arguably applicable here: (1) 28 U.S.C. 2680(h), excluding certain specified torts from the ambit of the Act; (2) section 2680(b), exempting from the Act any liability for loss or miscarriage of mail; (3) section 2680(a), creating an exemption from liability for acts done pursuant to a discretionary function. If the claims in suit fall within one of the statutory exceptions, the district court lacks subject matter jurisdiction.

II. Although it appeared that the plaintiff was not touched physically or harmed financially, and that the sole damage claim was mental suffering, New York recognizes as "personal injury" mental suffering that results from invasion of the common law right to privacy. The activities of the Government in opening and reproducing plaintiffs' mail constituted such an intrusion into Birnbaum's privacy. As described by the Restatement, violation of the right against intrusion may occur through "opening private and personal mail."

III. We must now consider whether the Government may claim an exception from liability under the Federal Torts Claim Act. We will focus upon three exceptions: (1) section 2680(h), for certain specified torts; (2) section 2680(b), for miscarriage of mail; and (3) section 2680(a), for discretionary functions.

A. Section 2680(h)

Under this subsection of the Federal Tort Claims Act, there is an exception for: "Any claim arising out of assault, battery, false imprisonment, false arrest, malicious prosecution, abuse of process, libel, slander, misrepresentation, deceit, or interference with contract rights…." Although this exception might be construed as excepting all intentional torts, the Government does not urge that reading upon us. Thus, it has been held that the torts of trespass and invasion of privacy do not fall within the exception of section 2680(h).

B. Section 2680(b): The Postal Exception

The exception relates to "any claim arising out of the loss, miscarriage, or negligent transmission of letters or postal matter." The language of the exception itself indicates that it was not aimed to encompass intentional acts. Had Congress intended to bring Intentional disturbance of the integrity of a letter within the postal exception, it would not have used the term "negligent transmission." Nor were the letters lost or miscarried. "Miscarriage" in the context of mail means misdelivery. We hold, therefore, that the postal exception does not apply to save the United States from liability in these cases.

C. Section 2680(a): "Discretionary Function" Exception

Finally, we turn to consider whether the Government's mail opening project is removed from the scope of the Federal Tort Claims Act by section 2680(a), which provides an exception for: "Any claim based upon an act or omission of an employee of the Government, exercising due care, in the execution of a statute or regulation, whether or not such statute or regulation be valid, or based upon the exercise or performance or the failure to exercise or perform a discretionary function or duty on the part of a federal agency or an employee of the Government, whether or not the discretion involved be abused."

It is common ground that there is no statute or regulation which sanctions the mail opening procedure engaged in by the CIA. Our inquiry relates therefore only to whether the CIA personnel were engaging in a "discretionary function," rather than executing a policy required by "statute or regulation." The "discretionary function" exception is distinct from the exception based upon a statute or regulation. A discretionary function can derive only from properly delegated authority. Authority generally stems from a statute or regulation, or at least, from a jurisdictional grant that brings the discretionary function within the competence of the agency. Discretion may be as elastic as a rubber-band, but it, too, has a breaking point. An act that is clearly outside the authority delegated cannot be considered as an "abuse of discretion."

The Central Intelligence Agency was chartered by Legislative enactment in 1947. The scope of its authority and the limitations thereon were contained in the National Security Act of 1947, which provides specifically "(t)hat the Agency shall have no police, subpoena, law-enforcement powers, or internal-security functions." Furthermore, National Security Council Intelligence Directives, designed to guide the CIA, permitted so-called "overt" collection of foreign intelligence within the United States but not "clandestine" collection in the United States.

From 1958 on, the CIA began to examine intercepted mail not only to satisfy its own need for intelligence about the U.S.S.R., but to satisfy as well the FBI's requirements for counterespionage information and data on "peace organizations, antiwar leaders, black activists, and women's groups." By the mid-sixties, then, the CIA had undertaken an operation that involved broad and indiscriminate inspection of private mail with a view to obtaining information on matters of domestic, as well as foreign, concern. There was no room in the charter for a "policy judgment" that the CIA should involve itself in gathering secret data on domestic problems. Indeed the CIA knew this as well as anyone. An Agency internal memorandum admitted that "there is no legal basis for monitoring postal communications in the United States except during time of war or national emergency." We find, therefore, that the CIA was acting so far beyond its authority that it could not have been exercising a function which could in any proper sense be called "discretionary."

IV. Having determined that the United States is liable to these plaintiffs for harm caused by mail openings, we must review the District Court's award of $1000 in compensatory damages and of an apology to the plaintiff. Although damages under the Federal Torts Claim Act are governed by state law, the FTCA limits recovery to compensatory damages and provides that the United States shall not be liable for punitive damages. The question is whether the testimony of the plaintiffs sustains a finding of mental anguish under New York law, in which event the judgment for $1,000 each would not be excessive, or whether there was no actual damage, in which case only nominal damages of one dollar would have been proper.

The answer is not easy. There was no finding of physical injury and no loss of employment. There also was no mental injury in the sense of "permanent symptoms of anxiety." Although, in a sense, the plaintiffs brought their feelings of outrage upon themselves by seeking information, we do not believe, upon reflection, that this is a meaningful break in the chain of causation that links the mail openings to any anguish suffered. The mail opening was an intentional tort and it may be deemed to have been foreseeable that anguish might ensue if there were discovery.

More troublesome is the fact that plaintiffs should have been aware that their mail Might be opened by the Soviet officials. That could have convinced the trier of fact that there was no compensable damage. Indeed, the testimony of the plaintiffs with regard to their subjective feelings was both weak and meager. The nub of their testimony was that each felt "disappointment" that their own government could do such a thing. Such anguish is political rather than emotional, much as a member of a Senate investigating committee might feel toward the same revelation. The "injury" was principally to "their wounded faith in our democratic institutions," a loss of faith probably shared by many Americans who do not expect compensation for such intellectual injuries. The issue comes down to whether the plaintiff suffered any mental injury whatever from the knowledge that a single letter had been opened. The plaintiffs could not recover money damages as a vindication of the rights of the American people. Nor do we think that they may recover simply to deter future action, for this particular statute prohibits punitive damages.

The District Court did find, however, that "the emotional distress these plaintiffs suffered was the sort that would be experienced by reasonable people under the almost unprecedented circumstances of these cases." Though we could view this finding as one merely of damage presumed from the circumstances, worth only the nominal sum of one dollar, we interpret the finding more generously as determining that these plaintiffs actually suffered personal anguish. Though the question of damages is close, we affirm the money judgments for $1,000 each.

With regard to the Judge's order that the Government send a letter of apology to each plaintiff, though such letters might someday achieve monetary value as collectors' items, we do not view them as "money damages," the only form of relief provided in the Act. We accordingly reverse that part of the judgment ordering that letters of apology be sent.

The judgments on appeal, except for the order to send letters of apology, are affirmed.

PRENATAL

Remy v. MacDonald

Supreme Judicial Court of Massachusetts (2004)

Christine MacDonald was operating a motor vehicle when her vehicle was struck by a motor vehicle operated by Anna Ellis. MacDonald was thirty-two weeks pregnant with the plaintiff at that time, and the plaintiff was born, by emergency caesarian section, four days later. The plaintiff was hospitalized for twenty-three days and experienced multiple breathing difficulties associated with her premature birth. In the first few years of her life, she has had, and continues to suffer from, respiratory distress and asthma. The plaintiff alleges that her mother's negligent driving caused the accident that led to the plaintiff's premature birth and subsequent related injuries. The plaintiff contends that a jury could find her mother liable in negligence for the injuries she has incurred, and, therefore, the judge improperly allowed summary judgment.

In order to succeed on a claim of negligence, a plaintiff first must establish that the defendant owed a legal duty of care. We must decide whether a pregnant woman owes a legal duty of care to her unborn child to refrain from negligent conduct that may result in physical harm to that child. If no such duty exists, a claim of negligence cannot be brought.

Recognizing a pregnant woman's legal duty of care in negligence to her unborn child would present an almost unlimited number of circumstances that would likely give rise to litigation. Courts would be challenged to refine the scope of such a duty, including the degree of knowledge expected of a mother in order to pinpoint when such a duty would arise (e.g., at the point of pregnancy; at the point of awareness of pregnancy; or at the point of awareness that pregnancy is a possibility) or the particular standard of conduct to which a reasonably careful pregnant woman, in a single case, should be held. There is no consensus on if and when a duty such as the one sought by the plaintiff should be imposed, and there is considerable debate with respect to a mother's civil liability for injuries to her unborn fetus, including disagreement over whether the rights of the child should supersede the legal rights of the mother. No set of clear existing social values and customs exist, and no settled social policy can be identified, to justify the maintenance of the present lawsuit.

This court has recognized the right of a plaintiff to maintain an independent cause of action for prenatal injuries sustained as the result of the negligence of another. If the tortious conduct and the legal causation of the harm can be satisfactorily established, there may be recovery for any injury occurring at any time after conception. Moreover, a viable fetus, whether or not born alive, is considered a person for purposes of our wrongful death statute.

It is true that, had the plaintiff been injured while MacDonald was a passenger in an automobile negligently operated by another, the plaintiff (whether or not she survived) would have been able to recover damages against the operator of the vehicle. There is also no question that, had the plaintiff been born at the time of the accident, even if only one hour of age, she would have been able to recover against MacDonald for injuries sustained as a result of her mother's negligence. Our cases affirm the principle that children enjoy the same right to protection and to legal redress for wrongs done them as others enjoy.

We reject the plaintiff's argument that a rule permitting a child to recover for negligent injuries inflicted before birth by the child's mother could be restricted solely to a viable fetus claiming negligence in an automobile accident. There is nothing special about injuries incurred in automobile accidents that sets them apart from other negligently caused injuries, and the limitation sought by the plaintiff would be inconsistent with that law. The presence of automobile liability insurance does not create liability where none previously existed. Further, and more importantly, there is no meaningful way to limit such a rule to automobile accidents cases. It would be only a matter of time before the rule could be extended to a myriad of situations that would make pregnant women liable to their viable fetuses for all manner of allegedly negligent conduct.

We conclude that there are inherent and important differences between a fetus, in utero, and a child already born, that permits a bright line to be drawn around the zone of potential tort liability of one who is still biologically joined to an injured plaintiff.

Renslow v. Mennonite Hospital

Supreme Court of Illinois (1977)

There is but one issue: Does a child, not conceived at the time negligent acts were committed against its mother, have a cause of action against the tortfeasors for its injuries resulting from their conduct?

Plaintiff's complaint alleges that in October of 1965, when her mother was 13 years of age, the defendants, on two occasions, negligently transfused her mother with Rh-positive blood. The mother's Rh-negative blood was incompatible with, and was sensitized by, the Rh-positive blood. Her mother had no knowledge of an adverse reaction from the transfusions and did not know she had been improperly transfused or that her blood had been sensitized.

In December 1973 she first discovered her condition when a routine blood screening was ordered by her physician in the course of prenatal care. Plaintiff further asserts that the defendants discovered they had administered the incompatible blood, but at no time notified her mother or the mother's family.

The resulting sensitization of the mother's blood allegedly caused prenatal damage to plaintiff's hemolytic processes, which put her life in jeopardy and necessitated her induced premature birth. Plaintiff was born on March 25, 1974, jaundiced and suffering from hyperbilirubinemia. She required an immediate, complete exchange transfusion of her blood and another such transfusion shortly thereafter. It is further alleged that, as a result of the defendants' acts, plaintiff suffers from permanent damage to various organs, her brain, and her nervous system.

The trial court dismissed plaintiff's cause of action because she was not at the time of the alleged infliction of the injury conceived. The appellate court, in a careful and well-reasoned opinion, emphasized that the defendants were a doctor and a hospital, and held that there was no showing that the defendants could not reasonably have foreseen that the teenage girl would later marry and bear a child and that the child would be injured as the result of the improper blood transfusion. Here, the negligent force, which had its impact upon the infant in its prenatal state, was set in motion years prior to plaintiff's conception. The court observed that in other types of tort cases liability has not been barred because the allegedly wrongful conduct occurred long before the resultant injury when duty and causation can be established. The appellate court found no reason to deny a cause of action to a person simply because he had not yet been conceived at the time of the wrongful conduct.

The rule permitting a cause of action only where the child is viable at the time of the injury has been criticized as a most unsatisfactory criterion, since viability is a relative matter, depending on the health of mother and child and many other matters in addition to the stage of development. Furthermore, it has been pointed out that denial of claims for injuries to the previable fetus may indeed cut off some of the most meritorious claims, for there is substantial medical authority that congenital structural defects caused by factors in the prenatal environment can be sustained only early in the previable stages. Upon reconsideration, we henceforth reject viability as a criterion to a common law action for prenatal injuries. Thus the failure to allege that plaintiff was viable at the time she sustained her injuries does not bar this action. This conclusion, however, does not fully answer the ultimate question of whether a cause of action exists on behalf of a live born infant, although the infant's injuries resulted from a negligent act occurring prior to her conception. The defendants assert they owed no duty to plaintiff because her injuries were not reasonably foreseeable at the time of the act.

Historically, negligence could not be founded upon the breach of a duty owed only to some person other than the plaintiff. "Negligence in the air, so to speak, will not do." As medical science progressed, the courts took notice that a fetus is a separate human entity prior to birth. It is by now commonly accepted that at conception the egg and sperm unite to jointly provide the genetic material requisite for human life. Thus, various courts have gradually come to recognize that the embryo, from the moment of conception, is a separate organism that can be compensated for negligently inflicted prenatal harm. In the case at bar, the wrongful conduct took place prior to plaintiff's conception; the plaintiff at the time of the conduct was in no sense a separate entity to whom the traditional duty of care could be owed. Plaintiff herein asks us to reexamine our notions of duty, and to find, in essence, a contingent prospective duty to a child not yet conceived but foreseeably harmed by a breach of duty to the child's mother.

We reaffirm the utility of the concept of duty as a means by which to direct and control the course of the common law. But examples of changing notions of legal duty, as well as the progressive expansion of duty in prenatal cases already documented, demonstrate that duty is not a static concept.

The cases allowing relief to an infant for injuries incurred in its pre-viable state make it clear that a defendant may be held liable to a person whose existence was not apparent at the time of his act. We therefore find it illogical to bar relief for an act done prior to conception where the defendant would be liable for this same conduct had the child, unbeknownst to him, been conceived prior to his act. We believe that there is a right to be born free from prenatal injuries foreseeably caused by a breach of duty to the child's mother.

Albala v. City of New York

Court of Appeals of New York (1981)

On December 27, 1971, Ruth Albala underwent an abortion at Bellevue Hospital during the course of which her uterus was perforated. In June of 1973 she commenced a malpractice action which was ultimately settled in June of 1979. Jeffrey Albala, the infant plaintiff in the case now before us, was conceived sometime in September of 1975, while his mother's malpractice case was still pending. He was born on June 3, 1976, four years after the alleged malpractice and three years before that lawsuit was settled.

This action was commenced on behalf of Jeffrey on September 26, 1978. It is contended that as a result of the alleged malpractice of defendants in negligently perforating Ruth's uterus, seven years prior to this lawsuit, plaintiff was born with a damaged brain.

It is clear from a review of our prior decisions that we are presented with a question of first impression in this State. Assuming the allegations in the complaint to be true, had the alleged negligence not occurred and Ruth Albala's uterus not been perforated, plaintiff would have in all likelihood been born normal. Here, the defendants' alleged negligence made the difference between life in an impaired state and life in an unimpaired state.

We are not unmindful of the point made by the dissent that at the time Ruth Albala underwent an abortion in 1971 it was foreseeable that she would again conceive and that the health of children born thereafter could be adversely affected by damage to her uterus. We disagree, however, that this foreseeability alone established a duty to plaintiff on the part of defendants. We determined long ago in a case involving policy issues as sensitive as the ones at bar that foreseeability alone is not the hallmark of legal duty for if foreseeability were the sole test we could not logically confine the extension of liability.

Thus, were we to establish liability in this case, could we logically preclude liability in a case where a negligent motorist collides with another vehicle containing a female passenger who sustains a punctured uterus as a result of the accident and subsequently gives birth to a deformed child? Unlimited hypotheses accompanied by staggering implications are manifest. The perimeters of liability although a proper legislative concern, in cases such as these, cannot be judicially established in a reasonable and practical manner.

As a final consideration, it is worth noting that the recognition of a cause of action under the circumstances of this case would have the undesirable impact of encouraging the practice of defensive medicine. A physician faced with the alternative of saving a patient's life by administering a treatment involving the possibility of adverse consequences to later conceived offspring of that patient would, if exposed to liability of the magnitude considered in this case, undoubtedly be inclined to advise against the treatment rather than risk the possibility of having to recompense a child born with a handicap. Accordingly, society as a whole would bear the cost of our placing physicians in a direct conflict between their moral duty to patients and the proposed legal duty to those hypothetical future generations outside the immediate zone of danger.

While the temptation is always great to provide a form of relief to one who has suffered, it is well established that the law cannot provide a remedy for every injury incurred. In defining the common law, it is this court's duty to consider the consequences of recognizing a novel cause of action and to strike the delicate balance between the competing policy considerations which arise whenever tort liability is sought to be extended beyond traditional bounds.

IV. VICARIOUS LIABILITY

Fruit v. Schreiner

Supreme Court of Alaska (1972)

At the time of the accident, Fruit, a life insurance salesman, was attending a sales convention of his employer, Equitable Life Assurance Society (Equitable). Sales employees of the company were required to attend the convention. The agency manager decided that participants should travel by private transportation, and that they would be reimbursed a lump sum for their expenses. Clay Fruit chose to drive his own automobile.

Insurance experts from California and Washington were also invited as guests to the convention, and the Alaska salesmen were encouraged to mix freely with these guests to learn as much as possible about sales techniques during the three-day gathering. Scheduled events included business meetings during morning hours, evening dinners and at least two cocktail parties. District managers entertained their own sales personnel at other cocktail parties.

At some time between 10:00 p.m. and 11:30 p.m. following a seafood dinner, members of the group awoke Fruit who, accompanied by his wife and two couples, walked to the Salty Dawg Bar. The others were tired and went to bed but Fruit decided to drive to another town as he was under the impression that the out-of-state guests were at the Waterfront Bar and Restaurant. Fruit then drove his car to Homer but departed when he did not find any of his colleagues.

His return route took him past the Salty Dawg Bar where Schreiner's automobile was disabled. At approximately 2:00 a.m. Fruit applied his brakes and skidded across the dividing line of the highway, colliding with the front of Schreiner's car. The hood of Schreiner's automobile had been raised and Schreiner was standing in front of his car. The collision crushed his legs.

EQUITABLE'S LIABILITY UNDER THE DOCTRINE OF RESPONDEAT SUPERIOR

The jury found that Fruit was an employee acting within the course and scope of his employment for Equitable at the time and place of the accident. Under the doctrine of respondeat superior (which simply means 'let the employer answer') Equitable would thus be liable for Fruit's of negligence despite lack of fault on Equitable's part.

Equitable argues, however, that the evidence was insufficient to establish that Fruit was acting within the course and scope of his employment. Equitable contends that any business purpose was completed when Fruit left the Waterfront Bar and Restaurant. It cites cases holding that an employee traveling to his home or other personal destination cannot ordinarily be regarded as acting in the scope of his employment. But Fruit was not returning to his home. He was traveling to the convention headquarters where he was attending meetings as a part of his employment.

A truly imaginative variety of rationale have been advanced by courts and glossators in justification of this imposition of liability on employers. Among the suggestions are the employer's duty to hire and maintain a responsible staff of employees, to control the activities of his employees and thus to insist upon appropriate safety measures; the belief that the employer should pay for the inherent risks which result from hiring others to carry on his business; the observation that the employer most often has easier access to evidence of the facts surrounding the injury; and the metaphysical identification of the employer and employee as a single persona jointly liable for the injury which occurred in the context of the business. One legal scholar more cynically states: "in hard fact, the reason for the employers' liability is the damages are taken from a deep pocket."

The concept of vicarious liability is broad enough to include circumstances where the master has been in no way at fault; where the work which the servant was employed to do was in no sense unlawful or violative of the plaintiff's rights; where there has been no delegation of a special duty; where the tortious conduct of the servant was neither commanded nor ratified; but nevertheless the master is made responsible. This liability arises from the relationship of the enterprise to society rather than from a misfeasance on the part of the employer.

Scope of employment as a test for application of respondeat superior would be insufficient if it failed to encompass the duty of every enterprise to the social community which gives it life and contributes to its prosperity. The basis of respondeat superior has been correctly stated as the desire to include in the costs of operation inevitable losses to third persons incident to carrying on an enterprise, and thus distribute the burden among those benefited by the enterprise.

Consistent with these considerations, it is apparent that no categorical statement can delimit the meaning of "scope of employment" once and for all times. Applicability of respondeat superior will depend primarily on the findings of fact in each case. In this particular case, Clay Fruit's employment contract required that he attend the sales conference. Each employee was left to his own resources for transportation, and many of the agents, including

Fruit, chose to drive their own automobiles. By the admission of Equitable's agency manager, the scope of the conference included informal socializing as well as formal meetings. Social contact with the out-of-state guests was encouraged, and there is undisputed evidence that such associations were not limited to the conference headquarters at Land's End. Some agents, including Fruit, gathered with the guests in Homer the evening before the accident, and groups of agents and their wives visited the Salty Dawg on various occasions.

When Fruit left for the Waterfront Bar and Restaurant his principal purpose was to join the out-of-state guests. This testimony of his was further confirmed by the fact that once he discovered that they were not present at the Waterfront he departed immediately.

Because we find that fair-minded men in the exercise of reasonable judgment could differ as to whether Fruit's activities in returning from Homer to the convention headquarters were within the scope of his employment, we are not disposed to upset the jury's conclusion that liability for damages may be vicariously imputed to Equitable.

Hinman v. Westinghouse Electric Company

Supreme Court of California (1970)

Plaintiff, a Los Angeles policeman, was standing on the center divider of a freeway inspecting a possible road hazard when he was struck by a car driven by Frank Allen Herman, an employee of defendant Westinghouse. As a result of the accident he received permanent injuries.

At the time of the accident, Herman was employed by Westinghouse and was returning home from work. He did not go to the office before or after work but instead went from home directly to the job site and after work returned home from the job site. The union contracts under which Herman worked provided for the payment of carfare and travel time in certain circumstances depending on the location of the job site in relation to the Los Angeles City Hall. As to this job, which was 15 to 20 miles from the city hall, Herman received an hour and a half per day as his roundtrip travel time and $1.30 for his travel expense. The employer had no control over the method or route of transportation used by Herman.

Liability of the employer may not be avoided on the basis of the "going and coming" rule. Under the "going and coming" rule, an employee going to and from work is ordinarily considered outside the scope of employment so that the employer is not liable for his torts. The "going and coming" rule is sometimes ascribed to the theory that the employment relationship is suspended from the time the employee leaves until he returns, or that in commuting he is not rendering service to his employer. Exceptions will be made to the "going and coming" rule where the trip involves an incidental benefit to the employer, not common to commute trips by ordinary members of the work force.

There is a substantial benefit to an employer in one area to be permitted to reach out to a labor market in another area or to enlarge the available labor market by providing travel expenses and payment for travel time. It cannot be denied that the employer's reaching out to the distant or larger labor market increases the risk of injury in transportation. In other words, the employer, having found it desirable in the interests of his enterprise to pay for travel time and for travel expenses and to go beyond the normal labor market or to have located his enterprise at a place remote from the labor market, should be required to pay for the risks inherent in his decision.

We are satisfied that, where, as here, the employer and employee have made the travel time part of the working day by their contract, the employer should be treated as such during the travel time, and it follows that so long as the employee is using the time for the designated purpose, to return home, the doctrine of Respondeat superior is applicable. The facts relating to the applicability of the doctrine of Respondeat superior are undisputed in the instant case, and we conclude that as a matter of law the doctrine is applicable.

Bryan v. Bunis

New York Supreme Court, Appellate Division (1924)

Solomon Bunis, one of the defendants, directed Charles Evans, an employee, to take him from the shop to the Bunis home in the truck owned by defendants. The hour was about noon. Bunis then told Evans to take the truck back to the shop. Instead of returning directly, Evans started to go home for his lunch. This involved a deviation from the direct route. About one-half mile from the Bunis residence, the truck collided with the plaintiff. The latter has recovered damages from the defendants for injuries sustained.

Since 1834, when Baron Parke, in discussing the liability of a master, made a distinction between a "frolic" and a "detour," the question as to just what constitutes a frolic and what a detour has been a perplexing one. In the one case the master is not liable for his servant's misconduct; in the other, the doctrine of respondeat superior is applied. There is in such cases no broad line of demarcation separating the doctrine of liability and nonliability. It often becomes shadowy and indistinct. To a large extent each case must be decided upon its own peculiar facts.

In general, to hold the master liable, the servant must be definitely engaged in the master's work. Mere deviation from the ordinary route, or from that selected by the master, even for a purpose conceived by the servant, does not relieve the master from liability, if his business, generally speaking, is still being carried on. And if the work, though temporarily abandoned, has been resumed, the same rule applies. A deviation for a casual visit constitutes merely misconduct in the servant's employment and not an abandonment thereof. The deviation by a servant of a few blocks for ends of his own, does not relieve the master of liability.

But the mere fact that the injuries were caused by the servant during his period of employment does not make the master liable, where it clearly appears that at the time he was not acting for the master or within the scope of his employment. Nor is the master liable if the servant has abandoned his work and engaged in an independent enterprise of his own. Where there is a long and unnecessary divergence from the course prescribed, the master is relieved from liability.

In determining whether or not liability exists under given circumstances, no hard and fast rule on the subject, either of time or space, can be applied. The choice of a different way back does not, constitute an abandonment of the master's work. Courts will not be limited by tests that are merely mechanical or formal; and its judgment, though it may be guided by location in time and space, will not be controlled by such circumstances, if there are others that characterize the intent of the transaction.

In this case the defendant, directing the servant's movements, knew that the usual hour of meal time was at hand. He knew where the employee lived. Certain employees are by law given a fixed period for the noonday meal. Custom has decreed a similar period for others. This defendant knew that Evans was allowed the time from 12 to 1 for lunch. The comparatively slight deviation by Evans of a half mile from the direct route back to the shop, in order that he might obtain his usual noonday meal, was not an engagement in a new, independent enterprise, or an abandonment of his master's work. It was a part of his daily duty, and when his employer took him from the shop at the noon hour, and, after his immediate errand was performed, directed him to return, it was within his contemplation that the ambit of the chauffeur's duty would not require him to be back at the shop until 1 o'clock, and that in the meantime at some place, presumptively his home, he would obtain his midday meal. His employment was not changed, at least as a matter of law, by going to his home on this errand. To go at the usual time for a meal and to his home after the day's work is done are incidents of employment.

We have recently held that a slight deviation, even for the servant's own benefit, from the course of work required by the master, will not necessarily relieve the master from the liability for an accident occurring during such deviation. The jury has found here that Evans had not abandoned the employment of the defendants when the accident occurred. The deviation, therefore, was but temporary, and the objective of Evans was the shop to which his duty and his master's direction called him at 1 o'clock. The judgment should be affirmed.

Johnson v. The News and Observer Publishing Company

Court of Appeals of North Carolina (2004)

Plaintiffs' personal injury claims arise out of an automobile accident involving plaintiffs and defendant Jack Roberts. Roberts worked as a newspaper carrier for the Smithfield Herald and was delivering newspapers when the accident occurred. Plaintiffs sought recovery from Roberts for negligence and from the Smithfield Herald, its affiliate, and its parent company (collectively "the Herald") on the basis of respondeat superior. The Herald denied liability for plaintiffs' accident based on its contention that Roberts was an independent contractor rather than an employee. After holding that Roberts was an independent contractor as a matter of law, the trial court ruled that the Herald had no vicarious liability in this case.

The record shows that when the accident occurred in 1999, Roberts had been delivering newspapers for the Herald for about ten years. In the employment contract, the Herald assigned Roberts a delivery route and permitted him to purchase newspapers from the Herald at a wholesale rate. However, the Herald reserved the right to renegotiate this wholesale rate upon thirty days notice to the carrier.

Roberts received as payment for his work the difference between the wholesale rate at which he bought the newspapers and the retail rate at which they were sold to customers. The Herald agreed to bill customers who prepaid by mail, but any amount a customer failed to pay would be deducted from Roberts's paycheck. The contract provided that Roberts could bill the other customers in any manner he chose.

The Herald authorized Roberts to use his own judgment and discretion as to whether and in what manner to do business with customers. The contract only required that he exert his best efforts to increase the number of customers for The Smithfield Herald and to keep those customers satisfied. Roberts could determine the means and manner in which he delivered newspapers to customers without control or supervision from the Herald. But the contract also provided that Roberts was responsible for the prompt and satisfactory delivery of the newspaper to customers on his route and required Roberts to deliver the papers in a dry and readable condition with delivery completed by 5:00 p.m.

Pursuant to the contract, Roberts used his own vehicle to complete his route and purchased his own liability insurance. He was designated as an independent contractor and had authority to hire assistants to help him, but those assistants were considered his employees and he was responsible for compensating them. The contract specifically assigned sole liability to Roberts for any third party claims arising out of tortious acts committed by him or his assistants.

Under the doctrine of respondeat superior, an employer can be held vicariously liable for a worker's negligence when an employer-employee relationship exists. Generally, an employer is not liable for the negligent acts of an independent contractor.

An independent contractor is defined as one who exercises an independent employment and contracts to do certain work according to his own judgment and method, without being subject to his employer except as to the results of his work. Although the contract with the Herald designates Roberts as an independent contractor and assigns to him sole liability for any third party claims against him, these types of contractual declarations are not determinative of the relationship or the rights of the parties. An employer cannot exonerate himself from his legally imposed liability to a third party for injury resulting from the tortious acts of his employee simply by contracting with the employee that he is to be free from the employer's control.

There are several factors to consider in determining whether a person is an independent contractor. These factors include whether the person:

(a) is engaged in an independent business, calling, or occupation; (b) is to have the independent use of his special skill, knowledge, or training in the execution of the work; (c) is doing a specified piece of work at a fixed price or for a lump sum or upon a quantitative basis; (d) is not subject to discharge because he adopts one method of doing the work rather than another; (e) is not in the regular employ of the other contracting party; (f) is free to use such assistants as he may think proper; (g) has full control over such assistants; and (h) selects his own time.

However, none of these factors are determinative, nor is the presence of all required to indicate an independent contractor relationship. The factors are considered along with the other circumstances of the employment relationship to determine whether the one employed possesses that degree of independence necessary to require his classification as an independent contractor rather than an employee.

Applying these factors, our Supreme Court has found that newspaper carriers typically do not exercise a sufficient degree of control over their work to be considered independent contractors as a matter of law. The Court stated that ordinarily, the day by day sale and delivery of newspapers under a cancellable agreement of indefinite duration may not be considered a specific job under a contract within the meaning of that phrase when used in defining an independent contractor. Considering these factors, we cannot conclude that Roberts was an independent contractor as a matter of law.

Roberts was not exercising an independent business, calling, or occupation by delivering newspapers for the Herald. The prompt delivery and circulation of newspapers is essential to the newspaper's success and is part of the regular business of the publisher. Newspaper carriers are just as much an integral part of the newspaper industry as are the typesetters and pressmen or the editorial staff.

While independent contractors usually have a special skill or knowledge, the duties performed by newspaper carriers are generally routine in nature, requiring diligence and responsibility rather than discretion and skill. The parties agree that the Herald had no real skill or education requirements for its carriers and that Roberts received little or no training when he started working for the Herald.

Also, the potential variations in time and manner in which a newspaper carrier could choose to deliver newspapers to customers on his route are considerably limited. Roberts had little discretion in how to complete his route since he was required to deliver the papers in a dry and readable condition promptly upon receipt by him and in a manner satisfactory to customers. Although the contract states that he could choose whether and in what manner to do business with any customer, if Roberts forgot or chose not to deliver to a customer, the Herald could opt to deliver the paper for him and penalize him with a fee of $3.00 per paper.

If Roberts breached any of the contract provisions, the Herald has the option of terminating his contract. Our courts have recognized that the right to fire is one of the most effective methods of control. Under the terms of the contract, Roberts was subject to discharge if he did not deliver the newspapers in a prompt and satisfactory manner. Although Roberts could hire assistants, his ability to hire employees has little significance since the Herald retained the right to fire Roberts at will for a broad range of reasons. It is worth noting that while Roberts could terminate the contract for a breach by the Herald, the contract contained very few provisions that placed any kind of duty on the Herald.

However, while not dispositive, the contract in the case is still evidence of the relationship between Roberts and the Herald. In addition, defendants presented evidence that would permit a jury to find that Roberts engaged in an independent business over which the newspaper did not exercise the requisite degree of control necessary to transform him into an employee. Thus, we hold that the entry of summary judgment should be reversed and the matter remanded to the trial court for further proceedings consistent with this opinion.

O'Banner v. McDonald's Corporation

Supreme Court of Illinois (1996)

Reginald O'Banner brought an action to recover damages for personal injuries he allegedly sustained when he slipped and fell in the bathroom of a McDonald's restaurant. In his complaint, O'Banner named as defendants McDonald's Corporation (McDonald's) and certain "unknown owners." McDonald's promptly moved for summary judgment on the grounds that the restaurant was actually owned by one of its franchisees and that it neither owned, operated, maintained, nor controlled the facility.

The trial court here entered summary judgment in favor of McDonald's based on the company's argument that it was merely the franchisor of the restaurant where O'Banner was injured and, as such, had no responsibility for the conditions that caused his accident. O'Banner challenged this conclusion in the appellate court by theorizing that even though McDonald's was a franchisor, it could nevertheless be held liable for the franchisee's negligence under principles of respondeat superior because there was sufficient evidence in the record to establish that the franchisee served as McDonald's actual agent. In the alternative, O'Banner contended that McDonald's could be vicariously liable for the acts and omissions of the franchisee based on the doctrine of apparent agency.

In the appeal before this court, the issue of actual agency has not been pursued. The sole question before us is whether the appellate court erred in reversing and remanding based on the theory of apparent agency.

Apparent agency, also known in Illinois as apparent authority, has long been recognized in this state. The doctrine is based on principles of estoppel. The idea is that if a principal creates the appearance that someone is his agent, he should not then be permitted to deny the agency if an innocent third party reasonably relies on the apparent agency and is harmed as a result.

Under the doctrine, a principal can be held vicariously liable in tort for injury caused by the negligent acts of his apparent agent if the injury would not have occurred but for the injured party's justifiable reliance on the apparent agency. The fundamental obstacle to O'Banner's recovery in this case concerns this element of reliance. Even if one concedes that McDonald's advertising and other conduct could entice a person to enter a McDonald's restaurant in the belief it was dealing with an agent of the corporation itself, that is not sufficient. In order to recover on an apparent agency theory, O'Banner would have to show that he actually did rely on the apparent agency in going to the restaurant where he was allegedly injured.

No amount of liberal construction can alter the fact that the record before us is devoid of anything remotely suggesting that the necessary reliance was present here. The pleadings and affidavit submitted by O'Banner in the trial court state only that he slipped and fell in the restroom of a McDonald's restaurant. They give no indication as to why he went to the restaurant in the first place. The fact that this was a McDonald's may have been completely irrelevant to his decision. For all we know, O'Banner went there simply because it provided the closest bathroom when he needed one or because some friend asked to meet him there.

If O'Banner had any basis to support his position, he was obliged to present it to the trial court. He did not do so, and the time for substantiating any claim of reliance has passed. The appellate court was therefore wrong to reverse the trial court's entry of summary judgment in McDonald's favor based on the apparent agency doctrine.

Trinity Lutheran Church v. Miller

Court of Appeals of Indiana (1983)

The Guild has maintained a Christmas program for sick and infirm members of the congregation who are confined in hospitals or nursing homes. During the Christmas holidays, Guild members bake cookies, place them in baskets made of Christmas cards, and deliver the baskets to the shut-in members of the Church. On December 15, 1980, Goodman, accompanied by his wife Valeda, a Guild member, was driving his automobile while in the process of delivering cookies. He turned his vehicle into Miller's motorcycle. As a result of the accident, Miller's left leg was amputated above the knee.

The facts established the Guild prepared a list of shut-in members who were to receive cookies, designated which Guild members would deliver cookies to specified recipients, and checked to see whether the shut-ins actually received the cookies. The Guild picked the delivery date.

Goodman had participated as a driver in the program for four or five years previously and the Guild knew Goodman would be driving his wife. Goodman testified his only purpose in driving on the day of the accident was to deliver the cookies, the Guild told him where to go, and he would have gone to any address which it had directed. He further testified "he was doing it for the Church-doing it for everyone", and that he would not have delivered the cookies if he had not been so instructed.

The following definitions will be helpful for this opinion:

A master is a principal who employs an agent to perform service in his affairs and who controls or has the right to control the physical conduct of the other in the performance of the service.

A servant is an agent employed by a master to perform service in his affairs whose physical conduct in the performance of the service is controlled or is subject to the right of control by the master.

Agency is the relationship which results from the manifestation of consent by the person to another that the other shall act on his behalf and subject to his control, and consent by the others so to act.

Generally, the doctrine of respondeat superior imposes liability upon a master for the torts of his servants committed while acting within the scope of the servant's employment. The general test in determining the existence of a master-servant relationship is the right to direct and control the conduct of the alleged servant at the time the negligent act occurred. In Indiana the phrase 'right to control' is used not in a specific sense but in a general sense. It refers only to the right and not to the exercise of control over the servant. This is especially true where the work is such as to not demand a great deal of supervision.

The Church argues the evidence is insufficient to support the verdict because there is no evidence that Goodman agreed to subject himself to the Guild's control. It alleges Miller is attempting to utilize the doctrine of respondeat superior based solely upon Goodman's membership in the Church.

The Church contends there is no direct evidence of an agreement between the Guild and Goodman. However, agency may arise by implication and be shown by circumstantial evidence. A master may have a gratuitous servant. The duty of an agent acting gratuitously is the same as other agents.

The facts establish that Goodman was acting within the scope of his employment when the accident occurred. The parties stipulated the cookie bake and delivery are the work of the Guild. Goodman testified his only purpose in driving was to deliver cookies. He was clearly within the scope of the Guild's activity when he struck Miller's motorcycle.

The judgment is affirmed.

V. STRICT LIABILITY

HISTORY

Weaver v. Ward

King's Bench (1616)

Weaver brought an action of trespass of assault and battery against Ward. The defendant pleaded, that he was amongst others by the commandment of the Lords of the Council a trained soldier in London, of the band of one Andrews captain; and so was the plaintiff, and that they were skirmishing with their muskets charged with powder for their exercise *in re militari*, against another captain and his band; and as they were so skirmishing, the defendant *casualiter & per infortunium* & *contra voluntatem suam*, in discharging of his piece did hurt and wound the plaintiff, which is the same, & c. *absque hoc*, that he was guilty *aliter sive alio modo.* And upon demurrer by the plaintiff, judgment was given for him; for though it were agreed, that if men tilt or tourney in the presence of the King, or if two masters of defense playing their prizes kill one another, that this shall be no felony; or if a lunatick kill a man, or the like, because felony must be done *animo felonico*: yet in trespass, which tends only to give damages according to hurt or loss, it is not so; and therefore if a lunatic hurt a man, he shall be answerable in trespass: and therefore no man shall be excused of a trespass (for this is the nature of an excuse, and not of a justification, *prout ei bene licuit*) except it may be judged utterly without his fault.

As if a man by force take my hand and strike you, or if here the defendant had said, that the plaintiff ran cross his piece when it was discharging, or had set forth the case with the circumstances, so as it had appeared to the Court that it had been inevitable, and that the defendant had committed no negligence to give occasion to the hurt.

Brown v. Kendall

Supreme Judicial Court of Massachusetts (1850)

This is an action of trespass, vi et armis, brought by George Brown against George K. Kendall, for a battery. The facts preclude the supposition, that the blow, inflicted by the hand of the defendant upon the person of the plaintiff, was intentional. The whole case proceeds on the assumption, that the damage sustained by the plaintiff, from the stick held by the defendant, was inadvertent and unintentional; and the case involves the question how far, and under what qualifications, the party by whose unconscious act the damage was done is responsible for it. We use the term unintentional rather than involuntary, because in some of the cases the act of holding and using a weapon or instrument, the movement of which is the immediate cause of hurt to another, is a voluntary act, although its particular effect in hitting and hurting another is not within the purpose or intention of the party doing the act.

It appears to us, that some of the confusion in the cases on this subject has grown out of the long-vexed question, under the rule of the common law, whether a party's remedy, should be sought in an action of the case, or of trespass. The result of these cases is, that if the damage complained of is the immediate effect of the act of the defendant, trespass vi et armis lies; if consequential only, and not immediate, case is the proper remedy.

We think the rule is correctly stated that the plaintiff must come prepared with evidence to show either that the intention was unlawful, or that the defendant was in fault; for if the injury was unavoidable, and the conduct of the defendant was free from blame, he will not be liable. If, in the prosecution of a lawful act, a casualty purely accidental arises, no action can be supported for an injury arising therefrom. In applying these rules to the present case, if both plaintiff and defendant at the time of the blow were using ordinary care, or if at that time the defendant was using ordinary care, and the plaintiff was not, or if at that time, both the plaintiff and defendant were not using ordinary care, then the plaintiff could not recover.

In using this term, ordinary care, what constitutes ordinary care will vary with the circumstances of cases. In general, it means that kind and degree of care, which prudent and cautious men would use, such as is required by the exigency of the case, and such as is necessary to guard against probable danger. A man, who should have occasion to discharge a gun, on an open and extensive marsh, or in a forest, would be required to use less circumspection and care, than if he were to do the same thing in an inhabited town, village, or city. To make an accident, or casualty, or as the law sometimes states it, inevitable accident, it must be such an accident as the defendant could not have avoided by the use of the kind and degree of care necessary to the exigency, and in the circumstances in which he was placed.

We have no doubt that the act of the defendant in attempting to part the fighting dogs, one of which was his own, and for the injurious acts of which he might be responsible, was a lawful and proper act, which he might do by proper and safe means. If, then, in doing this act, using due care and all proper precautions necessary to the exigency of the case, to avoid hurt to others, in raising his stick for that purpose, he accidentally hit the plaintiff in his eye, and wounded him, this was the result of pure accident, or was involuntary and unavoidable, and therefore the action would not lie. Or if the defendant was chargeable with some negligence, and if the plaintiff was also chargeable with negligence, we think the plaintiff cannot recover without showing that the damage was caused wholly by the act of the defendant, and that the plaintiff's own negligence did not contribute as an efficient cause to produce it.

Case and Davis v. Mark

Ohio Supreme Court (1825)

The error assigned in this case is, that the court of common pleas arrested the judgment, on the ground that the facts amounted to a trespass vi et armis, and that this action could not be sustained. It became necessary, therefore, to ascertain the distinction between trespass and case, and apply it to the facts and circumstances set out in the declaration.

The plaintiffs charge that the defendant was the owner and commander of a certain steamboat, called the Congress, navigating the Ohio river-that he so carelessly navigated, managed, and steered the said steamboat, that he run her foul of, struck, and broke a certain coal-boat, owned and navigated by the plaintiffs, by means of which the said coal-boat immediately sunk, and was lost.

The plaintiffs contend that the injury here described was consequential and not direct; but if direct, that it was the result of negligence, and that in either event, the action ought to be case.

The first part of this proposition certainly can not be sustained. The terms consequential and immediate are well understood. That is immediate which is produced by the act to which it is ascribed, without the intervention or agency of any distinct, immediate cause, but the effect of an intermediate cause is sometimes considered as a trespass, produced by a preceding cause, when the former is the immediate effect of the latter. Thus, the effect of pulling the trigger of a loaded gun is the production of fire, which causes the powder to burn, which gives motion to the ball, by which the injury is produced; here the whole transaction is considered as one act, and the trespass is ascribed to the pulling of the trigger, though the injury is the immediate effect of an intervening cause, which gave motion and force to the ball. In this case the defendant was at the helm, directing the course of his boat-the steam which gave it motion was under his control; the boat therefore received its motion and course from the defendant, by which it was made to strike the plaintiffs' boat, so that it was broken, and immediately sunk. Here there was no distinct intermediate agency. The injury was the breaking and sinking of the coal-boat-the cause of that injury was the act of the defendant, in running the steamboat against her. The injury, therefore, can not be considered as consequential-it was direct and immediate.

The second part of the proposition is equally untenable. The defendant could not shelter himself under the plea of negligence, and the plaintiffs are not at liberty to force on him an apology of which he could not avail himself. The character of the transaction, in reference to the form of the suit can not be affected by the presence or absence of negligence. That circumstance may, in some cases, have an impression on the amount of damages recovered, by varying the degree of malice, but it can not change the nature of the act. If it has the ingredient that stamps it with the character of a trespass, it must be treated as such. If a man shooting at game, does it so carelessly and negligently as to wound a person happening to be in the vicinity, the fact that it was done carelessly, and without design, will not protect him from an action of trespass. So if a man in self-defense, aims a blow at another, and by negligence or want of care strikes a third person, it is a trespass.

The proposition set up by the plaintiffs that where there is negligence, although the injury be immediate, the party may waive the immediate injury, and claim the damages only which is the consequence of the injury, amounts to this, that he may take up an entire, connected transaction by parts, and rely on as much of it as will answer his purpose, to the exclusion of the residue. This would be a convenient privilege, as it would often save a plaintiff from the unpleasant consequences of a nonsuit; but it would destroy established distinctions, and introduce an uncertainty in judicial proceedings which would be inconvenient and injurious. One of the reasons given for not sustaining actions on the case, where the circumstances amount to a clear trespass, and vice versa, is the necessity of preserving the boundary of actions, by which I understand the rules that prescribe what particular action or form of suit, shall be brought for each particular injury. These rules can not be uniform, if plaintiffs are permitted to garble their cases, so as to convert an unequivocal trespass, into trespass on the case. Were this permitted, I can not conceive of any trespass that may not be sued for in the form of case. What are the ordinary concomitants of a severe battery? They are plain, bodily and mental-incapacity for business-the expense of medical aid, and disgrace in the public estimation. If under the pretense of waiving the immediate injury, which is pain, the party may go for the consequential damage, which is the incapacity for business, expense, etc., it will be a matter of but little moment whether he sue in trespass or in case, as the only difference in the result would be the portion of damage that might be allowed for the pain inflicted. If this be conceded, the boundary between trespass and case is at once broken down-courts have no control over it-it is in the power of every plaintiff, and may be varied as the convenience of the moment may require. Should a party mistake his remedy, and sue in case for an undoubted trespass, he has only to turn on his opponent, and say, I waive the immediate injury, and he is perfectly safe. I have looked into the authorities cited to this point, and although some of them seem to be in opposition to the general tenor of the cases on the subject, I can not believe that they sustain the plaintiffs.

The uncertainty that exists in cases of this character, may be ascribed, in some measure, to the decisions that have been made in case for running down ships, where the force that causes the injury does not always proceed from the agency of the person having the management of the vessel. Winds, waves, and currents may counteract his designs, by moving the ship in a course he has endeavored to avoid. It may be easy to determine the presence of this agency, but difficult to ascertain the extent of its effect. On a supposition that the defendant's vessel has been taken to the point where the injury was done, without his agency, or in opposition to his efforts, honestly made to prevent it, it would be hard to declare him a trespasser. The impossibility of knowing with certainty the real extent of the extraneous cause, and how far it might have been in the power of the defendant to counteract it, or whether his efforts by miscalculation or design, did not co-operate with it, renders it difficult to apply a uniform rule. But this difficulty can not be found in cases that receive an unequivocal character from the certainty of the facts on which they depend.

Something may also be ascribed to the reluctance with which courts yield to the necessity of deciding against a just claim, on a technical objection, or of turning a party round, because he has mistaken his remedy. In some instances this feeling has induced judges to avail themselves of circumstances in support of a case, having justice and equity on its side, that do not form a legal distinction, or bring it within any established rule. The same circumstances are relied on in other cases, which tends to render the law apparently doubtful. For example, in some cases we find the lawfulness or unlawfulness of the act much insisted on, from which an inattentive reader might conclude that that circumstance formed the rule of distinction between trespass and case; but it is well known that acts strictly lawful frequently amount to trespass, while those that are not unlawful are attended with injuries, for which trespass can not be sustained. Thus, if a man shooting at a target, which is lawful, miss his aim and wound another, trespass will lie; but if he dig a pit in the highway, into which a traveler falls, trespass will not lie, although the act was unlawful.

In some cases, great stress is laid on the force that accompanies the act, by which an injury is done, but this is not a distinguishing fact-it forms no criterion by which to decide the character of the injury, or of the remedy. This will appear from the very familiar case of the log: if it be thrown into the highway with great force and violence, and afterward a traveler falls over it, he can not have trespass; but if it be laid very gently on his foot, by which he is injured, trespass will lie. So if a man quietly enters the inclosure of his neighbor and picks up an apple, trespass will lie; but if he should, by forcible and violent effort, obstruct a watercourse, whereby the water is caused to flow back on his neighhor's land, it would not be a trespass-he would be liable only in an action on the case.

It has also been contended, as it is in this case, that when the act from which the injury proceeds, was done willfully, trespass is the proper remedy; but not so when it is the effect of carelessness, or negligence. But this distinction can not be sustained, as will be evident from a little reflection. In the cases before mentioned, the log was thrown into the highway, and the water-course was obstructed intentionally, and it might be, to produce the very injury that ensued, but trespass could not be maintained. On the other hand, if, while a person is carelessly handling a loaded gun, he should unintentionally cause it to go off and wound another, trespass would lie, although the act was not willful, and the injury was the effect of negligence. So if a man should carelessly throw a brickbat from the scaffold and unintentionally wound another, trespass would lie. In Leame and Bray, it was proved that the accident happened from negligence, and not willfully, yet it was decided that trespass was the proper action. So in Weaver and Ward, where the defendant, exercising in the trained bands, fired his musket, and by accident hurt the plaintiff, it was trespass; and where a person suddenly turning round knocked another down, unintentionally and without seeing him, trespass was holden to lie.

The true distinction unquestionably is, whether the injury be immediate, or consequential, as will appear clearly from the authorities.

Taylor v. Rainbow, 2 Hen. & Munf. 436, was trespass on the case, for shooting off a gun in a place where many people were assembled, so carelessly and negligently, though without any design to injure the plaintiff, that the contents of the gun struck his leg, and wounded him, in consequence of which wound his leg was amputated-he was unable to attend to his business, and put to great expense, etc. It was contended that the plaintiff had mistaken his action, and that the defendant could be made answerable only in an action of trespass vi et armis. The whole court were of that opinion, on the ground that the injury was immediate, being occasioned by the discharge of the gun. Judge Roane remarked, that there was no position in the law more clearly established than this, that wherever the injury is committed by the immediate act complained of, the action must be trespass.

Covel v. Laming, 1 Camp. N. P. 497. In this case the defendant was the owner of a ship: being on board, and standing at the helm, he unintentionally, and through ignorance and want of skill, run her against the plaintiff's ship in the river Thames. The action was trespass. It was contended for defendant, that the action could not sustained, unless the act were willfully done, and that it was willfulness alone that court determine the nature of the act.

Lord Ellenborough declared he had always been of opinion, that the only just and intelligible criterion of trespass and case, was, whether the injury complained of arose directly, or followed consequentially from the act of the defendant. That as the defendant at the helm guided his vessel, the winds and waves being only instrumental in carrying her along, the force proceeded from him, and the injury was the immediate effect of that force.

Reynolds v. Clarke, 2 Ld. Raym. 1399, was an action of trespass for putting up spouts to the defendant's house by which the water was collected in great quantities, and thrown onto the plaintiff's land, by reason whereof, etc. The question was, whether case or trespass was the proper action. The court decided the distinction in law to be, where the immediate act itself occasioned a prejudice, or is an injury to the plaintiff, or where the act itself be not an injury, but a consequence from that act, is prejudicial to the plaintiff; that in the first case, trespass vi et armis will lie; in the last, it will not. And in remarking on the case of Preston v. Mason, cited at bar, from Hard. 61, the court observed, that case might be law, because it was laid, that the defendant made the water to run; which was the same as if it had been laid, that the defendant poured the water; in which case trespass would have lain, because the immediate act of pouring would have been a trespass. In the report of this case, as we find it in Stra. 634, the chief justice is represented as saying, if the action in the first instance be unlawful, trespass will lie; but if the act be prima facie lawful, and the prejudice to another is not immediate, but consequential, it must be an action on the case; but the chief justice, in his own report of the case lays no stress on the lawfulness, or unlawfulness of the act.

Savignar v. Roome, 6 Term, 125, was an action on the case, for driving willfully against the plaintiff's carriage, whereby it was injured. After verdict, judgment was arrested, because the injury was immediate, and the action, if any could be sustained, should have been trespass.

In the case of Scott v. Shepherd, as we have it reported in 2 Blac. and 3 Wils., where there was no diversity of opinion as to the rule, that where the injury is direct and immediate, the action should be trespass. The disagreement was as to the proper inference to be drawn from the facts of the case. Judge Blackstone considered the injury as proceeding from the person who last threw the squib, and not from the defendant. The other judge considered that after the first act of throwing the squib, the different directions which it received from other hands was a continuation of the first act of the defendant, and that the injury was the immediate consequence of that act, and on that ground the action of trespass was sustained.

In Howard v. Banks, 2 Burr. 1114, the distinction between trespass and case was recognized to be this: immediate damage to the plaintiff's property is a ground for trespass, consequential damage to it is a ground for case. The court decided that the damage was consequential, and sustained the action.

In 1 Swift's Digest, 540, it is laid down, that the criterion is not whether the act was accompanied with force, or whether there was an intent to do the injury, or whether the injury was occasioned by negligence; but the question always will be, whether the injury was the direct and immediate effect of the act complained of, or whether it was merely the consequence of some act or omission.

In Leame v. Bray, 3 East, 593, the whole court recognized the rule laid down in Scott v. Shepherd, that where the injury is direct and immediate, the remedy is trespass; where it is mediate and consequential, it is case. This was said to be the rule deducible from all the authorities, ancient and modern; and Le Blanc, Justice, declared that in all the books the invariable principle to be collected is, that where the injury is immediate on the act done, then trespass lies; but where it is not immediate, but consequential, then the remedy is case.

On the whole, we are well satisfied that whatever may be the apparent discrepancy between the cases, the rule is clearly and judiciously settled, that where the injury is direct and immediate, the action must be trespass, whether the act were done willfully or by negligence and want of care; and as the facts set out in the declaration show that such was the character of the injury complained of in this case.

ANIMALS

State v. Mathis

Supreme Court of North Carolina (1908)

Judge Battle says: "In England, where all, or nearly all, the lands were enclosed by the respective owners, the law requires that each proprietor shall keep his horses, cattle, and other livestock on his own premises, and if he permits them to go upon the land of another, it will be a trespass for which he will be responsible." He proceeds to give an interesting account of the change adopted in this country, by reason of the different conditions of things, concluding that, by the statutes requiring every planter to maintain, around his cultivated land, a fence of prescribed height, "general common, because of vicinage, throughout the state was established." It was upon this ground held that an owner of cattle was not required to fence them in, and therefore not liable for damages done by them in going upon the lands of another.

If the condition, in respect to the agricultural system of the people, so changes as to make it conducive to their interest to require all stock to be fenced in, and relieve the landowner of the duty to fence it out, we can see no good reason why the Legislature may not by appropriate legislation do so. For the past 25 years, such has been the policy of the state, as evidenced by our legislation. This being true, we do not see why the Legislature may not forbid stock running at large in the county, or any township thereof, and declare a mountain range, a creek, or other natural or political boundary a lawful fence, or the limit within which the law shall operate.

Rector v. Southern Coal Company

Supreme Court of North Carolina (1926)

The question of law presented by this case is, what duty does the owner of a mule owe to an employee who has charge of the mule and who goes into the stall where the mule is? A mule is a melancholy creature. It has been said that a mule has neither price of ancestry nor hope of posterity. Josh Billings remarked that if he had to preach the funeral of a mule he would stand at his head. Men love and pet horses, dogs, cats, and lambs. These domestic animals have found their way in literature. Shakespeare said of a horse: "I will not change my horse with any that treads but on four pasterns; when I bestride him I soar, I am a hawk; he trots the air; the earth sings when he touches it." *The Life of King Henry the Fifth*, Act 3, Scene 7.

But nobody loves or pets a mule. No poet has ever penned a sonnet or an ode to him, and no prose writer has ever paid a tribute to his good qualities. He is kicked and cuffed, and beaten and sworn at, and frequently underfed and forced to work under extremely adverse conditions; yet, withal, he has a grim endurance and a stubborn courage which survives his misfortunes and enables him to do a large portion of the world's rough work. It is a matter of common knowledge among men who know mules and deal with them that they are uncertain, moody, and morose. This particular mule, charged with injuring plaintiff, was referred to in the oral argument as an "unsafe mule" and as an "unsafe tool and appliance." The idealist may dream of the day when the world is safe for democracy, but this event will perhaps arrive long before the world will be safe from the heels of a mule.

The evidence in this case discloses that the mule of the defendant did not kick or bite or attack the plaintiff, but that as the plaintiff went behind the mule into the stall he whirled around and his rump pressed the plaintiff against a part or partition of the stall and mashed him.

The liability of an owner for injuries committed by domestic animals, such as dogs, horses and mules, depends upon two essential facts: (1) The animal inflicting the injury must be dangerous, vicious, mischievous, or ferocious, or one termed in the law as possessing a vicious propensity. (2) The owner must have actual or constructive knowledge of the vicious propensity, character, and habits of the animal.

The determinative inquiry, therefore, on this record, is whether or not there is any competent evidence that defendant's mule was "accustomed to do mischief." The testimony of the plaintiff is set out at length. It appears that the plaintiff testified:

"I cannot tell you now exactly what the vicious habits of the mule were. If you touched it or went to go by it, it would whirl to get away, and, if it could, it would catch you. It was just generally skittish and scared to death all the time. I don't know of any other bad or vicious act committed by the mule except the injury received by me. He nearly ran over me two or three times before. That mule had never injured any other person to my knowledge. If it did injure any person during the time I had charge of it I don't remember it."

It is true that the plaintiff testified:

"I told Mr. Parker that old mule was dangerous and that it would kill somebody some of these days. He said it had no sense."

This statement of plaintiff was a mere declaration of a conclusion and is not supported by his evidence, because it clearly appears that the mule had never injured anyone else before or since the injury to the plaintiff, and that the particular act of the mule in whirling around when the plaintiff went in the stall was the only "bad or vicious act" committed by him. This evidence would almost amount to giving the mule a "good character."

The defendant offered no evidence, and, after viewing the evidence of the plaintiff with that liberality which the law requires, it does not appear that the act complained of was in itself a vicious act or one flowing from a vicious propensity.

Upon the whole record, therefore, we are of the opinion that there was no sufficient evidence that the mule was "accustomed to do mischief," or that the owner had actual or constructive knowledge of any vicious or dangerous habit or propensity, and that the motion for nonsuit should have been allowed. If recovery could be permitted under the facts in this case, then every farmer or contractor in the state could ill afford to keep a mule.

Reversed.

NUISANCE

Page County Appliance Center v. Honeywell

Supreme Court of Iowa (1984)

Plaintiff Page County Appliance Center (Appliance Center), sued Honeywell, and ITT Electronic Travel Services (ITT), for nuisance.

Appliance Center has owned and operated an appliance store in Shenandoah, Iowa, since 1953. Before 1980 Pearson had no reception trouble with his display televisions. In early January 1980, however, ITT placed one of its computers with Central Travel Service in Shenandoah as part of a nationwide plan to lease computers to retail travel agents. Central Travel was separated by only one other business from the Appliance Center. This ITT computer was manufactured, installed, and maintained by Honeywell.

Thereafter many of Pearson's customers told him his display television pictures were bad; on two of the three channels available in Shenandoah he had a difficult time getting a picture that was fit to watch. After unsuccessfully attempting several remedial measures, in late January 1980, he finally traced the interference to the operations of Central Travel's computer. Both defendants concede Pearson's problems were caused by radiation leaking from the Honeywell computer.

Pearson discussed the problem with Kay Crowell, owner of Central Travel. She placed a call to ITT's president in New York. Although he was unavailable, ITT personnel apparently notified Honeywell. ITT's only contact with Pearson was through a telephone call some ten months later. At that time Pearson told ITT's sales representative that Honeywell was working on the problem; he made no effort to follow up on ITT's interest in the problem.

Honeywell indeed was working to correct the situation, and had been since February 1980. Honeywell technicians made repeated trips to make various unsuccessful adjustments to the computer. They found the computer was operating properly; the interference-causing radiation was a design and not a service problem. Pearson then telephoned Armando Benitez, the technicians' supervisor. Pearson testified Benitez told him Honeywell was "way over budget" on the Central Travel computer and that "if you don't like it, you can move."

Nonetheless, in early fall of 1980 Honeywell sent out Phil Brzozoski, one of its engineers from Boston. According to Pearson, when he asked Brzozoski why it had taken him so long to come, the latter replied he would not have been there at all had Pearson not instituted suit; that was the way big business worked. Kay Crowell, admittedly Pearson's friend, testified Brzozoski told her the delay was "good business." The Honeywell engineers effected a 70 percent improvement in the television reception by certain modifications of the computer in the fall of 1980. Pearson, still dissatisfied, started this action in December. While the suit was pending, Honeywell further modified the computer, finally alleviating Pearson's problems in May 1982.

The Appliance Center's case against Honeywell and ITT finally was submitted to the jury on the theories of nuisance and tortious interference with prospective business relations. The jury found for the Appliance Center against the remaining defendants on both theories, and further found the Appliance Center should recover $71,000 in compensatory damages and $150,000 in exemplary damages.

We note the Appliance Center is alleging a "private nuisance," that is, an actionable interference with a person's interest in the private use and enjoyment of his or her property. It also is apparent that if Central Travel's computer emissions constitute a nuisance it is a "nuisance per accidens, or in fact"—a lawful activity conducted in such a manner as to be a nuisance.

Principles governing our consideration of nuisance claims are well established. One's use of property should not unreasonably interfere with or disturb a neighbor's comfortable and reasonable use and enjoyment of his or her estate. A fair test of whether the operation of a lawful trade or industry constitutes a nuisance is the reasonableness of conducting it in the manner, at the place, and under the circumstances shown by the evidence. Each case turns on its own facts and ordinarily the ultimate issue is one of fact, not law. The existence of a nuisance is not affected by the intention of its creator not to injure anyone. Priority of occupation and location—who was there first—is a circumstance of considerable weight.

When the alleged nuisance is claimed to be offensive to the person, courts apply the standard of "normal persons in a particular locality" to measure the existence of a nuisance. This normalcy standard also is applied where the use of property is claimed to be affected. The plaintiff cannot, by devoting his own land to an unusually sensitive use, make a nuisance out of conduct of the adjoining defendant which would otherwise be harmless.

In the case before us, ITT asserts the Appliance Center's display televisions constituted a hypersensitive use of its premises as a matter of law, and equates this situation to cases involving light thrown on outdoor theater screens in which light-throwing defendants have carried the day. We cannot equate the rare outdoor theater screen with the ubiquitous television that exists, in various numbers, in almost every home. Clearly, the presence of televisions on any premises is not such an abnormal condition that we can say, as a matter of law, that the owner has engaged in a peculiarly sensitive use of the property. This consideration, as well as related considerations of unreasonableness, gravity of harm, utility of conduct, and priority of occupation, are factual determinations that should have been submitted to the jury in this case. We find no trial court error in refusing to direct a verdict on this ground.

Honeywell asserts trial court should have granted its motion for directed verdict because, even though it manufactured the computer, Central Travel and ITT were in control of the instrument at all relevant times; thus Honeywell did not have the legal right to terminate its use. Honeywell devotes ten and one-half pages of its brief to this thesis without mentioning that it had an ongoing contract to service and maintain the computer.

Honeywell's design permitted radiation to escape this computer, although technology was available to minimize this effect. Apparently factors of cost and ease of service access weighed more in the design decision. Honeywell was the only party with the technological know-how to control the radiation leakage. Its maintenance contract with ITT clearly absolved it of any liability if anyone else made any alterations or additions to the equipment, and reserved the right to terminate the agreement should that occur. As with ITT, we think Honeywell's material participation was an issue for the finder of fact.

Honeywell asserts there was no competent evidence the computer interference caused plaintiff any actual damages, therefore, its motion for directed verdict on this ground should have been sustained.

Appliance Center placed its 1976 through 1981 tax returns in evidence. Large decreases in income in 1980 and 1981 were posted, as contrasted to a growth in the prior years. There was testimony that color televisions constituted 60 percent of the gross sales, and that sales of these items dropped drastically in 1980 and 1981.

This evidence was not as precise as one might wish, nor was the effect, if any, of "a little bit of a downturn" in business generally in the community. Nonetheless, we hold it minimally was sufficient to take the issue to the jury, and that trial court did not err in refusing to direct a verdict on this ground.

Both Honeywell and ITT asserted there was no evidence to justify submitting the issue of punitive damages to the jury. The issue was submitted, and the jury fixed an award of $150,000 in favor of Appliance Center against both defendants.

Exemplary damages are not awarded as a matter of right; rather, their allowance rests with the fact finder. Their award depends upon whether under the facts in a particular case such an award is appropriate in order to punish an offending party or discourage others from similar wrongful conduct. This determination depends upon the existence of malice--either actual or legal malice. Legal malice may be established by showing wrongful or illegal conduct committed or continued with a willful or reckless disregard of another's rights.

The mere commission of a nuisance justifying an award of actual damages would be insufficient to justify the assessment of punitive damages as a penalty. In other words, to be liable for actual damages one need only create or commit a nuisance, but to be punished for it he must create and persistently maintain it with a reckless disregard for the rights of others.

In many controversies involving punitive damages, the fighting issue is the existence of legal malice. Viewed in a light most favorable to plaintiffs, it is to us evident some substantial evidence was presented disclosing defendant knowingly and intentionally, without just cause, persisted in the maintenance of a private nuisance despite repeated protests and complaints of its harmful consequences, thereby disclosing such willful disregard for plaintiffs' rights as to create a jury issue relative to punitive damages.

Under the record made in this trial, we cannot say trial court erred in submitting the punitive damage claim against Honeywell to the jury.

We do not reach the same decision, however, with respect to ITT. The record made here does not disclose substantial evidence that it was guilty of legal malice—a showing of wrongful or illegal conduct committed or continued with a willful or reckless disregard of another's rights.

ABNORMALLY DANGEROUS ACTIVITIES

Restatement First

An activity is ultrahazardous if it

(a) necessarily involves a risk of serious harm to the person, land or chattels of others which cannot be eliminated by the exercise of the utmost care, and

(b) is not a matter of common usage.

Restatement Second

In determining whether an activity is abnormally dangerous, the following factors are to be considered:

(a) existence of a high degree of risk of some harm to the person, land or chattels of others;

(b) likelihood that the harm that results from it will be great;

(c) inability to eliminate the risk by the exercise of reasonable care;

(d) extent to which the activity is not a matter of common usage;

(e) inappropriateness of the activity to the place where it is carried on; and

(f) extent to which its value to the community is outweighed by its dangerous attributes.

Restatement Third

(a) An actor who carries on an abnormally dangerous activity is subject to strict liability for physical harm resulting from the activity.

(b) An activity is abnormally dangerous if:

> (1) the activity creates a foreseeable and highly significant risk of physical harm even when reasonable care is exercised by all actors; and
>
> (2) the activity is not one of common usage.

Koos v. Roth

Supreme Court of Oregon (1982)

We are called upon to decide whether a farmer who employs field burning as an agricultural technique is strictly liable to pay damages when the fire enters upon and destroys a neighbor's property, without any need to show that the field burning was conducted negligently.

Defendant was engaged in the commercial production of grass seed. After the grass seed was harvested, a crew of men equipped with mobile water tanks burned the field by setting fire to dry straw, having first plowed a protective strip around the perimeter. While defendant's field was being burned, plaintiffs' adjoining field caught fire, causing damage to real and personal property. Although no one testified to seeing how the fire on plaintiffs' property started, the witnesses agreed that probably a whirlwind carried burning material from defendant's field.

The trial court denied plaintiffs' motion and directed a verdict for defendant on all counts. On appeal, the Court of Appeals concluded that the trespass resulted from an ultrahazardous activity.

I. Abnormally dangerous activities.

In Bedell v. Goulter, the court adopted the reasoning of Exner v. Sherman Power Co. (2nd Cir.1931), quoting extensively from the opinion of Judge Augustus Hand in that case. The chief issue was not so much whether an explosion of dynamite, intentional or accidental, results in strict liability but whether the harm must result from the tangible impact of debris scattered by the explosion, and this court followed Exner to reject that distinction. Strict liability followed simply from the intrinsic dangerousness of explosives. Justice Lusk's extensive review of the cases quoted from Exner:

"When a person engages in such a dangerous activity, useful though it be, he becomes an insurer. If damage is inflicted, there ordinarily is liability, in the absence of excuse. When, as here, the defendant, though without fault, has engaged in the perilous activity of storing large quantities of a dangerous explosive for use in his business, we think there is no justification for relieving it of liability, and that the owner of the business, rather than a third person who has no relation to the explosion, other than that of injury, should bear the loss."

The opinion then quoted the Restatement (First) of Torts, which at that time defined an activity as "ultrahazardous" if it "(a) necessarily involves a risk of serious harm to the person, land or chattels of others which cannot be eliminated by the exercise of the utmost care, and (b) is not a matter of common usage."

In McLane v. Northwest Natural Gas, Justice Holman's opinion made clear that the danger of an activity did not depend on the frequency with which it miscarries, though this could be an important indicator, and that the destructive effects of the activity need not occur beyond the defendant's premises. Also, the place in which the activity is carried on makes the locality in which the activity is carried on a relevant factor. The locality was said to be relevant to determining whether an activity is extraordinary, exceptional, or unusual.

In a subsequent case, the court equated the older terms "extra hazardous" or "ultrahazardous" with the phrase "abnormally dangerous" employed in the second Restatement of Torts. The change of phrasing from "extra hazardous" or "ultrahazardous" to "abnormally dangerous," though subtle, created an ambiguity. To what norm does "abnormally" refer? The older phrases kept the focus on the hazardous character of the activity, on its essentially irreducible potential for causing substantial harm. Like them, "abnormally dangerous" literally means extraordinarily dangerous, much more dangerous than other activities. But the newer phrase lends itself to invoking social as well as physical norms, as if it read "abnormal and dangerous activities," thereby mixing questions of cause and effect, or probabilities and magnitudes of harm in the natural world, with what may be called societal considerations.

Whether the danger is so great as to give rise to strict liability depends both on the probability and on the magnitude of the threatened harm. If the consequences of a mishap are potentially lethal or highly destructive of health or property, a slight likelihood that they will occur suffices, even if the harm in the actual occurrence is less severe. Conversely, we have held that even when the risk "only moderately threatens economic activities rather than harm to life, health, or property or environment," the activity may carry strict liability if the consequences are highly probable or, if the activity can be carried on only with a substantially uncontrollable likelihood that the damage will sometimes occur.

The assessment of extraordinary danger thus has been based on the magnitude of harmful events and their probability despite all reasonable precautions. The role of societal criteria in our decisions is more doubtful. The opinions have made no clear distinction between the notions of "common usage" and of appropriateness of an activity to the location, nor whether "common usage" and "appropriate location" are identical, overlapping, or cumulative tests for escaping strict liability for highly dangerous activities. The test of common or uncommon usage has been recited to mean not only an activity that is widely carried on by many persons but also one that is accepted as natural or necessary by the inhabitants of the locality, like the irrigation ditches, or the urban piping of gas. Likewise, a location may sometimes be called "appropriate" because the dangerous activity is useful or necessary, and sometimes because it is less likely to cause extreme harm in that location. The second meaning clarifies but adds nothing to the initial equation of danger.

The greater divergence from the "factors" quoted in Nicolai v. Day, concerns the value of the dangerous activity to the community. In the present case, defendant presses upon us the economic importance of the grass seed industry, which makes extensive use of field burning, and of the forest products industry, which is concerned about the potential implications for its practices of burning slash and debris. This consideration, however, has not been a factor in this court's assessment of strict liability for abnormally dangerous activities.

There are at least two reasons not to judge civil liability for unintended harm by a court's views of the utility or value of the harmful activity. One reason lies in the nature of the judgment. Utility and value often are subjective and controversial. They will be judged differently by those who profit from an activity and those who are endangered by it, and between one locality and another. The use of explosives to remove old buildings for a new highway or shopping center may be described as slum clearance or as the destruction of historic landmarks and neighborhoods. On a smaller scale, it may celebrate a traditional holiday which some may value more highly than either buildings or roads. Highly toxic materials may be necessary to the production of agricultural pesticides, or of drugs, or of chemical or bacteriological weapons, or of industrial products of all sorts; does liability for injury from their storage or movement depend on the utility of these products? Judges, like others, may differ about such values; they can hardly be described as conclusions of law.

The second reason why the value of a hazardous activity does not preclude strict liability for its consequences is that the conclusion does not follow from the premise. In the prior cases, the court did not question the economic value of blasting, crop-dusting, or storing natural gas. In an action for damages, the question is not whether the activity threatens such harm that it should not be continued. The question is who shall pay for harm that has been done. The loss has occurred. It is a cost of the activity whoever bears it. To say that when the activity has great economic value the cost should be borne by others is no more or less logical than to say that when the costs of an activity are borne by others it gains in value. This, in effect, is postulated in the argument that the industry which relies on field burning is highly valuable but could not survive the cost difference of insurance against strict liability instead of negligence.

Sometimes, moreover, the cost is borne by others engaged in the same or similar activity. That is true in this case, where plaintiffs and defendant farmed adjoining fields. The same can occur in crop-dusting, in burning forest debris, or in the escape of stored water. If the accidentally impoverished neighbor is told that in the long run the losses will balance out, he may answer, like one economist, that in the long run we are all dead. Society has other ways to lighten the burdens of costly but unavoidable accidents on a valued industry than to let them fall haphazardly on the industry's neighbors.

That, at least, has been this court's view of the common law in the absence of relevant legislation. The person conducting the activity can choose whether or not to chance the potentially costly consequences. If he also owned the adjoining property, he might choose not to take the risk of fire, or blasting, or aerial spraying of toxic chemicals, with any degree of care. The potential victim cannot make that choice. Thus, where one of two innocent persons must suffer, the loss should fall upon the one who created the risk causing the harm. Strict liability accompanies the decision to undertake the hazardous activity: The element of fault, if it can be called that, lies in the deliberate choice by the defendant to inflict a high degree of risk upon his neighbor, even though utmost care is observed in so doing.

In sum, the focus in our cases has been on assessing abnormal hazards by their potential for harm of exceptional magnitude or probability despite the utmost care. This potential may, of course, differ with the place where the activity is conducted; but an activity is not otherwise immune from strict liability because it is "appropriate" in its place. If there is an appropriate location for aerial crop-dusting, it is over open agricultural fields, however, mere frequency of usage by specialists in a particular field does not determine whether or not the activity should pay its own way. A danger that is only ordinary in an appropriate location may be abnormal where it exposes others to an extraordinary risk or magnitude of harm, but an extraordinary risk does not become ordinary because it occurs in its own appropriate place.

The societal qualification, rather, is that a dangerous activity is not an abnormal hazard, even though its intrinsic dangers cannot be prevented, if it is a "common usage." That term has been extended beyond its original meaning of widespread and accepted individual practice to embrace also essential service activities like the distribution of gas or electricity. In other words, a dangerous activity is not extraordinarily so if nearly everyone routinely does it or expects to have it done for him.

II. Fire as an abnormal hazard.

The use of fire, of course, is the aboriginal "dangerous activity." It should not be assumed that the common law demanded a showing of negligence to recover for losses from the spread of a fire intentionally set on another's property. The common law decisions were to the contrary, although exactly what rule of liability they established is disputed. An early common law action for letting one's fire escape and injure his neighbor is traced to the 1401 report of Beaulieu v. Finglam, Y.B. 2 Hen. IV. fo. 18, pl. 5. It applied equally to a fire set outdoors, for burning stubble in a field, as to fire in one's house. "Once it was established that the fire was ignis suus [i.e., the defendant's fire], and that it had spread, the defendant was strictly liable for consequent damage to the plaintiff's property. It was not necessary to show that the defendant had been careless. "

These principles do not lead to strict liability for the use of fire as such. The use must be abnormally dangerous, creating an effectively uncontrollable danger of serious harm beyond the ordinary risks associated with common uses of fire that are readily avoided by due care. It appears that field burning fits this description. It differs from other domestic and industrial uses of fire, including the spark-throwing steam locomotives whose incendiary propensities were a classic cost of industrial progress, because it is used specifically for destruction. Any fire means the destruction of raw material by oxidation, with attendant dangers; but in field burning, as in using explosives and herbicides, the same destruction that poses the danger to the user's neighbor is the user's very purpose. That alone does not make every backyard burner an abnormally dangerous activity. It is a matter of scale as well as location. When fire reaches the magnitude of burning essentially the whole surface of a large area open to the winds, the possibility that it will spread beyond its intended bounds cannot be excluded with any practical degree of care.

Also, the abnormal character of the danger is not negated because the field burning occurs in its appropriate location. Field burning is not a "common usage" in the sense that it is an ordinary activity that many people routinely expect to do for themselves, like domestic fires, or to have done for them, like the distribution of water, gas, electricity and other common goods. Even in farming, field burning is not a generalized use, though widely employed for certain kinds of crops.

VI. WORKERS' COMPENSATION

Jaeger Baking Company v. Kretschmann

Supreme Court of Wisconsin (1980)

The sole issue on review is whether sec. 102.03(1)(c)1, which provides workers compensation coverage to "any employee injured while going between an employer's designated parking lot and the employer's work premises while on a direct route and in the ordinary and usual way," covers an employee who, although he has made no use of the employer's parking lot, is injured on his way to work at a point on the direct path between the employer's parking lot and work premises. Stated another way, does the amended statute cover only those employees who are injured while proceeding to or from the employer's parking lot, or does it create a zone of coverage between the two portions of the employer's work premises.

Heinrich Kretschmann was injured while walking to work shortly before 2:00 a.m. the morning, when two unknown persons attacked him on a public sidewalk in the City of Milwaukee. On the night of the injury, he took a city bus to work. Upon alighting at the bus stop, Kretschmann walked directly toward the bakery's employee entrance. Kretschmann was walking on the public sidewalk adjacent to the bakery building and was about 50 feet from the employee entrance when attacked. The place where the attack occurred was on the direct route which an employee using the parking lot would have taken in travelling from the lot to the employee entrance. Had Kretschmann used the parking lot and then walked to the employee entrance, his route would have taken him to the point where he was attacked.

The department examiner denied Kretschmann's application for worker's compensation, finding that the injury did not occur on the premises of the employer and did not result from an occurrence on the premises; that at the time of the injury the employee was not performing service growing out of and incidental to his employment and the accident causing injury did not arise out of the employment.

Upon appeal to the Workers' Compensation Commission, the examiner's findings were set aside. The Commission explained its reasons for reversing the examiner as follows:

"Wisconsin Statute 102.03(1) does not state or infer that the injured employee must have used the designated parking lot. The applicant met the conditions of liability by the fact that at the time of this assault he was proceeding in the ordinary and usual way on a direct route between the designated parking lot and the employer's work premises. It is the opinion of the Commissioners that an employee arriving at work by bus is entitled to the same protection under the Wisconsin Workmen's Compensation Act as an employee who uses the designated parking lot, as long as the employee is on a direct route between the designated parking lot and the work premises."

Section 102.03 sets forth the conditions which must be satisfied to impose liability under the Worker's Compensation Act. In part, the statute provides:

"Liability under this chapter shall exist against an employer only where the following conditions concur: Where, at the time of the injury, the employee is performing service growing out of and incidental to his employment. Every employee going to and from his employment in the ordinary and usual way, while on the premises of his employer, or while in the immediate vicinity thereof if the injury results from an occurrence on the premises, shall be deemed to be performing service growing out of and incidental to his employment; so shall any employee going between an employer's designated parking lot and the employer's work premises while on a direct route and in the ordinary and usual way."

The general rule prior to the amendment was that employees going to or coming from work were ordinarily not performing services incidental to their employment and thus were not covered unless actually on the employer's premises when injured. In accordance with this general rule, we have held that the statute covered employees injured while in a parking lot owned or maintained by the employer for the convenience of its employees, but did not cover employees injured while walking from the employer's parking lot to the work premises. The legislature subsequently amended that statute to cover employees injured while crossing between an employer-owned parking lot and the work premises.

When the statutory language is unambiguous, the intention of the legislature must be arrived at by giving the language its ordinary and accepted meaning. The plain meaning of the phrase, "going between an employer's designated parking lot and the employer's work premises," was meant to cover employees injured while going directly from the one portion of the employer's premises to the other. The plain and simple meaning is that coverage may be allowed when an employee is traveling from the parking lot to the work premises, or vice versa, on a direct route.

It is strained to conclude as a matter of fact that a worker falls within the compensable category merely because his route to work intersected the route that would have been taken by an employee walking from the parking lot to the work premises. Protection is afforded by the statute for the journey undertaken by an employee when he is going between two portions of the employer's premises when one of such portions is the employee parking lot.

The court of appeals reasoned, and the department argues on appeal, that following the plain meaning of the statute will produce absurd results by distinguishing between employees injured in the same manner and place on the basis of how they got to work. Although the argument has superficial merit, the construction of the statute urged by the department would produce even more arbitrary results.

The department's construction would differentiate between two employees proceeding to work from the same bus stop if one happened to be injured at a location on the direct route between the employer's parking lot and work premises and the other, following the same route to work, was injured several inches, yards, or blocks off the "route between." It was fortuitous that Kretschmann was injured at a point on the direct route from the employee parking lot to the bakery.

We find Professor Larson's discussion of the problem presented by this case persuasive. Professor Larson is generally critical of judicial attempts to broaden the time tested premises rule. He notes that:

"It is a familiar problem of law, when a sharp, objective, and perhaps somewhat arbitrary line has been drawn, producing the kind of distinctions just cited, to encounter demands that the line be blurred a little to take care of the closest cases. For example, one writer says that there is no reason in principle why states should not protect employees for a reasonable distance before reaching or after leaving the employer's premises. This, however, only raises a new problem without solving the first. It raises a new problem because it provides no standard by which the reasonableness of the distance can be judged. It substitutes the widely-varying subjective interpretation of reasonable distance by different administrators and judges for the physical fact of a boundary line. At the same time, it does not solve the original problem, because each time the premises are extended a reasonable distance, there will inevitably arise new cases only slightly beyond that point and the cry of unfairness of drawing distinctions based on only a few feet of distance will once more be heard."

We agree with Professor Larson's analysis. Although worker's compensation laws should be liberally construed to effect the remedial purposes underlying such legislation, court interpretation of a statute is not to be used as a device for repealing it or changing its obvious meaning.

Accordingly, we resolve the question of statutory interpretation against Kretschmann and against the unwarranted broadening of coverage. We conclude that the legislature has not made the injury here compensable. The decision of the court of appeals is reversed and the circuit court's judgment dismissing the claim for compensation is affirmed.

Whitaker v. Town of Scotland Neck

North Carolina Supreme Court (2003)

The issue raised in the present appeal is whether plaintiffs presented sufficient evidence to trigger the narrowly defined *Woodson* exception to the general exclusivity provisions of the North Carolina Workers' Compensation Act (Act). See *Woodson v. Rowland*, 329 N.C. 330 (1991); see also N.C.G.S. § 97-10.1 (2001) (excluding all rights and remedies against employers other than those specifically set forth in the Workers' Compensation Act). For the reasons set forth below, we hold that plaintiffs did not meet this burden and that the trial court properly granted summary judgment in favor of defendants.

The Town of Scotland Neck (Town) is a North Carolina municipality that provides general governmental services including, among other things, garbage collection. Decedent Carlton Whitaker was employed by the Town as a general maintenance worker assigned to assist in the operation of a garbage truck. On 30 July 1997, decedent and two other maintenance workers were emptying a dumpster at a private school. As the dumpster was being hoisted, the latching mechanism on decedent's side of the garbage truck gave way, allowing the raised container to swing free of its restraints. The dumpster swung around to decedent's side of the truck, striking decedent and pinning him against the truck. Twenty-eight days after the accident, decedent died as a consequence of a crush injury to his chest.

On the day of the accident, Scotland Neck Safety Director C.T. Hasty began his investigation. He interviewed a number of decedent's co-workers, several of whom reported that both the dumpster and the truck's latching mechanism had been broken for at least two months and that such defects had been reported to their supervisor. The supervisor, however, denied any prior knowledge of defects in the truck or dumpster. Based upon his investigation, Hasty concluded that the broken latch and the bent dumpster were the direct cause of the accident.

In August 1997, the North Carolina Department of Labor's Division of Occupational Safety and Health (OSHANC) also investigated the accident and similarly concluded that defective equipment was the proximate cause of the accident and that the accident was a result of employment conditions that were not in compliance with the safety standards of OSHA. More specifically, the OSHANC investigator found five serious violations of state labor law. These violations included: failure to train employees in the safe operation of garbage truck equipment, failure to properly supervise employees in the operation of garbage truck equipment, failure to implement a program for inspection of garbage truck equipment, operation of defective garbage truck equipment, and unsafe operation of garbage truck equipment. As a result of these OSHANC violations, the Town was assessed penalties totaling $10,500.

The administrators of the estate of decedent, filed a civil action against the Town. Plaintiffs alleged willful, wanton, reckless, careless and gross negligence, and demanded compensatory and punitive damages. Defendants responded by claiming the action was barred by the North Carolina Workers' Compensation Act, which limits remedies for work-related injuries to those expressly provided by the Act. The trial court agreed that plaintiffs' claim was barred by the Workers' Compensation Act and granted defendants' motion for summary judgment. Plaintiffs thereafter appealed to the Court of Appeals, which reversed the trial court, concluding that plaintiffs had raised a genuine issue of material fact under *Woodson* as to whether defendants' actions were substantially certain to cause decedent's death.

After our thorough review of the facts in the present case, we conclude that the trial court properly granted defendants' motion for summary judgment. As this Court has often discussed, the North Carolina Workers' Compensation Act was created to ensure that injured employees receive sure and certain recovery for their work-related injuries without having to prove negligence on the part of the employer or defend against charges of contributory negligence. In exchange for these limited but assured benefits, the employee is generally barred from suing the employer for potentially larger damages in civil negligence actions and is instead limited exclusively to those remedies set forth in the Act.

This Court, however, recognizes an important exception to the general exclusivity provisions of the Workers' Compensation Act where an employee is injured or killed as a result of the intentional misconduct of the employer. In *Woodson*, this Court slightly expanded this exception to include cases in which a defendant employer engaged in conduct that, while not categorized as an intentional tort, was nonetheless substantially certain to cause serious injury or death to the employee. In such cases, the injured employee may proceed outside the exclusivity provisions of the Act and maintain a common law tort action against the employer.

In *Woodson v. Rowland*, the defendant-employer was a construction company that specialized in trench excavation. An employee of the defendant-employer was killed when a fourteen-foot-deep trench in which he was working collapsed. In flagrant disregard of safety regulations and industry-wide standards, the defendant-employer's president had knowingly directed his employees to work in a deep trench with sheer, unstable walls that lacked proper shoring. The hazard of a cave-in was so obvious that the foreman of another construction crew working on the project had emphatically refused to send his men into the trench until it was properly shored. Moreover, the defendant-employer had been cited at least four times in the preceding six and a half years for multiple violations of trenching-safety regulations. Thus, there was sufficient evidence from which a reasonable juror could determine that upon placing a man in this trench serious injury or death as a result of a cave-in was a substantial certainty rather than an unforeseeable event, mere possibility, or even substantial probability. Based on these specific facts, this Court in *Woodson* defined a narrow exception to the general exclusivity provisions of the North Carolina Workers' Compensation Act. We specifically held that when an employer intentionally engages in misconduct knowing it is substantially certain to cause serious injury or death to employees and an employee is injured or killed by that misconduct, that employee, or the personal representative of the estate in case of death, may pursue a civil action against the employer. Such misconduct is tantamount to an intentional tort, and civil actions based thereon are not barred by the exclusivity provisions of the Act.

In the present case, there is insufficient evidence to reasonably support plaintiffs' contention that defendants intentionally engaged in misconduct knowing that it was substantially certain to cause serious injury or death to decedent. Indeed, the facts of the present case are readily distinguishable from those that gave rise to our holding in *Woodson*. In the present case, there is no similar evidence that defendants were manifestly indifferent to the health and safety of their employees. The Town has a long history of garbage collection, yet there is no evidence of record that the Town had been previously cited for multiple, significant violations of safety regulations, as in *Woodson*. On the day of the accident, none of the Town's supervisors were on-site to monitor or oversee the workers' activities. Decedent was not expressly instructed to proceed into an obviously hazardous situation as in *Woodson*. There is no evidence that defendants knew that the latching mechanism on the truck was substantially certain to fail or that if such failure did occur, serious injury or death would be substantially certain to follow. As discussed in *Woodson*, simply having knowledge of some possibility, or even probability, of injury or death is not the same as knowledge of a substantial certainty of injury or death. The facts of this case involve defective equipment and human error that amount to an accident rather than intentional misconduct.

We therefore conclude that plaintiffs failed to raise a genuine issue of material fact as to defendants' civil liability under the *Woodson* exception to the general exclusivity provisions of the North Carolina Workers' Compensation Act. Accordingly, we reverse the ruling of the Court of Appeals and instruct that court to reinstate the original order of the Superior Court granting summary judgment in favor of defendants.

VII. PRODUCTS LIABILITY

PRODUCT OR SERVICE

Newmark v. Gimbel

New Jersey (1969)

The defendants operated a number of beauty parlors where permanent waves were offered to the public. For about a year and a half prior to the incident in question, Mrs. Newmark had been a patron of one of defendants' shops where she had a standing appointment every week to have her hair washed and set. She was usually attended by the same operator, William Valante.

During an appointment, Mrs. Newmark went to the beauty parlor where she inquired of Valante about a permanent wave that was on special sale. He told her that her fine hair was not right for the special permanent and that she needed a "good" permanent wave. She agreed to accept the wave suggested by him. Valante conceded that the wave she received was given at his suggestion and that in accepting it she relied on his judgment as to what was good for her hair. Both Valante and Mrs. Newmark testified there was nothing wrong with her hair or scalp before the wave was given.

About three to five minutes after the last of the waving solution had been applied, Mrs. Newmark experienced a burning sensation on the front part of her head. She complained to Valante who added more cream along the hairline. When the dryer operation was completed her hair was combed, and she left the parlor. That evening her head reddened, and during the following day her entire forehead was red and blistered. A large amount of hair fell out when it was combed. Six days after the permanent wave Mrs. Newmark consulted a dermatologist who diagnosed her condition as contact dermatitis of the scalp and loss of hair resulting therefrom. On the basis of his experience, he concluded that the sole cause of her condition was the permanent wave solution. When he last saw her the loss of hair on the top of her head was still present and he could not estimate the time it would take for replacement.

Valante applied the solution as it came from the original package or container, and his experience had shown that a tingling or burning sensation, the degree varying with different persons, was fairly common. The label on the package contained a caveat for the beauty operator. It said:

"Always wear rubber gloves when giving a wave. Make sure patron's hair and scalp are in condition to receive a cold wave. Never brush or rub the scalp vigorously either before or after shampooing. If the scalp is excessively tender or shows evidence of sores or abrasions, the wave should not be given. Ask the patron her previous experience with cold waves to be sure she does not have a sensitivity to waving lotion."

Mrs. Newmark did not see this label, and there is nothing in the record to indicate Valante asked her about any previous experience with cold waves. It does appear, however, that she had four permanent waves without ill effects after the incident involved here.

If the permanent wave lotion were sold to Mrs. Newmark by defendants for home consumption or application or to enable her to give herself the permanent wave, unquestionably an implied warranty of fitness for that purpose would have been an integral incident of the sale. Basically defendants argue that if, in addition to recommending the use of a lotion or other product and supplying it for use, they applied it, such fact (the application) would have the effect of lessening their liability to the patron by eliminating warranty and by limiting their responsibility to the issue of negligence. There is no just reason why it should. On the contrary by taking on the administration of the product in addition to recommending and supplying it, they might increase the scope of their liability, if the method of administration were improper.

The transaction, in our judgment, is a hybrid partaking of incidents of a sale and a service. It is really partly the rendering of service, and partly the supplying of goods for a consideration. Obviously in permanent wave operations the product is taken into consideration in fixing the price of the service. The no-separate-charge argument puts excessive emphasis on form and downgrades the overall substance of the transaction. If the beauty parlor operator bought and applied the permanent wave solution to her own hair and suffered injury thereby, her action in warranty or strict liability in tort against the manufacturer-seller of the product clearly would be maintainable because the basic transaction would have arisen from a conventional type of sale It does not accord with logic to deny a similar right to a patron against the beauty parlor operator or the manufacturer when the purchase and sale were made in anticipation of and for the purpose of use of the product on the patron who would be charged for its use. Common sense demands that such patron be deemed a consumer as to both manufacturer and beauty parlor operator.

A beauty parlor operator in soliciting patronage assures the public that he or she possesses adequate knowledge and skill to do the things and to apply the solution necessary to produce the permanent wave in the hair of the customer. When a patron responds to the solicitation she does so confident that any product used in the shop has come from a reliable origin and can be trusted not to injure her. She places herself in the hands of the operator relying upon his or her expertise both in the selection of the products to be used on her and in the method of using them. The ministrations and the products employed on her are under the control and selection of the operator; the patron is a mere passive recipient.

Defendants suggest that there is no doctrinal basis for distinguishing the services rendered by a beauty parlor operator from those rendered by a dentist or a doctor, and that consequently the liability of all three should be tested by the same principles. On the contrary there is a vast difference in the relationships. The beautician is engaged in a commercial enterprise; the dentist and doctor in a profession. The former caters publicly not to a need but to a form of aesthetic convenience or luxury, involving the rendition of non-professional services and the application of products for which a charge is made. The dentist or doctor does not and cannot advertise for patients; the demand for his services stems from a felt necessity of the patient. In response to such a call the doctor, and to a somewhat lesser degree the dentist, exercises his best judgment in diagnosing the patient's ailment or disability, prescribing and sometimes furnishing medicines or other methods of treatment which he believes, and in some measure hopes, will relieve or cure the condition. His performance is not mechanical or routine because each patient requires individual study and formulation of an informed judgment as to the physical or mental disability or condition presented, and the course of treatment needed. Neither medicine nor dentistry is an exact science; there is no implied warranty of cure or relief. There is no representation of infallibility and such professional men should not be held to such a degree of perfection. There is no guaranty that the diagnosis is correct. Such men are not producers or sellers of property in any reasonably acceptable sense of the term. In a primary sense they furnish services in the form of an opinion of the patient's condition based upon their experienced analysis of the objective and subjective complaints, and in the form of recommended and, at times, personally administered medicines and treatment.

Practitioners of such callings, licensed by the State to practice after years of study and preparation, must be deemed to have a special and essential role in our society, that of studying our physical and mental ills and ways to alleviate or cure them, and that of applying their knowledge, empirical judgment and skill in an effort to diagnose and then to relieve or to cure the ailment of a particular patient. Thus their paramount function — the essence of their function — ought to be regarded as the furnishing of opinions and services. Their unique status and the rendition of these sui generis services bear such a necessary and intimate relationship to public health and welfare that their obligation ought to be grounded and expressed in a duty to exercise reasonable competence and care toward their patients.

Strict liability to the injured consumer does not leave the dealer without remedy. He has an action over against the manufacturer who should bear the primary responsibility for putting defective products in the stream of trade. Considering the overall problem of prosecuting products liability cases, it would seem to make sense procedurally to have the plaintiff's cause of action whenever possible adjudicated in one action against manufacturer and retailer. If the plaintiff sues the dealer alone, the dealer in his own interest should implead the manufacturer and thus avoid circuity of action. Service of process on the manufacturer may present a problem occasionally. But here recourse may be had to the long-arm service rule, with its obvious implications of liberal application. Its use may overcome the difficulty in most cases.

Accordingly, a factual issue was presented at trial for jury determination as to (1) whether the permanent wave solution was defective, and (2) whether it was the proximate cause of the dermatitis. Remanded for a new trial.

CONTRACT OR TORT

Moorman Manufacturing Co. v. National Tank

Supreme Court of Illinois (1982)

The issues raised on appeal before us are whether plaintiff can recover for the cost of repairs and loss of use of the tank under tort law.

Defendant designed, manufactured and sold storage tanks. In 1966, plaintiff purchased a bolted-steel grain-storage tank from defendant for use at its feed-processing plant in Alpha, Illinois. In the last few months of 1976 or the first months of 1977, a crack developed in one of the steel plates on the second ring of the tank. Count I alleged that the tank was not reasonably safe due to certain design and manufacturing defects. Count II asserted that defendant had made certain representations, which were in fact untrue, in connection with the sale of the tank. Count III accused defendant of negligently designing the tank. On April 9, 1979, plaintiff filed an amendment to the complaint, adding count IV, claiming it had relied upon an express warranty made by the defendant at the time of the sale.

The tort law of products liability stems from the contract cause of action for breach of warranty. In MacPherson v. Buick Motor Co. (1916), liability in negligence was imposed upon a manufacturer to an ultimate consumer without privity of contract. Subsequently, courts began to hold manufacturers liable for personal injuries without negligence; the theory generally utilized to reach the manufacturers was based upon the law of sales warranty. However, recognition of the difficulties facing consumers with respect to items such as notice and privity led most courts to abandon the privity requirement in implied-warranty actions and to ultimately abandon the fiction of warranty in favor of strict liability in tort.

This State adopted the tort theory of strict liability to allow a plaintiff to recovery from a manufacturer for personal injuries. However, we did not address the question of whether a consumer could recover under a strict liability in tort theory for solely economic loss. In Seely v. White Motor Co. (1965), the Supreme Court of California rejected strict liability in tort for economic loss. In Seely, plaintiff purchased a truck manufactured by defendant. After he took possession, Seely discovered that the truck bounced violently. Nine months later, the truck overturned after brake failure, causing damage to the truck but no personal injury to Seely. Plaintiff had the damage repaired and subsequently stopped making his installment payments. Defendant repossessed the truck, at which time plaintiff sued on theories of breach of express warranty and strict tort liability, and sought damages for the repair of the truck, for money paid on the purchase price, and for profits lost by virtue of the truck's unsuitability for normal use. The court affirmed the trial court's award to Seely for money paid on the purchase price and for lost profits on the basis of express warranty. The court, however, went on to state that these economic losses are not recoverable under strict liability in tort.

Like the California Supreme Court, in adopting the strict liability in tort theory we emphasized the unreasonably dangerous nature of the product. The focus upon the unreasonably dangerous condition of the product in cases involving strict liability has been consistently followed by this court. The unreasonably dangerous nature of a product has particular relevance when a personal injury results and to some degree when property damage occurs. It has little relevance to economic loss when neither personal injury nor property damage is involved.

The law of sales has been carefully articulated to govern the economic relations between suppliers and consumers of goods. The framework provided by the UCC includes the parol evidence rule, express warranties, implied warranties, rules on disclaimers, notice requirements, limitations on the extent of a manufacturer's liability, and a statute of limitations. Although warranty rules frustrate just compensation for physical injury, they function well in a commercial setting. These rules determine the quality of the product the manufacturer promises and thereby determine the quality he must deliver.

We note, for example, section 2-316 of the UCC, which permits parties to a sales contract to limit warranties in any reasonable manner, or to agree that the buyer possesses no warranty protection at all. The parties may even agree to exclude the implied warranties of merchantability and fitness if they do so in writing, and may modify the implied warranty by clear and conspicuous language. Yet, a manufacturer's strict liability for economic loss cannot be disclaimed because a manufacturer should not be permitted to define the scope of its own responsibility for defective .Thus, adopting strict liability in tort for economic loss would effectively eviscerate section 2-316 of the UCC.

Further, application of the rules of warranty prevents a manufacturer from being held liable for damages of unknown and unlimited scope. If a defendant were held strictly liable in tort for the commercial loss suffered by a particular purchaser, it would be liable for business losses of other purchasers caused by the failure of the product to meet the specific needs of their business, even though these needs were communicated only to the dealer. Finally, a large purchaser, such as plaintiff in the instant case, can protect itself against the risk of unsatisfactory performance by bargaining for a warranty. Or, it may choose to accept a lower purchase price for the product in lieu of warranty protection. Subsequent purchasers may do likewise in bargaining over the price of the product. We believe it is preferable to relegate the consumer to the comprehensive scheme of remedies fashioned by the UCC, rather than requiring the consuming public to pay more for their products so that a manufacturer can insure against the possibility that some of his products will not meet the business needs of some of his customers.

A common argument advanced by those favoring imposition of strict liability in tort for solely economic loss is the arbitrariness in allowing one who has suffered a personal injury to recover for all types of harm, yet preventing one from recovering for economic loss because he fortuitously escaped personal injury. Although the argument has some appeal, we find Justice Traynor's response to that contention in his majority opinion in Seely more persuasive. Justice Traynor stated:

"The distinction that the law has drawn between tort recovery for physical injuries and warranty recovery for economic loss is not arbitrary and does not rest on the 'luck' of one plaintiff in having an accident causing physical injury. The distinction rests, rather, on an understanding of the nature of the responsibility a manufacturer must undertake in distributing his products. He can appropriately be held liable for physical injuries caused by defects by requiring his goods to match a standard of safety defined in terms of conditions that create unreasonable risks of harm. He cannot be held for the level of performance of his products in the consumer's business unless he agrees that the product was designed to meet the consumer's demands. A consumer should not be charged at the will of the manufacturer with bearing the risk of physical injury when he buys a product on the market. He can, however, be fairly charged with the risk that the product will not match his economic expectations unless the manufacturer agrees that it will. Even in actions for negligence, a manufacturer's liability is limited to damages for physical injuries and there is no recovery for economic loss alone."

Our examination of the considerable number of arguments advanced on both sides of the issue leads us to reject imposition of a strict liability in tort theory for recovery of solely economic loss.

We do hold, however, that when a product is sold in a defective condition that is unreasonably dangerous to the user or consumer or to his property, strict liability in tort is applicable to physical injury to plaintiff's property, as well as to personal injury. When an unreasonably dangerous defect is present, such as the truck's nonfunctioning brakes, and physical injury does, in fact, result, then physical injury to property is so akin to personal injury that there is no reason to distinguish them. This comports with the notion that the essence of a product liability tort case is not that the plaintiff failed to receive the quality of product he expected, but that the plaintiff has been exposed, through a hazardous product, to an unreasonable risk of injury to his person or property. On the other hand, contract law, which protects expectation interests, provides the proper standard when a qualitative defect is involved, i.e., when a product is unfit for its intended use.

"Economic loss" has been defined as "damages for inadequate value, costs of repair and replacement of the defective product, or consequent loss of profits-without any claim of personal injury or damage to other property as well as "the diminution in the value of the product because it is inferior in quality and does not work for the general purposes for which it was manufactured and sold." These definitions are consistent with the policy of warranty law to protect expectations of suitability and quality.

The demarcation between physical harm or property damage on the one hand and economic loss on the other usually depends on the nature of the defect and the manner in which the damage occurred. As one commentator observed in applying the definition of economic loss with respect to damage to the product:

"When the defect causes an accident 'involving some violence or collision with external objects,' the resulting loss is treated as property damage. On the other hand, when the damage to the product results from deterioration, internal breakage, or other non-accidental causes, it is treated as economic loss. It is also important to distinguish between 'direct' and 'consequential' economic loss. Direct economic loss also may be measured by costs of replacement and repair. Consequential economic loss includes all indirect loss, such as loss of profits resulting from inability to make use of the defective product."

In cases such as the present one where only the defective product is damaged, the majority approach is to identify whether a particular injury amounts to economic loss or physical damage. In drawing this distinction, the items for which damages are sought, such as repair costs, are not determinative. Rather, the line between tort and contract must be drawn by analyzing interrelated factors such as the nature of the defect, the type of risk, and the manner in which the injury arose. These factors bear directly on whether the safety-insurance policy of tort law or the expectation-bargain protection policy of warranty law is most applicable to a particular claim.

We hold that, where only the defective product is damaged, economic losses caused by qualitative defects falling under the ambit of a purchaser's disappointed expectations cannot be recovered under a strict liability theory. Here, a crack developed in one of the steel plates on the second ring of the tank; such crack was not discovered by plaintiff until such tank was being emptied. This was not the type of sudden and dangerous occurrence best served by the policy of tort law that the manufacturer should bear the risk of hazardous products. Rather, the harm resulted from a qualitative defect relating to the purchaser's expectation in terms of the product's fitness to perform its intended function. Plaintiff suffered a commercial loss of the type that the law of warranty is designed to protect. Consequently, repair and reinforcement of the tank and loss of the tank's use constitute economic losses for which plaintiff cannot recover under a theory of strict liability in tort.

Our conclusion that qualitative defects are best handled by contract, rather than tort, law applies whether the tort theory involved is strict liability or negligence. Tort theory is appropriately suited for personal injury or property damage resulting from a sudden or dangerous occurrence of the nature described above. The remedy for economic loss, loss relating to a purchaser's disappointed expectations due to deterioration, internal breakdown or nonaccidental cause, on the other hand, lies in contract.

In summary, extension of the tort theories of strict liability, negligence or innocent misrepresentation to cover solely economic losses would, in effect, make a manufacturer the guarantor that all of its products would continue to perform satisfactorily throughout their reasonably productive life. Subjecting a manufacturer to liability under those tort theories for a purchaser's solely economic losses would encroach upon the decision by our legislature to enact the sales provisions, sections 2-101 to 2-725, of the Uniform Commercial Code.

STRICT LIABILITY

Leichtamer v. American Motors Corp.

Ohio Supreme Court (1981)

Paul Vance and his wife, Cynthia, invited Carl and Jeanne Leichtamer, brother and sister, to go for a ride in the Vance's Jeep Model CJ-7. The Vances and the Leichtamers drove together to the Hall of Fame Four-Wheel Club, of which the Vances were members. The Vances were seated in the front of the vehicle and the Leichtamers rode in the back. The club, located near Dundee, Ohio, was an "off-the-road" recreation facility. The course there consisted of hills and trails about an abandoned strip mine.

While the Vance vehicle was negotiating a double-terraced hill, an accident occurred. An expert witness for American Motors Corporation, testified that the vehicle had to be travelling between 15 and 20 miles per hour, the vehicle having flown about 47 feet in the air and having fallen approximately 23.5 feet.

The accident killed the driver, Paul Vance, and his wife, Cynthia. Carl Leichtamer sustained a depressed skull fracture. The tail gate of the vehicle presumably struck Jeanne Leichtamer. Jeanne was trapped in the vehicle after the accident and her position was described by her brother as follows: "She was like laying on her stomach although her head was sticking out of the jeep and the she was laying on her stomach like and the tailgate of the jeep like, was laying lower, just a little bit lower or right almost on her shoulders and then the back seat of the jeep was laying on her lower part of her back. Her legs were twisted through the front seat." Jeanne Leichtamer is a paraplegic as a result of the injury.

Carl and Jeanne Leichtamer subsequently sued American Motors Corporation, American Motors Sales Corporation and Jeep Corporation for injuries they sustained in the accident. The amended complaint averred that the permanent trauma to the body of Jeanne Leichtamer and the other injuries to her brother, Carl, were causally related to the displacement of the "roll bar" on the vehicle. They claimed that Paul Vance's negligence caused the accident, but alleged that their injuries were "substantially enhanced, intensified, aggravated, and prolonged" by the roll bar displacement.

The focus of appellees' case was that the weakness of the sheet metal housing upon which the roll bar had been attached was causally related to the trauma to their bodies. Specifically, when the vehicle landed upside down, the flat sheet metal housing of the rear wheels upon which the roll bar tubing was attached by bolts gave way so that the single, side-to-side bar across the top of the vehicle was displaced to a position twelve inches forward of and fourteen and one-half inches lower than its original configuration relative to the chassis. The movement of the position of the intact roll bar resulting from the collapse of the sheet metal housing upon which it was bolted was, therefore, downward and forward. The roll bar tubing did not punch through the sheet metal housing, rather the housing collapsed, taking the intact tubing with it. That this displacement or movement of the intact roll bar is permitted by the thin nature of the sheet metal wheel housing to which it is attached and the propensity of the bar to do so when the vehicle lands upside down is central to appellees' case.

The appellants' position concerning the roll bar is that, from an engineering point of view, the roll bar was an optional device provided solely as protection for a side-roll. A side-roll, as opposed to pitch-over, was described by the Court of Appeals as "a roll of the vehicle around its longitudinal axis. The roll bar was never tested for the pitch-over; appellants assert it was provided solely as protection against the side-roll.

The other principal element of appellees' case was that the advertised use of the vehicle involves great risk of forward pitch-overs. The accident occurred at the Hall of Fame Four-Wheel Club, which had been organized, among others, by Norman Petty, the vendor of the Vance vehicle. Petty allowed the club to meet at his Jeep dealership. He showed club members movies of the performance of the Jeep in hilly country. This activity was coupled with a national advertising program of American Motors Sales Corporation, which included a multi-million dollar television campaign. The television advertising campaign was aimed at encouraging people to buy a Jeep, as follows: "Ever discover the rough, exciting world of mountains, forest, rugged terrain? The original Jeep can get you there, and Jeep guts will bring you back."

The campaign also stressed the ability of the Jeep to drive up and down steep hills. One Jeep CJ-7 television advertisement, for example, challenges a young man, accompanied by his girlfriend: " You guys aren't yellow, are you? Is it a steep hill? Yeah, little lady, you could say it is a steep hill. Let's try it. The King of the Hill, is about to discover the new Jeep CJ-7." Moreover, the owner's manual for the Jeep CJ-5/CJ-7 provided instructions as to how "a four-wheel drive vehicle can proceed in safety down a grade which could not be negotiated safely by a conventional 2-wheel drive vehicle." Both appellees testified that they had seen the commercials and that they thought the roll bar would protect them if the vehicle landed on its top.

Appellants' principal argument was that the roll bar was provided solely for a side-roll. Appellants' only testing of the roll bar was done on a 1969 Jeep CJ-5, a model with a wheel base ten inches shorter than the Jeep CJ-7. Evidence of the test was offered in evidence and refused. With regard to tests for either side-rolls or pitch-overs on the Jeep CJ-7, appellants responded to interrogatories that no "proving ground," "vibration or shock," or "crash" tests were conducted.

The jury returned a verdict for both appellees. Damages were assessed for Carl Leichtamer at $100,000 compensatory and $100,000 punitive. Damages were assessed for Jeanne Leichtamer at $1 million compensatory and $1 million punitive.

Opinion

We turn to the question of what constitutes an unreasonably dangerous defective product.

Section 402A subjects to liability one who sells a product in a "defective condition unreasonably dangerous" which causes physical harm to the ultimate user. Comment g defines defective condition as "a condition not contemplated by the ultimate consumer which will be unreasonably dangerous to him." Comment i states that for a product to be unreasonably dangerous, "(t)he article sold must be dangerous to an extent beyond that which would be contemplated by the ordinary consumer who purchases it, with the ordinary knowledge common to the community as to its characteristics."

With regard to design defects, the product is considered defective only because it causes or enhances an injury. "In such a case, the defect and the injury cannot be separated, yet clearly a product cannot be considered defective simply because it is capable of producing injury." Rather, in such a case the concept of "unreasonable danger" is essential to establish liability under strict liability in tort principles.

The concept of "unreasonable danger," as found in Section 402A, provides implicitly that a product may be found defective in design if it is more dangerous in use than the ordinary consumer would expect. Another way of phrasing this proposition is that "a product may be found defective in design if the plaintiff demonstrates that the product failed to perform as safely as an ordinary consumer would expect when used in an intended or reasonably foreseeable manner."

Moreover, a consumer-expectation test of unreasonable danger recognizes the legitimacy of one of the fundamental values in the law of torts: "the protection of the individuality of persons, by according formal respect for their fairly developed expectations of product safety."

Thus, we hold a cause of action for damages for injuries "enhanced" by a design defect will lie in strict liability in tort. In order to recover, the plaintiff must prove by a preponderance of the evidence that the "enhancement" of the injuries was proximately caused by a defective product unreasonably dangerous to the plaintiff.

A product will be found unreasonably dangerous if it is dangerous to an extent beyond the expectations of an ordinary consumer when used in an intended or reasonably foreseeable manner.

WARRANTY

Dewitt v. Eveready Battery Company

Supreme Court of North Carolina (2002)

Plaintiff purchased a Coleman battery-powered lantern and eight Eveready "Energizer" size D batteries from a Wal-Mart store. The batteries, manufactured by defendant, were sold in sealed packages containing two batteries each. Plaintiff read the instructions accompanying the lantern explaining proper battery installation. He did not remember if these instructions included warnings of potential hazards that could result from incorrect battery placement, nor did he read or see any warnings on the battery packages or on the batteries themselves. However, because his occupation involved installing fire alarms and security systems, he was familiar with the characteristics of such batteries. He knew that it could be dangerous to install the batteries incorrectly and that the contents of damaged or leaking batteries could cause injury.

Plaintiff inserted the eight batteries in the bottom of the lantern. Plaintiff then operated the lantern for approximately five minutes. He was not satisfied with the meager illumination provided by the lantern, however, so he set it aside. The next day, plaintiff decided to remove the batteries and return the lantern. At that point, the batteries had been in the lantern for approximately twenty-four hours. Plaintiff held the lantern between his ankles for three to four minutes while he removed the batteries. As he did so, he noticed fluid on some of the batteries. As plaintiff stated during his deposition, "I noticed on one for sure, there was like a slimy feeling." Plaintiff also noticed some "slimy" moisture on the bottom of the lantern. However, he did not realize that the moisture on the batteries or the lantern came from the batteries themselves. Instead, he "didn't know if it was like condensation or what it could be" and simply washed his hands.

Shortly thereafter, plaintiff felt a tingling on his ankle and noticed that it was slightly red. Because he was not in any discomfort and had not experienced any tingling in his fingers prior to washing his hands, he thought he had been bitten by an insect. He also noticed that his sock was moist but, because the weather was warm, assumed the moisture came from perspiration. He added, "The last place I would have thought it had come from was the batteries." Accordingly, he did not wash his ankle or remove his sock, but put the lantern back in its box and returned it to Wal-Mart. He kept the batteries and later gave them to his attorney.

While driving home, plaintiff felt an uncomfortable warm sensation, "almost like a burning," on his ankle. Once inside his house, he removed his right shoe and sock and discovered that the entire heel of his right foot was black.

Plaintiff was diagnosed with having third- and fourth-degree alkaline chemical burns to his right ankle caused by potassium hydroxide, a chemical that leaked from the batteries. As a result of his injuries, plaintiff has undergone surgeries on his ankle, requiring skin grafts from his thighs and wrist.

William Wayne Beaver, an electrical engineer specializing in forensic analysis of failed structures and products, gave deposition testimony describing the design of the Eveready "Energizer" size D battery. Beaver examined and took x-rays of the eight batteries used by plaintiff in the Coleman lantern. He testified that leakage had occurred and opined that several possibilities could explain the leakage. Two of these possibilities were manufacturing defects: either (1) a small hole in the positive metal case or negative metal top on the batteries, or (2) a gap or tear in the nonmetallic insulating seal between the positive metal case and the negative metal top (in other words, a loose connection where the batteries were crimped). Another possible cause of leakage was an increase of pressure in the battery. Such an increase can result from creating a charge if a battery is installed backwards, that is, with the positive and negative ends pointed in the incorrect direction. Although Beaver agreed with defendant's counsel that initiation of the venting mechanism in the batteries would be "strong evidence that the batteries worked as they were supposed to," he later added that an activated venting mechanism could work improperly by venting at the wrong place if part of the battery casing is thinner than designed. Beaver also stated that the venting mechanism could have operated at too low a pressure or that the chemicals in the batteries could have been of the wrong mixture, causing an increase in pressure and subsequent venting. Ultimately, though, Beaver could not tell from the x-rays where the leakage originated, whether the venting mechanism in the batteries had been initiated, or whether the batteries vented properly or instead leaked as the result of a defect. He stated that he needed to conduct intrusive testing in order to reach such conclusions.

Dr. Richard G. Pearson, a professor of industrial engineering at North Carolina State University, submitted a detailed affidavit relating to the adequacy of the warning on the batteries used by plaintiff. He noted that plaintiff acted reasonably. Pearson also stated that the labeling of the batteries failed to address the specific consequences of chemical exposure and the actions a user should take upon exposure. He added that these warnings failed to comply with industry practice, published standards, and the federal code. Pearson also expressed concerns that defendant has no written policy or procedure for the design of warnings and the content of hazard labels, does not test warning comprehension by consumers, and emphasizes marketing rather than industry standards and practice in determining the format of warnings.

Products Liability

This case is governed by North Carolina's Products Liability Act. Under the Act, a product liability action is defined as any action brought for or on account of personal injury, death or property damage caused by or resulting from the manufacture, construction, design, formulation, development of standards, preparation, processing, assembly, testing, listing, certifying, warning, instructing, marketing, selling, advertising, packaging or labeling of any product. Pursuant to the Act, a plaintiff may base a products liability action against a manufacturer or seller on contract principles of breach of warranty.

An action for breach of implied warranty of merchantability is established by the North Carolina Uniform Commercial Code and is a product liability action if, as here, the action is for injury to a person resulting from a sale of a product. To establish a breach of implied warranty of merchantability under the statute, a plaintiff must prove the following elements: (1)that the goods bought and sold were subject to an implied warranty of merchantability; (2)that the goods did not comply with the warranty in that the goods were defective at the time of sale; (3)that his injury was due to the defective nature of the goods; and (4)that damages were suffered as a result. Here, the parties do not dispute that the first, third, and fourth elements have been established in plaintiff's allegations. At issue is the second element, whether the batteries were defective at the time of sale.

Plaintiff does not argue that this element has been satisfied by evidence of a specific defect in the batteries, but instead asserts that a defect may be inferred from evidence that the batteries were put to their ordinary use and subsequently malfunctioned. Additionally, when a plaintiff does not produce evidence of a specific defect, a product defect may be inferred from evidence the product was put to its ordinary use and the product malfunctioned. We agree.

This rule, allowing a plaintiff to prove a product defect circumstantially, has been accepted by a majority of jurisdictions that have considered the issue. When advancing a theory of strict product liability, a plaintiff has the burden of showing that the product was defective, that the defect was the proximate cause of his or her injuries and that the defect existed at the time the product left the manufacturer. In certain cases of alleged manufacturing defects, however, the plaintiff need not present direct evidence of the defect. When proceeding on a malfunction theory, the plaintiff may "present a case-in-chief evidencing the occurrence of a malfunction and eliminating abnormal use or reasonable, secondary causes for the malfunction." From this circumstantial evidence, a jury may be permitted to infer that the product was defective at the time of sale.

Although proof of a specific defect is not essential to establish liability under this theory, the plaintiff cannot depend upon conjecture or guesswork. The mere fact that an accident happens, even in this enlightened age, does not take the injured plaintiff to the jury. The malfunction theory, thus, does not relieve the burden of establishing a defect. However, the malfunction itself is circumstantial evidence of a defective condition.

Thus, in a products liability case the plaintiff seeks to prove, through whatever means he or she has available under the circumstances of the case, that a product was defective when it left the hands of the manufacturer. In some cases, the plaintiff may be able to prove that the product suffered from a specific defect by producing expert testimony to explain to the jury precisely how the product was defective and how the defect must have arisen from the manufacturer or seller. In cases of a manufacturing defect, such expert testimony is certainly desirable from the plaintiff's perspective, but it is not essential. The plaintiff, even without expert testimony articulating the specific defect, may be able to convince a jury that the product was defective when it left the seller's hands by producing circumstantial evidence. Such circumstantial evidence includes (1) the malfunction of the product; (2) expert testimony as to a variety of possible causes; (3) the timing of the malfunction in relation to when the plaintiff first obtained the product; (4) similar accidents involving the same product; (5) elimination of other possible causes of the accident; and (6) proof tending to establish that the accident does not occur absent a manufacturing defect. However the plaintiff chooses to present his or her case, the goal is the same: to prove that the product was not only defective, but that such a defect existed when it left the hands of the seller.

In a typical case involving a claim for breach of implied warranty of merchantability, the plaintiff will attempt to establish the precise manner in which the product failed. However, sometimes the product will be destroyed in the accident, or proof of how the product failed to operate safely will otherwise be unavailable. In such malfunction cases, the plaintiff may still rely on the merchantability warranty and need not necessarily show with particularity the precise nature of the defect or the precise physical mechanism which caused the product to fail. Thus, it is sufficient for the plaintiff merely to show the malfunction, regardless of the cause. When machinery malfunctions, it obviously lacks fitness regardless of the cause of the malfunction. Under the theory of warranty, the "sin" is the lack of fitness as evidenced by the malfunction itself rather than some specific dereliction by the manufacturer in constructing or designing the machinery.

1. *Malfunction*

Plaintiff testified that he purchased the batteries, which were contained in their original blister packaging; read the instructions accompanying the lantern; inserted the batteries in the lantern; and tested the lantern for only five minutes, all on the day of purchase. He removed the batteries within twenty-four hours after purchasing them. Although the batteries were brand new and used for but a minimal time, two leaked. Viewing all facts and inferences in plaintiff's favor, we hold this evidence presents a genuine issue of material fact such that a reasonable person could find that the batteries at issue malfunctioned.

2. *Expert Testimony*

Plaintiff's expert, William Beaver, testified at his deposition that there were several possible explanations for the batteries' leakage. Two of the possible explanations were manufacturing defects, described in the facts of this opinion, while another possibility was misuse by plaintiff. Beaver also described several ways that a battery could malfunction even if the venting mechanism had been initiated. We hold this testimony was sufficient to raise a genuine issue of material fact such that a reasonable mind might accept that there were possible causes of the leakage attributable to defects, which were defendant's responsibility.

3. *Use of the Batteries and Timing of the Malfunction*

In his deposition, plaintiff indicated that he was not certain whether he put the batteries into the lantern correctly but that he knew which end of a battery was the positive end and, based on his experience, assumed he placed them in the lantern correctly.

Q. Did you notice whether you put them all in correctly or did you not pay any attention to that?
A. No, I always pay attention to that because I know the side with the dimples is always your positive side on a battery. And that was towards your plus on the device you're installing it in.

Q. As you-and when did you notice that? When you were putting the batteries in or taking them out?
A. What was that?

Q. Notice that you had all the batteries in the right way.
A. I don't even think I really looked to notice, to say honestly.

Q. Just assume you'd done it right?
A. Yeah, yeah, I've put so many batteries in and out of things over the years with raising kids and everything.

Q. So I take it after you put them in there and the light wasn't bright enough, you didn't double check to make sure they were all in right.
A. I can't really say for sure that I did or not.

Defendant argues that plaintiff's assumption that he placed the batteries into the lantern correctly is fatal to his claim because it does not constitute substantial evidence necessary to survive a motion for summary judgment. We note that neither plaintiff nor defendant presented evidence as to whether the lantern would illuminate at all if one or more batteries were inserted backward. Despite this deficiency in the record, we believe plaintiff presented sufficient additional circumstantial evidence to support his assumption that he positioned the batteries correctly. He testified that he read the instructions accompanying the lantern relating to placement of the batteries in the lantern and knew that inserting them backwards could be dangerous because "the current isn't flowing in the direction that the batteries would accept." He also testified that he was familiar with handling batteries through his work installing fire alarms and security systems, "usually working with batteries a couple times a week."

5. *Elimination of Other Possible Causes*

Defendant argues that plaintiff must eliminate the possibility that he incorrectly charged the batteries before he can establish by inference a defect in the batteries. We do not adopt this suggestion. Plaintiff need not negate every theoretically conceivable secondary cause for the malfunction. Rather the plaintiff fails to establish a prima facie case only if the plaintiff does not negate evidence of other reasonable, secondary causes or abnormal use that is actually introduced during plaintiff's case-in-chief.

6. *Proof Tending to Establish that the Accident Does Not Occur Absent a Manufacturing Defect*

Finally, evidence was presented that the accident would not have occurred even if plaintiff did install the batteries backwards. Telzrow and his staff simulated the circumstances of the accident for defendant by purchasing a duplicate lantern at Wal-Mart and placing two

"Energizer" size D batteries into the lantern backwards while placing the other six batteries into the lantern correctly. Telzrow testified that the simulated test was conducted to determine the current when one or more batteries is reversed to see if our analysis of how long it would take the vent to react is consistent with what plaintiff is saying it took to burn him. Although Telzrow is not sure how long his employee simulated the test, he did know that the employee took it past the peak current and let it stabilize. Notably, when asked if he knew whether any of the batteries leaked under those simulated conditions, Telzrow responded no. Telzrow later added that defendant had never received any reports that a battery had leaked while it was being used in a Coleman lantern.

Viewing all of these circumstances in a light most favorable to plaintiff and drawing every reasonable inference in his favor, we hold that this evidence presents a genuine issue of material fact such that a reasonable person could conclude that a defect in the batteries caused plaintiff's injuries.

MANUFACTURING DEFECT

Lee v. Crookston Coca-Cola Bottling Company

Minnesota Supreme Court (1971)

Plaintiff Helen Lee, a waitress, while working at the Norman Steak House at Ada, Minnesota, was injured when a quart (26-ounce) glass Coca-Cola bottle exploded in her hand and a glass fragment of the bottle punctured the median nerve at the level of her right wrist.

The evidence relating to the injury-producing incident is not in substantial dispute. Defendant's driver delivered a 12-bottle case of Coca-Cola and other beverages to the steak house shortly before noon on the day of the accident. Using a handcart, he stacked the Coca-Cola case in the dining room area of the steak house behind a bar or counter about 2 feet from a waist-high, sliding-top-three-door-type, refrigerated cooler. The case and the bottles remained undisturbed until between 12:30 and 1 p.m., when Mrs. Lee (hereafter plaintiff) undertook to transfer the bottles from the Coca-Cola case into the cooler. Without moving the case, she grasped one bottle at a time with her right hand, moved it laterally to her right, and lowered it into the cooler. While she was lowering the third bottle into the cooler, it 'exploded' in her hand, the neck of the bottle with a cap intact remaining in her hand. According to the testimony of plaintiff and the manager of the steak house, the only two women present at the time, the bottle exploded with a 'loud bang,' which the manager heard while working in the kitchen separated from the dining area. She saw plaintiff standing by the cooler holding the cap and neck of the bottle and found glass fragments from the bottle scattered in and about the cooler and adjacent area, some being found approximately ten or twelve feet away and some around the other end of the dining area. Since plaintiff and the manager considered the accident of little consequence, requiring only the application of a band-aid to the wound after the bleeding had been stopped, the bottle fragments were swept up and discarded.

Plaintiff testified that she was 'positive' and there was 'not one bit' of question in her mind that she had not 'struck' the 'bottle on anything' as she was transferring it to the cooler. She insisted that the bottle had exploded sponstaneously while in her hand, and this testimony was uncontroverted.

The narrow question presented here is whether circumstantial evidence, the core of the res ipsa loquitur doctrine, is sufficient to take the case to the jury on the theory of strict liability as well as on the theory of negligence. When a plaintiff has proved that he was injured by a product claimed to have been defective, and where the claimed defect is such that there is circumstantial evidence from which it can be inferred that it is more probable than not that the product was defective when it left defendant's hands, absent plaintiff's own want of care or misuse of the product, there is an evidentiary basis for submitting the issue of liability to the jury on both the theory of negligence and strict liability in tort.

It surely must be conceded that circumstantial evidence of the type present in this case justifies submission of the issue of liability on the theory of res ipsa. Moreover, where the case is submitted on res ipsa, under this type of circumstantial evidence it would be strange indeed if the arguments to the jury did not include conflicting contentions by counsel as to whether the evidence established that the bottler's use of a defective bottle was the cause of the bottle's failure. That such may be the only plausible cause of an exploding bottle is demonstrated by the evidence in this case. As testified to by defendant's expert, there are three fundamental causes of bottle failure: Thermo-shock, internal pressure, and external force. According to the expert's testimony, failure because of thermo-shock could only result from drastic changes in temperature applied to the outside of the bottle, such as would be produced by placing a bottle containing hot liquid in cold water. Failure caused by external force, of course, usually results from an impact, such as striking or dropping the bottle. Failure because of internal pressure due to excessive carbonation is ordinarily unlikely because the bottle is designed to withstand approximately four times the pressure created by the gas introduced, and after the carbonated liquid is added to the syrup mixture, any excessive carbonation is equalized by exposure to atmospheric pressure during the interval between carbonation and capping. The capacity of different bottles to withstand internal pressure varies, however, in part due to bottlers' customary reuse of bottles. Some bottles have been refilled for years and might have been subjected to 'rough' handling numerous times, thereby increasing the probability that even though they are designed to withstand such handling, some could develop defects which would escape detection by the most careful bottler. This may be the only plausible explanation for the bottle's failure in this case, since there is uncontradicted evidence dispelling the probability that the failure was attributable to thermo-shock or external force. Absent expert opinion, as in a case of this type, circumstantial evidence may be the only available means of establishing a claim of either negligence or a defective product.

Under the theory of strict liability, the elements of proof as noted above are few and uncomplicated. The significant difference is that under strict liability the jury need not infer from the circumstantial evidence that defendant was negligent in order to impose liability. It is sufficient that the evidence establishes that the manufacturer placed a dangerously defective product on the market, knowing that it is to be used without inspection for defects. Defendant's evidence that it exercised the highest degree of care to guard against the use of a defective product may refute plaintiff's circumstantial evidence of the injury-producing incident and support a finding that the product was not defective. Thus, in many product liability cases—especially those involving exploding bottles—, under both the theory of negligence and the theory of strict liability, the injured party, in practical effect, has the burden of proving a defect at the time the product left the manufacturer's control. To argue that the same circumstantial evidence could not support a finding of a defective bottle sufficient to justify submission on the theory of strict liability seems clearly untenable and cannot be supported by reason or authority.

Where res ipsa is relied upon as the theory of recovery, plaintiff is not required to allege or prove specific claims of negligence or, as in this case, a specific defect. Indeed, plaintiff's inability to determine the specific defect or cause, coupled with the fact that the defendant is in a better position to present evidence as to the cause of the accident, is itself a fundamental reason for the res ipsa rule. The same reasoning applies with equal force to excuse plaintiff from proving a specific defect when pursuing recovery on the theory of strict liability. This is especially true in exploding-bottle cases and similar situations where the product is destroyed by reason of the defect, which is also obliterated, or where the defective part alone is destroyed by the incident. In short, under the theory of strict liability plaintiff should not be required to prove specifically what defect caused the incident, but may rely upon circumstantial evidence from which it can reasonably be inferred that it is more probable than not that the product was defective when it left defendant's control.

Reversed and new trial granted.

Mexicali Rose v. Superior Court

Supreme Court of California (1992)

Real party in interest (plaintiff), Jack A. Clark, was a customer at petitioners' (defendants') restaurant. He ordered a chicken enchilada and sustained throat injuries when he swallowed a one-inch chicken bone contained in the enchilada. He brought an action for damages based on theories of negligence, breach of implied warranty, and strict liability. He alleged defendant Mexicali Rose negligently left the bone in the enchilada and the food was unfit for human consumption. He also asserted he did not expect to find a bone, and it is not common knowledge there may be bones in chicken enchiladas.

The question we address is whether a restaurant keeper may be held liable for serving food containing substances natural to the product that, when consumed by the patron, cause injury. As explained below, we agree with plaintiff that a "reasonable expectation" test is applicable in this context and, in part at least, is consistent with the development of tort law in our jurisdiction. Accordingly, we adopt that test as our own. As we further explain, although we conclude that under a reasonable expectation test plaintiff may not state a cause of action under the theories of strict liability or breach of the implied warranties of merchantability or fitness, we conclude that under the same test, he may state a cause of action in negligence based on defendants' asserted failure to exercise due care in the preparation of the chicken enchilada.

1. The Mix Rule: The foreign natural test and the reasonable expectations of the consumer

In Mix, the plaintiff swallowed a fragment of chicken bone contained in a chicken pot pie he consumed in the defendant's restaurant. We held there could be no liability under either an implied warranty or negligence theory, explaining that the statutory implied warranty of fitness of food does not make the purveyor an insurer, but merely requires that food be reasonably fit for human consumption. Although we conceded that it is frequently a question for the jury to determine whether an injury-producing substance present in food makes the food unfit for consumption, we maintained that a court in appropriate cases may find as a matter of law that an alleged harmful substance in food does not make the food defective or unfit for consumption. We explained our holding as follows:

"Bones which are natural to the type of meat served cannot legitimately be called a foreign substance, and a consumer who eats meat dishes ought to anticipate and be on his guard against the presence of such bones. At least he cannot hold the restaurant keeper whose representation implied by law is that the meat dish is reasonably fit for human consumption, liable for any injury occurring as a result of the presence of a chicken bone in such chicken pie."

As for the negligence claim, we concluded that because the restaurateur had no duty to offer a perfect chicken pie, he or she was not negligent in serving a pie with a bone in it. After recognizing the duty of care, however, the Mix court observed that injury due to a chicken bone in a chicken pie did not establish a lack of due care amounting to a breach of that duty. The court observed that the negligence issue involved "a question of whether or not a restaurant keeper in the exercise of due care is required to serve in every instance a perfect chicken pie, in that all bones are entirely eliminated. If the customer has no right to expect such a perfect product, and we think he is not so entitled, then it cannot be said that it was negligence on the part of the restaurant keeper to fail to furnish an entirely boneless chicken pie."

2. The evolution of the Mix rule

More recently, however, courts addressing the foreign-natural distinction have deviated from strict application of Mix, to conclude that the ultimate issue of liability should not be based on a determination whether the object causing injury was either foreign or natural, but instead should be based on whether the consumer reasonably should have anticipated the natural injury-producing substance in the food.

The trend developing in courts recently considering the issue whether a plaintiff may recover for injuries caused by a natural or foreign substance can be summarized as follows: If the injury-producing substance is natural to the preparation of the food served, it can be said that it was reasonably expected by its very nature and the food cannot be determined to be unfit for human consumption or defective. Thus, a plaintiff in such a case has no cause of action in implied warranty or strict liability. The expectations of the consumer do not, however, negate a defendant's duty to exercise reasonable care in the preparation and service of the food. Therefore, if the presence of the natural substance is due to a defendant's failure to exercise due care in the preparation of the food, an injured plaintiff may state a cause of action in negligence. By contrast, if the substance is foreign to the food served, then a trier of fact additionally must determine whether its presence (i) could reasonably be expected by the average consumer and (ii) rendered the food unfit for human consumption or defective under the theories of the implied warranty of merchantability or strict liability.

As adopted in most of the preceding decisions, the "reasonable expectation" test differs from the foreign-natural rule in two important respects. First, whether bones or other injurious substances ought to be anticipated in a particular dish becomes a question for the trier of fact, unless as a matter of law the food was fit for consumption because the substance was natural to the food served. Second, and more important, this reasonable expectation test focuses not on the components of the dish, but on the final item sold to the consumer and the expectations that are engendered by the type of dish and the type of preparation used in making the dish. Thus, courts rejecting the exclusive application of the foreign-natural test, which by definition bars a negligence claim, have frequently identified the failure to focus on food preparation and the consumer expectation that is created by processing or by the nature of the dish sold.

Defendants contend that allowing a plaintiff to recover even in negligence for an injury caused by a natural substance is unreasonable because, they assert, this would place a burden on all restaurants to remove all bones. Defendants claim the better policy is "to encourage consumers to be careful."

As noted above, we agree with defendants to the extent they reason that a restaurant patron cannot expect a chicken pie to be free of all bones. Such an expectation would be unreasonable and unrealistic to the ordinary consumer and would not conform to either federal or state health and safety standards. Moreover, the implied warranties of merchantability and fitness are based on cases imposing liability for foreign objects in food, and the Restatement Second of Torts, section 402A, emphasizes that the doctrine of strict liability applies in the limited situation arising when foreign objects or ingredients not characteristic of food cause harm. Under these guidelines, therefore, a reasonable plaintiff cannot expect a chicken enchilada always to be free of bones, and defendants owe no duty to provide a perfect enchilada.

On the other hand, we disagree with defendants that we should continue to preclude a plaintiff from attempting to state a cause of action in negligence when a substance natural to the preparation of the food product has caused injury. We instead depart from our foreign-natural rule to the extent it precludes an action against defendants for the failure to exercise due care in the preparation of the chicken enchilada.

Such a new rule, expanding a restaurateur's potential liability and allowing an action in negligence for injuries caused by both natural and foreign substances in food, corresponds to modern developments in tort law. This court has recognized that traditional tort law principles support imposition of a duty of care when one is in a position to exercise custody or control over another. In light of our health and safety, we believe a patron can reasonably expect that a restaurateur will exercise reasonable care in preparing chicken enchiladas so that any natural substances contained in the food will not be either of such size, shape or quantity to cause injury when consumed. It is reasonably foreseeable that a sizable bone could cause the unsuspecting patron substantial injury if swallowed. Under these principles, we believe it is a question for the trier of fact to determine whether the presence of the injury-producing substance was caused by the failure of the defendants to exercise reasonable care in the preparation of the food, and whether the breach of the duty to exercise such care caused the consumer's injury. In so concluding, we emphasize that restaurateurs have available all the traditional defenses to a negligence cause of action, including comparative negligence.

Conclusion

The strict foreign-natural test should be rejected as the exclusive test for determining liability when a substance natural to food injures a restaurant patron. We conclude instead that in deciding the liability of a restaurateur for injuries caused by harmful substances in food, the proper tests to be used by the trier of fact are as follows:

If the injury-producing substance is natural to the preparation of the food served, it can be said that it was reasonably expected by its very nature and the food cannot be determined unfit or defective. A plaintiff in such a case has no cause of action in strict liability or implied warranty. If, however, the presence of the natural substance is due to a restaurateur's failure to exercise due care in food preparation, the injured patron may sue under a negligence theory.

If the injury-causing substance is foreign to the food served, then the injured patron may also state a cause of action in implied warranty and strict liability, and the trier of fact will determine whether the substance (i) could be reasonably expected by the average consumer and (ii) rendered the food unfit or defective.

DESIGN DEFECT

Honda, Inc. v. Norman

Court of Appeals of Texas (2003)

This is a products liability suit. A jury awarded Brian Norman, individually and as sole administrator of the estate of Karen Leslie Vivienne Norman, deceased, and Mary Norman, individually, (the Normans) $65 million in compensatory damages in a suit the Normans brought against Honda, Inc. after the Normans' daughter, Karen Norman, drowned in her Honda Civic automobile. The jury found that a design defect in the car's seatbelt was the producing cause of Karen's death.

At approximately 2:00 a.m. on December 2, 1992, Karen attempted to back her car up to turn around, and she accidentally backed down a boat ramp into the water in Galveston Bay. Her passenger, Josel Woods, was not wearing a seatbelt and was able to get out of the car by crawling out the passenger side window. After escaping, Woods reached back into the sinking car to get her purse. Woods testified that Karen was calm and did not appear scared. As Woods was swimming to the ramp, she heard Karen say, "Help me. I can't get my seatbelt undone." Woods testified that, after she reached the ramp, she heard Karen yell to her again that she could not get out of her seatbelt.

A dive team located Karen's car at 8:53 a.m. All of the windows were rolled up, including the one Woods testified she had escaped through, and all the doors were closed. Karen's body was found in the back seat. An autopsy revealed Karen's blood-alcohol level was .17

At the time of the accident, Karen's four-door 1991 Honda Civic was equipped with a two-point passive restraint system—an automatic seatbelt that was mechanically drawn up over the shoulder when the door was closed—supplemented with a manual lap belt. The automatic seatbelt fastened itself with no action on behalf of the occupant. Robert Hellmuth, a former National Highway Traffic Safety Administration employee, testified that, in 1990, all cars were required to have either a passive belt system or an air bag. Hellmuth also testified that a two-point passive restraint system was the most expensive seatbelt system in use at the time Karen's car was manufactured.

The shoulder belt on both front seats was attached to a "mouse" that ran along a rail above the door. When the door was closed, the mouse moved from its starting position, near the front of the car, along the length of the door and then part-way down the pillar between the front and back doors, pulling the belt over the shoulder of the driver. When the door was opened or the ignition was turned off, the mouse moved forward, allowing the occupant to get out of the car. The shoulder belt could be manually disengaged by pressing an emergency release button located at the juncture of the belt and the mouse. Like most seatbelts, the shoulder belt was naturally taut across the body, but it was easy to spool out more belt to allow the occupant to lean forward and/or sideways.

The Normans contend that the emergency locking retractor locked as Karen backed down the ramp and that she pulled on the door latch, causing the mouse to move and then stall and the seatbelt to pin her to her seat. Because she was pinned to the seat, Karen was unable to reach the emergency release button located over her left shoulder. The Normans argue that the evidence showed the seatbelt system was defectively designed because (1) the mouse was able to move even when the retractor was locked, allowing the seatbelt to pin an occupant in the seat; (2) the seatbelt, when fully extended, could not be released easily and rapidly by pressing the emergency release button; and (3) the emergency release button was improperly located, in that Honda failed to provide an easy and rapid way to get out of the seatbelt under conditions it knew would occur.

Two elements—a safer alternative design and producing cause—that must be proved, but are not alone sufficient, to establish liability for a defectively designed product. A claimant not only must meet the proof requirements of the statute but must show, under the common law, that the product was defectively designed so as to be unreasonably dangerous, taking into consideration the utility of the product and the risks involved in its use.

Honda argues that the Normans failed to meet their threshold statutory burden because they failed to prove there was a safer alternative design to the Honda's seatbelt restraint system. To prove a design defect, the Normans had to show, among other things, that (1) there was a safer alternative; (2) the safer alternative would have prevented or significantly reduced the risk of injury, without substantially impairing the product's utility; and the safer alternative was both technologically and economically feasible when the product left the control of the manufacturer. The Normans had the burden of demonstrating by a preponderance of the evidence that a safer alternative design existed at the relevant time. In addition, a plaintiff complaining of a design defect is required to show that the safety benefits from its proposed design are foreseeably greater than the resulting costs, including any diminished usefulness or diminished safety—that is, that the alternative design not only would have reduced the risk of harm in the instant case, but also would not, under other circumstances, impose an equal or greater risk of harm. Thus, the Normans had to prove that an economically and technologically feasible alternative seat belt and release system was available and would have prevented or significantly reduced the risk of Karen's death without substantially reducing the utility to the "intended users" of the product—namely, all automobile drivers. If no evidence is offered that a safer design existed, a product is not unreasonably dangerous as a matter of law.

The Normans elicited testimony from several experts, but only two of these experts commented on alternative designs for the seatbelt. Although they did not agree about the feasibility of the various alternative designs, two of the Normans' experts, Thomas Horton, a mechanical engineer, and Kenneth Ronald Laughery, a human factors expert, testified that there were three potential alternative seatbelt system designs: (1) the mouse could be on a timer; (2) the release button could be located on the hip level, as in Toyota cars; and (3) there could be two release buttons—one near the hip and one over the shoulder.

The Normans failed to show that the mouse timer, the hip release design used by Toyota, or the two-release-button system existed, were technologically and economically feasible, and were safer under relevant circumstances than the seat belt release system present in the Honda. There was, therefore, no evidence that a reasonably safer alternative design existed for Honda's passive restraint system when the car was manufactured. Having failed to present such evidence, the Normans failed to carry their threshold statutory burden of proving a safer alternative design. We reverse and render a take-nothing judgment.

Knitz v. Minster Machine Company

Ohio Supreme Court (1982)

Virginia Mae Knitz, appellant, began work at the Toledo Die and Manufacturing Company on August 16, 1976. For approximately the first week of her employment she operated punch presses. On August 23, 1976, she was assigned to operate a 60-ton Open Back Inclinable Press designed and manufactured by the Minster Machine Company, appellee.

That press functions to supply power in bringing two halves of a die together. The top half of the press is attached to a ram, which when the press is activated, descends five inches with sixty tons of force onto a bolster plate. The two die halves are, therefore, brought into contact and thereby shape the metal stock between them. The ram then ascends to its original position until again activated. The amount of time required for the ram to descend from its top position to its lower position is three quarters of one second.

On August 23, 1976, appellant was operating the press on a production run that required her to pick up and place a blank piece of metal stock in the space between the two halves of the die with her hand. The press ram was then activated to descend by pushing down on the pedal of a foot switch attached to the press at floor level. After two hours of operation of the press, appellant stopped and left it in search of a more comfortable stool. When she returned, she found that a scrap bin beneath the press had been emptied and the foot switch had been moved. Appellant leaned on the bolster plate with her right hand and attempted to move the pedal back into place with her foot. While so doing, appellant activated the foot pedal, and the ram descended amputating two fingers of her right hand.

The press was delivered to the Toledo Die and Manufacturing Company on October 15, 1971. It was manufactured and shipped with a two-hand, button-tripping device, which is comprised of two buttons that are placed at shoulder level above the die ram area. Both buttons must be depressed in order for the press to be activated, so that the device prevents an operator from placing either hand in the die area while the ram is descending. Appellant's employer had also ordered an optional foot pedal tripping device, also designed by appellee, which was shipped with the press at that time. On the date of the accident, the foot pedal was attached to the press and was the sole method of activating the ram. The two-hand, button-tripping device, however, was disconnected and rendered inoperable.

Subsequent to shipment of the press but prior to the August 23, 1976, accident, appellant's employer had installed on this press a pull-back guard (a Posson type). A Posson pull-back guard is attached to the wrists of the operator and physically pulls his hands and arms out of the die area when the ram descends. At the time of the accident, appellant did not have the pull-back guard attached to her wrists.

In Leichtamer we reviewed the policy underlying the development of strict liability in tort and concluded that application of a varying tort standard based upon "(a) distinction between defects resulting from manufacturing process and those resulting from design, and a resultant difference in the burden of proof on the injured party, would only provoke needless questions of defect classification, which would add little to the resolution of the underlying claims. A consumer injured by an unreasonably dangerous design should have the same benefit of freedom from proving fault provided by Section 402A as the consumer injured by a defectively manufactured product which proves unreasonably dangerous."

The focus of the inquiry in Leichtamer was what constituted a "defective condition unreasonably dangerous" as formulated by Section 402A of the Restatement of Torts. We adopted a variation of the familiar "consumer expectation test" of Section 402: "A product is in a defective condition unreasonably dangerous to the user or consumer if it is more dangerous than an ordinary consumer would expect when used in an intended or reasonably foreseeable manner."

Unlike the factual setting in Leichtamer, there are situations in which "the consumer would not know what to expect, because he would have no idea how safe the product could be made." Difficulty could arise, for example, where the injured party is an innocent bystander who is ignorant of the product and has no expectation of its safety, or where a new product is involved and no expectation of safety has developed. Conversely, liability could be barred hypothetically where industrial workmen "gradually learn of the dangers involved in the machinery they must use to make a living and come to 'expect' the dangers." In such cases, the policy underlying strict liability in tort, requires that "a product may be found defective in design, even if it satisfies ordinary consumer expectations, if through hindsight the jury determines that the product's design embodies 'excessive preventable danger,' or, in other words, if the jury finds that the risk of danger inherent in the challenged design outweighs the benefits of such design."

Accordingly, we hold that a product design is in a defective condition to the user or consumer if (1) it is more dangerous than an ordinary consumer would expect when used in an intended or reasonably foreseeable manner, or (2) if the benefits of the challenged design do not outweigh the risk inherent in such design. Factors relevant to the evaluation of the defectiveness of the product design are the likelihood that the product design will cause injury, the gravity of the danger posed, and the mechanical and economic feasibility of an improved design.

Applying this standard to both the facts of record and to the principles of strict liability in tort discussed, supra, we conclude that appellant has made out genuine issues of fact of whether appellee's press design was defective by allowing accidental tripping of the foot pedal control and in failing to provide a point of operation guard when the foot pedal is operative. Specifically, appellant provided an affidavit of James J. McCarthy, a former safety engineer for General Motors Corporation, involved with analysis of machine accident potential. McCarthy's affidavit states, inter alia, that in his opinion the press is defective "because of inadequate guarding at the point of operation caused by failure to attach a barrier or interlock gate guard to prevent entry of the operator's hands into the danger area while the ram is descending the press is defective because of inadequate guarding of the foot pedal of the foot switch to prevent inadvertent entry and tripping."

Appellant also offered the deposition of Simon Tammy, a mechanical engineer, in which he testified that the foot switch creates unique hazards which should be prevented by use of a point of operation guard. Appellant's own deposition indicates the accident occurred when she was attempting to pull the foot switch toward her by use of her foot, but that she was not intentionally attempting to activate the foot switch.

Construing this evidence most strongly in favor of appellant, we hold that reasonable minds cannot come to but one conclusion on the defectiveness of the design of the foot switch and the absence of a point of operation guard. Accordingly, for the foregoing reasons, the judgment of the Court of Appeals is reversed. Verdict in favor of Virginia Mae Knitz, appellant.

McCarthy v. Olin Corporation

United States Court of Appeals, Second Circuit (1997)

On December 7, 1993, Colin Ferguson boarded the Long Island Railroad's commuter train departing from New York City and opened fire on the passengers. Six people, including Dennis McCarthy, were killed and nineteen others, including Kevin McCarthy and Maryanne Phillips, were wounded in the vicious attack. Ferguson was armed with a 9mm semiautomatic handgun, which was loaded with Winchester "Black Talon" bullets (Black Talons). The injuries to Dennis and Kevin McCarthy and Maryanne Phillips were enhanced by the ripping and tearing action of the Black Talons because, unfortunately, the bullets performed as designed.

The Black Talon is a hollowpoint bullet designed to bend upon impact into six ninety-degree angle razor-sharp petals or "talons" that increase the wounding power of the bullet by stretching, cutting and tearing tissue and bone as it travels through the victim. The Black Talon bullet was designed and manufactured by Olin Corporation (Olin) through its Winchester division and went on the market in 1992. Although the bullet was originally developed for law enforcement agencies, it was marketed and available to the general public. In November 1993, following public outcry, Olin pulled the Black Talon from the public market and restricted its sales to law enforcement personnel. Colin Ferguson allegedly purchased the ammunition in 1993, before it was withdrawn from the market.

Plaintiffs brought this action against Olin, Sturm, Ruger & Company Inc., the manufacturer of the handgun used by Ferguson, and Ram–Line Inc., the manufacturer of the fifteen round capacity magazine used with the handgun. Olin moved to dismiss the complaint pursuant to Fed.R.Civ.P. 12(b)(6) for failure to state a claim upon which relief can be granted. The district court granted the motion.

DISCUSSION

Strict Liability

Appellants' first argument is that Olin should be held strictly liable for their injuries because the Black Talon ammunition was defectively designed and the design and manufacture of the bullets were inherently dangerous.

A. Design Defect

A manufacturer who places into the stream of commerce a defective product which causes injury may be held strictly liable. In New York, there are three distinct claims for strict products liability: (1) a manufacturing defect, which results when a mistake in manufacturing renders a product that is ordinarily safe dangerous so that it causes harm; (2) a warning defect, which occurs when the inadequacy or failure to warn of a reasonably foreseeable risk accompanying a product causes harm; and (3) a design defect, which results when the product as designed is unreasonably dangerous for its intended use. Appellants argue that the Black Talons were defectively designed because the expansion mechanism of the bullets, which causes ripping and tearing in its victims, results in enhanced injuries beyond ordinary bullets. The district court rejected this argument because the expanding of the bullet was an intentional and functional element of the design of the product. We agree.

To state a cause of action for a design defect, plaintiffs must allege that the bullet was unreasonably dangerous for its intended use. "[A] defectively designed product is one which, at the time it leaves the seller's hands, is in a condition not reasonably contemplated by the ultimate consumer." "This rule, however, is tempered by the realization that some products, for example knives, must by their very nature be dangerous in order to be functional." The very purpose of the Black Talon bullet is to kill or cause severe wounding. Here, plaintiffs concede that the Black Talons performed precisely as intended by the manufacturer and Colin Ferguson.

Sadly it must be acknowledged that: [m]any products, however well-built or well-designed may cause injury or death. Guns may kill; knives may maim; liquor may cause alcoholism; but the mere fact of injury does not entitle the [person injured] to recover ... there must be something wrong with the product, and if nothing is wrong there will be no liability.

Appellants have not alleged that the bullets were defective. "As a matter of law, a product's defect is related to its condition, not its intrinsic function." The bullets were not in defective condition nor were they unreasonably dangerous for their intended use because the Black Talons were purposely designed to expand on impact and cause severe wounding.

Appellants next argue that under the risk/utility test analysis applied by New York courts, appellee should be held strictly liable because the risk of harm posed by the Black Talons outweighs the ammunition's utility. The district court properly held that the risk/utility test is inapplicable "because the risks arise from the function of the product, not any defect in the product." "There must be 'something wrong' with a product before the risk/utility analysis may be applied in determining whether the product is unreasonably dangerous or defective."

The purpose of risk/utility analysis is to determine whether the risk of injury might have been reduced or avoided if the manufacturer had used a feasible alternative design. However, the risk of injury to be balanced with the utility is a risk not intended as the primary function of the product. Here, the primary function of the Black Talon bullets was to kill or cause serious injury. There is no reason to search for an alternative safer design where the product's sole utility is to kill and maim. Accordingly, we hold that appellants have failed to state a cause of action under New York strict products liability law.

Inherently Dangerous Product

Appellants also argue that Olin should be held strictly liable because the Black Talon ammunition is "unreasonably dangerous per se." According to the appellants' theory, a product is unreasonably dangerous per se if a reasonable person would conclude that the danger of the product, whether foreseeable or not, outweighs its utility. As the district court held, this is essentially a risk/utility analysis, which we have refused to apply. Under New York's strict products liability jurisprudence, there is no cause of action for an unreasonably dangerous per se product. Thus, this claim was properly dismissed.

CONCLUSION

Because we hold that the Black Talon bullets were not defectively designed, we must affirm the dismissal of appellants' strict liability claims. Although appellants are the victims of a horrible tragedy, under New York law, they have failed to state a cause of action upon which relief can be granted—in sum, New York law does not afford them a remedy. Accordingly, we affirm the judgment of the district court.

WARNING / INFORMATION DEFECT

Liriano v. Hobart Corporation

United States Court of Appeals, Second Circuit (1999)

Luis Liriano was severely injured on the job when his hand and arm were amputated in a meat grinder manufactured by Hobart Corporation ("Hobart") and owned by his employer, Super Associated ("Super"). The meat grinder had been sold to Super with a safety guard, but the safety guard was removed while the machine was in Super's possession and was not affixed to the meat grinder at the time of the accident. The machine bore no warning indicating that the grinder should be operated only with a safety guard attached. Liriano sued Hobart under several theories, including failure to warn and the jury returned a verdict for Liriano on that claim.

Most New Yorkers would probably appreciate the danger of meat grinders. Any additional warning might seem superfluous. On the other hand, Liriano was only seventeen years old at the time of his injury and had only recently immigrated to the United States. He had been on the job at Super for only one week. He had never been given instructions about how to use the meat grinder, and he had used the meat grinder only two or three times. And the mechanism that injured Liriano would not have been visible to someone who was operating the grinder. It could be argued that such a combination of facts was not so unlikely that a court should say, as a matter of law, that the defendant could not have foreseen them or, if aware of them, need not have guarded against them by issuing a warning.

Nevertheless, it remains the fact that meat grinders are widely known to be dangerous. Given that the position of the New York courts on the specific question before us is anything but obvious, we might well be of two minds as to whether a failure to warn that meat grinders are dangerous would be enough to raise a jury issue.

But to state the issue that way would be to misunderstand the complex functions of warnings. As two distinguished torts scholars have pointed out, a warning can do more than exhort its audience to be careful. It can also affect what activities the people warned choose to engage in. And where the function of a warning is to assist the reader in making choices, the value of the warning can lie as much in making known the existence of alternatives as in communicating the fact that a particular choice is dangerous. It follows that the duty to warn is not necessarily obviated merely because a danger is clear.

To be more concrete, a warning can convey at least two types of messages. One states that a particular place, object, or activity is dangerous. Another explains that people need not risk the danger posed by such a place, object, or activity in order to achieve the purpose for which they might have taken that risk. Thus, a highway sign that says "Danger—Steep Grade" says less than a sign that says "Steep Grade Ahead—Follow Suggested Detour to Avoid Dangerous Areas."

If the hills or mountains responsible for the steep grade are plainly visible, the first sign merely states what a reasonable person would know without having to be warned. The second sign tells drivers what they might not have otherwise known: that there is another road that is flatter and less hazardous. A driver who believes the road through the mountainous area to be the only way to reach her destination might well choose to drive on that road despite the steep grades, but a driver who knows herself to have an alternative might not, even though her understanding of the risks posed by the steep grade is exactly the same as those of the first driver. Accordingly, a certain level of obviousness as to the grade of a road might, in principle, eliminate the reason for posting a sign of the first variety. But no matter how patently steep the road, the second kind of sign might still have a beneficial effect. As a result, the duty to post a sign of the second variety may persist even when the danger of the road is obvious and a sign of the first type would not be warranted.

One who grinds meat, like one who drives on a steep road, can benefit not only from being told that his activity is dangerous but from being told of a safer way. As we have said, one can argue about whether the risk involved in grinding meat is sufficiently obvious that a responsible person would fail to warn of that risk, believing reasonably that it would convey no helpful information. But if it is also the case—as it is—that the risk posed by meat grinders can feasibly be reduced by attaching a safety guard, we have a different question. Given that attaching guards is feasible, does reasonable care require that meat workers be informed that they need not accept the risks of using unguarded grinders? Even if most ordinary users may—as a matter of law—know of the risk of using a guardless meat grinder, it does not follow that a sufficient number of them will—as a matter of law—also know that protective guards are available, that using them is a realistic possibility, and that they may ask that such guards be used. It is precisely these last pieces of information that a reasonable manufacturer may have a duty to convey even if the danger of using a grinder were itself deemed obvious.

Consequently, the instant case does not require us to decide the difficult question of whether New York would consider the risk posed by meat grinders to be obvious as a matter of law. A jury could reasonably find that there exist people who are employed as meat grinders and who do not know (a) that it is feasible to reduce the risk with safety guards, (b) that such guards are made available with the grinders, and (c) that the grinders should be used only with the guards. Moreover, a jury can also reasonably find that there are enough such people, and that warning them is sufficiently inexpensive, that a reasonable manufacturer would inform them that safety guards exist and that the grinder is meant to be used only with such guards. Thus, even if New York would consider the danger of meat grinders to be obvious as a matter of law, that obviousness does not substitute for the warning that a jury could, and indeed did, find that Hobart had a duty to provide. It follows that we cannot say, as a matter of law, that Hobart had no duty to warn Liriano in the present case. We therefore decline to adopt appellants' argument that the issue of negligence was for the court only and that the jury was not entitled, on the evidence, to return a verdict for Liriano.

Carruth v. Pittway Corp.

Supreme Court of Alabama (1994)

These cases involve a fire at the home of Coy Carruth and his wife, Shirley Carruth. The plaintiffs, as the administrators of the estates of seven Carruth family members who perished in the fire, brought wrongful death actions against the manufacturer of the Carruths' smoke detector, Pittway Corporation. The actions were based on failure to adequately warn.

The fire occurred on August 27, 1990. Two days before the fire, Carruth had installed a Pittway brand "First Alert Smoke and Fire Detector." The smoke detector was accompanied by a pamphlet explaining its installation, operation, and limitations as a safety device. Carruth says that Pittway inadequately warned consumers about where to locate the smoke detector in regard to wall-ceiling junctions, and that as a result of that inadequate warning he installed it too high on a wall surface for it to sound a timely alarm. According to Carruth, he inadvertently located the smoke detector within a "dead air space." Carruth alleges that because the detector was placed in a dead air space, it failed to sound a timely alarm, and he alleges that the failure to sound a timely alarm resulted in the deaths.

Carruth testified that he did not read the Pittway pamphlet "in depth" before he installed the smoke detector and that he installed it near the ceiling on a first floor wall adjacent to the staircase to the second floor. After installing the detector on August 25, 1990, Carruth said, he tested the detector by depressing an alarm testing button on the unit, and he said he tested it again on the following day.

On August 27, 1990, Shirley Carruth had already left the house to go to work when Coy Carruth awakened at 4:30 a.m. Carruth left the house to go to work at 5:00 a.m. At that time, six family members were sleeping upstairs. Another, Brian Carruth, was awake in an upstairs bedroom. Sometime between 5:00 a.m. and 5:30 a.m. a fire started in the kitchen on the first floor of the house. Six of the family members, including Brian, perished in their bedrooms; one escaped the house with severe burns and died two days later.

Carruth sued on a negligent-failure-to-adequately-warn theory, averring that Pittway had inadequately warned consumers about locating the detector at wall-ceiling junctions. The trial court entered a judgment against Carruth on Pittway's motion for summary judgment.

Negligent–Failure–to–Adequately–Warn Claim

The elements of a claim based on a negligent failure to adequately warn are duty, breach, causation, and damages. "[T]he plaintiff must provide ... evidence that [the] defendant breached a duty, and that the breach proximately caused the plaintiff's injury."

The issues raised by the parties as to Carruth's claim that Pittway negligently failed to adequately warn relate to the negligence elements of breach and causation. Pittway does not contend that it had no duty to warn about installation in dead air space, but, rather, that it did not breach its duty.

We will first address the parties' arguments as to the breach question—whether the Pittway pamphlet conveyed an inadequate warning about installation in dead air space.

As stated, Carruth concedes that he did not read "in depth" the pamphlet he complains of. He suggests that he was unaware of information about locating the detector in dead air space, even after casually scanning the pamphlet and observing information on the box the detector came in regarding where to locate the detector. He argues that the instructions in the Pittway pamphlet were so formidable in general that a consumer is discouraged from reading them fully. Carruth says that the breach of duty in this case comes from the Pittway pamphlet's presentation of information about dead air space concerns; he says those concerns were presented in a manner not calculated to attract the user's attention.

If a vital warning is not read by the user of a product because it is conveyed in such a way that it is not calculated to attract the user's attention, due to its position, size, and ... coloring, then it can constitute a legally inadequate warning. The law does not require that necessary warnings be conveyed in the best way possible, but does require that they not be conveyed in a manner that effectively prevents a consumer from reading them and being warned.

Turning to an examination of that instructional material, the pamphlet, we observe the following:

The pamphlet covers such matters as installation of the detector, general fire protection advice, special effectiveness limitations for the hard-of-hearing, information on use in a recreational vehicle or mobile home, and wide-ranging cautionary statements. The size of the pamphlet's text print is approximately half to two-thirds the size of typical print in a newspaper and could be fairly characterized as tightly spaced. Section headings are approximately the size of print in a newspaper. The pamphlet is seven pages in length, with the first page alone containing over 900 words, inclusive of a table of contents. The words "warning," "caution," and "danger" are interspersed throughout the pamphlet, but no section of the pamphlet covers all cautionary statements or directs the user to the locations of all cautionary statements. Cautionary statements and information about dead-air-space matters are interspersed in the text of the pamphlet. The pamphlet is in black ink on a white background. None of the statements related to dead-air-space is captioned by the words "warning," "caution," or "danger," as are other cautionary statements.

We observe also that a diagram on the box the detector came in—that diagram, Carruth said, was where he got "a general idea of where would be the place, I thought, to put this [detector]"—could reasonably be understood to convey all the information one needs regarding where to locate the detector.

Specifically, the box has a colored, and highly visible, diagram that unequivocally purports to show effective "Detector ... Locations in Typical 2–Story Home." This diagram clearly suggests that the area immediately below a wall-ceiling junction—an area indicated by the record to constitute a potential dead air space—is a suitable location for the detector.

Viewing the evidence most favorably to Carruth, one could reasonably infer that Pittway conveyed important cautionary information about dead-air-space concerns in a way "not calculated to attract the user's attention." Most particularly, from the pamphlet's format and print size, and the seemingly sufficient diagram on the box, a fair-minded person could reasonably infer that a user would be induced to only scan the pamphlet and thereby not get from the pamphlet the information about dead-air-space.

Accordingly, we hold that the evidence presents a jury question as to whether the Pittway pamphlet provided a legally adequate warning about dead-air-space concerns.

REVERSED AND REMANDED.

DEFENSES

Bowling v. Heil Company

Supreme Court of Ohio (1987)

Heil is engaged in the business of manufacturing and selling dump truck beds and hydraulic dump hoist systems designed to be installed on the chassis of trucks produced by various truck manufacturers. Heil does not install its dump beds and hoist systems; rather, it sells them to authorized distributors who install them onto the chassis of trucks selected by their customers.

In May 1979, Ralph Rogers purchased the dump truck at issue from Jake Sweeney Chevrolet, Inc. ("Sweeney"), for use in his backhoe business. The truck was equipped with a Heil DL dump hoist system, which included a dump bed, a hydraulic hoist, and a hydraulic pump valve assembly. This system had initially been installed on the truck's chassis by J.W. Devers & Son, Inc. ("Devers"), a Heil distributor.

As originally mounted, the 1617 DL system utilized a cable control system linking the truck cab controls to the hydraulic pump valve. Rogers was dissatisfied with the operation of the cable control system, however, and returned the truck to Sweeney, requesting that a lever control system be installed. Sweeney contacted Robco, Inc. ("Robco"), another Heil distributor, and Robco replaced the cable control system with a lever control system, which had also been manufactured by Heil. The failure of one of Robco's welds made while installing the lever control system triggered the tragic series of events culminating in David Bowling's death.

On April 26, 1980, one of Rogers' employees made the truck available to Timothy Brashear for his personal use. Brashear's brother, David, learned that Timothy had use of the truck for the day and called his friend, David Bowling, knowing that Bowling needed gravel for his driveway. All three men went to a gravel bed and purchased five tons of gravel, which they loaded into the truck. When they arrived at the Bowling residence, Timothy Brashear backed the dump truck into the driveway and then slowly drove forward with the bed raised, spreading the gravel.

When the truck reached the end of the driveway, Timothy Brashear pushed the in-cab control lever forward to lower the dump bed, but due to the failure of Robco's weld, the bed would not come down. Bowling and David Brashear leaned over the chassis, underneath the raised bed, to investigate the problem. Bowling reached in with his hand and grabbed the control lever on the pump valve assembly, and when he manually manipulated it the dump bed rapidly descended upon him, killing him instantly. David Brashear was able to move out from under the dump bed just before Bowling reached for the control lever, thereby avoiding injury.

Appellant proceeded against Heil on theories of negligence and strict liability in tort, and against Sweeney on a strict liability theory only. At the close of the evidence, the trial judge granted a directed verdict in favor of Sweeney on its cross-claim for indemnity against Heil. The jury returned a verdict in favor of appellant against Heil and Sweeney, and assessed damages at $1.75 million. Upon written interrogatories, the jury determined that Heil was both negligent and strictly liable, that Bowling was contributorily negligent but that he had not assumed a known risk, and that the following percentages of fault were attributable to Heil, Bowling, and Robco: to Heil, forty percent; to Bowling, thirty percent; and to Robco, thirty percent.

Two related issues are presented in this case: first, whether principles of comparative negligence or comparative fault are applicable to a products liability action based upon strict liability in tort; and second, whether the enactment of Ohio's Contribution Among Joint Tortfeasors Act abolished the doctrine of joint and several liability. For the reasons that follow, we answer both questions in the negative.

The court of appeals below held that Ohio's comparative negligence statute does not apply to a products liability action grounded upon strict liability in tort because that statute is limited to negligence actions. We agree.

In Ohio and elsewhere, products liability law, although an outgrowth of the laws of contracts and negligence, has evolved as a separate, identifiable body of law. Products liability cases decided by this court have often involved issues of negligence as well as strict liability. However, a review of those cases demonstrates that those two doctrines have consistently been regarded as complementary, but distinct.

In Leichtamer v. American Motors Corp. we said:

" A distinction between defects resulting from manufacturing processes and those resulting from design, and a resultant difference in the burden of proof on the injured party, would only provoke needless questions of defect classification, which would add little to the resolution of the underlying claims. A consumer injured by an unreasonably dangerous design should have the same benefit of freedom from proving fault provided by Section 402A as the consumer injured by a defectively manufactured product which proves unreasonably dangerous."

The doctrine of strict liability evolved to place liability on the party primarily responsible for the injury occurring, that is, the manufacturer of the defective product. Any distinction based upon the source of the defect undermines the policy underlying the doctrine that the public interest in human life and safety can best be protected by subjecting manufacturers of defective products to strict liability in tort when the products cause harm.

Thus, in Leichtamer, we widened the chasm between theories of negligence and strict liability in tort.

The following year, in Knitz v. Minster Machine Co. we elaborated on the standard for determining whether a product design is defective. We held in the syllabus:

"A product design is in a defective condition if it is more dangerous than an ordinary consumer would expect when used in an intended or reasonably foreseeable manner or if the benefits of the challenged design do not outweigh the risk inherent in such design."

It is obvious that neither prong of this test is grounded upon negligence; rather, the standard is calculated to guard against defective products by subjecting manufacturers and sellers to strict liability in tort.

Thus, a separate body of products liability law has evolved in Ohio, apart from the laws of contracts and negligence. Further, it is apparent that the negligence concept of ordinary care is not a part of the products liability doctrine, which is governed instead by the distinct principles of strict liability in tort. These principles require liability even where a manufacturer has exercised "all possible care."

Included in the body of Ohio law governing products liability is an analysis of the defenses available in actions involving allegedly defective products. Currently, two affirmative defenses based upon a plaintiff's misconduct are recognized. First, an otherwise strictly liable defendant has a complete defense if the plaintiff voluntarily and knowingly assumed the risk occasioned by the defect. Second, such a defendant is also provided with a complete defense if the plaintiff misused the product in an unforeseeable manner.

In this case, the jury found that Bowling was contributorily negligent but that he had not assumed a known risk. Therefore, his contributory negligence did not provide Heil with a defense to appellant's strict liability claim.

Of course, the absence of support in either the Restatement or existing Ohio law for the recognition of comparative negligence as a defense to strict liability does not preclude this court from adopting comparative negligence principles as part of the law of products liability. This court, having developed that body of law, remains inherently vested with the power to modify it. We now turn to a consideration of the public policy underlying the application of strict liability in tort to products liability cases, in order to demonstrate why such modification is not appropriate.

On whatever theory, the justification for the strict liability has been said to be that the seller, by marketing his product for use and consumption, has undertaken and assumed a special responsibility toward any member of the consuming public who may be injured by it; that the public has the right to and does expect, in the case of products which it needs and for which it is forced to rely upon the seller, that reputable sellers will stand behind their goods; that public policy demands that the burden of accidental injuries caused by products intended for consumption be placed upon those who market them, and be treated as a cost of production against which liability insurance can be obtained; and that the consumer of such products is entitled to the maximum of protection at the hands of someone, and the proper persons to afford it are those who market the products.

Under negligence principles, on the other hand, liability is determined according to fault. In negligence, we seek to make the person or persons responsible for causing a loss pay for it. In other words, we "blame" the loss on the negligent party or parties because it was they who could have avoided the loss by conforming to due care. Conversely, in strict liability in tort we hold the manufacturer or seller of a defective product responsible, not because it is "blameworthy," but because it is more able than the consumers to spread that loss among those who use and thereby benefit from the product.

We recognize that strict liability cannot be absolutely divorced from traditional concepts of fault. In a sense we "blame" the loss on the manufacturer or seller because it introduced the defective product into the marketplace. However, it must be reemphasized that strict liability is at odds with traditional notions of due care. In sum, the public policy and goals underlying strict liability differ in important respects from those underlying the law of negligence.

Although some other jurisdictions have chosen to apply comparative negligence to products liability cases in our view the better-reasoned position is that comparative negligence has no application to products liability actions.

Products liability under § 402A does not rest upon negligence principles, but rather is premised on the concept of enterprise liability for casting a defective product into the stream of commerce. Thus, the focus is upon the nature of the product, and the consumer's reasonable expectations with regard to that product, rather than on the conduct either of the manufacturer or the person injured because of the product.

Based upon the foregoing analysis, we hold that principles of comparative negligence or comparative fault have no application to a products liability case based upon strict liability in tort. Strict liability, in focusing on the product rather than the conduct of its manufacturer or seller, does not seek to apportion a loss among all persons who have caused or contributed to it. Rather, it seeks to spread the loss among all users of the product. The concept of comparative fault is fundamentally inapplicable.

We therefore reverse the judgment of the court of appeals with respect to its reduction of appellant's verdict by the thirty percent found by the jury to be attributable to Bowling's contributory negligence.

Hughes v. Magic Chef, Inc.

Supreme Court of Iowa (1980)

Plaintiff Vincent E. Hughes was severely burned on March 9, 1976, when a stove manufactured by defendant Magic Chef, Inc., exploded in his mobile home. The propane gas tank which fueled the stove had run dry on March 7, 1976. After the propane tank was refilled that evening, two pilot lights on the top of the stove were re-lit but a third pilot light in the oven broiler cavity was not re-ignited. Experts testified that a resultant buildup of propane gas in the stove produced an explosion and fire when Hughes attempted to use the stove on the evening of March 9th.

Hughes and his wife Eileen brought this strict liability action against Magic Chef, alleging the stove was unreasonably dangerous in several respects. Magic Chef raised affirmative defenses of assumption of risk and misuse of product. The jury found for Magic Chef and the trial court overruled the Hugheses' motion for new trial.

Instruction on misuse. Hughes claims that the trial court's instruction on misuse was erroneous in two respects. First, he argues that the misuse of product and assumption of risk defenses should not both be submitted in strict liability actions. Second, he argues that the trial court's misuse instruction erroneously holds him to a "reasonableness" standard in the use of the product.

A. As to Hughes' first argument, this court held in Rosenau that in an ordinary negligence case in which the defendant raises the issue of the plaintiff's own negligence, assumption of risk is not to be pled and submitted as a separate defense. Instead, the essential elements of assumed risk, if supported by substantial evidence, are to be included in the contributory negligence instruction. Separate instructions on those defenses might result in the jury's rendering inconsistent verdicts and in the trial court's overemphasizing a particular aspect of a case.

Hughes' argument that the Rosenau reasoning applies equally to the products liability defenses of misuse of product and assumption of risk does not recognize the differing natures of those two issues. Misuse precludes recovery when the plaintiff uses the product "in a manner which defendant could not reasonably foresee." Assumption of risk is a defense to a strict liability action when the plaintiff has "voluntarily and unreasonably proceeded to encounter a known danger. . . ." The misuse of product doctrine has to do with the producer's responsibility in the first place; he has no liability at the outset if the product is misused. The assumption of risk doctrine has to do with the user's culpability; he bars himself from recovering if he voluntarily proceeds in the face of known danger. Although we recognize that in certain cases a plaintiff might have both used the product in a manner which the defendant could not reasonably foresee and voluntarily and unreasonably proceeded to encounter a known risk, we reject the idea that a plaintiff cannot do one without doing the other.

Despite our rejection of Hughes' attempt to apply Rosenau by analogy to this case, we agree with his basic contention that the trial court should not have given an instruction on misuse as a defense in this strict liability action. Misuse is not an affirmative defense but rather has to do with an element of the plaintiff's own case.

If we continued to treat misuse as an affirmative defense distinct and additional to the plaintiff's burden of proving that the product was used in a reasonably foreseeable manner, we would create the potential for inconsistent jury findings in the same case. In addition we would create the possibility of a shifting burden of proof on the issue. The burden of proof regarding the use made of the product should not shift depending on the subtle distinction of whether the defendant offers evidence of misuse to rebut the plaintiff's evidence or instead offers it "to support an affirmative defense he is attempting to raise."

The committee of The Iowa State Bar Association which compiled the uniform Iowa jury instructions, and whose comments were not available when this court decided some of the earlier strict liability cases, had the following to say regarding this specific question:

It is submitted that simply because a defendant pleads and offers proof negating an issue that the plaintiff must prove, it should not be treated as an affirmative defense. Instructions to juries become unnecessarily complicated and illogical when the burden of proof is placed upon the plaintiff to prove the affirmative of an issue and on the defendant to prove the negative of the same issue.

We approve the committee's comment. Misuse of product is no longer to be considered an affirmative defense in products liability actions but is rather to be treated in connection with the plaintiff's burden of proving an unreasonably dangerous condition and legal cause. By adopting this view we do not imply that a defendant may not be entitled to jury instructions on misuse.

B. Hughes' second challenge to the misuse instruction. The problem with the misuse instruction here is that it specifically directed the jury to consider what Hughes knew or ought reasonably to have known. What Hughes knew or should have known about the pilot light has slight relevance to the issue of whether Magic Chef should reasonably have foreseen the use to which the stove was put. The personal characteristics of users or, in this case, knowledge of users, becomes relevant to foreseeability of use only when the characteristics are attributable to a substantial group of users. By including a specific reference to what Hughes knew or should have known, the misuse instruction invited the jury to consider a matter of little relevance to the issue it had to resolve whether Magic Chef should reasonably have foreseen that users would attempt to operate the stove after an interruption in gas service without first igniting all the pilot lights.

We thus hold that on retrial misuse is not to be treated in the jury instructions as an affirmative defense. Instead, the instructions with respect to the use to which the stove was put must place the burden of proof on Hughes to establish by a preponderance of the evidence that the use made of the stove was reasonably foreseeable by Magic Chef. Reference to knowledge reasonably attributable to the ordinary user may be made, but the instruction must make clear that such knowledge is one factor to be weighed in determining whether Hughes' manner of using the product was reasonably foreseeable by Magic Chef. If on retrial Hughes proves by a preponderance of the evidence that the use made of the stove was reasonably foreseeable and that the stove was unreasonably dangerous when so used, then he will have established the first element of his case; otherwise the case is over.

III. Instruction on assumption of risk.

Hughes contends finally that the trial court's assumption of risk instruction was erroneous in not requiring Magic Chef to prove he was aware of the danger involved in attempting to operate the stove as he did. Hughes' argument has merit that this instruction omitted an essential element of assumption of risk. That defense requires assumption of a known risk. The second paragraph of the instruction correctly stated that a plaintiff who assumes the risk must act with knowledge of the danger to himself but the following paragraph, which specifically stated what Magic Chef had to prove, made no mention of Hughes' awareness of danger. The instruction was fatally defective.

In addition the assumption of risk instruction failed to state that the user must unreasonably assume a known risk in order for the defense to apply. The instruction was also defective in that respect.

Hughes' motion for new trial should have been sustained.

REVERSED.

Reid v. Spadone Machine Company

Supreme Court of New Hampshire (1979)

This is a products liability case brought to recover for personal injuries allegedly suffered as a result of a defect in the design of an industrial guillotine-type cutting machine manufactured by the defendant, Spadone Machine Company. The case, which was tried on the theory of strict liability in tort, arose when the plaintiff suffered serious injury to one hand while operating the machine in the course of his employment at Davidson Rubber Company. A jury trial resulted in a verdict for the plaintiff in the amount of $150,000. The defendant requests a reversal of the verdict and, in the alternative, a reduction of the damages.

Plaintiff was a plastics demolder, meaning essentially that he emptied large rectangular molds of plastic and cut the plastic into uniformly sized squares. The demolding was originally done with a "hot knife," an electrical device used to score and then cut the plastic while still in the molding pan. In September 1974, however, Davidson replaced the hot knife with a new Spadone 24-10 bail cutting machine. It is the design of this machine that is the subject of this case.

The Spadone 24-10 is essentially a table-mounted guillotine. It is designed to cut a variety of materials. The machine's twenty-four-inch cutting blade is actuated by the simultaneous pressing of two palm buttons located on the side of the machine. In normal operation, the blade rests some fourteen inches above the flat cutting surface known as the "strike plate." When the buttons are depressed, compressed air fills a pressurized cylinder and the blade begins its descent; when the buttons are released, the blade returns to its uppermost position. The blade is also capable of producing a chopping action if the operator repeatedly presses the buttons before the blade returns to the top of its mount.

The Spadone 24-10 has been manufactured and sold by the defendant for nearly twenty-five years. Until 1972, the cutter was manufactured with the palm buttons on the front of the machine, facing the operator. In 1972 their position was changed to an arm at the machine's side away from the open cutting area. Defendant's witnesses testified that this change was made after the company learned that some operators were rigging a bar on the two buttons on the front, thereby facilitating one-handed operation of the machine. This, it was feared, would lead to dangerous machine operation and an increased possibility of hand injury. The change was designed, therefore, to require the operator to load the machine and then walk to the side of the machine to actuate the blade's descent. According to the defendant, the machine was known by Davidson and by industry in general as a low-volume, one-person utility cutter, and its redesign was never intended to change its use to a two-person machine.

The defendant sold the machine to Davidson on September 12, 1974. Included with the machine was a brochure describing the machine and its general use. No other literature or instructions were included. The brochure depicted and described the machine as it had existed prior to 1972, that is, with the buttons on the front of the machine. Neither the brochure nor the initial correspondence between Davidson and the defendant stated that the machine was to be operated by one person only. It appears, however, that Davidson's engineers recognized the machine's intended one-person use when they inspected it upon its arrival.

Before putting the machine in use, Davidson's engineers added a safety screen around the area of the blade, fashioned a plastic push stick to be used by the operator for removal of material that had previously been cut, and conducted an instructional demonstration of the machine's operation for the employees of the New Products Division. During the instruction period the employees were directed to use the cutter as a one-person operation only. The plaintiff, however, was not present at the demonstration, and testified that he was never personally instructed that two-person operation was forbidden.

After the machine was placed in service, management became aware of the fact that the machine was occasionally used by two men, one as a feeder and one as a button pusher. Initially, those found using it in such fashion were stopped. Even so, plaintiff's testimony indicates that it was used as a two-person machine approximately ten to thirteen percent of the time. Supervisors testified that "things got out of hand" as far as the two-person use went, one supervisor even admitting that he occasionally engaged in the practice himself.

Plaintiff's injury occurred while he and another employee were using the machine on November 15, 1974. Plaintiff's twelve hour shift was nearly over when a fellow employee, decided to assist him in the demolding operation. The two men alternated positions, one feeding the plastic mold under the blade from one direction, the other then rotating the mold ninety degrees and pushing it back through the machine's blade. When one was feeding, the other was pressing the buttons to actuate the blade. While the blade was rising, plaintiff reached underneath the blade and, without using the push stick, shoved the cut material back through to the front of the machine. His coworker pressed the buttons once more. The blade immediately ceased its upward motion and began its cutting descent. Plaintiff lost portions of three fingers from his right hand.

Plaintiff brought this personal injury action based on strict liability alleging that the defendant had defectively designed the bail cutter, that the machine was unreasonably dangerous, and that his injuries were proximately caused by its design. Plaintiff's claim of defect was that by moving the buttons to the machine's side, the operator was required to step away from the feeding area and walk to the side to actuate the blade, thus leaving the feeding area open for another person and encouraging two-person use.

The evidence supports a finding that the machine was defectively designed. Placement of the buttons on the side required the operator to leave the feeding area open while he actuated the blade. This could be found not only to permit, but actually to encourage, two-person operation. This condition, coupled with inadequate warnings against two-person use, could properly be found to have made the machine "unreasonably dangerous." This condition certainly existed at the time of purchase.

The second issue relates to the court's ruling regarding the superseding cause defense. At trial, defendant sought to argue that Davidson's conduct, negligence, and misuse of the bail cutter was the sole proximate cause of plaintiff's injury. The position taken is not that plaintiff's damages should be apportioned by Davidson's comparative causation, but that plaintiff is not entitled to a verdict of any sort against the defendant, because Davidson's conduct and not the defendant's product was the sole proximate cause of the injury. A careful consideration of the facts in the case, however, convinces us to the contrary.

The manufacturer or seller faced with an allegation of strict liability in tort for a defective design may have several defenses against liability, for example, product misuse or abnormal use, and what was formerly termed contributory negligence or unreasonable assumption of the risk. These defenses relate to the comparative fault of the plaintiff and are now classified as "plaintiff's misconduct." With respect to a nonparty third person's conduct, however, the manufacturer's sole defense is that of total nonliability based upon the third person's conduct as a superseding cause. In the usual case, no reason of the law stands to prevent a defendant in a products liability action from arguing a third person's negligence or misuse of the product as the sole proximate cause of the plaintiff's injury. The availability of this defense depends, however, on the foreseeability of the alleged misuse or negligence and, on the nature of the alleged design defect.

In New Hampshire, the manufacturer is under a general "duty to design his product reasonably safely for the uses which he can foresee." This duty is necessarily limited to foreseeing the probable results of the normal use of the product or a use that can reasonably be anticipated. Thus, before a defendant may successfully argue a third person's negligence or misuse as a superseding cause, he must prove that the negligence or misuse was not reasonably foreseeable.

However, by finding the machine defective in design, the jury has found that two-person use was foreseeable. It was the failure to guard against such foreseeable use that made the machine's design defective. This being so, that same use cannot be a superseding cause, even assuming that Davidson was negligent in not preventing that use.

VIII. FAMILY TORTS

Nunn v. Allen

Court of Appeals of North Carolina (2002)

Donald Nunn married Vickie O'Brien Nunn, now Vickie Woods (hereinafter "Mrs. Nunn"), on 1 July 1978; three sons were born to the marriage. Mrs. Nunn moved out of the couple's home in April 1997. Plaintiff and Mrs. Nunn signed a separation agreement on 8 September 1997, and were divorced on 17 August 1998.

Mrs. Nunn had been employed for several years at Allen Brothers Timber Company ("Allen Brothers") as secretary of the corporation. Defendant is also employed by Allen Brothers; his father is president of the company and defendant is a vice-president.

Through the testimony of Mrs. Nunn and other witnesses, there was evidence that plaintiff had accused or suspected Mrs. Nunn of having affairs with other men during their marriage. Mrs. Nunn testified that rumors circulated that her youngest son, who was born in 1991, was, in fact, fathered by defendant's father Bruce Allen or his cousin Steve Allen, Jr. Plaintiff testified that when he confronted Steve Allen, Jr., about these rumors, Steve said, "Clay is your man."

Mrs. Nunn and defendant both testified that they had sexual intercourse for the first time in or about October 1997; Mrs. Nunn testified that it occurred after she and plaintiff had signed the separation agreement.

There was evidence that plaintiff had engaged in an extra-marital relationship with a co-worker in or about 1996. Although there was no evidence that the relationship was sexual, the two often had lunch together, and were seen by witnesses in physically close situations in plaintiff's truck and office. In the fall of 1996, Mrs. Nunn found greeting cards the co-worker had given to plaintiff. Mrs. Nunn and other witnesses testified that the cards appeared to be of a romantic nature and that Mrs. Nunn was upset by their discovery. Mrs. Nunn testified that she stopped sleeping in the same bed with her husband because he would not bathe after coming home from his job working on cars and before getting into bed, and that she was generally disgusted with him and other things going on in her life. She testified that defendant had nothing to do with her separation from plaintiff.

The jury answered the issues of alienation of affection and criminal conversation in favor of plaintiff and awarded compensatory damages of $50,000 and punitive damages of $50,000.

Defendant contends plaintiff failed to produce sufficient evidence as to the existence of each element of the tort of alienation of affection to warrant submission of the issue to the jury. A claim for alienation of affection requires that plaintiff present evidence: (1) there was a marriage with love and affection existing between the husband and wife; (2) that love and affection was alienated; and (3) the malicious acts of the defendant produced the loss of that love and affection.

With respect to the first element, the plaintiff need not prove that he and his spouse had a marriage free from discord, only that some affection existed between them. In terms of proving that alienation of affection occurred, plaintiff need only show that his spouse's affection for him was diminished or destroyed. The third element requires a showing of both malice and proximate cause. Malice is shown by evidence that defendant knew of the marriage and acted intentionally in a way likely to affect the marriage. Proximate cause does not require that defendant's acts be the sole cause of the alienation, as long as they were the controlling or effective cause.

Plaintiff offered substantial evidence from which a jury could find the existence of the first element. There was evidence that plaintiff and his wife had a loving marriage until 1996. Plaintiff testified that between 1993 and 1995, Mrs. Nunn's attention to housework and preparing family meals, as well as her interest in sexual relations with him, began to decline. She stopped attending church with plaintiff and their sons and did not want to take family trips in 1995 and 1996. In November 1996, Mrs. Nunn began sleeping separately from plaintiff and their sexual relationship ended except for one isolated incident of sexual intercourse before April 1997. In April 1997, she moved out of the marital home.

With respect, however, to the element that defendant maliciously engaged in conduct which proximately resulted in the alienation of Mrs. Nunn's affection from plaintiff, defendant argues that a claim for alienation of affection can only be based on pre-separation conduct by defendant, and the evidence shows that any wrongful conduct by defendant only occurred after Mrs. Nunn separated from plaintiff. We disagree. There was evidence tending to show that defendant and Mrs. Nunn worked together for a number of years prior to her separation from plaintiff and that she would occasionally go to defendant's brother's ranch on weekends to ride horses and defendant would be there. The evidence also showed that Allen Brothers Timber Company purchased a house for Mrs. Nunn's grandmother to rent and live in, and that Mrs. Nunn moved into that residence when she separated from plaintiff.

There was also evidence tending to show that after Mrs. Nunn separated from plaintiff, she would go to defendant's residence for drinks with defendant's brother and sister-in-law. Plaintiff testified that between April and September 1997, he observed Mrs. Nunn's car driving down the road to defendant's home in the late afternoon about half a dozen times. In September 1997, plaintiff and Mr. Searcey saw defendant and Mrs. Nunn hugging and kissing, and Mr. Searcey saw her performing oral sex on defendant. Post-separation conduct is admissible and relevant to corroborate evidence of pre-separation conduct, and the evidence of post-separation conduct here provides strong circumstantial evidence explaining and corroborating defendant's pre-separation conduct. In addition, defendant admitted to having sexual intercourse with Mrs. Nunn in October 1997 and continuing a sexual relationship with her thereafter. We hold that a jury could find from all the evidence, without having to engage in speculation, that defendant's conduct was the effective cause of the alienation of Mrs. Nunn's affection from plaintiff, and the trial court did not err in denying defendant's motions for directed verdict and judgment notwithstanding the verdict.

Jones v. Skelley

Court of Appeals of North Carolina (2009)

Beginning in January 2003, defendant and Mr. Jones began conversing with some regularity via cell phone. Both testified that their relationship began to deepen in the spring of 2003. Defendant testified that she and Mr. Jones began to talk frequently via cell phone in the spring of 2003 and that they would also occasionally meet in parking lots. Defendant and Mr. Jones both admitted that they concealed their phone conversations, these meetings, and their relationship from their respective spouses.

In May 2004, plaintiff discovered Mr. Jones and defendant in bed together in the middle of the night at a residence in South Carolina. Defendant and Mr. Jones both admitted that they engaged in sexual intercourse on that day, but claimed that it was the first time that they had done so. Both defendant and Mr. Jones admitted that approximately one month later, in June 2004, they went on a weekend trip to Wilmington and New Bern, North Carolina where they engaged in sexual intercourse. Defendant admitted to paying for the majority of expenses for this trip. Though Mr. Jones initially testified that he and defendant only had sex on these two occasions, he ultimately admitted that he and defendant began having sex on a regular basis beginning in May 2004 and that he was currently in a committed relationship with defendant.

On 21 January 2005, plaintiff and Mr. Jones signed a formal separation agreement, and on 4 March 2005, they divorced.

Plaintiff asserts the court erred with respect to her criminal conversation claim because North Carolina law is clear that she, not defendant, was entitled to summary judgment. Although defendant acknowledges case law to the contrary, she argues that a single occurrence of sexual intercourse between her and Mr. Jones in North Carolina in June 2004, which occurred while plaintiff and her husband were separated and subsequent to plaintiff telling her that she did not want Mr. Jones, does not constitute an interest of the State to give North Carolina subject matter jurisdiction. We agree with plaintiff.

To withstand a defendant's motion for summary judgment on a claim of criminal conversation, plaintiff must present evidence demonstrating: (1) marriage between the spouses and (2) sexual intercourse between defendant and plaintiff's spouse during the marriage. In addition, a plaintiff must also show that the tortious injuries the criminal conversation, occurred in North Carolina before North Carolina substantive law can be applied. Consequently, a plaintiff must show that a defendant engaged in sexual intercourse with her spouse in North Carolina. North Carolina law is clear that a claim for criminal conversation can be based solely on post-separation conduct. Even where spouses enter into a separation agreement containing provisions which purportedly address and waive their right to exclusive sexual intercourse with the other, this Court, reasoning that such provisions relate only to the spouse's rights against each other and not against third parties, has held that the existence of such a separation agreement between a plaintiff and her spouse does not shield a defendant from liability for criminal conversation based on a defendant's post-separation sexual relationship with the plaintiff's spouse. Finally, a plaintiff may recover for criminal conversation where the evidence merely shows a single encounter of sexual intercourse between a defendant and her spouse.

Here, there is no material question of fact that defendant engaged in sexual intercourse with Mr. Jones in North Carolina while he and plaintiff were still married and prior to the execution of a separation agreement. While defendant argues that North Carolina does not have subject matter jurisdiction because at the time the June 2004 intercourse occurred, neither the parties nor Mr. Jones were residents of North Carolina and because North Carolina has no interest in the exclusive right of the sexual relationship between South Carolina residents, we note that in actions arising in tort, North Carolina employs the doctrine of lex loci delicti which provides that the law of the state where the tort was allegedly committed controls the substantive issues of the case. Accordingly, we hold that the trial court erred in granting summary judgment based on lack of subject matter jurisdiction in defendant's favor and that the trial court should have entered summary judgment in plaintiff's favor as there is no issue of material fact regarding plaintiff's criminal conversation claim arising out of the June 2004 sexual intercourse and plaintiff was entitled to judgment as a matter of law.

Reversed and remanded.

IX. DAMAGES

COMPENSATORY

United States v. Hatahley

United States Court of Appeals, Tenth Circuit (1958)

This case is before us for the second time. It was brought by the plaintiffs, who are Indians of the Navajo tribe, to recover $100,000 as damages for the loss of horses and burros which they allege were wrongfully and unlawfully seized and destroyed in the State of Utah by agents of the United States. The trial court found for the plaintiffs and entered a lump sum judgment of $100,000. We reversed on the grounds that the horses and burros in question had been lawfully seized and disposed of under the Utah abandoned horse statute. The United States Supreme Court reversed. The case was remanded for specific findings as to damages.

Upon remand, the District Court took additional evidence on the issue of consequential damages, and without an amendment of the complaint, entered a judgment against the United States for the total sum of $186,017.50. The value of each horse or burro taken was fixed at $395; each plaintiff was awarded $3,500 for mental pain and suffering; and damages were given for one-half of the value of the diminution of the individual herds of sheep, goats and cattle between the date the horses and burros were taken in 1952, and the date of the last hearing in 1957.

The fundamental principle of damages is to restore the injured party, as nearly as possible, to the position he would have been in had it not been for the wrong of the other party. Applying this rule, the plaintiffs were entitled to the market value, or replacement cost, of their horses and burros as of the time of taking, plus the use value of the animals during the interim between the taking and the time they, acting prudently, could have replaced the animals.

The plaintiffs did not prove the replacement cost of the animals, but relied upon a theory that the animals taken were unique because of their peculiar nature and training, and could not be replaced. The trial court accepted this theory, and relying upon some testimony that a horse or a burro could be traded among Indians for sheep, goats or cattle worth a stated price, together with the owner's testimony of the value, arrived at a market value of $395 per head. No consideration was given to replacement cost. The court rejected evidence of the availability of like animals in the immediate vicinity, and their value. This was error. It is true that animals of a particular strain and trained for a special purpose are different from animals of another strain and not so trained, but that does not mean that they cannot be replaced by animals similarly developed and trained, or which may be trained after acquisition. Ordinarily every domestic animal is developed and trained for the purpose to which the owner intends to use it. This development and training adds to its usefulness and generally increases the market value of the animal. In arriving at a fair market value of destroyed animals, the court should consider evidence of the availability of like animals, together with all other elements which go to make up market value.

Likewise, we think the court applied an erroneous rule, wholly unsupported by the evidence, in arriving at the amount of loss of use damage. There was testimony by the plaintiffs that because of the loss of their horses and burros they were not able to maintain and look after as much livestock as they had been able to before the unlawful taking, consequently the size of their herds was reduced. If the unlawful taking of the animals was the proximate cause of the herd reductions, the measure of damages would be the loss of profits occasioned thereby.

Plaintiffs' evidence indicated that the loss of their animals made it difficult and burdensome for them to obtain and transport needed water, wood, food, and game, and curtailed their travel for medical care and to tribal council meetings and ceremonies. Plaintiffs also testified that because of the loss of their animals they were not able to grow crops and gardens as extensively as before. These were factors upon which damages for loss of use could have been based. This does not exclude the right to damages for loss of profits which may have resulted from reduction of the number of livestock, or actual loss of the animals, if the unlawful acts of the defendant agents were the proximate cause of the loss and were proved to a reasonable degree of certainty. But the right to such damages does not extend forever, and it is limited to the time in which a prudent person would replace the destroyed horses and burros. The law requires only that the United States make full reparation for the pecuniary loss which their agents inflicted.

The District Court awarded each plaintiff the sum of $3,500 for mental pain and suffering and stated: "It is not possible for the extent of the mental pain and suffering to be separately evaluated as to each individual plaintiff. It is evident that each and all of the plaintiffs sustained mental pain and suffering. Nor is it possible to say that the plaintiffs who lost one or two horses sustained less mental pain and suffering than plaintiffs who lost a dozen horses. The mental pain and suffering sustained was a thing common to all the plaintiffs. It was a community loss and a community sorrow shared by all. On this basis, the Court finds and awards the sum of $3,500.00 to each of the plaintiffs as a fair and reasonable approximation of the mental pain and suffering sustained by each, as a proximate result of the taking of the horses by the defendant."

There is no evidence that any plaintiff was physically injured when his horses and burros were taken. There was evidence that because of the seizure of their animals and the continued activity of government agents and white ranchers to rid the public range of trespassers, the plaintiffs and their families were frightened, and after the animals were taken, they were sick at heart, their dignity suffered, and some of them cried. There was considerable evidence that some of the plaintiffs mourned the loss of their animals for a long period of time. We think it quite clear that the sum given each plaintiff was wholly conjectural and picked out of thin air. The District Court seemed to think that because the horses and burros played such an important part in the Indians' lives, the grief and hardships were the same as to each. The equal award to each plaintiff was based upon the grounds that it was not possible to separately evaluate the mental pain and suffering as to each individual, and that it was a community loss and a community sorrow.

Apparently the court found a total amount which should be awarded to all plaintiffs for pain and suffering, and divided it equally among them. There was no more justification for such division than there would have been in using the total value of the seized animals and dividing it equally among the plaintiffs. Pain and suffering is a personal and individual matter, not a common injury, and must be so treated. While damages for mental pain and suffering, where there has been no physical injury, are allowed only in extreme cases, they may be awarded in some circumstances. Any award for mental pain and suffering in this case must result from the wrongful taking of plaintiffs' animals by agents of the United States, and nothing else.

Plaintiffs' claims are asserted under the Federal Tort Claims Act. In applying this Act, everyone should be treated the same. Racial differences merit no concern. Feelings of charity or ideological sympathy for the Indians must be put to one side. The deep concern which the executive and legislative branches of the government should have for the plaintiffs does not justify the court in giving them any better or worse treatment than would be given to anyone else.

Reversed, and remanded for a new trial as to damages only.

McDougald v. Garber

Court of Appeals of New York (1989)

This appeal raises fundamental questions about the nature and role of nonpecuniary damages in personal injury litigation. By nonpecuniary damages, we mean those damages awarded to compensate an injured person for the physical and emotional consequences of the injury, such as pain and suffering and the loss of the ability to engage in certain activities. Pecuniary damages, on the other hand, compensate the victim for the economic consequences of the injury, such as medical expenses, lost earnings and the cost of custodial care.

The specific questions raised here deal with assessment of nonpecuniary damages and are (1) whether some degree of cognitive awareness is a prerequisite to recovery for loss of enjoyment of life and (2) whether a jury should be instructed to consider and award damages for loss of enjoyment of life separately from damages for pain and suffering.

On September 7, 1978, plaintiff Emma McDougald, then 31 years old, underwent a Caesarean section and tubal ligation. During the surgery, Mrs. McDougald suffered oxygen deprivation which resulted in severe brain damage and left her in a permanent comatose condition.

A jury found all defendants liable and awarded Emma McDougald a total of $9,650,102 in damages, including $1,000,000 for conscious pain and suffering and a separate award of $3,500,000 for loss of the pleasures and pursuits of life. The balance of the damages awarded to her were for pecuniary damages—lost earnings and the cost of custodial and nursing care. Her husband was awarded $1,500,000 on his derivative claim for the loss of his wife's services.

We note at the outset that the defendants' liability for Emma McDougald's injuries is unchallenged here. Also unchallenged are the awards in the amount of $770,978 for loss of earnings and $2,025,750 for future custodial care. What remains in dispute, primarily, is the award to Emma McDougald for nonpecuniary damages. At trial, defendants sought to show that Mrs. McDougald's injuries were so severe that she was incapable of either experiencing pain or appreciating her condition. Plaintiffs, on the other hand, introduced proof that Mrs. McDougald responded to certain stimuli to a sufficient extent to indicate that she was aware of her circumstances.

We begin with the familiar proposition that an award of damages to a person injured by the negligence of another is to compensate the victim, not to punish the wrongdoer. The goal is to restore the injured party, to the extent possible, to the position that would have been occupied had the wrong not occurred. To be sure, placing the burden of compensation on the negligent party also serves as a deterrent, but purely punitive damages—that is, those which have no compensatory purpose—are prohibited unless the harmful conduct is intentional, malicious, outrageous, or otherwise aggravated beyond mere.

Damages for nonpecuniary losses are, of course, among those that can be awarded as compensation to the victim. This aspect of damages, however, stands on less certain ground than does an award for pecuniary damages. An economic loss can be compensated in kind by an economic gain; but recovery for noneconomic losses such as pain and suffering and loss of enjoyment of life rests on the legal fiction that money damages can compensate for a victim's injury. We accept this fiction, knowing that although money will neither ease the pain nor restore the victim's abilities, this device is as close as the law can come in its effort to right the wrong. We have no hope of evaluating what has been lost, but a monetary award may provide a measure of solace for the condition created.

Our willingness to indulge this fiction comes to an end, however, when it ceases to serve the compensatory goals of tort recovery. When that limit is met, further indulgence can only result in assessing damages that are punitive. The question posed by this case, then, is whether an award of damages for loss of enjoyment of life to a person whose injuries preclude any awareness of the loss serves a compensatory purpose. We conclude that it does not.

Simply put, an award of money damages in such circumstances has no meaning or utility to the injured person. An award for the loss of enjoyment of life cannot provide such a victim with any consolation or ease any burden resting on him. He cannot spend it upon necessities or pleasures. He cannot experience the pleasure of giving it away.

Accordingly, we conclude that cognitive awareness is a prerequisite to recovery for loss of enjoyment of life. We do not go so far, however, as to require the fact finder to sort out varying degrees of cognition and determine at what level a particular deprivation can be fully appreciated. With respect to pain and suffering, the trial court charged simply that there must be "some level of awareness" in order for plaintiff to recover. We think that this is an appropriate standard for all aspects of nonpecuniary loss. We turn next to the question whether loss of enjoyment of life should be considered a category of damages separate from pain and suffering.

There is no dispute here that the fact finder may, in assessing nonpecuniary damages, consider the effect of the injuries on the plaintiff's capacity to lead a normal life. Traditionally, in this State and elsewhere, this aspect of suffering has not been treated as a separate category of damages; instead, the plaintiff's inability to enjoy life to its fullest has been considered one type of suffering to be factored into a general award for nonpecuniary damages, commonly known as pain and suffering.

Recently, however, there has been an attempt to segregate the suffering associated with physical pain from the mental anguish that stems from the inability to engage in certain activities, and to have juries provide a separate award for each. Some courts have resisted the effort, primarily on the ground that duplicative and therefore excessive awards would result. Other courts have allowed separate awards, noting that the types of suffering involved are analytically distinguishable. Still other courts have questioned the propriety of the practice but held that, in the particular case, separate awards did not constitute reversible error.

We do not dispute that distinctions can be found or created between the concepts of pain and suffering and loss of enjoyment of life. If the term "suffering" is limited to the emotional response to the sensation of pain, then the emotional response caused by the limitation of life's activities may be considered qualitatively different. But suffering need not be so limited—it can easily encompass the frustration and anguish caused by the inability to participate in activities that once brought pleasure. Traditionally, by treating loss of enjoyment of life as a permissible factor in assessing pain and suffering, courts have given the term this broad meaning.

If we are to depart from this traditional approach and approve a separate award for loss of enjoyment of life, it must be on the basis that such an approach will yield a more accurate evaluation of the compensation due to the plaintiff. We have no doubt that, in general, the total award for nonpecuniary damages would increase if we adopted the rule. That separate awards are advocated by plaintiffs and resisted by defendants is sufficient evidence that larger awards are at stake here. But a larger award does not by itself indicate that the goal of compensation has been better served.

We are not persuaded that any salutary purpose would be served by having the jury make separate awards for pain and suffering and loss of enjoyment of life. We are confident, furthermore, that the trial advocate's art is a sufficient guarantee that none of the plaintiff's losses will be ignored by the jury.

Martin v. United States

United States District Court of Arizona (1979)

This is a Federal Tort Claims case. By oral opinion, I found in favor of plaintiffs on the issue of the government's negligence; in addition, I found against the government on the issue of contributory negligence. Liability having been established, I requested the parties to submit post-trial memoranda concerning damages.

The facts of this near-fatal accident are simple. Plaintiffs, each a grade school youngster, were riding home from school on a motorbike when they struck a sagging or "down" power line negligently maintained by the government. Plaintiff Jeffrey Martin was operating, and Plaintiff Melvin Burrows was a rear passenger on the bike. Each suffered tragically severe and permanent injuries. The damage elements are:

1) Past medical expenses, which are agreed;

2) Future medical expenses, also agreed, save for minor aspects;

3) Present value of lost future earning capacity;

4) Pain and suffering, and interference with normal and usual activities.

I. MELVIN E. BURROWS II.

Plaintiff Melvin E. Burrows II sustained severe burns to his face, head, back, buttocks, arms and legs.

A. Past Medical Expenses

This plaintiff has submitted uncontested documentation of past medical expenses totaling $48,130.97.

B. Future Medical Expenses

This plaintiff originally sought an award of $55,000 for future medical expenses based upon the testimony of Dr. Alan Sacks that each of 11 further contemplated plastic surgeries will cost about $3,000; that the operations should be performed at intervals of approximately six months; that hospital costs have doubled over the past five years; and that future cost increases will be about 12-15% Per year. The defendant objected to plaintiff's suggestion that I take judicial notice of the asserted rate of inflation in hospital costs. Defendant also noted that the award could be immediately invested by the plaintiff to generate a return that would at least partially offset future medical care cost inflation. Following my letter of March 20, 1979, to the parties seeking clarification of this matter, the parties agreed to entry of an award for future medical expenses of $48,629. In addition, I award $5,000 for psychological treatments to accompany Melvin's additional surgeries, as recommended by Dr. Aaron Canter, a clinical psychologist who treated Melvin during and after his stay at the Maricopa County Hospital.

C. Loss of Earning Capacity

1. Probable Earning Capacity Absent the Accident

Clarence Martin is principal of the Florence middle school, owner of a roofing business that employs Melvin Burrows' father, and uncle of the other plaintiff in this case. He testified upon the basis of his observation of Melvin during the seven years he has known him and the month and a half that Melvin had attended the middle school prior to the accident. He believed that Melvin was average or above average in intelligence and probably would have become a skilled worker, perhaps a mechanic or a carpenter. Dr. Glenn Wilt, an associate professor of finance at Arizona State University and an investment counselor, stated:

(I)t can be reasonably presumed that, but for their injuries, both Melvin and Jeffrey would have gravitated into positions in one of the construction trades. Clearly, that is exactly what most of their uninjured classmates will do, and considering the general demand in this territory, due to the growth of population and need for attendant services in the construction field, a strong demand can be forecast for these jobs.

Dr. David Yandell, a clinical psychologist and vocational rehabilitation counselor called by the defendant, testified that the intelligence and aptitude tests administered by Dr. Donald Guinoud show that Melvin could not have pursued a career in the skilled crafts but instead probably would have become a laborer. Defendant's other witness, Dr. John Buehler, chairman of the department of economics at the University of Arizona, expressed his opinion that neither plaintiff probably would have become a worker in the skilled trades, but rather each would have earned average wages.

Based upon my evaluation of the testimony and the expertise and credibility of the witnesses, I conclude that Melvin Burrows probably would have become a skilled worker. Dr. Wilt stated that a carpenter would, at 1978 wage rates, earn about $9,450 per year during a four-year apprenticeship and during a subsequent 42-year career as a journeyman carpenter would earn about $18,900 annually in wages and $3,900 annually in fringe benefits. I accept these figures as reasonable approximations of Melvin's lifetime earnings had he not experienced this accident.

2. Probable Earning Capacity

Dr. Guinourd testified that Melvin might be employable as a night watchman or night diesel mechanic not involved with the public interaction aspect of either business. Dr. Wilt concluded that, because of Melvin's disfigurement and intolerance to sunlight and perspiration, he would probably be unable to find a job suited to his handicap. Dr. Canter testified that Melvin would benefit psychologically from working even at a lowly position.

Based upon the testimony and my own observation of Melvin Burrows, I conclude that he probably will be able to work at an entry-level position for at least half of his normal working life. According to Dr. Wilt, such work would generate an annual income of $3,120 in 1978 dollars. Thus, Melvin is entitled to recover in 1978 dollars $6,330 per year for four years (apprenticeship period), then $19,680 per year for the following 42 years (journeyman period).

3. Inflation Rate and Return on Investment

Dr. Wilt testified that it is reasonable to expect an annual wage inflation rate of 7% over Melvin's working lifetime and that a sum of money in the hundreds of thousands of dollars could earn 7% annually in relatively riskless investments. Dr. Buehler, on the other hand, stated that wages should be expected to increase only 5.5% annually over this period and that the award could presently be invested with essentially no risk yet earn more than 9% annually.

I find that the award can presently be invested at very little risk and return 7.5% Compounded annually. I find that 5.5% Is a reasonable annual rate of wage inflation to be expected during Melvin's working lifetime.

4. Amount of the Award

I award an amount for the loss of Melvin's earning capacity sufficient when invested at a 7.5% Annual rate of return to generate in 1978 dollars $6,330 per year for the four years 1983-86 (hypothetical apprenticeship period) and $19,680 per year for the following 42 years 1987-2028 (hypothetical journeyman period). These amounts in 1978 dollars are to be converted to current dollars for each year by application of a 5.5% Expected annual rate of wage inflation, then discounted at 7.5% Per year back to 1979. By this method of calculation, the award for loss of Melvin's earning capacity amounts to $548,029.

D. Pain and Suffering

The power line struck Melvin on the face, head and perhaps also on the back, causing severe and extensive burns on those areas and on "blowout holes" on his buttocks, legs, left arm and right hand, where the electric current left his body seeking the ground. More than 80% of his head and face was burned, 70% to the third degree or worse. He also suffered third degree burns on 40% of his back, on his entire left buttocks and on at least six blowout ulcers. Melvin regained consciousness soon after the accident and was found wandering in the desert near the scene. Dr. Williams Clemans, a general practitioner in Florence, treated Melvin briefly in the back of a pickup truck outside the local hospital before having him sent to the burn treatment unit at the Maricopa County Hospital in Phoenix. Dr. Clemans testified that Melvin appeared to be in critical condition. He doubted whether Melvin would survive long enough to reach the burn unit.

At the Maricopa County Hospital where Melvin remained for four months, the surgeons removed the charred layers of skin and tissue from Melvin's face, head, buttocks and other areas of his body. They performed numerous skin grafts and attempted to fashion a functioning right eyelid, which Melvin still cannot close. Melvin lost his right ear entirely and the top third of his left ear. To graft skin onto his left temple, which had been burned down to the skull, the doctors ground the skull down to granulation tissue that could accept a graft. Restoring hair growth to this area would require an additional series of scalp rotation operations. The operations have left Melvin's face and scalp severely scarred, his mouth permanently contorted into a sneer. Because his facial nerves and muscles have been burned away, even additional surgery will never restore to him the ability to smile.

Of the expected eleven future operations, Melvin will undergo eight additional operations to his face. Skin grafts not infrequently dry out, crack, become infected and ulcerated and must be replaced by new grafts. Sunlight darkens grafted skin permanently, highlighting the injured area. Grafted areas are also more susceptible to skin cancer than normal tissue. Melvin testified that the grafted areas hurt and itch constantly. Dr. Sacks testified that additional plastic surgeries and skin grafts will not restore a normal appearance to Melvin.

Melvin has suffered psychologically as well as physically. At the burn unit Dr. Canter treated Melvin by hypnosis to relieve pain, prevent regurgitation of food and restore a will to live. Since emerging from the hospital Melvin has faced teasing and ridicule from his peers and startle reactions and revulsion from strangers.

For several months Melvin wore a mask to protect his healing face from further injury. His schoolmates labeled him "Maskatron." During a school outing children from another school saw him and ran away in horror. Strangers often ask, "What happened to you?" Clarence Martin testified that Melvin has become reclusive, reluctant to attend school. Dr. Canter stated that Melvin has become somewhat detached from life, blames himself for his father's heart trouble and may develop schizophrenic tendencies as a result of his injuries. Nor is it likely that Melvin will have a normal social or sexual life, given the severity of the injuries.

Based upon the testimony and my own observation of Melvin, I award $1,000,000 in compensation for pain and suffering.

PUNITIVE

Clark v. Cantrell

Supreme Court of South Carolina (2000)

Shortly after dark on November 1, 1993, Cantrell, driving a late-model Mustang GT with hazard lights flashing, sped down Highway 24. The driver of a pickup truck that Cantrell passed on a two-lane stretch of road estimated Cantrell was traveling 75 to 80 mph, and she nearly collided with the pickup truck while swerving back into the right lane.

Cantrell sped through an intersection a short distance from a Hess gas station, entering a busy stretch of four-lane highway flanked by restaurants and other retail businesses. The speeding Mustang scared a man whose wife, accompanied by their three boys, was taking him to his night-shift textile job. The man estimated the Mustang was traveling 75 to 100 mph.

Anderson was making a left into the Hess gas station. She waited for a car or two to go by, then began turning left across two lanes of traffic. The front of her car was at the entrance of the service station lot when Anderson glimpsed a small "turbo car" speeding toward her. The textile worker, still watching Cantrell's speeding car from the nearby intersection, saw it strike the right rear side of Anderson's Oldsmobile. The impact flung Anderson's friend, David James, from the car, killing him.

A state Highway Patrol trooper who reconstructed the accident scene pegged the Mustang's speed at 67 to 71 mph when Cantrell first applied her brakes. An accident reconstruction expert hired by Cantrell estimated her car was traveling 57 mph. The posted speed limit was 35 mph. The trooper and Cantrell's expert testified that, if she had been traveling 35 mph, the accident probably would not have occurred.

When Cantrell emerged from her car, she was upset and screaming about the condition of her car, demanding that bystanders look at what had happened to it. She laughed as a trooper talked to her a short while later, although her laughter ended when she was informed someone had died in the accident. Cantrell told a trooper the next day that she was speeding because her car was low on gas and she was in a hurry to reach a station.

Anderson and Clark alleged that Cantrell had caused their injuries and damages by speeding on the busy highway. Cantrell's primary defense was that Anderson caused the accident by turning left in front of her. The jury found Anderson sixteen percent at fault and Cantrell eighty-four percent at fault in the accident. The jury awarded Anderson $75,000 in actual damages and $25,000 in punitive damages; and Clark, the vehicle's owner, $3,000 in actual damages and $750 in punitive damages. The trial judge reduced the actual damages, but not the punitive damages, by the proportion of Anderson's fault.

1. PUNITIVE DAMAGES

Cantrell contends the Court of Appeals erred in holding that punitive damages, unlike actual damages, are not reduced by the proportion of the plaintiff's negligence under comparative negligence. Cantrell argues punitive damages should be reduced proportionately because such damages serve, in part, a compensatory role. We disagree.

The purpose of actual or compensatory damages is to compensate a party for injuries suffered or losses sustained. The goal is to restore the injured party, as nearly as possible through the payment of money, to the same position he or she was in before the wrongful injury occurred.

The purposes of punitive damages are to punish the wrongdoer and deter the wrongdoer and others from engaging in similar reckless, willful, wanton, or malicious conduct in the future. This Court has explained the important role that punitive damages play in the American system of justice generally, and in South Carolina in particular since at least 1784. Exemplary or punitive damages go to the plaintiff, not as a fine or penalty for a public wrong, but in vindication of a private right which has been willfully invaded; and indeed, it may be said that such damages in a measure compensate or satisfy for the willfulness with which the private right was invaded, but, in addition thereto, operating as a deterring punishment to the wrongdoer, and as a warning to others.... Punitive damages have now come, however, to be generally, though not universally, regarded, not only as punishment for wrong, but as vindication of private right. This is the basis upon which they are now placed in this state.

We affirm the Court of Appeals' holding on this issue for four related reasons. First, allowing the defendant to shift a portion of the cost of a punitive award back to the plaintiff through comparative negligence would reduce the punishment and deterrent effect of the award. The defendant's punishment would be lessened simply because the plaintiff was somewhat negligent. That is illogical and violates the underlying rationale of punitive damages.

Second, any reduction in the defendant's punishment inflicts a corresponding amount of punishment on the plaintiff. Shifting a portion of the cost of the punitive award back to the plaintiff essentially would punish him or her along with the defendant. In this case,

Anderson would be punished by the loss of $4,000 (sixteen percent of $25,000 in punitive damages), money which the jury believed she rightly deserved. Yet Anderson in no way contributed to the willful or reckless nature of the defendant's conduct, and did nothing for which she should be punished.

Third, it would be inappropriate to reduce the punitive damages by comparing the plaintiff's negligence with the defendant's reckless or willful conduct. It is proper to reduce Anderson's actual damages in this case because the jury decided her negligent decision to turn left in front of Cantrell's speeding car contributed to causing the accident. But Anderson's negligent conduct was not willful or reckless. Conduct that is merely negligent should not be used to reduce damages the jury decided Cantrell should pay as a means of punishing her willful and reckless conduct, and deterring similar conduct by her and others in the future.

Fourth, when considering the negligence attributable to each party, the focus is on the actions of both plaintiff and defendant. What did each do, or not do, that contributed to the cause of an injury? With punitive damages, however, the focus is on only the defendant. The central inquiry is whether the defendant's conduct was so reckless, willful, wanton, or malicious that the defendant should be punished and deterred by requiring him or her to pay money to the plaintiff.

Cantrell also argues that the Court of Appeals erred because Anderson did not present clear and convincing evidence of Cantrell's reckless, willful, wanton, or malicious conduct. We conclude the Court of Appeals correctly reasoned that Cantrell's excessive speed, her disregard for the commercial nature of the highway, her lack of remorse, and her frivolous reason for speeding amply support the award of punitive damages.

In sum, we hold that punitive damages are not reduced by the proportion of the plaintiff's negligence under comparative negligence. We also affirm the award of punitive damages to Anderson and Clark.

State Farm v. Campbell

Supreme Court of the United States (2003)

Justice KENNEDY delivered the opinion of the Court.

We address once again the measure of punishment, by means of punitive damages, a State may impose upon a defendant in a civil case. The question is whether, in the circumstances we shall recount, an award of $145 million in punitive damages, where full compensatory damages are $1 million, is excessive and in violation of the Due Process Clause of the Fourteenth Amendment to the Constitution of the United States.

I. In 1981, Curtis Campbell (Campbell) was driving with his wife, Inez Preece Campbell, in Cache County, Utah. He decided to pass six vans traveling ahead of them on a two-lane highway. Todd Ospital was driving a small car approaching from the opposite direction. To avoid a head-on collision with Campbell, who by then was driving on the wrong side of the highway and toward oncoming traffic, Ospital swerved onto the shoulder, lost control of his automobile, and collided with a vehicle driven by Robert G. Slusher. Ospital was killed, and Slusher was rendered permanently disabled. The Campbells escaped unscathed.

In the ensuing wrongful death and tort action, Campbell insisted he was not at fault. Early investigations did support differing conclusions as to who caused the accident, but "a consensus was reached early on by the investigators and witnesses that Mr. Campbell's unsafe pass had indeed caused the crash." Campbell's insurance company, petitioner State Farm Mutual Automobile Insurance Company (State Farm), nonetheless decided to contest liability and declined offers by Slusher and Ospital's estate (Ospital) to settle the claims for the policy limit of $50,000 ($25,000 per claimant). State Farm also ignored the advice of one of its own investigators and took the case to trial, assuring the Campbells that "their assets were safe, that they had no liability for the accident, that [State Farm] would represent their interests, and that they did not need to procure separate counsel." To the contrary, a jury determined that Campbell was 100 percent at fault, and a judgment was returned for $185,849, far more than the amount offered in settlement.

At first State Farm refused to cover the $135,849 in excess liability. Its counsel made this clear to the Campbells: " 'You may want to put for sale signs on your property to get things moving.'" Nor was State Farm willing to post a supersedeas bond to allow Campbell to appeal the judgment against him. Campbell obtained his own counsel to appeal the verdict. During the pendency of the appeal, in late 1984, Slusher, Ospital, and the Campbells reached an agreement whereby Slusher and Ospital agreed not to seek satisfaction of their claims against the Campbells. In exchange the Campbells agreed to pursue a bad faith action against

State Farm and to be represented by Slusher's and Ospital's attorneys. The Campbells also agreed that Slusher and Ospital would have a right to play a part in all major decisions concerning the bad-faith action. No settlement could be concluded without Slusher's and Ospital's approval, and Slusher and Ospital would receive 90 percent of any verdict against State Farm.

In 1989, the Utah Supreme Court denied Campbell's appeal in the wrongful-death and tort actions. State Farm then paid the entire judgment, including the amounts in excess of the policy limits. The Campbells nonetheless filed a complaint against State Farm alleging bad faith, fraud, and intentional infliction of emotional distress. The trial court initially granted State Farm's motion for summary judgment because State Farm had paid the excess verdict, but that ruling was reversed on appeal. On remand State Farm moved to exclude evidence of alleged conduct that occurred in unrelated cases outside of Utah, but the trial court denied the motion. At State Farm's request the trial court bifurcated the trial into two phases conducted before different juries. In the first phase the jury determined that State Farm's decision not to settle was unreasonable because there was a substantial likelihood of an excess verdict.

Before the second phase of the action against State Farm we decided BMW of North America, Inc. v. Gore, 517 U.S. 559 (1996), and refused to sustain a $2 million punitive damages award which accompanied a verdict of only $4,000 in compensatory damages. Based on that decision, State Farm again moved for the exclusion of evidence of dissimilar out-of-state conduct. The trial court denied State Farm's motion.

The second phase addressed State Farm's liability for fraud and intentional infliction of emotional distress, as well as compensatory and punitive damages. The Utah Supreme Court aptly characterized this phase of the trial:

"State Farm argued during phase II that its decision to take the case to trial was an 'honest mistake' that did not warrant punitive damages. In contrast, the Campbells introduced evidence that State Farm's decision to take the case to trial was a result of a national scheme to meet corporate fiscal goals by capping payouts on claims company wide. This scheme was referred to as State Farm's 'Performance, Planning and Review,' or PP & R, policy. To prove the existence of this scheme, the trial court allowed the Campbells to introduce extensive expert testimony regarding fraudulent practices by State Farm in its nation-wide operations. Although State Farm moved prior to phase II of the trial for the exclusion of such evidence and continued to object to it at trial, the trial court ruled that such evidence was admissible to determine whether State Farm's conduct in the Campbell case was indeed intentional and sufficiently egregious to warrant punitive damages."

Evidence pertaining to the PP & R policy concerned State Farm's business practices for over 20 years in numerous States. Most of these practices bore no relation to third-party automobile insurance claims, the type of claim underlying the Campbells' complaint against the company. The jury awarded the Campbells $2.6 million in compensatory damages and $145 million in punitive damages, which the trial court reduced to $1 million and $25 million respectively. Both parties appealed.

The Utah Supreme Court sought to apply the three guideposts we identified in Gore, and it reinstated the $145 million punitive damages award. Relying in large part on the extensive evidence concerning the PP & R policy, the court concluded State Farm's conduct was reprehensible. The court also relied upon State Farm's "massive wealth" and on testimony indicating that "State Farm's actions, because of their clandestine nature, will be punished at most in one out of every 50,000 cases as a matter of statistical probability," and concluded that the ratio between punitive and compensatory damages was not unwarranted. Finally, the court noted that the punitive damages award was not excessive when compared to various civil and criminal penalties State Farm could have faced, including $10,000 for each act of fraud, the suspension of its license to conduct business in Utah, the disgorgement of profits, and imprisonment.

II. While States possess discretion over the imposition of punitive damages, it is well established that there are procedural and substantive constitutional limitations on these awards. The Due Process Clause of the Fourteenth Amendment prohibits the imposition of grossly excessive or arbitrary punishments on a tortfeasor. This constitutional concern, itself harkening back to the Magna Carta, arises out of the basic unfairness of depriving citizens of life, liberty, or property, through the application, not of law and legal processes, but of arbitrary coercion. The reason is that elementary notions of fairness enshrined in our constitutional jurisprudence dictate that a person receive fair notice not only of the conduct that will subject him to punishment, but also of the severity of the penalty that a State may impose. To the extent an award is grossly excessive, it furthers no legitimate purpose and constitutes an arbitrary deprivation of property.

Although these awards serve the same purposes as criminal penalties, defendants subjected to punitive damages in civil cases have not been accorded the protections applicable in a criminal proceeding. This increases our concerns over the imprecise manner in which punitive damages systems are administered. We have admonished that punitive damages pose an acute danger of arbitrary deprivation of property. Jury instructions typically leave the jury with wide discretion in choosing amounts, and the presentation of evidence of a defendant's net worth creates the potential that juries will use their verdicts to express biases against big businesses, particularly those without strong local presences. Our concerns are heightened when the decisionmaker is presented with evidence that has little bearing as to the amount of punitive damages that should be awarded.

In light of these concerns, in Gore, we instructed courts reviewing punitive damages to consider three guideposts: (1) the degree of reprehensibility of the defendant's misconduct; (2) the disparity between the actual or potential harm suffered by the plaintiff and the punitive damages award; and (3) the difference between the punitive damages awarded by the jury and the civil penalties authorized or imposed in comparable cases.

III. Under the principles outlined in BMW of North America, Inc. v. Gore, this case is neither close nor difficult. It was error to reinstate the jury's $145 million punitive damages award. We address each guidepost of Gore in some detail.

A. "[T]he most important indicium of the reasonableness of a punitive damages award is the degree of reprehensibility of the defendant's conduct." We have instructed courts to determine the reprehensibility of a defendant by considering whether: the harm caused was physical as opposed to economic; the tortious conduct evinced an indifference to or a reckless disregard of the health or safety of others; the target of the conduct had financial vulnerability; the conduct involved repeated actions or was an isolated incident; and the harm was the result of intentional malice, trickery, or deceit, or mere accident. The existence of any one of these factors weighing in favor of a plaintiff may not be sufficient to sustain a punitive damages award; and the absence of all of them renders any award suspect. It should be presumed a plaintiff has been made whole for his injuries by compensatory damages, so punitive damages should only be awarded if the defendant's culpability, after having paid compensatory damages, is so reprehensible as to warrant the imposition of further sanctions to achieve punishment or deterrence.

Applying these factors in the instant case, we must acknowledge that State Farm's handling of the claims against the Campbells merits no praise. The trial court found that State Farm's employees altered the company's records to make Campbell appear less culpable. State Farm disregarded the overwhelming likelihood of liability and the near-certain probability that, by taking the case to trial, a judgment in excess of the policy limits would be awarded. State Farm amplified the harm by at first assuring the Campbells their assets would be safe from any verdict and by later telling them, postjudgment, to put a for-sale sign on their house. While we do not suggest there was error in awarding punitive damages based upon State Farm's conduct toward the Campbells, a more modest punishment for this reprehensible conduct could have satisfied the State's legitimate objectives, and the Utah courts should have gone no further.

A State cannot punish a defendant for conduct that may have been lawful where it occurred. Nor, as a general rule, does a State have a legitimate concern in imposing punitive damages to punish a defendant for unlawful acts committed outside of the State's jurisdiction. Any proper adjudication of conduct that occurred outside Utah to other persons would require their inclusion, and, to those parties, the Utah courts, in the usual case, would need to apply the laws of their relevant jurisdiction.

The courts awarded punitive damages to punish and deter conduct that bore no relation to the Campbells' harm. A defendant's dissimilar acts, independent from the acts upon which liability was premised, may not serve as the basis for punitive damages. A defendant should be punished for the conduct that harmed the plaintiff, not for being an unsavory individual or business. Due process does not permit courts, in the calculation of punitive damages, to adjudicate the merits of other parties' hypothetical claims against a defendant under the guise of the reprehensibility analysis, but we have no doubt the Utah Supreme Court did that here. Punishment on these bases creates the possibility of multiple punitive damages awards for the same conduct; for in the usual case nonparties are not bound by the judgment some other plaintiff obtains.

B. Turning to the second Gore guidepost, we have been reluctant to identify concrete constitutional limits on the ratio between harm, or potential harm, to the plaintiff and the punitive damages award. We decline again to impose a bright-line ratio which a punitive damages award cannot exceed. Our jurisprudence and the principles it has now established demonstrate, however, that, in practice, few awards exceeding a single-digit ratio between punitive and compensatory damages, to a significant degree, will satisfy due process.

Nonetheless, because there are no rigid benchmarks that a punitive damages award may not surpass, ratios greater than those we have previously upheld may comport with due process where "a particularly egregious act has resulted in only a small amount of economic damages." The converse is also true, however. When compensatory damages are substantial, then a lesser ratio, perhaps only equal to compensatory damages, can reach the outermost limit of the due process guarantee. The precise award in any case, of course, must be based upon the facts and circumstances of the defendant's conduct and the harm to the plaintiff.

In sum, courts must ensure that the measure of punishment is both reasonable and proportionate to the amount of harm to the plaintiff and to the general damages recovered. In the context of this case, we have no doubt that there is a presumption against an award that has a 145–to–1 ratio. The compensatory award in this case was substantial; the Campbells were awarded $1 million for a year and a half of emotional distress. This was complete compensation. The harm arose from a transaction in the economic realm, not from some physical assault or trauma; there were no physical injuries; and State Farm paid the excess verdict before the complaint was filed, so the Campbells suffered only minor economic injuries for the 18–month period in which State Farm refused to resolve the claim against them. The compensatory damages for the injury suffered here, moreover, likely were based on a component which was duplicated in the punitive award. Much of the distress was caused by the outrage and humiliation the Campbells suffered at the actions of their insurer; and it is a major role of punitive damages to condemn such conduct. Compensatory damages, however, already contain this punitive element.

The Utah Supreme Court sought to justify the massive award by pointing to State Farm's purported failure to report a prior $100 million punitive damages award in Texas to its corporate headquarters; the fact that State Farm's policies have affected numerous Utah consumers; the fact that State Farm will only be punished in one out of every 50,000 cases as a matter of statistical probability; and State Farm's enormous wealth. Since the Supreme Court of Utah discussed the Texas award when applying the ratio guidepost, we discuss it here. The Texas award, however, should have been analyzed in the context of the reprehensibility guidepost only. The failure of the company to report the Texas award is out-of-state conduct that, if the conduct were similar, might have had some bearing on the degree of reprehensibility, subject to the limitations we have described. Here, it was dissimilar, and of such marginal relevance that it should have been accorded little or no weight. The award was rendered in a first-party lawsuit; no judgment was entered in the case; and it was later settled for a fraction of the verdict. With respect to the Utah Supreme Court's second justification, the Campbells' inability to direct us to testimony demonstrating harm to the people of Utah (other than those directly involved in this case) indicates that the adverse effect on the State's general population was in fact minor.

The remaining premises for the Utah Supreme Court's decision bear no relation to the award's reasonableness or proportionality to the harm. They are, rather, arguments that seek to defend a departure from well-established constraints on punitive damages. While States enjoy considerable discretion in deducing when punitive damages are warranted, each award must comport with the principles set forth in Gore. Here the argument that State Farm will be punished in only the rare case, coupled with reference to its assets (which, of course, are what other insured parties in Utah and other States must rely upon for payment of claims) had little to do with the actual harm sustained by the Campbells. The wealth of a defendant cannot justify an otherwise unconstitutional punitive damages award. The principles set forth in Gore must be implemented with care, to ensure both reasonableness and proportionality.

C. The third guidepost in Gore is the disparity between the punitive damages award and the "civil penalties authorized or imposed in comparable cases." We note that, in the past, we have also looked to criminal penalties that could be imposed. The existence of a criminal penalty does have bearing on the seriousness with which a State views the wrongful action. When used to determine the dollar amount of the award, however, the criminal penalty has less utility. Great care must be taken to avoid use of the civil process to assess criminal penalties that can be imposed only after the heightened protections of a criminal trial have been observed, including, of course, its higher standards of proof. Punitive damages are not a substitute for the criminal process, and the remote possibility of a criminal sanction does not automatically sustain a punitive damages award.

Here, we need not dwell long on this guidepost. The most relevant civil sanction under Utah state law for the wrong done to the Campbells appears to be a $10,000 fine for an act of fraud, an amount dwarfed by the $145 million punitive damages award. The Supreme Court of Utah speculated about the loss of State Farm's business license, the disgorgement of profits, and possible imprisonment, but here again its references were to the broad fraudulent scheme drawn from evidence of out-of-state and dissimilar conduct. This analysis was insufficient to justify the award.

IV. An application of the Gore guideposts to the facts of this case, especially in light of the substantial compensatory damages awarded (a portion of which contained a punitive element), likely would justify a punitive damages award at or near the amount of compensatory damages. The punitive award of $145 million, therefore, was neither reasonable nor proportionate to the wrong committed, and it was an irrational and arbitrary deprivation of the property of the defendant. The proper calculation of punitive damages under the principles we have discussed should be resolved, in the first instance, by the Utah courts.

The judgment of the Utah Supreme Court is reversed, and the case is remanded for further proceedings not inconsistent with this opinion.

It is so ordered.

COLLATERAL SOURCE RULE

Badgett v. Davis

Court of Appeals of North Carolina (1991)

Defendant, Dr. Davis, admitted plaintiff, Mr. Badgett, to a detoxification center where plaintiff was given medication to prevent seizures. Plaintiff developed an allergic reaction, toxic epidermal necrolysis, which plaintiff attributed to Dilantin. Plaintiff filed suit against Dr. Davis on 23 November 1988 alleging negligent prescription of a drug which defendant knew plaintiff to be allergic. Plaintiff presented photographs of his blotched and blistered skin to prove his pain and suffering, but was unable to produce an itemized bill to prove his medical expenses as the hospital in which he was treated kept itemized bills for only five years. Mr. Badgett's bill was destroyed in 1987. The hospital had retained a cash ledger which documented the time, date, and amount of all payments made on each patient's account.

The court held an examination outside the jury's presence in which the ledger was examined through its custodian. During this conference, the custodian indicated that Mr. Badgett's hospital costs were reconstructed from the cash ledger entries by combining the amounts actually paid with the amounts written off. Plaintiff asked the court to mark the ledger plaintiff's exhibit 10 for purposes of identification, but did not request that it be admitted into evidence. Defendant questioned the use of the exhibit without its being admitted. The court indicated that it would be unfair to permit testimony as to the total bill without evidence to show how the custodian arrived at this total. The ledger was admitted and plaintiff objected to the admission of exhibit 10 based upon the collateral source rule and requested that the court's clerk delete the exhibit's reference to Medicare. This was not done.

On direct examination before the jury, plaintiff asked the custodian to give the total cost of Mr. Badgett's hospitalization. She testified that the total was $17,270.52 and that Medicare had paid these bills in part. She testified that according to the hospital's contract with Medicare, the unpaid balance was written off and could not thereafter be collected from the plaintiff. Over defendant's objection the custodian testified that Medicare had a lien for the amounts it expended on Mr. Badgett's medical bills. The jury awarded plaintiff $18,000.00 in damages. Plaintiff moved to set aside the damage award as having been improperly influenced by the prejudicial admission of evidence that plaintiff's medical bills were paid by Medicare and because the damage award was inadequate as a matter of law. This motion was denied. Plaintiff appeals the denial of this motion.

The collateral source rule is a protective device normally invoked to shield a plaintiff from a defendant's attempts to lower the damage award. Because we believe that the plaintiff's shield was pierced by the court's admission of the cash ledger in unredacted form despite the plaintiff's request to the contrary, we reverse and remand for a new trial on the issue of damages.

Exclusion of prejudicial evidence is the foundation of the collateral source rule. This rule provides that evidence of a plaintiff's receipt of benefits for his or her injury or disability from sources collateral to defendant generally is not admissible. These benefits include payments from both public and private sources. This rule gives force to the public policy which prohibits a tortfeasor from reducing "his own liability for damages by the amount of compensation the injured party receives from an independent source." Evidence of collateral source payments violate the rule whether admitted in the defendant's case-in-chief or on cross examination of the plaintiff's witness. The erroneous admission of collateral source evidence often must result in a new trial. This evidentiary admission was so likely to have prejudiced plaintiff's recovery that we remand the case for a new trial on the issue of damages.

SUBROGATION

Erie Insurance Company v. Kaltenbach

Court of Appeals of Ohio (1998)

Kaltenbach was an insured of Erie under an automobile insurance policy. The Erie policy contained the following subrogation provision: "After we make a payment under this policy, we will have the right to recover from anyone else held responsible. Anyone we protect is required to transfer this right to us, and do nothing to harm this right. Anyone receiving payment from us and from someone else for the same accident or loss will reimburse us up to our payment."

Kaltenbach was injured in an automobile accident allegedly caused by the actions of Ben Parsons. The tortfeasor, Parsons, was insured by Allstate Insurance Company. Kaltenbach received chiropractic treatments for his injury, incurring over $5,000 in medical expenses. Erie paid the medical bills up to the maximum policy medical limit of $5,000. Without first filing a complaint against either Parsons or Allstate, Kaltenbach entered into settlement negotiations with them. Allstate offered to pay $4,462 to Kaltenbach in exchange for a release of all claims against Allstate and Parsons stemming from the accident. Kaltenbach contacted Erie, notifying it of the negotiations and proposed settlement. Kaltenbach stated that he would not himself pursue litigation against the tortfeasor because that would be too costly, and instead asked Erie to file suit on his behalf.

Erie informed Kaltenbach that it did not consent to the proposed settlement agreement. Erie also stated that it would not file suit on Kaltenbach's behalf, and reminded him that settlement and release of his claims against Allstate and Parsons would harm its subrogation rights against those parties. Thereafter, in order to protect its subrogation rights, Erie filed its own suit against Allstate and Parsons.

Still not having filed suit against Allstate and Parsons, and with the time in which to file suit running out, Kaltenbach settled with Allstate and Parsons for $4,462, releasing all of his claims against them. Erie dismissed its action against Allstate and Parsons due to Kaltenbach's settlement and release. Erie then filed suit against Kaltenbach, claiming breach of contract and demanding reimbursement for the medical payments paid under the policy. In the court below, both parties filed motions for summary judgment. The trial court denied Kaltenbach's motion and granted the motion of Erie, ordering Kaltenbach to pay Erie the settlement amount of $4,462, plus interest and costs. This appeal followed.

The right of an insurer to be subrogated to the rights of the insured arises either from the right of conventional subrogation, that is, subrogation by agreement between the parties, or equitable subrogation by operation of law. Conventional subrogation is premised on the contractual obligations of the parties, either express or implied. Contractual subrogation clauses in an insurance policy are controlled by contract principles, including those of interpretation of the contract language.

Here, the language of the policy agreement between Kaltenbach and Erie is plain and unambiguous. Under the policy, Erie reserved the right to pursue an action for recovery from anyone responsible for injury to the insured. The insured promised not to harm the recovery rights of Erie against the third parties who were deemed responsible for the injury. Under the provisions of the policy, Kaltenbach had to transfer his rights of recovery against Allstate and Parsons to Erie. Additionally, Kaltenbach was obligated to reimburse Erie for Erie's payments made to him out of any recovery gained from a third party, based on the same accident or loss.

An insurer-subrogee cannot succeed to or acquire any right or remedy not possessed by its insured-subrogor. Once Kaltenbach settled, he released his rights to claim injury against Allstate or Parsons. Kaltenbach's release extinguished all recovery or remedy rights he had against the tortfeasor, and thereby barred the subrogated recovery rights of Erie. Therefore, by virtue of the settlement and release of his claims, Kaltenbach breached his agreement with Erie under the policy by harming its right of recovery. By the terms of the policy, Kaltenbach then was obligated to reimburse Erie for the medical payments made on his behalf, up to $5,000, out of the other accident-related payments he received. Therefore, Kaltenbach owed Erie the $4,462 he had received in settlement from Allstate and Parsons.

In the instant case, the Erie policy subrogation provisions convey the right of recovery against any third-party wrongdoer to Erie, to the extent of the payment by the insurer to the insured. Under the policy, Erie is entitled to reimbursement from the settlement amount up to $5,000 medical payments made on Kaltenbach's behalf. Kaltenbach argues that Erie is not entitled to recovery because Erie did not cooperate or assist in proceedings against the tortfeasor.

The evidence shows that Erie advised Kaltenbach not to settle without Erie's consent. Erie initiated its own action against Allstate and Parsons in order to preserve its subrogation rights against the tortfeasor, even though no action was filed by Kaltenbach. Therefore, to the extent that it was required and able to, Erie did cooperate and assist Kaltenbach in proceedings against the tortfeasor, thereby permitting it to be fully reimbursed for its payments under the policy.

We hold, therefore, that Erie was entitled to subrogation; that Kaltenbach was fully compensated for his injury, and even if he was not, the full-compensation rule does not apply because of Kaltenbach's interference with Erie's recovery rights; and that Erie was owed the full amount of settlement proceeds received by Kaltenbach, up to $5,000, without application of a pro rata distribution or setoff for Kaltenbach's costs in pursuing settlement.

X. ECONOMIC AND DIGNITARY TORTS

BUSINESS TORTS

Auvil v. CBS

United States Court of Appeals, Ninth Circuit (1995)

On February 26, 1989, CBS's weekly news show "60 Minutes" aired a segment on daminozide, a chemical growth regulator sprayed on apples. The broadcast, entitled "A is for Apple," also addressed the slow pace of government efforts to recall the chemical. The broadcast was based largely on a Natural Resources Defense Council ("NRDC") report, entitled Intolerable Risk: Pesticides in Our Children's Food ("Intolerable Risk "), which outlined health risks associated with the use of a number of pesticides on fruit, especially the risks to children. "A is for Apple" focused on the NRDC report's findings concerning daminozide, as well as the EPA's knowledge of daminozide's carcinogenity. Scientific research had indicated that daminozide, more commonly known by its trade name, Alar, breaks down into unsymmetrical dimethylhydrazine (UDMH), a carcinogen.

The segment opened with the following capsule summary from Ed Bradley, a "60 Minutes" commentator:

> The most potent cancer-causing agent in our food supply is a substance sprayed on apples to keep them on the trees longer and make them look better. That's the conclusion of a number of scientific experts. And who is most at risk? Children, who may someday develop cancer from this one chemical called daminozide. Daminozide, which has been sprayed on apples for more than 20 years, breaks down into another chemical called UDMH.

Following the "60 Minutes" broadcast, consumer demand for apples and apple products decreased dramatically. The apple growers and others dependent upon apple production lost millions of dollars. Many of the growers lost their homes and livelihoods.

In November 1990, eleven Washington State apple growers, representing some 4,700 growers in the Washington area, filed a complaint in Washington State Superior Court against CBS. The growers asserted a claim for product disparagement.

DISCUSSION

To establish a claim of product disparagement, also known as trade libel, a plaintiff must allege that the defendant published a knowingly false statement harmful to the interests of another and intended such publication to harm the plaintiff's pecuniary interests. Accordingly, for a product disparagement claim to be actionable, the plaintiff must prove the falsity of the disparaging statements. As a tort whose actionability depends on the existence of disparaging speech, the tort is substantively similar to defamation.

"A is for Apple" was based on Intolerable Risk, a scientific report disseminated by the NRDC. The report discussed the findings of cancer research studies on various chemicals used on fruit and questioned the EPA's hesitance in removing Alar from the market. The broadcast contained a number of factual assertions, several of which are pointed out by the growers to support their claim that the broadcast falsely disparaged their product.

The growers offered evidence showing that no studies have been conducted to test the relationship between ingestion of daminozide and incidence of cancer in humans. The growers' only challenge to the scientific studies is their claim that animal studies cannot be relied on to indicate cancer risk for humans. Because animal studies can be relied upon, their evidence that no studies have been conducted on the effects of daminozide on humans does not create a genuine issue for trial on the falsity of the broadcast's assertions regarding daminozide's carcinogenicity.

The growers offered evidence showing that no scientific study has been conducted on cancer risks to children from the use of pesticides. However, CBS based its statements regarding cancer and children on the NRDC's findings that the daminozide found on apples is more harmful to children because they ingest more apple products per unit of body weight than do adults. The growers have provided no affirmative evidence that daminozide does not pose a risk to children. The fact that there have been no studies conducted specifically on the cancer risks to children from daminozide does nothing to disprove the conclusion that, if children consume more of a carcinogenic substance than do adults, they are at higher risk for contracting cancer. The growers' evidence, therefore, does not create a genuine issue as to the falsity of the broadcast's assertion that daminozide is more harmful to children.

Despite their inability to prove that statements made during the broadcast were false, the growers assert that summary judgment for CBS was improper because a jury could find that the broadcast contained a provably false message, viewing the broadcast segment in its entirety. They further argue that, if they can prove the falsity of this implied message, they have satisfied their burden of proving falsity.

The growers' contentions are unavailing. Their attempt to derive a specific, implied message from the broadcast as a whole and to prove the falsity of that overall message is unprecedented and inconsistent with Washington law. No Washington court has held that the analysis of falsity proceeds from an implied, disparaging message. It is the statements themselves that are of primary concern in the analysis. Defamatory meaning may not be imputed to true statements. The defamatory character of the language must be apparent from the words themselves. Washington courts are bound to invest words with their natural and obvious meaning and may not extend language by innuendo or by the conclusions of the pleader. Therefore, we must reject the growers' invitation to infer an overall message from the broadcast and determine whether that message is false.

CONCLUSION

Because the growers have failed to raise a genuine issue of material fact regarding the falsity of statements made during the broadcast of "A is for Apple," the district court's decision granting CBS's motion for summary judgment is AFFIRMED.

Carolina Overall v. East Carolina Linen Supply

Court of Appeals of North Carolina (1970)

Plaintiff and defendant are corporate competitors in the industrial laundry business. Defendant induced one Bill Lowe to breach an employment contract as a route salesman with plaintiff and to enter the employment of defendant; and defendant, acting through Bill Lowe and other agents, solicited the business of fourteen of plaintiff's customers and induced them to breach their contracts with plaintiff for laundry service. Further, the actions of defendant were without justification and constituted tortious interference with plaintiff's contracts.

It is well established in this jurisdiction that an action lies against one who, without legal justification, knowingly and a contract to breach that contract and cause damage to the other contracting party. The elements necessary to establish a cause of action for tortious interference with a contract are: (1) that a contract existed between him and a third person which conferred upon plaintiff some contractual right against the third person; (2) that defendant had knowledge of plaintiff's contract with such third person; (3) that defendant intentionally induced the third person not to perform his contract with plaintiff; (4) that in so doing the defendant acted without justification; and (5) that defendant's acts caused plaintiff actual damages.

Defendant concedes the general principles but argues that competition is legal justification for interference by a party with a contract between his competitor and a third person. The following general rule is set forth in the Restatement of the Law of Torts:

(1) One is privileged purposely to cause a third person not to enter into or continue a business relation with a competitor of the actor if

> *(a) the relation concerns a matter involved in the competition between the actor and the competitor, and*
>
> *(b) the actor does not employ improper means, and*
>
> *(c) the actor does not intend thereby to create or continue an illegal restraint of competition, and*
>
> *(d) the actor's purpose is at least in part to advance his interest in his competition with the other.*

(2) The fact that one is a competitor of another for the business of a third person does not create a privilege to cause the third person to commit a breach of contract with the other even under the conditions stated in Subsection (1).

The theory of the doctrine which permits recovery for the tortious interference with a contract is that the right to the performance of a contract and to reap the profits therefrom are property rights which entitle each party to protection and to seek compensation by action in court for an injury to such contract. We see no valid reason for holding that a competitor is privileged to interfere wrongfully with contractual rights. If contracts otherwise binding are not secure from wrongful interference by competitors, they offer little certainty in business relations, and it is security from competition that often gives them value. It is true that a party to a contract which is breached by another has a cause of action for breach of contract. This, however, affords little remedy where the party breaching the contract is insolvent; or where, as alleged here, numerous contracts involving nominal amounts of money are breached as a result of wrongful inducement by a competitor.

In our opinion the complaint states a cause of action for compensatory damages for tortious interference with plaintiff's contracts. If plaintiff is entitled to recover at all, its recovery will be for the actual value of the contracts interfered with, and will not extend to such speculative matters alleged in the complaint as loss of patronage and good will.

Sturges v. Wal-Mart Stores

Court of Appeals of Texas (1998)

Harry W. Sturges, III, Dick Ford, Bruce Whitehead, and J.D. Martin, III, individually and on behalf of Gulf Coast Investment Group, brought suit against Wal–Mart for breach of contract and tortious interference with prospective business relations. A jury awarded them $1,000,000 in actual damages, and $500,000 in exemplary damages.

This case involves a dispute concerning commercial property, referred to as "tract 2". In 1982, Wal–Mart owned tract 2, which was adjacent to tract 1, the property where the Wal–Mart Store was located. In 1984, Whitehead purchased tract 2 on behalf of Texas Southwest Gulf Coast Partnership. In connection with the purchase of tract 2, and as part of the consideration of the sale, Texas Southwest executed a document reflecting restrictions on the property, entitled Easements With Covenants and Restrictions Affecting Land. In 1988, Gulf Coast and Wal–Mart entered into and executed a document modifying the earlier agreement (ECR). Appellants contend the ECR evidenced an agreement between Gulf Coast and Wal–Mart to act reasonably regarding any future requested modifications to the ECR.

Whitehead and Martin, individually and on behalf of Gulf Coast entered an agreement whereby Ford and Sturges would participate in the marketing and development of tract 2. In January of 1990, Sturges reached an agreement with Fleming Foods of Texas, Inc, (Fleming) under which the appellants would construct and lease to Fleming a supermarket on tract 2. A letter of intent evidenced the agreement between Fleming and Sturges, acting on behalf of appellants and signed January 31, 1990.

Fleming furnished a lease form and would have executed a definitive lease agreement, provided that Wal–Mart approved requested revisions to the ECR. These modifications dealt primarily with a minor variation in the ratio of parking spaces to square footage of the Fleming supermarket, and approval of a new site plan which provided for a larger supermarket and eliminated the other retail space on tract 2. Sturges then contacted the appropriate officials of Wal–Mart and requested the changes necessary to consummate the Fleming lease. Wal–Mart personnel were supportive of a supermarket on tract 2. Appellants' plans were enthusiastically received at both the local and corporate level of Wal–Mart. On January 8, 1990, Sturges sent a site plan to Delee Wood, property manager of Wal–Mart, for the purpose of obtaining approval of the changes necessary to accommodate the Fleming lease. Shortly thereafter, Wood represented to Sturges that she had obtained approval from the necessary people at Wal–Mart for the requested changes and that Sturges should submit documentation for execution by Wal–Mart to memorialize the revisions.

Around July of 1989, the Wal–Mart property division began efforts to purchase tract 2. In approximately November of 1989, Tom Hudson, acting as real estate agent for Wal–Mart, contacted Bank One and was informed by Bank One that tract 2 was already under contract. In early January of 1990, Hudson informed officials of Wal–Mart that if the ECR modification requested by the appellants were withheld it would in all probability "kill" the sale of tract 2 from Bank One to appellants, and the lease arrangement involving the Appellants and Fleming. Wal–Mart never revealed to appellants their efforts to reacquire tract 2 but instead encouraged appellants to proceed with their plans for development of a supermarket on tract 2.

Prior to the time appellants and Fleming could finalize their lease arrangement, Wal-mart informed Fleming that they wanted to acquire tract 2 for expansion; and that if they did not obtain this land on which to expand, Wal–Mart would move its store. Wal–Mart then refused to approve modification of the parking ratio or to approve a new site plan allowing for a larger supermarket and eliminating the other retail space on tract 2. Appellants were then unable to consummate their transaction with Fleming. They then brought suit against Wal–Mart for breach of contract and tortious interference with prospective business relations.

Wal–Mart argues there was no evidence or insufficient evidence to show that it intentionally prevented appellants from contracting with Fleming. In response, appellants urge that Hudson's call to Callaway, Fleming's manager of store development of the Houston area, resulted in Fleming's cancellation of its proposed business transaction with appellants. The evidence at trial indicated that Hudson, Fuller, Watson and Wood conspired to destroy the transaction with Fleming. Hudson phoned Callaway in the early part of 1990. Hudson indicated to Callaway that he was representing Wal–Mart and gave him an ultimatum not to build the store. Hudson said that if the supermarket were built, Wal–Mart would relocate and close the existing store. Callaway, relying on that information, called Sturges and told him the deal was off. Anthony Fuller, the director of Wal–Mart Realty Company, acted as Wal–Mart's designated corporate representative at trial. He testified regarding Hudson's call to Callaway, that whatever Hudson said, he did on behalf of Wal–Mart. Hudson stated at trial that Fuller and Watson instructed him to call Fleming.

In a letter by Hudson dated January 3, 1990, to Wal–Mart's real estate manager Sandra Watson, Hudson told Watson that appellants would drop their contract to purchase tract 2 from Bank One, if Wal–Mart denied appellants' request for ECR revisions. Wal–Mart did in fact deny the request for ECR revisions.

Wal–Mart's exultation in the success of its plan to destroy appellants' transaction is evidenced by a thank you note by Watson to Fuller, thanking Fuller for his help in destroying appellants' prospective agreement with Fleming.

MISREPRESENTATION

Follo v. Florindo

Supreme Court of Vermont (2009)

In 2000, defendants formed a Vermont limited liability company, Cranberry Farm, LLC. Defendant Morency owned 51% of the LLC and was president and treasurer while defendant Florindo owned 49% and was vice-president, secretary, and assistant treasurer of the company. Defendants created Cranberry Farm, LLC to acquire an inn in Vermont, and soon after it was formed, the company purchased an inn on twenty-seven acres of land in Rockingham, Vermont (the Inn) for $825,000. Defendants' lenders required an appraisal of the parcel, and the appraised value was the same as the purchase price. In the same year, 2000, but acting as individuals instead of through either of their companies, defendants purchased a single-family house (the Cottage) on twenty acres of land adjacent to the Inn for $175,000.

Over the next two years, defendants redecorated and operated the Inn while also separately renting out the Cottage. Defendants split their duties in running the Inn. Even though Ms. Morency was Cranberry Farm LLC's President and Treasurer, Mr. Florindo handled most of the finances for the Inn, including the bookkeeping and filing tax returns. Ms. Morency's responsibilities included decorating, operating the front desk, planning private parties, and managing housekeeping and guest relations. Defendants operated the Inn for close to two years, and in the summer of 2002, defendants decided to sell the Inn and the Cottage. Defendants listed the properties with a real estate company, Hospitality Consultants. Hospitality Consultants marketed the Inn and the Cottage together in one brochure, listing the Inn for $1,195,000 and the Cottage for $225,000.

When plaintiff decided he wanted to buy a bed and breakfast, he began researching methods for evaluating inns listed for sale. During his research, plaintiff learned about a "gross revenue multiplier" approach to calculating sales prices for inns. Under this approach, a prospective buyer multiplies the inn's gross earnings by a number between three and seven to determine an appropriate sales price. Plaintiff decided he would buy only an inn that showed it was profitable, that he could acquire for a maximum of five times the inn's gross sales, and that would cost less than $1 million.

Plaintiff entered into negotiations to purchase defendants' Inn late in 2002. He specifically pursued the Inn, even though the listed sales price was above his $1 million limit, because the profit-and-loss statement included in the marketing brochure for the Inn showed that it was a solid business. During negotiations, plaintiff asked for and received reports, including tax returns, from defendants (via the real estate agent) on the revenues, sales, expenses, and net income of the Inn during 2001 and 2002. Relying on these reports, plaintiff used the "gross revenue multiplier" approach to calculate that the property was worth $1,130,000 by multiplying the Inn's reported 2001 sales of $226,000 by five. Plaintiff then offered $1,080,000 for the Inn. However, in order to succeed with his bid for the Inn, plaintiff felt it was necessary to bid simultaneously on the Cottage because another bidder was prepared to make a bid on both properties at the same time. Plaintiff discussed with the real estate agent and defendant Florindo whether they thought he could raise sufficient revenue from the Cottage to cover its purchase price if he remodeled the Cottage to contain three suites, then rented those as part of the Inn business. According to plaintiff, both the real estate agent and Florindo expressed the opinion that he would "absolutely" get his money back using that plan, at least in part due to the occupancy rates and demand during certain times of the year as represented by defendants when they operated the Inn. Plaintiff purchased both the Inn and the Cottage for $1,245,000 in March 2003.

As he began to operate the Inn during the spring of 2003, plaintiff realized that the Inn's sales for the first few months of his ownership were less than one-quarter of the sales figures he expected based on the information defendants provided prior to sale. To boost sales, plaintiff decided to try a mailing directed at the Inn's former customers and requested guest registration information from defendant Florindo. Subsequent communications between the parties led plaintiff to suspect that defendants had not truthfully represented the Inn's actual revenues and occupancy rates in the realtor's marketing brochure and the various reports and tax returns defendants provided plaintiff during sale negotiations. His exchanges with defendants eventually led plaintiff to file this lawsuit in early 2004.

After trial, but before the case went to the jury, plaintiff dropped all claims except for common law and consumer fraud claims. The jury returned a verdict against defendants Florindo and Morency for common-law fraud and consumer fraud, but found in favor of the realtor and its agents. The jury awarded damages for plaintiff in the amount of $645,000.

In order to prove fraud, plaintiffs must demonstrate the following essential elements. One, that defendants misrepresented an existing fact which affected the essence of the transaction with plaintiffs or knowingly allowed another to make such a representation on defendants' behalf; two, that defendants did so intentionally; three, that the misrepresentation was false when made and known at the time to be false by a defendant, or that the representation was recklessly made as being within the defendants' own knowledge without defendant in fact knowing whether it was true or not.

Plaintiff's decision to buy the Inn and Cottage for $1,245,000 was founded in large part on his belief that the Inn generated certain levels of revenue and maintained certain occupancy rates during the years of defendants' operation. Plaintiff's beliefs on these subjects came from several documents that were either created by defendants or by third parties based on information that defendants provided. One of the documents was the brochure produced by the real estate agency, misrepresenting the Inn's profits and losses, occupancy information, and room rates for 2001. Another document was a separate profit-and-loss statement for the Inn for 2002, which the real estate agent provided plaintiff. The real estate agent also provided plaintiff with Cranberry Farm, LLC's 2001 income tax return. These documents indicated that the Inn had over $226,000 in gross revenue in 2001 and over $250,000 in gross revenue in 2002. In discussions with the real estate agency, plaintiff was told that those numbers represented the Inn's revenues without including the additional nine percent rooms-and-meals tax. At trial, the real estate agents testified that all of the financial information about the Inn that they presented to plaintiff came from defendants, although their direct dealings were with defendant Florindo.

Data gathered by plaintiff after he purchased the Inn, and in discovery after commencing this lawsuit, contradicted the representations contained in the brochure, the profit-and-loss statements, and the 2001 tax return. Before filing this suit, plaintiff obtained from defendants the original guest-information forms defendants kept for the Inn's 2002 reservations, which revealed the actual room sales for 2002 amounted to only about one-fifth of the sales defendants claimed in the 2002 profit-and-loss statement provided to plaintiff via the real estate agency. During discovery, plaintiff received defendants' room-assignment book for August 2002 through January 2003. According to defendants' bookkeeping system, the guest-information forms and room-assignment book should have contained duplicative information regarding room sales and occupancy. However, trial testimony by both plaintiff and defendant Morency revealed that the guest-information forms, which defendants had provided plaintiff before this lawsuit was commenced, listed many customers not corroborated by the room assignment book. As noted above, even the occupancy rates culled by plaintiff from the guest-information forms fell far short of the occupancy rate represented in the documents provided by defendants before plaintiff purchased the Inn.

Moreover, Mr. Florindo's testimony supplied evidence that his misrepresentations were knowingly or recklessly made. The trial court found that Mr. Florindo's testimony could be construed as unresponsive or evasive by a reasonable jury. The court concluded that a reasonable jury could imply from this evasiveness that defendant Florindo intentionally falsified the figures shared with plaintiff. Additionally, the court concluded that even if the jury would not find that Mr. Florindo was being evasive or that he had provided false numbers intentionally, the jury could believe that it was reckless for him to provide the revenue numbers for potential buyers of the property given how little understanding he claimed to have about the revenues and sales, and how little data and supporting evidence he could provide for those numbers. We agree with the trial court that, based on his testimony, there is clear and convincing evidence to support finding that Mr. Florindo at least recklessly disregarded the truth to a level amounting to fraud when he made these statements regarding the Inn's sales, occupancy, and revenues.

Ms. Morency argues that all of the trial testimony, including that of plaintiff's and her co-defendants', revealed that she, personally, never made any representations to plaintiff regarding the Inn's finances. She notes that there was no evidence that she communicated any financial information about the Inn to the real estate agents who marketed the Inn and Cottage to plaintiff. Further, Ms. Morency claims that she never knew that the companies' tax returns contained any inaccuracies or that defendant Florindo provided the tax returns to the real estate agents for use in marketing the Inn. Ms. Morency argues that all of this evidence shows that she did not take any actions that could be considered fraudulent and that she did not have the requisite knowledge of the misrepresentations of the Inn's finances made to plaintiff to be liable for fraud.

We agree that the record does not reveal any evidence that Ms. Morency made misrepresentations directly to plaintiff or directly to the real estate agents, as Mr. Florindo did. Instead, the evidence of fraud by defendant Morency subsists in her documented involvement in the companies and the business of operating the Inn and in her trial testimony. Ms. Morency was the majority owner of Cranberry Farm, LLC, was both president and treasurer of that company with defendant Florindo, as well as the long-term girlfriend and business associate of Mr. Florindo. She had owned rental property in Massachusetts with defendant Florindo prior to their buying the Inn and Cottage, and at the time of trial she still owned excavating equipment that she leased to Mr. Florindo.

Ms. Morency testified at trial that she did not take part in paying the Inn's bills and that she had little to do with the Inn's operation. However, in response to questions, she revealed that she had written many checks to pay for materials to renovate the Inn, to pay expenses, and to pay for the mortgages on the Inn and the Cottage. She also testified that she did not review the Inn's finances or tax returns, but acknowledged that she was the person who signed the companies' tax returns. Ms. Morency admitted that by signing the returns she was declaring that she had examined the return and that it was "true, correct and complete." Nonetheless, she maintained that she never looked at any of the numbers on those returns. Even if the jury believed Ms. Morency that she had no idea whether the figures in the tax returns were accurate, it could have found that, by swearing to the information in the tax returns without knowing whether those returns were true or accurate, defendant Morency made false statements "recklessly" without regard to whether they were true or false. That level of knowledge is sufficient for fraud.

Additionally, the guest-information forms and room-assignment book that plaintiff introduced at trial were filled out, for the most part, in Ms. Morency's handwriting. Even though she had filled out those forms, she could not explain why the 2002 guest-information forms contained many customer names and reservations that never appeared in the corresponding room-assignment book. This provides sufficient information for a reasonable jury to conclude that defendant Morency made misrepresentations by aiding in supplying false statements of occupancy rates to plaintiff while he was deciding to purchase the Inn.

All of these facts, coupled with her close relationship with Mr. Florindo, provide a sound basis for the jury to have concluded that Ms. Morency was enmeshed in the companies, the Inn's operation, and in Mr. Florindo's decision-making. Further, the trial provided sufficient clear and convincing evidence that Ms. Morency knowingly or recklessly made false statements regarding the Inn's occupancy and revenues, which plaintiff relied on in purchasing the Inn. Although she testified that she had no idea that Mr. Florindo supplied the false documentation to plaintiff, a reasonable jury simply could have discredited her testimony, under the circumstances, as a false, and inculpatory, protestation of innocence.

DEFAMATION

Bryson v. News America Publications

Supreme Court of Illinois (1996)

A short story entitled "Bryson," written by defendant Logsdon, was published by the defendant News America in the March 1991 issue of Seventeen magazine. The story, written in the style of a first-person narrative, recounts a conflict between the unidentified speaker and her high school classmate, Bryson. According to the speaker, Bryson, "a platinum-blond, blue-eye-shadowed, faded-blue-jeaned, black polyester-topped shriek" who lives "on the other side of town" was "after" her. In the course of describing events that led up to an after-school fight between Bryson and the speaker, the speaker discusses an incident that occurred two months earlier:

"About two months ago Bryson was at a bonfire with these two guys that nobody knew. One had a tattoo, and they were all drinking. Lots. Who knows what guys like that made Bryson do. The next day she came into school with a black eye. Later that afternoon, as Bryson shouted down the hallways like always, I remembered what a slut she was and forgot about the sorriness I'd been holding onto for her." A footnote at the end of the story identifies the author, Lucy Logsdon, as a native of southern Illinois.

Defamation

A statement is considered defamatory if it tends to cause such harm to the reputation of another that it lowers that person in the eyes of the community or deters third persons from associating with her. A statement or publication may be defamatory on its face. However, even a statement that is not defamatory on its face may support a cause of action for defamation if the plaintiff has pled extrinsic facts that demonstrate that the statement has a defamatory meaning.

Only certain limited categories of defamatory statements are deemed actionable *per se.* If a defamatory statement is actionable *per se,* the plaintiff need not plead or prove actual damage to her reputation to recover. Rather, statements that fall within these actionable *per se* categories are thought to be so obviously and materially harmful to the plaintiff that injury to her reputation may be presumed. If a defamatory statement does not fall within one of the limited categories of statements that are actionable *per se,* the plaintiff must plead and prove that she sustained actual damage of a pecuniary nature ("special damages") to recover.

Defamation Per Se

We first consider whether the disputed statements may be considered actionable *per se.* The plaintiff alleges that the article is actionable *per se* because it referred to her as a "slut" and implied that she was an "unchaste" individual. Under our common law, four categories of statements are considered actionable *per se* and give rise to a cause of action for defamation without a showing of special damages. They are: (1) words that impute the commission of a criminal offense; (2) words that impute infection with a loathsome communicable disease; (3) words that impute an inability to perform or want of integrity in the discharge of duties of office or employment; or (4) words that prejudice a party, or impute lack of ability, in his or her trade, profession or business. The Slander and Libel Act has enlarged the classifications enumerated above by providing that false accusations of fornication and adultery are actionable as a matter of law. Specifically, section 1 of that statute provides: "If any person shall falsely use, utter or publish words, which in their common acceptance, shall amount to charge any person with having been guilty of fornication or adultery, such words so spoken shall be deemed actionable, and he shall be deemed guilty of slander." Here, the plaintiff's complaint alleges that the defendants, by using the word "slut," implied that she was "unchaste."

Identity of Bryson as the Plaintiff

The defendants next argue that the article may reasonably be construed as referring to someone other than the plaintiff. The defendants note that the complaint does not allege any facts to demonstrate that third persons would reasonably conclude that the character "Bryson" is the plaintiff, Kimberly Bryson. The defendants argue that where an allegedly defamatory statement does not mention the plaintiff by name, the plaintiff must plead extrinsic facts to demonstrate that third persons believed that the libelous statement referred to the plaintiff.

We agree with the general proposition that, where a libelous article does not name the plaintiff, it should appear on the face of the complaint that persons other than the plaintiff and the defendant must have reasonably understood that the article was about the plaintiff and that the allegedly libelous expression related to her. The article at issue did, of course, use the plaintiff's last name. The name "Bryson" is not so common that we must find, as a matter of law, that no reasonable person would believe that the article was about the plaintiff. Under the present facts, we reject the defendants' claim that the story must be innocently construed as referring to someone other than the plaintiff.

One of the interrogatories propounded by the defendants asked the plaintiff to identify why she believed that she was the character described in the story. The plaintiff's response identified more than 25 alleged similarities between herself and the physical attributes, locations and events attributed to the character "Bryson" in the story. Had the trial court considered this interrogatory answer, it certainly would have rejected the defendants' claim that the article must be innocently construed as referring to someone other than the plaintiff. Under the circumstances, we conclude that the plaintiff should be allowed the opportunity to prove that, despite the fictional label, the character "Bryson" bears such a close resemblance to the plaintiff that reasonable persons would understand that the character was actually intended to portray the plaintiff. Whether the article was actually understood by third parties to be about the plaintiff is, of course, a question of fact for the jury.

Dissent:

The plaintiff in this cause is not a public figure or well known for any other reason. She does not allege or claim to be known or publicly recognizable for any reason. Nowhere in the complaint does plaintiff establish her identity as the fictitious Bryson. It is only in her answer to interrogatories that plaintiff claims 25 similarities between the fictitious Bryson and herself. None of the similarities are unique or conclusive. For example, the author of the story describes the Bryson character as a "Brass Blonde" and a "Platinum Blonde." According to plaintiff, "her mother owned a beauty salon" and she and "her friend, Susie Patton, were always changing their hair color." Plaintiff also refers to one incident in the story wherein another character, Anita, is grounded for refusing to tell her father what she had done with his Willie Nelson tapes. Plaintiff claims that she had a friend named Anita, and that Anita's brother was named Nelson. In my opinion, these are not similarities which establish the identity of plaintiff as the Bryson in the fictional story.

The innocent construction rule provides that an allegedly defamatory statement is not actionable *per se* if it is reasonably capable of an innocent construction. This rule requires courts to consider a written or oral statement in context, giving the words and implications there from their natural and obvious meaning. The focus of the rule is on whether the statement, when so considered, may reasonably be innocently interpreted. That determination is a question of law for the court to decide.

As a general rule, it is not actionable to call a woman a "slut" unless the word is used in such a manner as to impute whoredom. This rule recognizes that the word itself does not always impute a breach of chastity, but carries with it such nonactionable connotations as brazen or shameless. Indeed, as defendants point out, and the majority concedes, the American Heritage Dictionary contains several definitions of the word "slut," such as a "slovenly, dirty woman," "a woman of loose morals," a "prostitute," "a bold, brazen girl," or "a female dog." Consequently, because the word has many different meanings, most of which are not defamatory per se, context is crucial; for as noted above, if a word "may reasonably be innocently interpreted," it is not actionable *per se.*

The narrator relates that during one particular week Bryson had been slamming lockers, cutting classes and dropping water balloons. The narrator, bemoaning the fact that "it was only a matter of time before her attention swung my way," proceeds to describe the following scene, which takes place in the high school restroom in the presence of another girl, Sue Barton: "I heard a voice behind me like I've heard a million times, in a high-pitched, brassy voice, 'Well look who's here.' Bryson had just walked in. Without turning around I knew she was talking straight to me. 'You usually got cigarettes.' 'Not today.' 'Not today?' Bryson looked at Sue and didn't say anything. Good. If she wasn't saying anything, she wasn't looking for a scene. I put my comb in my bag and edged for the door. 'Hey, I *was talking* to you.' She placed one arm on the wall's peeling green paint. Then, instead of doing what I'd always done--what I've learned was the only thing to do--stand there, quiet, looking at my feet until her attention went somewhere else, I walked straight up to her arm, put my hands together in a sort of hammer, and knocked it down. Then she smiled and said, 'So meet me by the baseball field after school today then.' "

Later that morning, the narrator telephoned her friend Anita who was sick at home. Anita cautioned, "You can't fight her. She broke Beth Harper's two front teeth." Then, the narrator states: "About two months ago Bryson was at a bonfire with these two guys that nobody knew. One had a tattoo, and they were all drinking. Lots. Who knows what guys like that made Bryson do. The next day she came into school with a black eye. Beth Harper looked at her too long, and Bryson slammed her up against a glass door and cracked her one clean in the mouth. Later that afternoon, as Bryson shouted down the hallways like always, I remembered what a slut she was and forgot about the sorriness I'd been holding onto for her."

In this case, the majority submits that the sexual implication underlying the use of slut is intensified with the commentary "who knows what guys like that made Bryson do." I disagree. In my opinion, not only can the word slut as used here be construed in the nondefamatory sense connoting brazenness, it is the only way it can be construed. There is nothing lascivious or licentious in the word slut when used to describe the fictional Bryson's less than decorous or mannerly behavior. Indeed, Bryson's sexual drive is neither the focal point of the story, nor a digression.

Because I believe that the word slut as used in this context is clearly capable of a nondefamatory construction, and because I also find that our defamation law is ill-served by the majority's decision, I cannot join in the majority's reinstatement of plaintiff's claim for libel *per se*.

New York Times v. Sullivan

Supreme Court of the United States (1964)

We are required in this case to determine for the first time the extent to which the constitutional protections for speech and press limit a State's power to award damages in a libel action brought by a public official against critics of his official conduct. Respondent L. B. Sullivan is one of the three elected Commissioners of the City of Montgomery, Alabama. He testified that he was Commissioner of Public Affairs and the duties are supervision of the Police Department. He brought this civil libel action against the four individual petitioners and against petitioner the New York Times. A jury in the Circuit Court of Montgomery County awarded him damages of $500,000 and the Supreme Court of Alabama affirmed.

Respondent's complaint alleged that he had been libeled by statements in a full-page advertisement that was carried in the New York Times on March 29, 1960. The advertisement began by stating that "As the whole world knows by now, thousands of Southern Negro students are engaged in widespread non-violent demonstrations in positive affirmation of the right to live in human dignity as guaranteed by the U.S. Constitution and the Bill of Rights." It went on to charge that 'in their efforts to uphold these guarantees, they are being met by an unprecedented wave of terror by those who would deny and negate that document which the whole world looks upon as setting the pattern for modern freedom."

Although the statements did not mention respondent by name, he contended that the word "police" referred to him as the Montgomery Commissioner who supervised the Police Department, so that he was being accused of ringing the campus with police. He further claimed that the paragraph would be read as imputing to the police, and hence to him, the padlocking of the dining hall in order to starve the students into submission. As to the sixth paragraph, he contended that since arrests are ordinarily made by the police, the statement "they have arrested Dr. King seven times" would be read as referring to him; he further contended that the "they" who did the arresting would be equated with the "they" who committed the other described acts and with the "Southern violators." Thus, he argued, the paragraph would be read as accusing the Montgomery police, and hence him, of answering Dr. King's protests with "intimidation and violence," bombing his home, assaulting his person, and charging him with perjury. Respondent and six other Montgomery residents testified that they read some or all of the statements as referring to him in his capacity as Commissioner.

On the premise that the charges in the paragraph could be read as referring to him, respondent was allowed to prove that he had not participated in the events described. Although Dr. King's home had in fact been bombed twice when his wife and child were there, both of these occasions antedated respondent's tenure as Commissioner, and the police were not only not implicated in the bombings, but had made every effort to apprehend those who were. Three of Dr. King's four arrests took place before respondent became Commissioner. Although Dr. King had in fact been indicted (he was subsequently acquitted) on two counts of perjury, each of which carried a possible five-year sentence, respondent had nothing to do with procuring the indictment.

The question before us is whether this rule of liability, as applied to an action brought by a public official against critics of his official conduct, abridges the freedom of speech and of the press that is guaranteed by the First and Fourteenth Amendments.

The general proposition that freedom of expression upon public questions is secured by the First Amendment has long been settled by our decisions. The constitutional safeguard, we have said, was fashioned to assure unfettered interchange of ideas for the bringing about of political and social changes desired by the people. The maintenance of the opportunity for free political discussion to the end that government may be responsive to the will of the people and that changes may be obtained by lawful means, an opportunity essential to the security of the Republic, is a fundamental principle of our constitutional system. The First Amendment, said Judge Learned Hand, "presupposes that right conclusions are more likely to be gathered out of a multitude of tongues, than through any kind of authoritative selection. To many this is, and always will be, folly; but we have staked upon it our all."

Thus we consider this case against the background of a profound national commitment to the principle that debate on public issues should be uninhibited, robust, and wide-open, and that it may well include vehement, caustic, and sometimes unpleasantly sharp attacks on government and public officials. The present advertisement, as an expression of grievance and protest on one of the major public issues of our time, would seem clearly to qualify for the constitutional protection. The question is whether it forfeits that protection by the falsity of some of its factual statements and by its alleged defamation of respondent.

What a State may not constitutionally bring about by means of a criminal statute is likewise beyond the reach of its civil law of libel. The fear of damage awards under a rule such as that invoked by the Alabama courts here may be markedly more inhibiting than the fear of prosecution under a criminal statute. Alabama, for example, has a criminal libel law which subjects to prosecution "any person who speaks, writes, or prints of and concerning another any accusation falsely and maliciously importing the commission by such person of a felony, or any other indictable offense involving moral turpitude," and which allows as punishment upon conviction a fine not exceeding $500 and a prison sentence of six months. Presumably a person charged with violation of this statute enjoys ordinary criminal-law safeguards such as the requirements of an indictment and of proof beyond a reasonable doubt. These safeguards are not available to the defendant in a civil action. The judgment awarded in this case—without the need for any proof of actual pecuniary loss—was one thousand times greater than the maximum fine provided by the Alabama criminal statute.

The state rule of law is not saved by its allowance of the defense of truth. A rule compelling the critic of official conduct to guarantee the truth of all his factual assertions—and to do so on pain of libel judgments virtually unlimited in amount—leads to a comparable self-censorship. Allowance of the defense of truth, with the burden of proving it on the defendant, does not mean that only false speech will be deterred. Even courts accepting this defense as an adequate safeguard have recognized the difficulties of adducing legal proofs that the alleged libel was true in all its factual particulars. Under such a rule, would-be critics of official conduct may be deterred from voicing their criticism, even though it is believed to be true and even though it is in fact true, because of doubt whether it can be proved in court or fear of the expense of having to do so. They tend to make only statements which steer far wider of the unlawful zone. The rule thus dampens the vigor and limits the variety of public debate. It is inconsistent with the First and Fourteenth Amendments.

The constitutional guarantees require, we think, a federal rule that prohibits a public official from recovering damages for a defamatory falsehood relating to his official conduct unless he proves that the statement was made with 'actual malice'—that is, with knowledge that it was false or with reckless disregard of whether it was false or not.

As to the Times, we conclude that the facts do not support a finding of actual malice. The statement by the Times' Secretary that, apart from the padlocking allegation, he thought the advertisement was 'substantially correct,' affords no constitutional warrant for the Alabama Supreme Court's conclusion that it was a 'cavalier ignoring of the falsity of the advertisement from which, the jury could not have but been impressed with the bad faith of The Times, and its maliciousness inferable therefrom.' The statement does not indicate malice at the time of the publication; even if the advertisement was not 'substantially correct'—although respondent's own proofs tend to show that it was—that opinion was at least a reasonable one, and there was no evidence to impeach the witness' good faith in holding it.

Finally, there is evidence that the Times published the advertisement without checking its accuracy against the news stories in the Times' own files. The mere presence of the stories in the files does not, of course, establish that the Times 'knew' the advertisement was false, since the state of mind required for actual malice would have to be brought home to the persons in the Times' organization having responsibility for the publication of the advertisement. With respect to the failure of those persons to make the check, the record shows that they relied upon their knowledge of the good reputation of many of those whose names were listed as sponsors of the advertisement, and upon the letter from A. Philip Randolph, known to them as a responsible individual, certifying that the use of the names was authorized. There was testimony that the persons handling the advertisement saw nothing in it that would render it unacceptable under the Times' policy of rejecting advertisements containing 'attacks of a personal character'; their failure to reject it on this ground was not unreasonable. We think the evidence against the Times supports at most a finding of negligence in failing to discover the misstatements, and is constitutionally insufficient to show the recklessness that is required for a finding of actual malice.

The judgment of the Supreme Court of Alabama is reversed.

Gertz v. Robert Welch, Inc.

Supreme Court of the United States (1974)

In 1968 a Chicago policeman named Nuccio shot and killed a youth named Nelson. The state authorities prosecuted Nuccio for the homicide and ultimately obtained a conviction for murder in the second degree. The Nelson family retained petitioner Elmer Gertz, a reputable attorney, to represent them in civil litigation against Nuccio.

Respondent publishes American Opinion, a monthly outlet for the views of the John Birch Society. Early in the 1960's the magazine began to warn of a nationwide conspiracy to discredit local law enforcement agencies and create in their stead a national police force capable of supporting a Communist dictatorship. As part of the continuing effort to alert the public to this assumed danger, the managing editor of American Opinion commissioned an article on the murder trial of Officer Nuccio. For this purpose he engaged a regular contributor to the magazine. In March 1969 respondent published the resulting article under the title "FRAME-UP: Richard Nuccio And The War On Police." The article purports to demonstrate that the testimony against Nuccio at his criminal trial was false and that his prosecution was part of the Communist campaign against the police.

In his capacity as counsel for the Nelson family in the civil litigation, petitioner attended the coroner's inquest into the boy's death and initiated actions for damages, but he neither discussed Officer Nuccio with the press nor played any part in the criminal proceeding. Notwithstanding petitioner's remote connection with the prosecution of Nuccio, respondent's magazine portrayed him as an architect of the "frame-up." The article stated that petitioner had been an official of the "Marxist League for Industrial Democracy, originally known as the Intercollegiate Socialist Society, which has advocated the violent seizure of our government." It labeled Gertz a "Leninist" and a "Communist-fronter." It also stated that Gertz had been an officer of the National Lawyers Guild, described as a Communist organization that "probably did more than any other outfit to plan the Communist attack on the Chicago police during the 1968 Democratic Convention."

These statements contained serious inaccuracies. The implication that petitioner had a criminal record was false. Petitioner had been a member and officer of the National Lawyers Guild some 15 years earlier, but there was no evidence that he or that organization had taken any part in planning the 1968 demonstrations in Chicago. There was also no basis for the charge that petitioner was a Leninist or a Communist-fronter. And he had never been a member of the Marxist League for Industrial Democracy or the Intercollegiate Socialist Society.

The managing editor of American Opinion made no effort to verify or substantiate the charges against petitioner. Instead, he appended an editorial introduction stating that the author had conducted extensive research into the Richard Nuccio Case. And he included in the article a photograph of petitioner and wrote the caption that appeared under it: "Elmer Gertz of Red Guild harasses Nuccio." Respondent placed the issue of American Opinion containing the article on sale at newsstands throughout the country and distributed reprints of the article on the streets of Chicago.

After all the evidence had been presented at trial but before submission of the case to the jury, the court ruled in effect that petitioner was neither a public official nor a public figure. It added that, if he were, the resulting application of the New York Times standard would require a directed verdict for respondent. Because some statements in the article constituted libel per se, the court submitted the case to the jury under instructions that withdrew from its consideration all issues save the measure of damages. The jury awarded $50,000 to petitioner.

The principal issue in this case is whether a newspaper or broadcaster that publishes defamatory falsehoods about an individual who is neither a public official nor a public figure may claim a constitutional privilege against liability for the injury inflicted by those statements.

Under the First Amendment there is no such thing as a false idea. However pernicious an opinion may seem, we depend for its correction not on the conscience of judges and juries but on the competition of other ideas. But there is no constitutional value in false statements of fact. Neither the intentional lie nor the careless error materially advances society's interest in uninhibited, robust, and wide-open' debate on public issues. They belong to that category of utterances which are no essential part of any exposition of ideas, and are of such slight social value as a step to truth that any benefit that may be derived from them is clearly outweighed by the social interest in order and morality.

Our decisions recognize that a rule of strict liability that compels a publisher or broadcaster to guarantee the accuracy of his factual assertions may lead to intolerable self-censorship. Allowing the media to avoid liability only by proving the truth of all injurious statements does not accord adequate protection to First Amendment liberties. Allowance of the defense of truth, with the burden of proving it on the defendant, does not mean that only false speech will be deterred. The First Amendment requires that we protect some falsehood in order to protect speech that matters.

The legitimate state interest underlying the law of libel is the compensation of individuals for the harm inflicted on them by defamatory falsehood. We would not lightly require the State to abandon this purpose, for the individual's right to the protection of his own good name reflects no more than our basic concept of the essential dignity and worth of every human being—a concept at the root of any decent system of ordered liberty. The protection of private personality, like the protection of life itself, is left primarily to the individual States under the Ninth and Tenth Amendments. But this does not mean that the right is entitled to any less recognition by this Court as a basic of our constitutional system.

The New York Times standard defines the level of constitutional protection appropriate to the context of defamation of a public person. Those who, by reason of the notoriety of their achievements or the vigor and success with which they seek the public's attention, are properly classed as public figures and those who hold governmental office may recover for injury to reputation only on clear and convincing proof that the defamatory falsehood was made with knowledge of its falsity or with reckless disregard for the truth. This standard administers an extremely powerful antidote to the inducement to media self-censorship of the common-law rule of strict liability for libel and slander. And it exacts a correspondingly high price from the victims of defamatory falsehood. Plainly many deserving plaintiffs, including some intentionally subjected to injury, will be unable to surmount the barrier of the New York Times test. Despite this substantial abridgment of the state law right to compensation for wrongful hurt to one's reputation, the Court has concluded that the protection of the New York Times privilege should be available to publishers and broadcasters of defamatory falsehood concerning public officials and public figures. We think that these decisions are correct, but we do not find their holdings justified solely by reference to the interest of the press and broadcast media in immunity from liability. Rather, we believe that the New York Times rule states an accommodation between this concern and the limited state interest present in the context of libel actions brought by public persons. For the reasons stated below, we conclude that the state interest in compensating injury to the reputation of private individuals requires that a different rule should obtain with respect to them.

We conclude that the States should retain substantial latitude in their efforts to enforce a legal remedy for defamatory falsehood injurious to the reputation of a private individual. The extension of the New York Times test would abridge this legitimate state interest to a degree that we find unacceptable. We hold that, so long as they do not impose liability without fault, the States may define for themselves the appropriate standard of liability for a publisher or broadcaster of defamatory falsehood injurious to a private individual. This approach provides a more equitable boundary between the competing concerns involved here. It recognizes the strength of the legitimate state interest in compensating private individuals for wrongful injury to reputation, yet shields the press and broadcast media from the rigors of strict liability for defamation. At least this conclusion obtains where, as here, the substance of the defamatory statement makes substantial danger to reputation apparent. This phrase places in perspective the conclusion we announce today.

Our accommodation of the competing values at stake in defamation suits by private individuals allows the States to impose liability on the publisher or broadcaster of defamatory falsehood on a less demanding showing than that required by New York Times. This conclusion is not based on a belief that the considerations which prompted the adoption of the New York Times privilege for defamation of public officials and its extension to public figures are wholly inapplicable to the context of private individuals. Rather, we endorse this approach in recognition of the strong and legitimate state interest in compensating private individuals for injury to reputation. But this countervailing state interest extends no further than compensation for actual injury. For the reasons stated below, we hold that the States may not permit recovery of presumed or punitive damages, at least when liability is not based on a showing of knowledge of falsity or reckless disregard for the truth.

Reversed and remanded.

INVASION OF PRIVACY

Solano v. Playgirl, Inc.

United States Court of Appeals, Ninth Circuit (2002)

Solano appeared bare-chested wearing his red trunks, dominating the cover. In the upper left corner was a red circle containing the words, "TV Guys," followed by the headline, "Primetime's Sexy Young Stars Exposed," which ran across the top of Solano's head. Immediately to the left of Solano's picture, the magazine proclaimed, "12 Sizzling Centerfolds Ready to Score With You." The "s" in "Centerfolds" was superimposed on Solano's right shoulder. Also placed to the left of Solano, running down the left margin, the cover touted "Countdown to Climax: Naughty Ways to Ring in the New Year," "Toyz in the Hood: The Best in Erotic Home Shopping" and "Bottoms Up!: Hot Celebrity Buns." In the cover's lower right-hand corner was the headline, "Baywatch's Best Body, Jose Solano."

[**STUDENTS:** COVER & PAGE 21 APPEARS ON LAST PAGE OF THIS CASE]

Solano's sole appearance inside the magazine was on page 21, in a quarter-page, head-and-shoulders photograph—showing him fully dressed in a tee shirt and sweater—alongside a brief, quarter-page profile of the actor. Solano's profile included information about his "Baywatch" character, facts about his life before he began acting and a quote in which he says that with two younger brothers he strives to be a positive role model and hopes to encourage others to pursue their dreams. Significantly, Playgirl issues are displayed on newsstands packaged in plastic wrap to prevent potential customers from flipping through the pages to view the magazine's contents.

Solano filed suit against the magazine's publisher, Playgirl, Inc., in California Superior Court, alleging Playgirl invaded his privacy by portraying him in a false light and by misappropriating his likeness in violation of California Civil Code § 3344 and common law. The district court granted Playgirl's motion for summary judgment. The court found that the use of Solano's photograph in Playgirl did not create a false impression and, in any event, as a public figure he could not show actual malice. Solano timely appealed.

DISCUSSION

I. The False Light Claim

Solano argues that Playgirl's use of his photograph along with suggestive headlines on the cover conveyed the false message that Solano voluntarily posed nude for the magazine and, in doing so, implicitly endorsed the magazine and its sexually explicit content. To prevail on this false light claim, Solano must show that: (1) Playgirl disclosed to one or more persons information about or concerning Solano that was presented as factual but that was actually false or created a false impression about him; (2) the information was understood by one or more persons to whom it was disclosed as stating or implying something highly offensive that would have a tendency to injure Solano's reputation; (3) by clear and convincing evidence, Playgirl acted with constitutional malice; and (4) Solano was damaged by the disclosure.

A. False Impression and Injury to Reputation

Solano contends that when the photograph and headlines on the cover are viewed in context—that of a magazine that features sexually suggestive nude pictures of men-there is a triable issue of fact regarding the falsity of the message conveyed by Playgirl. We agree.

It is well-established that "[a] defendant is liable for what is insinuated as well as for what is stated explicitly." As the Seventh Circuit observed in Douglass v. Hustler Magazine, 769 F.2d 1128 (7th Cir.1985), where an actress asserted a false light claim based on Hustler magazine's insinuation that she was the kind of person to pose nude for Hustler: "To be depicted as voluntarily associated with such a sheet ... is unquestionably degrading to a normal person...."

That Solano's profile inside the magazine was of a relatively innocent and nonsexual nature is of little significance. Here, the Solano profile appeared 21 pages away from the cover—with plenty of graphic frontal male nudity to traverse before reaching "TV Guys" and Solano's tame profile. "[O]ur inquiry is not to determine whether the publication may have an innocent meaning but rather to determine if it reasonably conveys a defamatory meaning. In making that determination we look to what is explicitly stated as well as what insinuation and implication can reasonably be drawn from the publication." Selleck v. Globe Int'l, 166 Cal.App.3d 1123 (1985). Given the record before us—especially when we recall that the magazine is displayed for sale in plastic wrapping, making the cover the key to what a reader can expect to find inside the magazine.

A jury reasonably could conclude that the Playgirl cover conveyed the message that Solano was not the wholesome person he claimed to be, that he was willing to—or was "washed up" and had to—sell himself naked to a women's sex magazine.

B. Actual Malice

Although Solano has established a genuine issue as to whether the cover created a false impression, to survive summary judgment he must, as a public figure, also establish by clear and convincing evidence that Playgirl's editors knowingly or recklessly created this false impression. The third element necessary to establish a claim for false light, therefore, is the constitutional requirement of actual malice. Specifically, Solano must show that Playgirl "either deliberately cast [its] statements in an equivocal fashion in the hope of insinuating a [false] import to the reader, or that [it] knew or acted in reckless disregard of whether [its] words would be interpreted by the average reader as[false] statements of fact."

[T]he actual malice standard is not satisfied merely through a showing of ill will or 'malice' in the ordinary sense of the term.... Nor can the fact that the defendant published the defamatory material in order to increase its profits suffice to prove actual malice. ... Actual malice, instead, requires at a minimum that the statements were made with a reckless disregard for the truth. And although the concept of 'reckless disregard' 'cannot be fully encompassed in one infallible definition,' we have made clear that the defendant must have made the false publication with a 'high degree of awareness of ... probable falsity,' or must have 'entertained serious doubts as to the truth of his publication.'

Against this backdrop, we now turn to the conflicting evidence regarding the existence of actual malice on the part of Playgirl editors in assembling the January 1999 issue. Playgirl associate editor Theresa O'Rourke testified in her deposition that at an October 1998 meeting to discuss the January 1999 cover, Playgirl senior vice president Carmine Bellucci generally instructed the editorial staff to "sex up" the magazine to imply that there was more nudity in the magazine than actually was there. She stated that Bellucci wanted to "bang [readers] over the head with something like, hey, this is sexy young stars exposed" so that "people are going to want to pick up the magazine more." According to O'Rourke, "we definitely weren't trying to be subtle, and we knew it." She stated that there had been discussion in the cover meetings that the cover layout implied Solano appeared nude in a centerfold inside the magazine. She said the "Primetime's Sexy Young Stars Exposed" headline specifically sparked debate at the meetings "[b]ecause some of us did not feel like it was fair to do that." Editor-in-chief Claire Viguerie Harth testified that the magazine's intent with the headline was "to make a line that was sexy enough [that] people would be intrigued and want to look inside, but not to say something that the magazine was showing something that it didn't have."

Playgirl art director Joanne Chiaramonte emphasized that if the magazine had contained a nude photograph of Solano, the cover explicitly would have said so. She stated that she never thought readers would expect to see Solano in a centerfold photograph because the headline, "Baywatch's Best Body, Jose Solano" clearly referred to Solano's presence in the magazine. Additionally, she explained that "[e]xposed and nude are really two different things." Associate art director Serena Spiezio disagreed. She testified that she thought it would be reasonable for a reader to expect to see Solano nude inside the magazine "[b]ecause it says TV Guys and they're being exposed. And it's Playgirl Magazine. What else would they be exposing but their bodies?"

O'Rourke also recalled that someone raised a concern about the "12 Sizzling Centerfolds: Ready to Score with You" headline because it occupied the space where the headline relating to the cover subject often is placed. She believed "someone's going to think that he's naked in there." O'Rourke said that Bellucci tended to just "blow off" such comments and concerns. Bellucci agreed in his deposition that Solano was a "primetime sexy young star" as those words were used in the cover headline, but denied that the editors used Solano's photograph and the cover headlines falsely to imply that Solano appeared nude in the magazine.

Even if, as Playgirl asserts, Chiaramonte and Bellucci were the final decisionmakers as to the content of the cover, the testimony of O'Rourke and Spiezio serve to prove that during the editorial process someone raised concerns about the use of Solano's photograph alongside the suggestive headlines; both Bellucci and Chiaramonte were aware of some staffers' concerns that the cover might falsely imply that Solano appeared nude inside the magazine. Given that awareness and the evidence that Bellucci wanted to "sex up" the magazine to imply nudity, plainly to promote magazine sales, a jury could conclude Playgirl's editors knowingly or recklessly published the misleading cover. Such evidence is sufficient to satisfy the actual malice standard.

C. Damages

The final element necessary to prove a case for false light is damages. A plaintiff may collect actual damages and general damages for humiliation and mental anguish and suffering. Playgirl argues that Solano cannot prove any damages. Solano admitted in his deposition that he did not seek therapy or any other type of treatment from any medical professional, although he did seek spiritual counseling from his father, a minister. He testified to both personal and familial humiliation and embarrassment because of the publication of his picture in the magazine. He claimed that several possibilities for appearing on various television programs failed to materialize after the publication of the Playgirl issue, yet he was unable to provide evidence that any lost job was related to his appearance in the magazine. Solano's current and previous agent and previous manager all stated that no one ever has mentioned the Playgirl issue to them—especially in relation to a job for Solano. Solano also argues that his invitations to charity events declined after the publication of the Playgirl issue, but again he admitted that he could only speculate—and had no proof—that there is a connection between the two events. In light of precedent, Solano's testimony regarding his humiliation and embarrassment is sufficient to establish a genuine issue with respect to damages and precludes summary judgment. (We make no predictions about whether this evidence alone will suffice to sustain the damages element at trial.)

REVERSED and REMANDED.

COVER PAGE

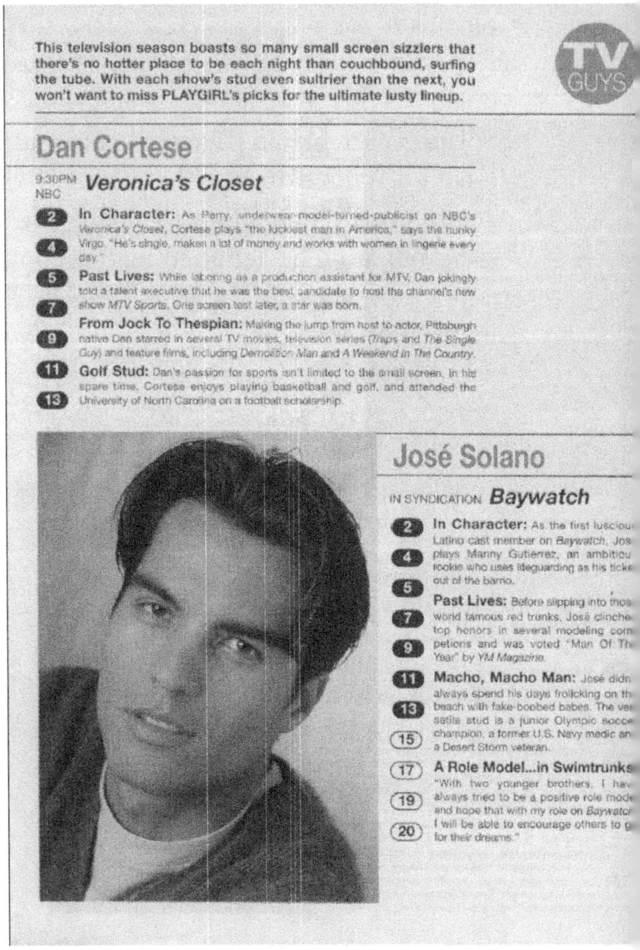

This television season boasts so many small screen sizzlers that there's no hotter place to be each night than couchbound, surfing the tube. With each show's stud even sultrier than the next, you won't want to miss PLAYGIRL's picks for the ultimate lusty lineup.

TV GUYS

Dan Cortese

9:30PM NBC *Veronica's Closet*

2 4 **In Character:** As Perry, underwear-model-turned-publicist on NBC's *Veronica's Closet*, Cortese plays "the luckiest man in America," says the hunky Virgo. "He's single, makes a lot of money and works with women in lingerie every day."

5 7 **Past Lives:** While laboring as a production assistant for MTV, Dan jokingly told a talent executive that he was the best candidate to host the channel's new show *MTV Sports*. One screen test later, a star was born.

9 **From Jock To Thespian:** Making the jump from host to actor, Pittsburgh native Dan starred in several TV movies, television series (*Traps* and *The Single Guy*) and feature films, including *Demolition Man* and *A Weekend in The Country*.

11 13 **Golf Stud:** Dan's passion for sports isn't limited to the small screen. In his spare time, Cortese enjoys playing basketball and golf, and attended the University of North Carolina on a football scholarship.

José Solano

IN SYNDICATION *Baywatch*

2 4 **In Character:** As the first lusciou Latino cast member on *Baywatch*, Jos plays Manny Gutierrez, an ambitiou rookie who uses lifeguarding as his ticke out of the barrio.

5 7 9 **Past Lives:** Before slipping into thos world famous red trunks, José clinche top honors in several modeling com petions and was voted "Man Of Th Year" by *YM Magazine*.

11 13 15 **Macho, Macho Man:** José didn always spend his days frolicking on th beach with fake-boobed babes. The ve satile stud is a junior Olympic socce champion, a former U.S. Navy medic an a Desert Storm veteran.

17 19 20 **A Role Model...in Swimtrunks** "With two younger brothers, I hav always tried to be a positive role mode and hope that with my role on *Baywatc* I will be able to encourage others to g for their dreams."

PAGE 21

* These are the only two pages where Jose Solano appears.

Godbehere v. Phoenix Newspapers, Inc.

Supreme Court of Arizona (1989)

Richard G. Godbehere, a former Maricopa County Sheriff, and several deputies and civilian employees of the sheriff's office (plaintiffs) brought this action against Phoenix Newspapers, Inc., the publisher of The Arizona Republic and Phoenix Gazette, for libel and false light invasion of privacy.

FACTS

In the spring and summer of 1985, publishers printed over fifty articles, editorials, and columns (the publications) about plaintiffs' various law enforcement activities. The publications stated that the plaintiffs engaged in illegal activities, staged narcotics arrests to generate publicity, illegally arrested citizens, misused public funds and resources, committed police brutality, and generally were incompetent at law enforcement. Plaintiffs alleged in their eighteen-count complaint that the publications were false, damaged their reputations, harmed them in their profession, and caused them emotional distress.

DISCUSSION

In 1890, Samuel Warren and Louis Brandeis published an article advocating the recognition of a right to privacy as an independent legal concept. Warren & Brandeis, The Right to Privacy, 4 HARV.L.REV. 193 (1890). Explaining how courts traditionally recognized claims involving injury to a person's private thoughts or feelings, they also described how courts used contract and property law to protect thoughts, ideas, or expressions from wrongful appropriation. Warren and Brandeis contended these were nothing more than instances and applications of a general right to privacy. Hence, they supported recognition of the right to be let alone.

In 1960, Dean Prosser concluded that four separate torts had developed under the right of privacy rubric: (1) intrusion on the plaintiff's seclusion or private affairs; (2) public disclosure of embarrassing private facts; (3) publicity placing the plaintiff in a false light in the public eye; and (4) appropriation of the plaintiff's name or likeness for the defendant's advantage. Although each tort is classified under invasion of privacy, they otherwise have almost nothing in common except that each represents an interference with the right of the plaintiff to be let alone.

Privacy in Arizona

The publishers argue that there is no need for an independent tort of false light invasion of privacy because the action overlaps two other recognized torts: defamation and intentional infliction of emotional distress. These, publishers contend, cover the field and permit recovery in meritorious cases, thus making the false light action an unnecessary burden on the media's first amendment rights. To consider this argument, we must examine the distinctions between the false light action and the torts of intentional infliction of emotional distress and defamation.

False Light Invasion of Privacy and Intentional Infliction of Emotional Distress

Intentional infliction of emotional distress, also known as the tort of outrage, is defined as: one who by extreme and outrageous conduct intentionally or recklessly causes severe emotional distress to another is subject to liability for such emotional distress, and if bodily harm to the other results from it, for such bodily harm.

Publishers emphasize that actions for both intentional infliction of emotional distress and invasion of privacy provide compensation for emotional distress or damage to sensibility. Thus, the injury from both torts is similar. Although this may be true, the fact that two different actions address the same injury is no reason to refuse to recognize torts that protect against different wrongful conduct. For example, three victims may suffer broken legs in the following ways: (1) a defendant negligently drives a car into the first victim's car; (2) a defendant's defective product injures the second victim; and (3) a defendant, without justification, attacks the third. Each victim would have a different tort claim: negligence, strict liability, and battery. The fact that each victim suffers the same type of injury does not preclude recognizing separate tort actions. Each tort theory developed separately to deter and provide redress against a different type of wrongful conduct.

Thus, the fact that outrage and invasion of privacy both provide redress for emotional injury does not persuade us that the actions are merged or that plaintiffs should be required to prove the former in an action for the latter. The outrage tort protects against conduct so extreme that it would induce an average member of the community to exclaim, "outrageous!" False light invasion of privacy, however, protects against the conduct of knowingly or recklessly publishing false information or innuendo that a reasonable person would find highly offensive. Although false publication may constitute outrageous conduct and vice versa, it is also true that the same wrongful conduct will not always satisfy the elements of both tort actions. Because each action protects against a different type of tortious conduct, each has its place, and the common injury should not abrogate the action.

Nor do we believe that recognizing the false light action without requiring plaintiffs to prove outrage will circumvent the stringent standards of the emotional distress tort. The standards for proving false light invasion of privacy are quite stringent by themselves. For example, the plaintiff in a false light case must prove that the defendant published with knowledge of the falsity or reckless disregard for the truth. This standard is as stringent as the intentional infliction of emotional distress requirement that the plaintiff prove the defendant intentionally or recklessly caused the emotional distress.

We conclude, therefore, that the two torts exist to redress different types of wrongful conduct. Situations exist where a jury could find the defendant's publication of false information or innuendo was not outrageous but did satisfy the false light elements. Thus, we believe the tort action for false light invasion of privacy provides protection against a narrow class of wrongful conduct that falls short of outrage, but nevertheless should be deterred.

Invasion of Privacy and Defamation

A second argument advanced by publishers is that little distinction exists between a tort action for false light invasion of privacy and one for defamation. Again, we disagree.

Although both defamation and false light invasion of privacy involve publication, the nature of the interests protected by each action differs substantially. A defamation action compensates damage to reputation or good name caused by the publication of false information. To be defamatory, a publication must be false and must bring the defamed person into disrepute, contempt, or ridicule, or must impeach plaintiff's honesty, integrity, virtue, or reputation.

Privacy, on the other hand, does not protect reputation but protects mental and emotional interests. Indeed, the gravamen of a privacy action is the injury to the feelings of the plaintiff, the mental anguish and distress caused by the publication. The remedy is available to protect a person's interest in being let alone and is available when there has been publicity of a kind that is highly offensive. Under this theory, a plaintiff may recover even in the absence of reputational damage, as long as the publicity is unreasonably offensive and attributes false characteristics. However, to qualify as a false light invasion of privacy, the publication must involve a major misrepresentation of the plaintiff's character, history, activities or beliefs, not merely minor or unimportant inaccuracies.

Another distinction between defamation and false light invasion of privacy is the role played by truth. To be defamatory, a publication must be false, and truth is a defense. A false light cause of action may arise when something untrue has been published about an individual, or when the publication of true information creates a false implication about the individual. In the latter type of case, the false innuendo created by the highly offensive presentation of a true fact constitutes the injury.

Thus, although defamation and false light often overlap, they serve very different objectives. The two tort actions deter different conduct and redress different wrongs. A plaintiff may bring a false light invasion of privacy action even though the publication is not defamatory, and even though the actual facts stated are true.

Free Speech Considerations

As in defamation, a public official in a false light action must always show that the defendant published with knowledge of the false innuendo or with reckless disregard of the truth. Any doubt about the application of the actual malice element of the false light tort to public figures has been eliminated. In Hustler Magazine, Inc. v. Falwell (1988), the Supreme Court held that a public figure plaintiff must prove actual malice in order to recover for intentional infliction of emotional distress. Although Hustler was an intentional infliction case, the language used by the Court is so broad that it applies to any tort action relating to free speech, particularly in the area of public debate about public figures.

Is False Light Available in This Case?

Finally, publishers contended that even if we recognize false light actions, the action does not lie in this case. They argue that not only do the publications discuss matters of public interest, but plaintiffs have no right of privacy with respect to the manner in which they perform their official duties. We agree.

We have specifically held that the right of privacy does not exist where the plaintiff has become a public character. In addition, privacy rights are absent or limited in connection with the life of a person in whom the public has a rightful interest, or where the information would be of public benefit.

A number of jurisdictions take the position that because false light is a form of invasion of privacy, it must relate only to the private affairs of the plaintiff and cannot involve matters of public interest. It is difficult to conceive of an area of greater public interest than law enforcement. Certainly the public has a legitimate interest in the manner in which law enforcement officers perform their duties. Therefore, we hold that there can be no false light invasion of privacy action for matters involving official acts or duties of public officers.

Consequently, we adopt the following legal standard: a plaintiff cannot sue for false light invasion of privacy if he or she is a public official and the publication relates to performance of his or her public life or duties. We do not go so far as to say, however, that a public official has no privacy rights at all and may never bring an action for invasion of privacy. Certainly, if the publication presents the public official's private life in a false light, he or she can sue under the false light tort, although actual malice must be shown. The sheriff and the deputies here are public officials. The publications at issue concern the discharge of their public duties and do not relate to private affairs. Therefore, plaintiffs have no claim for false light invasion of privacy.

This page left intentionally blank

ABOUT THE AUTHOR

Professor H. Beau Baez is on the law faculty at Ohio Northern University Pettit College of Law. He began his teaching career in 2000 and has taught thousands of students at seven law schools. In addition, he has worked one-on-one with law students at many law schools throughout the United States, the United Kingdom, Canada, and Australia. Courses he has taught include Torts, Federal Income Tax, State & Local Tax, Business Associations, Wills & Trusts, Estate Planning, Contracts, Civil Procedure, Legal Writing, and Criminal Procedure.

In addition to teaching, Professor Baez is a YouTube creator at YouTube.com/LearnLawBetter This is the first popular channel hosted by a law professor, with videos viewed millions of times and subscribers in over 150 countries. A prolific author, he has written several books and numerous scholarly articles.

His undergraduate degrees are in Speech Communications, Accounting, and Religion. At Georgetown University he earned the JD and LLM (tax) degrees. After law school, he practiced law for eight years with the Multistate Tax Commission in Washington, DC. At the Commission he administered a successful voluntary compliance program and assisted in preparing briefs before State supreme courts and the United States Supreme Court—he has attended over a hundred oral arguments at the Supreme Court. For nearly a decade he served on the North Carolina General Statutes Commission, where he worked on revising legislation.

This page left intentionally blank

ADDITIONAL RESOURCES

Resource	*URL*
Website	LearnLawBetter.com
YouTube Channel	YouTube.com/LearnLawBetter
Facebook	Facebook.com/LearnLawBetter
Instagram	Instagram.com/LearnLawBetter
LinkedIn	LinkedIn.com/company/LearnLawBetter

This page left intentionally blank

Made in the USA
Coppell, TX
21 August 2026

87745810R00210